TM

References for the Rest of Us!™

BESTSELLING BOOK SERIES

Do you find that traditional reference books are overloaded with technical details and advice you'll never use? Do you postpone important life decisions because you just don't want to deal with them? Then our *...For Dummies*® business and general reference book series is for you.

...For Dummies business and general reference books are written for those frustrated and hard-working souls who know they aren't dumb, but find that the myriad of personal and business issues and the accompanying horror stories make them feel helpless. *...For Dummies* books use a lighthearted approach, a down-to-earth style, and even cartoons and humorous icons to dispel fears and build confidence. Lighthearted but not lightweight, these books are perfect survival guides to solve your everyday personal and business problems.

> **"More than a publishing phenomenon, 'Dummies' is a sign of the times."**
>
> — *The New York Times*

> **"...you won't go wrong buying them."**
>
> — *Walter Mossberg, Wall Street Journal, on IDG Books' ...For Dummies books*

> **"A world of detailed and authoritative information is packed into them..."**
>
> — *U.S. News and World Report*

Already, millions of satisfied readers agree. They have made *...For Dummies* the #1 introductory level computer book series and a best-selling business book series. They have written asking for more. So, if you're looking for the best and easiest way to learn about business and other general reference topics, look to *...For Dummies* to give you a helping hand.

IDG
BOOKS
WORLDWIDE

1/99

by Peter Haugen

IDG Books Worldwide, Inc.
An International Data Group Company

Foster City, CA ◆ Chicago, IL ◆ Indianapolis, IN ◆ New York, NY

World History For Dummies®

Published by:
IDG Books, Inc.
909 Third Avenue
New York, NY 10022
www.idgbooks.com (IDG Books Worldwide Web site)
www.dummies.com (Dummies Press Web site)

Library of Congress Control Number: 00-112134

ISBN: 0-7645-5242-2

Printed in the United States of America

10 9 8 7 6 5 4 3 2

1B/RU/QS/QR/IN

Distributed in the United States by IDG Books, Inc.

Distributed by CDG Books Canada Inc. for Canada; by Transworld Publishers Limited in the United Kingdom; by IDG Norge Books for Norway; by IDG Sweden Books for Sweden; by IDG Books Australia Publishing Corporation Pty. Ltd. for Australia and New Zealand; by TransQuest Publishers Pte Ltd. for Singapore, Malaysia, Thailand, Indonesia, and Hong Kong; by Gotop Information Inc. for Taiwan; by ICG Muse, Inc. for Japan; by Intersoft for South Africa; by Eyrolles for France; by International Thomson Publishing for Germany, Austria and Switzerland; by Distribuidora Cuspide for Argentina; by LR International for Brazil; by Galileo Libros for Chile; by Ediciones ZETA S.C.R. Ltda. for Peru; by WS Computer Publishing Corporation, Inc., for the Philippines; by Contemporanea de Ediciones for Venezuela; by Express Computer Distributors for the Caribbean and West Indies; by Micronesia Media Distributor, Inc. for Micronesia; by Chips Computadoras S.A. de C.V. for Mexico; by Editorial Norma de Panama S.A. for Panama; by American Bookshops for Finland.

For general information on IDG Books' products and services please contact our Customer Care department; within the U.S. at 800-762-2974, outside the U.S. at 317-572-3993 or fax 317-572-4002.

For sales inquiries and resellers information, including discounts, premium and bulk quantity sales and foreign language translations please contact our Customer Care department at 800-434-3422, fax 317-572-4002 or write to IDG Books, Inc., Attn: Customer Care department, 10475 Crosspoint Boulevard, Indianapolis, IN 46256.

For information on licensing foreign or domestic rights, please contact our Sub-Rights Customer Care department at 650-653-7098.

For information on using IDG Books' products and services in the classroom or for ordering examination copies, please contact our Educational Sales department at 800-434-2086 or fax 317-572-4005.

Please contact our Public Relations department at 212-884-5163 for press review copies or 212-884-5000 for author interviews and other publicity information or fax 212-884-5400.

For authorization to photocopy items for corporate, personal, or educational use, please contact Copyright Clearance Center, 222 Rosewood Drive, Danvers, MA 01923, or fax 978-750-4470.

Library of Congress Cataloging-in-Publication Data

About the Author

Peter Haugen, a journalist with wide-ranging interests, has always been fascinated with how yesterday became today and how today becomes tomorrow. As a feature writer and critic, he has written about human culture in eras ranging from prehistory to ancient Greece, from Elizabethan England to the present.

In addition to teaching writing at the University of Wisconsin, Haugen works in the book-publishing industry as a contributing writer, consulting editor, and researcher. In a chapter of the upcoming book *Total Billiards* (Total/Sports Illustrated) he touches on Louis XIV's role in popularizing the pastime.

Haugen has served on the staffs of several newspapers, both as an editor and reporter. He has been the theater critic of the *Sacramento Bee* and a regional news editor at the *St. Petersburg Times*. He is a former fellow of the National Critics Institute in New London, Connecticut, a graduate of the University of California, Berkeley, and a U.S. Army veteran. He lives in Madison, Wisconsin, with his wife and two sons.

ABOUT IDG BOOKS WORLDWIDE

Welcome to the world of IDG Books Worldwide.

IDG Books Worldwide, Inc., is a subsidiary of International Data Group, the world's largest publisher of computer-related information and the leading global provider of information services on information technology. IDG was founded more than 30 years ago by Patrick J. McGovern and now employs more than 9,000 people worldwide. IDG publishes more than 290 computer publications in over 75 countries. More than 90 million people read one or more IDG publications each month.

Launched in 1990, IDG Books Worldwide is today the #1 publisher of best-selling computer books in the United States. We are proud to have received eight awards from the Computer Press Association in recognition of editorial excellence and three from Computer Currents' First Annual Readers' Choice Awards. Our best-selling ...*For Dummies*® series has more than 50 million copies in print with translations in 31 languages. IDG Books Worldwide, through a joint venture with IDG's Hi-Tech Beijing, became the first U.S. publisher to publish a computer book in the People's Republic of China. In record time, IDG Books Worldwide has become the first choice for millions of readers around the world who want to learn how to better manage their businesses.

Our mission is simple: Every one of our books is designed to bring extra value and skill-building instructions to the reader. Our books are written by experts who understand and care about our readers. The knowledge base of our editorial staff comes from years of experience in publishing, education, and journalism — experience we use to produce books to carry us into the new millennium. In short, we care about books, so we attract the best people. We devote special attention to details such as audience, interior design, use of icons, and illustrations. And because we use an efficient process of authoring, editing, and desktop publishing our books electronically, we can spend more time ensuring superior content and less time on the technicalities of making books.

You can count on our commitment to deliver high-quality books at competitive prices on topics you want to read about. At IDG Books Worldwide, we continue in the IDG tradition of delivering quality for more than 30 years. You'll find no better book on a subject than one from IDG Books Worldwide.

John Kilcullen
Chairman and CEO
IDG Books Worldwide, Inc.

*Eighth Annual
Computer Press
Awards ➢ 1992*

*Ninth Annual
Computer Press
Awards ➢ 1993*

*Tenth Annual
Computer Press
Awards ➢ 1994*

*Eleventh Annual
Computer Press
Awards ➢ 1995*

Dedication

To my loved ones: Deborah, Marcus, and Lucas.

Author's Acknowledgments

Many people helped me write this book and some don't even know that they helped. Thanks to: John Thorn and George Schlukbier for showing me the way to the world of book publishing; David Pietrusza and Kenneth Shouler for patiently guiding my orientation into that world; and to the late Mike Gershman for encouragement.

Thanks to my agent, B. Devereux Barker IV ("Skip") for insisting that I could write this book, even after I told him it was impossible; to David McDonald for excellent advice and much-needed reassurances, and for saving me from many embarrassing errors; to my editor, Kathleen Dobie, for guiding me through the writing and revision process and steadfastly curbing my wilder inconsistencies; to copy editor Esmeralda St. Clair, for asking good questions and making good suggestions; and to all the other fine minds at IDG Books Worldwide who contributed to this project.

I'd also like to thank Keith and Liz Anderson for soothing hospitality and a much-needed chance to blow off steam at a critical moment; David and Helen Haugen for understanding (among many other gifts); Pamela Johnson and Treaka Haugen for caring; Murray and Ann Blum for easing my family through a crucial week; and Rob Kane and Jeff Hudson for listening.

Thank you, Marcus and Lucas, for making me proud and grateful every day; and Dodger for faithfully keeping me company as I made revisions. Above all, I thank Deborah, who makes everything possible.

Publisher's Acknowledgments

We're proud of this book; please register your comments through our IDG Books Worldwide Online Registration Form located at http://my2cents.dummies.com.

Some of the people who helped bring this book to market include the following:

Acquisitions, Editorial, and Media Development

Project Editor: Kathleen A. Dobie

Acquisitions Editor: Susan Decker

Copy Editor: Esmeralda St. Clair

Technical Editor: David McDonald

Editorial Manager: Christine Meloy Beck

Editorial Assistant: Jennifer Young

Cover Photos:

Production

Project Coordinator: Nancee Reeves

Layout and Graphics: Jackie Nicholas, Kristin Pickett, Jill Piscitelli, Jacque Schneider, Kendra Span, Brian Torwelle, Jeremey Unger

Proofreaders: Andy Hollandbeck, Susan Moritz, Nancy Price, Charles Spencer York Production Services, Inc.

Indexer: York Production Services, Inc.

General and Administrative

IDG Books Worldwide, Inc.: John Kilcullen, CEO; Bill Barry, President and COO

IDG Books Consumer Reference Group

Business: Kathleen A. Welton, Vice President and Publisher; Kevin Thornton, Acquisitions Manager

Cooking/Gardening: Jennifer Feldman, Associate Vice President and Publisher

Education/Reference: Diane Graves Steele, Vice President and Publisher; Greg Tubach, Publishing Director

Lifestyles: Kathleen Nebenhaus, Vice President and Publisher; Tracy Boggier, Managing Editor

Pets: Dominique De Vito, Associate Vice President and Publisher; Tracy Boggier, Managing Editor

Travel: Michael Spring, Vice President and Publisher; Suzanne Jannetta, Editorial Director; Brice Gosnell, Managing Editor

IDG Books Consumer Editorial Services: Kathleen Nebenhaus, Vice President and Publisher; Kristin A. Cocks, Editorial Director; Cindy Kitchel, Editorial Director

IDG Books Consumer Production: Debbie Stailey, Production Director

IDG Books Packaging: Marc J. Mikulich, Vice President, Brand Strategy and Research

◆

The publisher would like to give special thanks to Patrick J. McGovern, without whom this book would not have been possible.

◆

World History For Dummies®

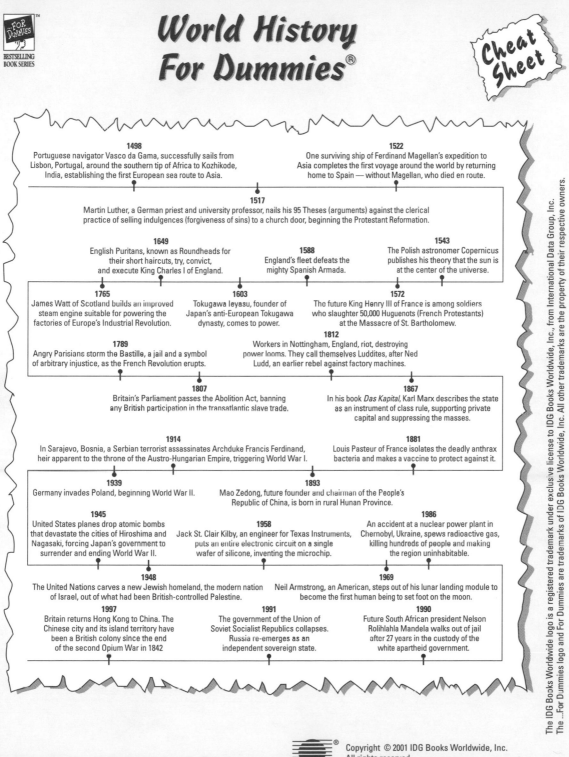

1498
Portuguese navigator Vasco da Gama, successfully sails from Lisbon, Portugal, around the southern tip of Africa to Kozhikode, India, establishing the first European sea route to Asia.

1522
One surviving ship of Ferdinand Magellan's expedition to Asia completes the first voyage around the world by returning home to Spain — without Magellan, who died en route.

1517
Martin Luther, a German priest and university professor, nails his 95 Theses (arguments) against the clerical practice of selling indulgences (forgiveness of sins) to a church door, beginning the Protestant Reformation.

1649
English Puritans, known as Roundheads for their short haircuts, try, convict, and execute King Charles I of England.

1588
England's fleet defeats the mighty Spanish Armada.

1543
The Polish astronomer Copernicus publishes his theory that the sun is at the center of the universe.

1765
James Watt of Scotland builds an improved steam engine suitable for powering the factories of Europe's Industrial Revolution.

1603
Tokugawa Ieyasu, founder of Japan's anti-European Tokugawa dynasty, comes to power.

1572
The future King Henry III of France is among soldiers who slaughter 50,000 Huguenots (French Protestants) at the Massacre of St. Bartholomew.

1789
Angry Parisians storm the Bastille, a jail and a symbol of arbitrary injustice, as the French Revolution erupts.

1812
Workers in Nottingham, England, riot, destroying power looms. They call themselves Luddites, after Ned Ludd, an earlier rebel against factory machines.

1807
Britain's Parliament passes the Abolition Act, banning any British participation in the transatlantic slave trade.

1867
In his book *Das Kapital*, Karl Marx describes the state as an instrument of class rule, supporting private capital and suppressing the masses.

1914
In Sarajevo, Bosnia, a Serbian terrorist assassinates Archduke Francis Ferdinand, heir apparent to the throne of the Austro-Hungarian Empire, triggering World War I.

1881
Louis Pasteur of France isolates the deadly anthrax bacteria and makes a vaccine to protect against it.

1939
Germany invades Poland, beginning World War II.

1893
Mao Zedong, future founder and chairman of the People's Republic of China, is born in rural Hunan Province.

1945
United States planes drop atomic bombs that devastate the cities of Hiroshima and Nagasaki, forcing Japan's government to surrender and ending World War II.

1958
Jack St. Clair Kilby, an engineer for Texas Instruments, puts an entire electronic circuit on a single wafer of silicone, inventing the microchip.

1986
An accident at a nuclear power plant in Chernobyl, Ukraine, spews radioactive gas, killing hundreds of people and making the region uninhabitable.

1948
The United Nations carves a new Jewish homeland, the modern nation of Israel, out of what had been British-controlled Palestine.

1969
Neil Armstrong, an American, steps out of his lunar landing module to become the first human being to set foot on the moon.

1997
Britain returns Hong Kong to China. The Chinese city and its island territory have been a British colony since the end of the second Opium War in 1842

1991
The government of the Union of Soviet Socialist Republics collapses. Russia re-emerges as an independent sovereign state.

1990
Future South African president Nelson Rolihlahla Mandela walks out of jail after 27 years in the custody of the white apartheid government.

The IDG Books Worldwide logo is a registered trademark under exclusive license to IDG Books Worldwide, Inc., from International Data Group, Inc. The ...For Dummies logo and For Dummies are trademarks of IDG Books Worldwide, Inc. All other trademarks are the property of their respective owners.

For Dummies™: Bestselling Book Series for Beginners

World History For Dummies®

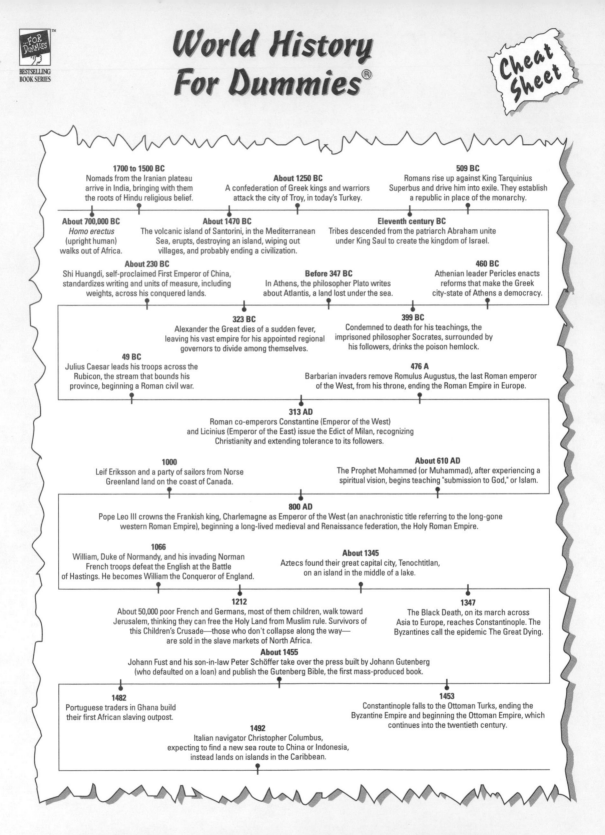

1700 to 1500 BC
Nomads from the Iranian plateau arrive in India, bringing with them the roots of Hindu religious belief.

About 1250 BC
A confederation of Greek kings and warriors attack the city of Troy, in today's Turkey.

509 BC
Romans rise up against King Tarquinius Superbus and drive him into exile. They establish a republic in place of the monarchy.

About 700,000 BC
Homo erectus (upright human) walks out of Africa.

About 1470 BC
The volcanic island of Santorini, in the Mediterranean Sea, erupts, destroying an island, wiping out villages, and probably ending a civilization.

Eleventh century BC
Tribes descended from the patriarch Abraham unite under King Saul to create the kingdom of Israel.

About 230 BC
Shi Huangdi, self-proclaimed First Emperor of China, standardizes writing and units of measure, including weights, across his conquered lands.

Before 347 BC
In Athens, the philosopher Plato writes about Atlantis, a land lost under the sea.

460 BC
Athenian leader Pericles enacts reforms that make the Greek city-state of Athens a democracy.

323 BC
Alexander the Great dies of a sudden fever, leaving his vast empire for his appointed regional governors to divide among themselves.

399 BC
Condemned to death for his teachings, the imprisoned philosopher Socrates, surrounded by his followers, drinks the poison hemlock.

49 BC
Julius Caesar leads his troops across the Rubicon, the stream that bounds his province, beginning a Roman civil war.

476 A
Barbarian invaders remove Romulus Augustus, the last Roman emperor of the West, from his throne, ending the Roman Empire in Europe.

313 AD
Roman co-emperors Constantine (Emperor of the West) and Licinius (Emperor of the East) issue the Edict of Milan, recognizing Christianity and extending tolerance to its followers.

1000
Leif Eriksson and a party of sailors from Norse Greenland land on the coast of Canada.

About 610 AD
The Prophet Mohammed (or Muhammad), after experiencing a spiritual vision, begins teaching "submission to God," or Islam.

800 AD
Pope Leo III crowns the Frankish king, Charlemagne as Emperor of the West (an anachronistic title referring to the long-gone western Roman Empire), beginning a long-lived medieval and Renaissance federation, the Holy Roman Empire.

1066
William, Duke of Normandy, and his invading Norman French troops defeat the English at the Battle of Hastings. He becomes William the Conqueror of England.

About 1345
Aztecs found their great capital city, Tenochtitlan, on an island in the middle of a lake.

1212
About 50,000 poor French and Germans, most of them children, walk toward Jerusalem, thinking they can free the Holy Land from Muslim rule. Survivors of this Children's Crusade—those who don't collapse along the way— are sold in the slave markets of North Africa.

1347
The Black Death, on its march across Asia to Europe, reaches Constantinople. The Byzantines call the epidemic The Great Dying.

About 1455
Johann Fust and his son-in-law Peter Schöffer take over the press built by Johann Gutenberg (who defaulted on a loan) and publish the Gutenberg Bible, the first mass-produced book.

1482
Portuguese traders in Ghana build their first African slaving outpost.

1453
Constantinople falls to the Ottoman Turks, ending the Byzantine Empire and beginning the Ottoman Empire, which continues into the twentieth century.

1492
Italian navigator Christopher Columbus, expecting to find a new sea route to China or Indonesia, instead lands on islands in the Caribbean.

Contents at a Glance

Cartoons at a Glance

By Rich Tennant

page 257

"Oh great - it's the Huns. Have you ever seen what these guys do to a salad bar?"

page 9

page 349

"And believe it or not children, some of your ancestors could be related to this fellow right here."

page 297

page 155

page 33

Cartoon Information:
Fax: 978-546-7747
E-Mail: richtennant@the5thwave.com
World Wide Web: www.the5thwave.com

Table of Contents

Introduction

• •

*T*he complete history of the world boiled down to about 330 pages and crammed between yellow paperback covers? The idea is preposterous, outrageous. I'd be crazy to attempt it. So here goes. . . .

No, wait. This book doesn't claim to be "complete." It can't. There are hundreds of other volumes devoted to a measly decade or two — World War II comes to mind. To plumb thousands of years in one little book would be impossible. To skim across the surface, however, is another matter. If, while reading the following chapters, you hit upon an era, a personality, a civilization, that you'd like to know more about, there's no lack of places to find out more. I point you toward more complete accounts in this excellent *...For Dummies* series. If you're interested in the history of the United States, for example, try *U.S. History For Dummies* by Steve Wiegand (published by Hungry Minds, Inc.). But if you want a collection of short, easy-to-read glimpses into the major players and events that have made the world what it is today, this is your first-stop reference.

History: The Ultimate Soap Opera

If history scares you, or if it bores you silly, that's probably because a teacher once required you to memorize dates — when things like the Magna Carta and the Versailles Treaty were signed, for example. Admittedly, dates are a big part of history, but only because historical events happened in a certain order. If Columbus hadn't sailed the ocean blue in fourteen hundred and ninety-two, the *Mayflower* Pilgrims might not have looked west for a place to practice their Puritan religion almost 130 years later. The eventual outcome? No day-after-Thanksgiving mob scenes at the mall. One thing leads to another, just as it does on *The Young and the Restless* (eventually).

History is a record of what happened; of who did what to whom. The word *history* is from the same Latin root that, by a slightly different path, came down to us as "story." That's what history is made of, the stories of people who changed things.

The history of the world is kind of like a soap opera that's been running ever since the invention of writing. It's a really lurid soap opera, full of dirty tricks and murder, romances and sexual deceptions, adventures, and wars and revolutions. (And, yes, treaties and dates.) Or maybe a better analogy is that history is like hundreds of soap operas with thousands of crossover characters jumping out of one story and into another — too many for even the most devoted fan to keep straight. All the more reason for an easy-to-use overview.

The most important thing to remember when paging through this book is that history is fun — or should be. It's not as if this is life-and-death stuff . . . No, wait. It *is* life-and-death — on a humongous scale. It's just that so many of the lives and deaths happened long ago. And that's good. I can pry into private affairs without getting sued. History is full of vintage gossip and antique scandal, peppered heavily with high, old adventure (swords and spears and canons and stuff). The more you get into it, the better you'll do when the neighbors drag out the home version of *Jeopardy*. Renaissance Italy for $500, please.

Getting to the Truth — or Something Close

History must be true, or at least reasonably close to what really happened. (Although historians often disagree about the details.) History is also understood to be a written account (or at least on videotape). There is *oral history,* but until the tale is set down in some permanent form, it's too easy for facts to get lost or changed. Things written down aren't immune to exaggeration, but there's something about the spoken word that invites outlandish embroidering. (Think about fishing stories or campaign speeches.) That's how history gets mangled and myths get made — that, and the TV miniseries.

Some of the first stories ever written down had been passed on by word-of-mouth for centuries before they ever were etched in mud or stone or on papyrus. They had gotten pretty wild over the years. Homer, a blind Greek poet, passed down a tale of the Trojan War that is based on a real military campaign. But many of his details are obviously myth. That stuff about Achilles' mom being a water nymph, for example, and the way she supposedly dipped him in the River Styx to make him invulnerable — forgive me if I don't buy that as exactly the way things went down. (Now, if Homer had told us Achilles was an alien from the planet Krypton . . .)

Positively post-historic

Because history needs to be set down in some kind of permanent record, it dates back only about as far as the written word, which some scholars say the Sumerians invented, at least in pictograph (or picture-writing) form, around 3500 BC. Among the best early record keepers were the Egyptians, who invented their own form of writing (hieroglyphs) around 3000 BC. Before written history it was *prehistoric* times.

A few words about biases

History took a beating in the late twentieth century. No, not just because of the Monica Lewinsky scandal. I'm talking about the way some university professors and political activists questioned the very concept of "history." "Whose history are we talking about?" they asked. Human beings are subjective, they said, so there's no such thing as "truth." If the victors write history, why do we accept those big bullies' tainted point of view as true? What about the victims? What about the indigenous peoples (American Indians, for example, and Australian Aborigines)? What about the women? Aside from Cleopatra, Joan of Arc, Elizabeth I of England, and Catherine the Great of Russia, females don't get a whole lot of credit. Doesn't it stink that so much of history is so overwhelmingly about white men?

It's true that history is slanted. It's about people, by people, so prejudice goes without saying. There are the biases of the time in which events happened, the biases of the time when they were written down — and the prejudices of the scholars who turn them over and over again decades, and often centuries, later. I can't change the fact that so many conquerors, politicians, soldiers, explorers and yes, historians, have been men. (Short of postmortem sex changes, that is.) It's just as true that conventionally taught world history focuses on Europe — how it was shaped and how it shaped other parts of the world, including the Americas.

Are there other stories worth telling, other points of view, other "truths"? You bet. You find some of them in this book, lightly touched upon, just like everything else here. But to be honest, the tilt is toward a male-centered history of what has been called Western Civilization. Why? Because that view is built on firmly set-down, well documented, widely disseminated tales of how the world became as it is — how twenty-first century humans got to be the way they are. And even if you want to change the world — or just change the history books — it helps to know what you're up against.

Conventions Used in This Book

Every field from brain surgery to refuse collection has a special vocabulary. History is no exception, but I tried to steer clear of historians-only words in this book. When such a word is unavoidable, I explain it. If historical labels, such as the names of eras ("medieval" and so on) worry you, check out

Chapter 2 to for a discussion of what they're for and why you can relax. If you still think you may get lost amid the dates, facts, quotes, and other details coming up, read on for an explanation of how tell the centuries apart, and how to use handy, helpful icons to find your way through the chapters.

Making sense of AD, BC, CE, and BCE

The years 1492, when Columbus sailed, and 1620, when the *Mayflower* Pilgrims arrived in Massachusetts, are AD, just like this year. It means *Ano Domini*. That's Latin for "Year of Our Lord," referring to the Christian era, or the time since Jesus was born. Before that, I designate years as BC, or Before Christ. Historians now prefer CE, for "Common Era," instead of AD, and BCE, for "Before the Common Era," instead of BC. The new initials aren't tied into just one religion. AD and BC, however, are what most people are used to. They're widely understood and deeply ingrained, so I stick with them here.

Remember that the years BC are figured by counting backwards. That's why the year that Alexander the Great died, 323 BC, is a smaller number than the year that he was born, 356 BC.

Yet Alexander didn't think of himself as living in backward-counting years three centuries before Christ, any more than Augustus Caesar of Rome wrote the date 1 AD on his checks. This system of dating years came about a lot later and it was superimposed on earlier times. Since most modern scholars think Jesus actually may have been born a little earlier than 1 AD — perhaps in about 6 BC (other historians estimate his birth as late as 7 AD) — the system isn't even particularly accurate. Perhaps the world didn't come to an end when we hit the year 2000 because the year 2000 occurred exactly 2,000 years after nothing in particular.

In this book, you can safely assume that a four-digit year without two capital letters following it is AD. For example: William the Conqueror invaded England in 1066. For the years 1 to 999 AD, I use the AD to remind you that I'm referring to a date. Example: The teenage boy who grew up to become St. Patrick was captured by pirates and sold into slavery in about 401 AD. I also include the initials for all the BC years. Examples: Saul was anointed the first king of the Israelites in about 1050 BC. The Roman general Marc Antony died in 30 BC.

The reason I say "about" when giving the dates of Patrick's kidnapping and King Saul's coronation is that nobody knows for sure. That's why, especially when dealing with ancient times, you often see a "c." in front of a date, or the word *circa,* which is Latin for "about." In this book, I use "about" and some-times "around."

Another thing that confuses some people when reading history is the way centuries are named. When you say the nineteen hundreds it doesn't mean the same thing as the nineteenth century. The nineteen hundreds are the twentieth century. This may sound stupid, but it's not. And it's amazing how many intelligent people are thrown by it, so let's take it slowly.

The twenty-first century is the one in which four-digit year numbers start with 20. The nineteenth century was the one in which years started with 18, and so on. Why isn't the century with the 20 starting every year the twentieth? Because the first century began in the year 1. When the numbers got up to 100 (or technically, 101), it became the second century. When they got up to 201 it was the third century, and so on. So the eleven hundreds were the twelfth century and the nineteen hundreds were the twentieth century. To figure the centuries BC, it works the same way (in reverse, of course) The twenty-first century BC is the one with years starting with 20, just like the twenty-first century AD — except that the people living at the time had no idea it was 2001 BC. Lucky for them. If you think *you're* confused, just imagine having to count backward to look forward.

Keeping an eye out for icons

In the margins of this book, you can see little picture road signs that clue you into what's going on in that particular paragraph or section. Some may warn you what to skip. Others may help you find just what you're interested in.

This icon clues you into an event, decision, or discovery that changed the world.

Screenwriters, perpetually hungry for plots, are always mining history for story ideas. This icon alerts you to Hollywood versions of real stories.

Okay, the quote in this icon is from Abraham Lincoln, who I barely mention in this book. But you do recognize it as a quote, which is the point. This icon marks memorable sayings worth repeating over coffee or cocktails.

This icon marks major historical concepts, as well as the key theme of a chapter — or the book.

This icon clues you in to when, where, and/or how things were made and to how things got done. For example, this icon marks paragraphs that tell you what society invented paper, and who came up with a more accurate compass.

How to Read This Book

You can start here and read to the end, but I don't recommend it. The parts are organized so that you can jump in any place you want. As you page through and browse, note that you can look at the same era from different perspectives. Part III, for example, is about philosophy and religion and how they shaped history. There you can find the religious wars that followed the Protestant Reformation. But if you're more interested in the weaponry and strategies of war, jump to Part IV. And if you just want browse through a sampling of people from history, check out Part V. Not sure? Part I is a good place to get a general feel for history. The table of contents and index, along with this short but sweet explanation of what I cover in each Part, should get you to the page you need.

Part 1: Getting Into History

How do you get "into" history? This part includes perspective to help you connect with the past. Your ancestors of decades, centuries, millennia past were essentially the same as you, except that they didn't have cell phones and Web sites. They may not have showered very often, either, but they can still show you things about yourself.

Part II: Civilizations

How did human society get to be a worldwide, interconnected network of cultures? This part of the book traces the growth from the earliest civilizations to today's global community.

Part III: Mind, Soul, Heart

You can glimpse ways that thoughts, ideas, and feelings — and the way people express and explore them in religion and philosophy — have always been a fundamental part of history.

Part IV: War

History isn't all conflict between nations — or between the government and the governed — but violent clashes and upheavals have immediate, often widespread and sometimes long-lasting global consequences.

Part V: People

This part includes an extremely incomplete collection of capsule biographies of people who changed history, along with a few who were changed by it.

Part VI: The Part of Tens

In the grand tradition of *For Dummies* books, this part contains easy-to-digest lists of history's unforgettable dates and indelible documents.

Part I
Getting Into History

The 5th Wave By Rich Tennant

"Oh great - it's the Huns. Have you ever seen what these guys do to a salad bar?"

In this part. . .

You may adjust your sense of scale about human experience.

Browsing through history can be like looking at the stars. Even if you don't know a planet from a supernova or the name of a single constellation, the first thing you're likely to get from gazing at the night sky is a sense of how small you are, what a tiny part of a tiny point in a vastness. That's a good place to begin in astronomy, and it's not a bad place to find yourself when peering into world history. Early in a new century and a new millennium, it's easy to think of a hundred years as "a long time," and a thousand years as "a long, long time." The modern habit is to chop up history and social trends into little decade-sized chunks — *the 1980s, the 1990s, the 2000s,* and so on. But if you step back a bit, and consider how long people have been doing a lot of the same things you and I do — buying, selling, cooking, falling in love, traveling, and fighting wars (okay, so I've never fought in a war, but I know people who have) — it can be both humbling and enriching.

Now — whether you define *now* as a day, a year, or a decade — is such a miniscule sliver of history, but it is *part* of the larger thing. There's a sense of *belonging* about that. The human species is a continuum. One of the best parts of being human is that you have more than your own experience to rely on; you have history: Language, lore, reading, writing, and, more recently, microchips, DVDs, and a few other technological tricks help people build on what their ancestors discovered — generations, centuries, and millennia ago. History is a big part; some might say the biggest part, of what defines humanity.

Chapter 1

Finding the Bodies: Real Stories, Real People

*T*wo hundred years is a long time. Two thousand years ago is impossibly ancient. What do I have in common with anybody who lived back then? How can I be interested in somebody that distant, that strange, and that unreal?

They wore funny clothes. They spoke languages nobody speaks anymore. They worshipped cruel gods in flying chariots. They had no computers, no fuel injectors, no freeways, and no digital anything except for fingers. They were too worried about survival to watch *Survivor.* Yet they are me. I know it. It's not that I believe in reincarnation and past lives; I don't. Rather, it's that I'm able to reach back through years, decades, centuries, and millennia, using great tools — hard evidence and my imagination.

If you think of history as lists of facts, dates, battles, and key civilizations, you may discover a lot, but you'll never experience the past's thrill. If, on the other hand, you're able to make the leap — to identify with people who are long dead, to imagine what living their lives must have been like — you may be among those for whom the past becomes a passion, perhaps even an addiction.

To do that, you must realize on a gut level that real people walked the earth long ago, and that they carried within them dreams and fears not so unlike yours. It's not so hard, especially with the aid of what the past's people left behind — their cities, art that shows them looking eerily familiar, and even their exquisitely preserved bodies.

Homing in on Homer

The *Iliad* and the *Odyssey,* epic poems passed down from the ancient Greek singer Homer, tell fantastic stories about a war between Greeks and Trojans, and the journey home from that war. They're *so* fantastic — full of vengeful gods and supernatural peril — that it's hard for modern people to credit any part of them as true.

Yet history is in them, history that became more tantalizing in the late nineteenth century, when the city of Troy turned out to be a real place, one of many ancient Troys built in just the place Homer described. Each rose and fell. Another rose on top of it. The old one was forgotten.

What happened to show that any of them were ever real? An eccentric German businessman dug them up.

Greeks attacked Troy more than 3,200 years ago, in the thirteenth century BC. The stories about that war were already ancient by the time of the philosopher Aristotle and Alexander the Great in the fourth century BC. Nobody knows for sure who Homer was or when he lived (although the ninth century BC is likely — more than 2,800 years ago). As centuries and millennia went by, the real Trojan War faded so far into the past that the legends and myths of Homer's poems were all that was left.

That was until Germany's Heinrich Schliemann, a wealthy amateur archeologist, decided to find Troy. With little but his faith in Homer to go on, he dug up not just one, but a stack of nine Troys built one on top of another. Then he went to Greece and discovered the mighty civilization of Mycenae, which also figures in Homer's saga.

Telling the Troy story

Sure that the *Iliad* was true, Schliemann fixed on an ancient mound at a place called Hissarlik that is close enough to the Aegean Sea for the invading Greeks to have jogged back and forth between it and their camp on the shore, just as Homer's story says they did.

Schliemann hired workers and started digging. Ironically, he hardly slowed down as he passed through what later archeologists identified as the probable Troy of the Trojan War (about 1250 BC), only three levels down.

Schliemann burrowed to an earlier layer of the ancient city, one from before 2000 BC — maybe 700 years earlier than the Troy in Homer's stories. In 1874, he found priceless gold artifacts that he erroneously pronounced must have been the treasures of King Priam, the Trojan king in the *Iliad*.

Not satisfied, Schliemann went back to Greece, looking for the palace of King Agamemnon, the leader of the Greeks in the *Iliad*. Unbelievably, he not only found evidence of a Mycenaean civilization that thrived long before the Classical Greeks (a name historians have assigned to Greeks who lived between about 479 and 323 BC), but he again came up with golden treasure, this time dating from 1550 BC.

Living his odyssey

Schliemann's life was fantastic in itself. Born poor in 1822, he survived a ship-wreck on his way to making a fortune as a commodities trader. By the 1860s, he had more than enough money and decided to pursue his obsession with Homer.

He went to Greece and married a 17-year-old village girl (he was 47); then set out for Turkey to look for ancient Troy.

As an amateur archeologist, Schliemann made mistakes. He may even have cheated. Later experts accused him of planting some of the artifacts he claimed to have unearthed. Still, his success is beyond dispute. With the discovery of Mycenae, he opened up the Greek mainland to waves of fruitful archeological exploration.

Schliemann paved the way for later scientists, such as Arthur Evans (1851 to 1941), an Englishman who uncovered the remains of the great Minoan civilization. (The Minoans were a vigorous, powerful people who thrived on Crete and other Aegean Islands between 3000 and 1450 BC.) Ultimately, Schliemann's work led to discoveries worldwide and to a broader perspective on history. After his finds, discounting ancient stories as mere legend or assuming that a *lost* city was make-believe wasn't as easy. Modern notions of when and where human societies grew into complex civilizations got a kick in the pants.

Raising Atlantis

Archeologists have found many forgotten cities (see the preceding section, also Chapter 3). They keep finding them. Does that mean that *every* lost civilization was for real? Does it mean, for example, that scientists or explorers will someday find the sunken nation of Atlantis? Oops. Did I just mention Atlantis? That's probably a mistake, because there isn't room in this book to delve into even a small fraction of the theories about where and what was Atlantis — if it ever existed.

A land of peace and plenty, destroyed in an overnight cataclysm, Atlantis is remembered only through the writings of Greek philosopher Plato (about 428 to 347 BC), who was making a point about social order and good government. But Plato's descriptions leave room for interpretation, and people have been interpreting wildly for more than 2,000 years.

If Atlantis wasn't in the Atlantic Ocean, just past Gibraltar on your way out of the Mediterranean (and geology seems to dictate that it couldn't have been there), then where was it?

Historians, archeologists, aerial photo experts, mystics, and self-appointed prophets have argued vociferously over the site. Dueling proponents put the *lost continent* everywhere from Britain to Bermuda to Bolivia, from Colorado to the China Sea. One theory claims it was on another planet. And then there are comic books that depict Atlantis still thriving in a giant Plexiglas bubble on the ocean floor. Virtually every theory has to make allowances for Plato getting the story of Atlantis indirectly from an Athenian statesman, Solon, who supposedly got it from scholar-priests on a visit to Egypt in about 590 BC. Because Plato wrote his version almost two centuries later, in about 360 BC, details may have changed along the way, or so many Atlantis seekers have rationalized.

One of the least outrageous theories is that the story of Atlantis is an interpretation of the volcanic disaster that destroyed Santorini, an island in the Mediterranean. Modern archeologists and geologists have studied the way the Santorini cataclysm caused flooding and ashfall that devastated Minoan civilization on nearby Crete.

Santorini (also known as Thera) lies about 45 miles north of Crete, which was the center of the vigorous and apparently peaceful Minoan culture. Minoan ruins are plentiful on what's left of Santorini, but that's only a small remnant of what the island was until about 1470 BC, when the 5,000-foot volcano in its middle exploded and collapsed into the sea. Ever since, the island has been a crescent surrounding a volcanic-crater lagoon.

The volcano started erupting about 1500 BC, and eruptions continued for 30 years, building up to a devastating climax of smoke, ash, hail, lightning, and a tidal wave. It knocked down buildings on islands throughout the region.

The waves, or tsunamis, must have flooded and destroyed coastal villages on Crete. The great palace at Knossos, capital of the Minoan Civilization, was apparently far enough inland to survive in remarkably good shape (as Arthur Evans, one of those who followed in Schliemann's wake, discovered when he dug it up more than 3,000 years later), but some experts theorize that the volcanic ash that soon settled over virtually everything hastened the civilization's end. Plants died. Crops failed. Famine followed. It wasn't long, this theory goes, before Myceneans from Greece overran the starving Minoans who remained, and Knossos finally fell. Is this really what happened? Nobody knows for sure. And nobody really knows if the sinking of Santorini had anything to do with launching a lasting legend of a capsized civilization.

Egypt traded with the Minoans. Egyptians were river people who took much of what they knew about the world beyond the Nile from traders who crossed the Mediterranean. When the Minoan traders stopped coming, when word of the island cataclysm came up the river, as it surely did, was the story of Atlantis born?

Seeing with Ancient Eyes

In 1999, an exhibition at the Metropolitan Museum of Art in New York featured a sculpture of Pharaoh Menkure and one of his wives. Experts have called the stone carving from about 2490 BC, a time that historians assign to Egypt's *Old Kingdom* (the time when the great pyramids were built), one of the finest examples of Egyptian sculpture ever found. You can see it for yourself in Figure 1-1.

Figure 1-1:
King
Menkure
and his
bride:
Egypt's royal
couple in
2490 BC —
young,
happy, and
in love.

Courtesy of the Museum of Fine Arts, Boston. Reproduced
with permission. ©2000 Museum of Fine Arts, Boston.
All Rights Reserved.

Regardless of what the art crowd sees in it, the sculpture is an eye-popper because it's so, well, real. The royal couple stands like people posing for a formal portrait, but then you notice that her left hand is bent at the elbow, across her bare torso (fashions change, okay?), with her hand pressed against the biceps of his right arm. Where's her other arm? It's wrapped behind him in an embrace, her wrist to his side and her left hand pressed to his lean, bare belly. Now look at the queen's face, the close-lipped smile, the happy crescent eyes over cheeks raised in what might be a suppressed giggle. The king looks pretty glad himself, although maybe a bit more contained about it.

You can't help but look at the pair and think they're just people — happy, in love. Okay, so they're royal, but royal status didn't stop millions of twentieth-century commoners from identifying with Britain's Princess Diana. The Menkures, judging by their demeanor, find this whole business of posing pretty ridiculous.

Put a bikini top on the queen and they're your neighbors, dressed up for Halloween or Mardi Gras (except that their costumes aren't outrageous enough) — a fun-loving young couple. And that's what's so great about the statue.

The ultimate thrill of history comes in the moment when you see historical people not as musty names from long ago but as individuals — real people with feelings like your own.

Reading the Body Language of the Dead

Some people who lived hundreds and thousands of years ago left more than their images. Preserved bodies are reminders that the people in ancient paintings were flesh and blood and bone. Everybody knows that, of course. Yet the mere fact that a human body from thousands of years past is still intact — more or less — and still recognizably the same as this year's model can help open your mind to the connection between then and now.

There's something about being in the presence of a mummy, or even seeing a photo of one, that helps your imagination bridge all the generations since that puckered flesh was taut, upright, and dancing. It sparks the imagination, one of the best things that history can do.

In history books — especially ones that cover big expanses of time — you have to adjust your perspective so that a century becomes a relatively small unit of history. In this book, you can breeze through a thousand years here, a thousand years there. Thinking of the Byzantine Empire as one civilization, a single station on the history train, is easy to do. Yet, it grew and receded, changed governments, and restructured policies over a stretch of centuries more than five times longer than the United States has been a nation.

When you back up far enough to take that in, you may lose sight of individual lives. They flicker past so quickly. I find that contemplating mummies is a helpful tool for hooking into the perspective of a single life span, a single individual, so long ago. Strangely, you can easily identify with a mummy, if you don't find that too macabre.

Mummies have turned up all over the world. Some were preserved naturally, by something in the environment where the body came to rest. Others, as in the celebrated tombs of ancient Egypt, were artfully prepared for their voyage into death.

Freezing facts

Two hikers, enjoying the Otzal Alps on the border between Austria and Italy in the unusually warm European summer of 1991, spotted what seemed to be a body melting out of the high-altitude ice. Alarmed, they suspected a climbing accident, common in those parts, and notified a nearby innkeeper. A forensic team responded a few days later. (Bodies of accident victims in the Alps have lain frozen for 40 or even 50 years, so there seemed little rush.)

When the corpse — which appeared to be naturally freeze-dried — proved too firmly stuck to the rocks for them to lift out, members of the forensic team borrowed a ski pole and an ax. Using these tools to clear away ice, they saw that the remains were of a bearded man, dressed in leather. Perhaps he was a back-to-nature hippie whose 1960s wanderings went tragically awry? No, there were other curious things that emerged as the team worked — things such as the man's hand-made knife, with its blade of flint. And those clumps of animal hair around the body showed that his clothes were furs.

Instead of the morgue, local authorities shipped the freeze-dried body to the University of Innsbruck in Austria, where initial estimates placed its age at 4,000 years. Further research moved the date of death back by 1,300 years, meaning that "Otzi," as scientists nicknamed him, was journeying over the mountain pass in about 3300 BC when he fell or lay down and was quickly covered by falling snow.

Otzi — now carefully kept in Italy's Museo Archologico dell'Alto Adige in Bolzano — is a natural mummy, a body preserved by nature. Scientists find out all kinds of things about the ways people lived and died from mummies, especially those preserved whole. Otzi suffered from a number of chronic illnesses, and his medicine pouch contained herbal prescriptions for what ailed him. Researchers even probed the corpse's stomach to find out what his last meal was. It was mostly grain.

Otzi's mummified body and the things found with it prompted scholars to rethink assumptions about the roots of European civilization. For one thing, Otzi carried a copper-headed ax, showing that the transition from stone technology to metal happened much earlier than archeologists used to believe. Grains of processed wheat sticking to his clothing showed that he was in contact with agriculture. If Otzi wasn't a farmer, he was among farmers.

The rest of his gear — a longbow, a quiver of arrows, a waterproof cape woven of grass, even his lightweight wooden pack frame — show that Otzi, aged between 40 and 50 when he died, was well equipped for his trek across the mountains. The stress patterns in his leg bones suggested he took such journeys routinely. If a chance storm hadn't caught Otzi, he probably would have completed his trip and eventually been buried among loved ones instead of being mummified in an Alpine snow bank to become an ambassador from an unremembered past.

Salting away something for the future

Mummies occur not just in ice, but in other environments. In the dry climate of Chinese Turkestan (between Russia and Mongolia) bodies buried in the salty soil near the towns of Cherchen and Loulan as long as 4,000 years ago turned into mummies rather than rotting away.

The Turkestan mummies appear to be of Caucasian ancestry, a fact that challenges latter-day assumptions about the range of certain ethnic groups four millennia ago. Based on their well-made, colorful clothing, they may have been related to the Celts, whose culture would later flourish all over Europe, and whose descendents include the Irish, Scots, and Welsh. The fabrics show weaving techniques similar to those still practiced in rural Ireland in the twentieth century AD.

Getting bogged down

Surprisingly, mummies aren't always dry. The watery peat bogs of northern Europe also made many mummies. Tannins in the *peat* (partially decayed plant matter) and the cold water preserved bodies in such startlingly good condition that Danish villagers have sometimes mistaken a 2,500-year-old body for that of someone they knew only decades before.

The bodies, though discolored by the tannins, look much as they did when the people died. Some people fell into the bogs, but many were killed and dumped there, probably as ritual sacrifices or as victims of another kind of execution. Mummies of young women wear blindfolds, and some appear to have been drowned alive. Some mummies have ropes around their necks and others' throats were slit.

Most have skin, hair, fingernails, and even facial expressions intact. And their jewelry and clothing sometimes look unsettlingly like something that could hang in your twenty-first-century closet. If you think of a pleated, plaid woolen skirt, for example, as a timeless style, you're more right than you know. Danish women wore them in 500 BC.

Staying dry and well preserved

The 500-year-old bodies of Inca children in the Argentine Andes that archeologist Johan Reinhard and a team from the National Geographic Society discovered in the 1990s atop Mount Llullaillaco are among the best-preserved mummies ever found. Apparently killed in a religious ritual sacrifice, the boy and two girls — aged between 8 and 15 — were so perfectly frozen (rather than freeze-dried like Otzi) that the scientist said they looked as if they had just drawn their last breaths.

The Argentine discoveries are more than fascinating and informative; they're also terribly sad. The idea of killing an 8-year-old is so repellent to people today that you may recoil in horror. You may grieve a bit for the long-dead child and wonder what can possibly possess a culture to do such a thing — to worship gods that must have the blood of innocents. Yet that's another reason why the three preserved bodies are so compelling. They draw you into the past as you struggle to comprehend how these people — so startlingly similar to people today — understood the world in such a different way.

Mummies who were victims of (or willing volunteers for) sacrificial rites, can tell researchers many things about ancient religious practices. (Chapter 9 has more on religions.) Bodies that were carefully buried illuminate long-ago attitudes toward death. At least they give scientists a basis for speculation. Cultures without a written record, however, can be tough to figure out.

The Chachapoya people of what is now Northern Peru left hundreds of mummies, but researchers don't know why or even exactly how the bodies were preserved. Treasure hunters found a cache of 200 mummies in 1996, hidden away in dry caves where the wet mountain weather of Laguna de los Cóndores (Lake of the Condors), near the modern town of Leimebamba, couldn't penetrate. The Chachapoya, or Cloud People, apparently developed their own method of embalming skin. They removed internal organs and stuffed facial cavities with cotton, but much about the Chachapoya culture is lost. These mountain folk were conquered by the neighboring Inca about 500 years ago, not very long before the Inca, in turn, fought against and lost to the invading Spanish in the early sixteenth century.

Preserving pharaohs

Perhaps nobody devoted quite so much thought and energy to death and the afterlife as the ancient Egyptians. After burying their dead with great care and ceremony since perhaps 4000 BC (Chapter 3 has more on ancient Egypt), the Egyptians began artfully mummifying their pharaohs sometime before the twenty-fourth century BC.

By the year 2300 BC, the practice had spread beyond royalty. Any Egyptian who could afford it was dried and fortified for the trip into the afterlife. The mummy was buried with many possessions and even servants for the next world.

Egyptian mummies differ from many others in that researchers actually can figure out whose bodies many of them were in life.

Egypt's King Tutankhamen's identity is intact thanks to ancient Egyptian writings, called hieroglyphics. British Egyptologist Howard Carter dug up his magnificent and previously undisturbed underground tomb in 1922, making Tutankhamen the most famous pharaoh in the twentieth century AD, even though he was probably a long way from that in the fourteenth century BC.

The moment Carter first gazed by candlelight into the wonders of that tomb, unseen for more than 3,300 years, has been held up ever since as the ideal archeological breakthrough — completely unlike most great discoveries, which are scratched out of the ancient dust and pieced painstakingly together. Tutankhamen's tomb, by contrast, was a storehouse of perfectly kept treasures.

Carter said that he stood there for a long, long moment, allowing his eyes to penetrate the gloom, lit only by the candle he held. His patron and partner, George Herbert, Earl of Carnarvon, stood behind him in the dark, unable to stand the suspense.

"Do you see anything?" asked Carnarvon breathlessly. "Yes," replied Carter in a hushed tone. "Wonderful things."

Carter's sensational discovery made all the papers, and so did Carnarvon's untimely death. The earl died of an infected mosquito bite a few months after he helped Carter find the tomb. Naturally, somebody blamed his death on an ancient curse against anyone who disturbed the boy-king's eternal rest. (Grave robbers were the scourge of Egypt's royalty.)

The notion of the mummy's curse may have disappeared if it weren't for a 1932 horror movie called *The Mummy,* which is completely wrong on every point of archeology and Egyptian religion, but features a compellingly subtle performance by Boris Karloff in the title role. *The Mummy* was successful enough that remakes and variations followed, including a 1959 version with Christopher Lee as the undead Egyptian. A 1999 tongue-in-cheek version of *The Mummy* stars Brendan Fraser.

Judging by the likeness on his mummy case, Tutankhamen had movie star looks, but he may not have had the time or experience to make much of an impact as a monarch. Tutankhamen took the throne in 1361 BC, at about age 9, succeeding Akhenaton (who was a heretic by Egyptian standards of the time, and a controversial king). King Tut, as folks in the twentieth century dubbed him, reigned for only 11 years. He died young and left a terrific-looking corpse.

Not every Egyptian mummy has a name. Sometimes a historical figure goes unrecognized. That may have happened to Pharaoh Rameses (or Ramses) I, whose body some researchers think is one of ten unidentified mummies that Emory University in Atlanta bought from a Canadian museum in 1999. Although not much is known about the specific achievements of Rameses I, he ruled from 1340 to 1318 BC and founded the great Nineteenth Dynasty.

Rameses I's mummy may have been overlooked among those in the collection purchased by Emory's Michael C. Carlos Museum. At least, that's what some U.S. scientists decided, based in part on family resemblance: The scientists noticed how much one of the mummies in the group — entombed in the significantly regal, arms-crossed pose — looked like that of Seti I, Rameses' son and heir. The mummy in question is from the correct era, so it may be the long-lost king.

TECHNICAL STUFF

Wrapping up a mummy

If you got a job preparing wealthy and royal Egyptians for the afterlife, how would you go about it? Here's the recipe:

1. First, remove the internal organs. Wait! Leave the heart. Egyptians considered it the control center for thought and action, so they figured they'd need it in the afterlife. What to do with the other organs? Put them in jars decorated with the heads of gods, or maybe a likeness of the dearly departed. The jars go in the tomb along with the mummy.

2. Now bathe the disemboweled body with spices and palm wine. Next, cover it with *natron salts,* a pasty form of sodium found in drying lakebeds, to retard spoilage and dry out the skin. Let it sit awhile.

3. When it's good and dry, take wadded-up linens and stuff them inside where the organs were, kind of like stuffing a turkey with bread crumbs, celery, onions, and sage. See if you can't restore the person's shape to something resembling lifelike.

4. After you do that, wrap more linens, cut into neat strips, around the outside to create that creepy, bandaged look that will scare the pants off moviegoers a few millennia later.

5. All wrapped? Finally, put it in a coffin, preferably a double coffin, one inside another. If you're working on a Pharaoh, put the coffin inside a stone sarcophagus, inside a hidden tomb or a formidable pyramid.

If you do it right, with sufficient time for drying, it takes two months, perhaps more. That doesn't count the years spent building a pyramid. The most famous of those, the Great Pyramid at Giza, was a tomb for King Khufu (who ruled more than a thousand years before Tutankhamen or Rameses, from about 2551 to 2528 BC). It contained 2,300 blocks of stone and stood 486 feet tall.

Tracking the Centuries

About 4000 BC: Egyptians begin burying their dead with ritual care.

About 3300 BC: A well-equipped traveler, a man in his 40s hiking through the Italian Alps, lies down in the snow and freezes to death.

2490 BC: Menkure rules Egypt's Old Kingdom.

About 1470 BC: The volcanic island of Santorini erupts, destroying an island, wiping out villages and probably ending a civilization.

1352 BC: Tutankhamen, young king of Egypt, dies.

About 1250 BC: A confederation of Greek kings and warriors attack the city of Troy, in today's Turkey.

Ninth century BC: The bard Homer sings about the Trojan War.

Early fourth century BC: In Athens, the philosopher Plato writes about Atlantis, a land lost under the sea.

Fifteenth century AD: Inca Empire conquers the Chachapoya people of Northern Peru.

1870s: Heinrich Schliemann, a commodities broker and amateur archeologist, finds Homer's Troy.

1922: Britain's Howard Carter opens Tutankhamen's perfectly preserved tomb.

1991: Hikers in the Italian Alps discover the 3,300-year-old mummy of a well-outfitted traveler. Researchers nickname him Otzi.

Chapter 2
Making History Happen

This world formed almost six billion years ago. I find that hard to grasp. I know it to be an informed estimate derived from science, but my mind balks at of processing how long a billion years is. Six billion? Forget it.

Even a million years ago can stump me, but it's within range. In imagining what the world looked and felt like that long ago, I'm armed with the knowledge that there were beings not completely unlike me, members of a species called *Homo erectus* (human, upright), who saw it and felt it. It helps to have somebody to identify with.

If I really want to bring the past into perspective, I start with recent times. Okay, recent is a relative term. I'm talking 40,000 years ago. That number comes up when scientists discuss the transition from a recent model, *Homo sapiens* (human, wise), to the state of the art, *Homo sapiens sapiens* (human, double wise), also called *fully modern* people.

Being Human Beings

Humanity turned a corner about 40,000 years ago. They carved patterns into rocks and made rafts to cross water — things that mark them as more like you, less like their *Homo erectus* ancestors.

Modern is a relative term. You can assign it to this year's fashions or next year's software. Some evolution experts apply the word *modern* to *Homo sapiens*, whose skeletons indicate that they closely resembled people today. Others reserve the term *modern* for *Homo sapiens sapiens* the more recent development whose cave paintings and tools suggest that they had already become the people who would go on to build cathedrals, sailing ships, microchips, and space shuttles.

The evolutionary path toward being human diverged from that of apes more than four million years ago, as relatively small-brained creatures, not unlike chimpanzees, got up on their hind legs.

A familiar illustration shows successive ancestor species (*Australopithicus, Homo habilis,* and so on) marching single file, ever taller and less hairy, toward modern humanity. It didn't happen that way. Evolution is rarely that neat. Different kinds of more-or-less humanlike animals lived at the same time. Some died out — genetic dead ends. Others gave rise to people.

Early *Homo sapiens* developed in Africa perhaps as long as 600,000 years ago. Its skeleton was much like yours, but with key differences in brain size and head shape. By 120,000 years ago, skulls featured high, domed braincases and flat foreheads (instead of the old-fashioned sloping style). But when did these creatures become modern? When did the older models die out? Scientists know that by 50,000 BC some skeletons were just like those of people today; and around 40,000 BC, this latest model of human being was making art, such as etchings on rocks. This change marks *Homo sapiens sapiens* (the species so nice, they named themselves twice) as unique.

Modern humans, as a species, are quite young. *Homo erectus* was on the Earth much longer than modern people have been. *Homo erectus* appeared about 1.6 million years ago and started traveling by one million years ago. *Homo erectus* hung around until at least 300,000 BC.

If the entire time since early, upright-walking *hominid* (humanlike) species such as *Australopithecus* (southern ape) were represented as a single, 24-hour day, then *Homo erectus* lasted for about 8 hours. By that scale, modern humans have been here a bit more than 15 minutes.

Nearing the Neanderthal

Like *Homo erectus,* all earlier hominids are extinct — unless you buy the idea that the North American Sasquatch (Bigfoot) and the Tibetan Yeti (Abominable Snowman) are your reclusive country cousins.

The nearest relative who left much evidence was the Neanderthal of Ice Age Europe and Asia Minor, a big-brained branch of the family that died out perhaps 28,000 years ago. The Neanderthal, or *Homo sapiens neandertalensis,* arose about 150,000 years ago in Ice Age Europe, probably descended from the widely traveled *Homo erectus.* It was a robust offshoot, a species adapted to harsh northern conditions.

The Neanderthal lived for long ages apart from other human ancestors. But, after glaciers receded, anatomically modern types migrated into the Neanderthal's part of the world. The two kinds of humans coexisted for thousands of years, both leaving evidence of their camps among the same hills, valleys, and caves.

Nobody knows how, or if, they got along with one another. Did they fight? Did modern humans wipe out their cousins in long ages of brutal genocide? Or did the newcomers simply have better survival skills?

The idea that the two species mated is especially interesting, if unlikely. What if the rest of humankind absorbed Neanderthal characteristics? Most experts say it couldn't have happened. They say interbreeding was impossible between two such different species. Others won't let go of the idea. If it's true, it's nothing to worry about. Neanderthals wouldn't be such bad ancestors, despite the big brow ridges and sloping foreheads. Neanderthals had big brains — maybe bigger than yours — and they did some rather *modern* things, such as burying their dead with flowers and *ochre,* a reddish clay used for its color, like body paint. They had stone tool technology, although they may have learned the latest techniques from their modern neighbors.

The stupid, club-carrying brute stereotype is probably just that, a stereotype. In the 1985 movie clunker *Clan of the Cave Bear,* tall, blonde Daryl Hannah rejects uncouth Neanderthal advances, perpetuating the idea that those guys had nothing to offer the gene pool.

Some prehistorians have suggested that the mixing of species, Neanderthal and Cro-Magnon (another name for the earliest modern humans in Europe), brought an explosion of culture, perhaps the very invention of art. However the two kinds of people dealt with each other, somebody invented art. After about 35,000 BC, cave paintings were all the rage. And the new technology — making rocks really, really sharp — spread, too. By the time the Neanderthal vanished, humans had been fashioning ingenious stone tools for many millennia. People were using counting devices (notches on a bone) in South Africa, engraving rocks in Australia, and making axes in New Guinea.

One of the most remarkable things about *Homo sapiens sapiens* is that this upright-walking, tool-using creature spread so quickly and so far. Modern humans evolved in Africa, where earlier hominids also originated. Then they migrated on their two spindly legs, not just into Europe where the Neanderthals had been coping with ice ages, but over all the other continents except Antarctica, crossing land bridges (such as the ones that periodically linked Siberia and Alaska), until by 9000 BC there were people, at the southern tip of South America.

You Talkin' to Me?

Before counting devices and pictures on rocks, human beings accomplished a more remarkable feat — they talked. Other species communicate with noises and some — birds and certain monkeys, for example — have complex vocabularies. But no other creature has anything as versatile or expressive as human language.

Scientists don't know when language happened. Could the first physiologically modern humans make all the sounds that their descendants do? Who can tell? Soft tissues such as the tongue and larynx rot away, even when bones fossilize. Yet whenever it came about, language brought huge change. Not only could humans warn of leopards and call the children to dinner with unprecedented eloquence; they could also share information.

Imagining what life was like before the spoken word is difficult. Take a look at the 1981 film *Quest for Fire,* the title of which sums up the plot. Author Anthony Burgess, who also wrote *A Clockwork Orange,* composed grunts and gestures for the film's cavemen, but the result is less than convincing.

Language probably started out as imitative sounds or noises expressive of emotions such as fear (a cry) or anger (a roar), but as people gave specific meanings to combinations of vocal sounds, they were devising symbols. A sound stood for a thing or an action. People were discovering how to think in the abstract. Could this shift have brought about art?

Able to exchange information, people began to amass it — not just as individuals, but as societies. You always could learn by watching and doing. But now you could also understand by somebody telling you: The *how to* genre was born. You could benefit from hearing about experiences of tribe members no longer living.

After tribes built *lore* — a body of shared knowledge — they could embellish. They could spin hunting stories that did more than help successive generations find and kill large prey. Within several generations, tribes surely had more fanciful folktales — about heroes, creation, and gods who commanded the stars and earth. (See Chapter 9 for more on early religion.) After writing developed (Chapter 3 talks about the written word), it was possible for cultures to leave a permanent record of events. Early written history, as in Egypt, was often the official record of a battle, or even the passage of a law or tax.

Herodotus the Greek, credited as the father of history, took his subject to the level of intellectual inquiry in the fifth century BC as he gathered thousand-year-old stories from around the Mediterranean. As the body of history grew, there came a need to organize it.

Labeling Eras

If your high school history teacher told you that *medieval* means the Middle Ages, the period between the fall of Rome (476 AD) and the Renaissance (the fourteenth century), you could have thrown the author H.G. Wells at him.

Not literally, of course. Let Mr. Wells rest in peace. Yet it might surprise certain teachers that historians disagree about when the period called *medieval* began. Wells is better remembered today as a pioneering science fiction writer, author of *War of the Worlds,* but he also wrote a three-volume *Outline of History.* In this big, 1920 history of the world, he began the second volume, called *Medieval History,* at 300 BC, with the rise, not the fall, of Rome's empire.

So what, you ask? That's my point. History is full of periods divided by arbitrary lines etched in the shifting sands of time.

Historians have points of view. The good ones have really well-informed points of view, but that doesn't mean they all march in intellectual lockstep.

Sorting Ancient from Modern

"That's ancient history, pops." In American *youth* movies from the 1930s to the 1950s, a teenager often says something like that to an older guy — dismissing a relatively recent event as too long ago to matter.

Ancient is another relative term like *modern* and *medieval.* To a child born in 2001, the teenager in that 1950s movie may seem beyond ancient. But in history, *ancient* has more specific meanings.

In his *Outline of History,* England's H.G. Wells (1866 to 1946) defined *ancient* as "From the World Before Man to the Rise of the Roman Empire." The kid in the movie would laugh at Wells beginning the *Modern* period in 1567, when King Philip II of Spain sent Fernando, Duke of Alva, to put down a rebellion in the Netherlands.

Naming eras

Classifications can be helpful, as long as you don't get so hung up on drawing lines across time that you take the fun out of history.

Scholars name periods for an event, such as Columbus's arrival in the Americas. Times before that in the Western Hemisphere are frequently called *pre-Columbian.* Period labels are often based on the reign of a monarch, such as England's Elizabeth I. Events, fashions, and literature from her reign (1558 to 1603, a golden age of English culture) wear the designation *Elizabethan*. A label may cover much longer periods, as when they derive from Chinese dynasties. The Ming Dynasty ruled from 1368 to 1644.

Sometimes a label's meaning is fleeting. I was born and grew up in the postwar United States, but as World War II fades farther into history, the term *postwar* is less widely understood. What war are you talking about, anyway?

The labels on periods and eras are worthwhile only if they help readers understand. Some can seem more arbitrary than others. For example, only sixteenth-century England under the reign of Elizabeth I wears the tag *Elizabethan*. But *Victorian* sticks to nineteenth-century fashions, attitudes, and architecture, even in places that Victoria never ruled.

Elizabethan would never fit late-sixteenth-century China (Ming) or late-sixteenth-century Peru (ruled by the Spanish). Yet *Victorian,* a term for the period between 1837 and 1901, when Victoria I was queen of Great Britain and empress over its vast colonial holdings around the world, has been applied well outside her sphere. Victoria never ruled California, but San Francisco is recognized for its *Victorian* architecture. (See both queens in Figures 2-1 and 2-2.)

Figures 2-1 and 2-2: Queens who lent their names to eras: Elizabeth I (left) and Victoria (right).

© Archivo Iconografico, S.A./CORBIS

© Bettmann/CORBIS

Classical schmassical

Classical is another historical label. Applied to the years 479 to 323 BC, it refers to the Classical Greeks, hailed as founders Western civilization's core values — rationality, freedom of debate, individuality, and democracy. Yet the interpretation can be challenged.

Dr. Leslie Kurke, of the University of California, Berkeley, digs into Greek civilization to find the arguments that gave rise to classic ideas. She points out that Greeks did not get together and say, "Let's value rational thought." Greek city-states fought each other; Greek thinkers disagreed. To say that the Greeks originated modern ideas is to overlook how weird some of their ideas were. In Aristotle's time you could argue that women are "failed men," a lesser rendering of the same biological pattern as males. I don't recommend that you try that argument today, at least not in mixed company.

Kurke points out huge differences between the Greeks' notion of democracy — maybe 30 percent of the population, at most, were citizens, and all citizens were men — and today's ideal of democracy.

After historians reinterpret the period, the term *classical* may no longer be helpful to understanding the years 479 to 323 BC. And you know what? That's okay. You can look at the Greeks from any number of angles and they don't get any less fascinating.

As H.G. Wells wrote: "The subject [history] is so splendid a one that no possible treatment . . . can rob it altogether of its sweeping greatness and dignity."

Telling Good Guys from Bad

The founder of the Church of England, King Henry VIII, ordered people killed when it suited his agenda. He executed two of his six wives, as well as his high-minded Lord Chancellor, Sir Thomas More (made a saint by the Roman Catholic Church).

The most successful conqueror of the ancient world, Alexander III of Macedon, was a murderer. One of his victims was a former childhood playmate, close friend, and trusted general who dared to criticize him one night over drinks in Persia. Alexander grabbed a pike and drove it through his buddy.

Alexander continues to be known as *the Great*. (You can read about Henry VIII in Chapter 9. Alexander the Great shows up in Chapters 3 and 15.) History is full of people who had an impact that was frequently violent, often cruel, and even outright evil. *The Great* may refer to a great soldier, but the line between soldier and cold-blooded killer has never been as clear as people would like to think.

Another leader who earned the title *Great* by instituting sweeping reforms, Czar Peter I of Russia transformed a backward nation into a major European power during his 1682 to 1725 reign. But he implemented his reforms so brutally that many Russians hated him. The czar's agents tortured Peter's own son, Alexis, to death after Alexis was accused of conspiracy against the throne. Does history judge Peter an important leader? Without a doubt. Was he a nice person? What do you think?

Verifying virtue

History does recognize goodness, but it pays attention most often when goodness results in political or cultural change. Mohandas Karamchand Gandhi (1869 to 1948), known as the Mahatma or *great soul,* fought racial injustice in South Africa and then fought for his native India's independence from Great Britain — without striking a literal blow.

He adopted the idea of nonviolent civil disobedience espoused by American writer Henry David Thoreau (1817 to 1862) and, in turn, inspired American civil rights leader Dr. Martin Luther King, Jr. (1929 to 1968) to use similar nonviolent protest against racial discrimination in the United States. (See Chapter 21 for more about Gandhi and King.)

Richard Attenborough made a terrific film called *Gandhi* in 1981. Both the movie and its star, Ben Kingsley, won Academy Awards. No single movie, however, can possibly sum up the spiritual leader's life.

Gandhi and King brought about change and stirred resistance. (Assassins killed both men.) Each was arguably *good.* Each sought to make the world a better place.

Had their efforts been in vain Gandhi and King may have faded into the historical background as ineffectual idealists. As an admirer of both men, I'd like to think that their motives had more to do with serving posterity than posturing for it.

Turning traitors

The earliest history celebrates heroes. Homer's epic poems are about the determination, courage, resourcefulness, and persistence of Greek warriors. What if the Trojans had won that legendary war? What if Troy and its culture survived and handed a poem or song down through the ages? Perhaps, the same warriors would have been remembered in a different light — as vicious invaders. History, goes the saying, is written by victors.

How would history have treated George Washington if the American Revolution had failed? By British law, he was certainly a traitor. Guy Fawkes, an English traitor of nearly two centuries earlier, also fought for a cause he thought was just. Led by Robert Catesby, Fawkes and his fellow conspirators tried to stop the persecution of English Catholics.

After less-drastic efforts failed, the conspirators hatched a desperate plan to blow up King James I and Parliament in **1605.** The Gunpowder Plot, as it came to be known, was uncovered in the nick of time.

One conspirator warned his brother-in-law, a member of the House of Lords, not to attend the targeted session. That aroused suspicions. Authorities caught Fawkes in a room underneath the assembly hall, with piles of explosives. The government tried, convicted, and hanged him. Ever since, England marks November 5, the date of his arrest, as Guy Fawkes Night, celebrating with bonfires and fireworks. Effigies of the traitor Fawkes, known as *guys,* are set ablaze. The term *guy* came to refer to a dummy, an insulting thing to call a man. Eventually losing the negative connotation, *guy* became nonjudgmental, as in "you guys." Guy Fawkes, meanwhile, remains one of England's greatest villains — a bad Guy.

Blazing George?

George Washington came down in history a selfless public servant who declined an American crown when it was offered him. Much as Mahatma Gandhi inspired Martin Luther King, Jr., Washington inspired Venezuela's Simón Bolívar, the revolutionary hero of South America. (For more about Washington, see Chapter 18. For more on Bolívar, Chapter 21.) Yet it all could have gone very differently. Imagine an America in which children delighted at the burning of the traitorous *Georges* every July 4.

Hailing Hitler?

Had Germany prevailed in World War II, how would history books depict Adolf Hitler? (For more about Hitler, see Chapter 19.) After losing World War II, Hitler went down in the books as a mass murderer on an epic scale — a madman. More than half a century after he committed suicide in a Berlin bunker, it's hard to imagine him in any other light. Historians pointing out Hitler's domestic successes risk being seen as apologists for his brutal, racist, genocidal programs. Yet history has exalted bloodthirsty monsters before. Keep in mind the brutalities of Alexander and Peter I, both hailed as great. One era's monster may be another era's hero.

Tracking the Centuries

About 6 billion BC: Earth forms.

About 4 million BC: Early hominids (humanlike ancestors) walk on their hind legs.

About 700,000 BC: *Homo erectus* (human, upright) walks out of Africa.

About 40,000 BC: Human beings leave behind early examples of art.

479 to 323 BC: Greek *classical* era gives rise to democracy and rational thought.

1605: Gunpowder Plot against England's King James I is foiled when conspirator Guy Fawkes is caught with explosives.

1945: Adolf Hitler kills himself in a Berlin bunker.

1948: An assassin kills India's Mahatma Gandhi.

Part II
Civilizations

The 5th Wave · By Rich Tennant

In this part. . .

Many people say "civilized" when they mean nice, mannerly, or peaceful. Yet human civilizations, although they achieve peace, rarely sustain it. An often-contradictory concept, civilization started with people building together for community benefit — raising a wall for defense, erecting a tower for surveillance, or digging an irrigation ditch to water crops. It also involved people fighting together against a common foe. Civilization often proves brutally violent — even in the name of enforcing peace.

Working together eventually led to cities, nations, and groups of nations striving toward shared goals. Civilization now stretches worldwide, with no part of humanity completely cut off from society at large.

This part of the book is about how civilization progressed from the first isolated towns, the first public works projects, to the increasingly connected, potentially homogenous (although still diverse and quarrelsome) global society of today.

Chapter 3

Getting Civilized

• •

In This Chapter

▶ Running rivers begin civilization

▶ Writing things down: hieroglyphics and cuneiforms

▶ Conquering the world with Alexander

▶ Spreading the Greek love of wisdom

• •

*P*eople lived for many thousands of years before anybody built a city. Human beings lived *without* cities — with none of what people today call *civilization* — much longer than people have lived *with* cities and civilization. Fully modern people (an idea I talk about in Chapter 2) arose about 40,000 years ago, yet archeologists can't find evidence that anything remotely like a city existed until 11,000 years ago at most. That's almost 30,000 years of pre-urban humanity. And if you count your ancestors who were *almost*, but not quite, like the people of today (also discussed in the previous chapter), humanity got along without urban centers for much, much longer yet.

Human beings, just like you in virtually every genetic detail, made do with a hunter-gatherer lifestyle for generation after generation (and so on), never considering that there could be another way. The people of 20,000 years ago may have thought about large permanent settlements, if the idea ever occurred to them, as impractical. The way to get food reliably was to remain mobile. If you wanted to eat, you went where the plants were ripening, where the shellfish clung to the river rocks, and where the herds and flocks migrated. Depending on the latitude in which you lived, you followed some or all of those food sources every year, each in its appropriate season. And as you wandered, you took care not to merge your band of wanderers with other bands. It wasn't a good idea to have too many mouths to feed.

But when the practice of farming got people to settle down, cities followed. By 10,000 years ago, the town of Jericho (coming up in the next section) was either welcoming travelers who happened by its Middle Eastern desert oasis, or chasing them away with rocks and spears hailed down from its protective walls and tower.

Although they continue piecing together the record of where and how the earliest urban civilizations arose (a complicated story), archeologists know quite a bit about some of the first cities — especially those that rose along major rivers in Iraq and Egypt. For anybody wanting to find out about early civilizations, it helps that Iraq and Egypt are also where people first invented writing. When the written record began (also ahead in this chapter), prehistory turned into history.

Cities grew not just in the Middle East, but also in Pakistan, India, and China, where great civilizations have risen and receded as they interacted with the rest of the world over three or four thousand years. Cities also arose in the Americas, where European invaders wiped out large native civilizations in the sixteenth century AD (more about the European conquest of the Americas in Chapter 7).

Early civilizations, though diverse as humanity, nevertheless experienced common needs — for order, justice, and understanding. Laws, religion, and philosophy all took on forms that led, by a long, circuitous path that I trace in this chapter and throughout this book, to modern ways of thinking and governing. The civilized world that you and I know started to take shape in those first urban societies.

Building Walls for Mutual Defense

Joshua and the Israelites raised a ruckus that brought down the walls of Jericho, a city in Canaan. It says so right in the Bible. What the Bible doesn't say is that those walls of perhaps 3,200 years ago were built on top of walls that were built on top of walls. Maybe that's why Jericho's walls toppled so easily when Joshua and his posse arrived.

Jericho may be the world's oldest city — at least the oldest one found — predating even the early civilizations along the Tigris and Euphrates Rivers in modern-day Iraq. Okay, so some archeologists nit-pick that Jericho is really a town, rather than a city, because it shows no evidence of a large urban society. Even so, Jericho — at a spring-fed oasis that still quenches the thirst of residents in the Palestinian West Bank — offers a startlingly early example of a settlement built to last, and to keep outsiders out.

When Joshua and the gang arrived at its walls, Jericho was already a relic. Science dates the town's earliest buildings to before 8000 BC — at least 10,000 years ago. True, Jericho was abandoned and rebuilt maybe 20 times, but when you're talking all those millennia, what's 20 start-overs?

What kind of town was Jericho? Scientists know how it was built and the shapes of living quarters: first round, later rectangular. Researchers can speculate about the people's lifestyle, based on the stuff found lying around, such as human skulls fitted with realistic plaster faces. (Creepy reconstructions of dead loved ones?)

Most significantly, the walls and a tall stone tower tell a story. They show researchers that Jericho's residents worked together for a common goal — to build civic structures that provided community defense. Working together in such an organized way — whether voluntarily or under the orders of a hard-handed ruler — is a sign of civilization.

Archeologists don't know the names and stories passed from generation to generation by word of mouth in Jericho. Jericho started too soon for writing and too early for recorded history. Civilization didn't wait for a way to write things down so that later generations could read all about its beginnings.

Planting Cities along Rivers

Although Jericho, perhaps the world's first city (see the preceding section), grew at a desert oasis — a prehistoric pit stop — the best known among early large-scale civilizations formed along rivers in Mesopotamia (modern-day Iraq), Egypt, India, and China.

River floods spread rich, silt-laden mud. Besides being fun to squish around in, it enriched the soil and made for good farming, which led to other interesting developments.

Settling between two rivers

The Tigris and Euphrates Rivers must have been particularly attractive places for nomadic people to stop and settle. Coursing through today's Iraq, the twin flows empty into the sea as one. Thousands of years ago, the two rivers had separate mouths, but just as they still do, the lower rivers formed a great marsh. Late Stone Age people lived there in reed huts. As hunter-gatherers and herdsman who lived around the swamp and in the hills to the north turned increasingly toward that hot new lifestyle — farming (a gradual change that took thousands of years) — the fertile river valleys upstream beckoned.

By about 5000 BC, barley and flax farmers dug networks of irrigation canals and built villages along those canals. Their villages grew rapidly until about a dozen impressive cities became the incredible Sumerian civilization, followed after 2000 BC by the great city-state of Babylon (a *city-state* was a city that was a state in itself) and its successive empires.

This was Mesopotamia, the land between the rivers. In the part nearest the sea stood Ur, home to the Bible's Abraham, and the leading city-state in the region between about 2700 and 2300 BC. Like other cities in the region, Ur was built of mud bricks. Besides fertilizing the fields, mud proved the best building material in an area with little stone or wood.

Flooding on a mythic scale

Although made of mud, Sumer sometimes got too much mud: Floodwaters could rise disastrously high. Archeologists found, between the ruins of one Sumerian city and the ruins of the city that came before it, a thick layer of once-oozing, now-dry river mud — evidence of a terrible flood. To the Sumerians, a flood on that scale — one that swept away cities — must have seemed the end of their world. Mud tablets — the first *books* — found in the ruins of one of these cities tell a story of how the gods decided to wipe out mankind with a flood, and how only one man, with his family and animals, was saved. In this Sumerian story, the man's name was not Noah but Utnapishtim.

Growing up along the Nile

Northern Africa, where the great Sahara Desert is today, was once fertile grassland with generous rainfall. It was a good place for animals to graze, and — as was Mesopotamia — a great place for nomadic hunters, gatherers, and herders to wander, stop, try a little farming, and establish villages.

Don't think of the switch to farming as anything sudden. From gathering edible grass seeds for hundreds and probably thousands of years, tribal people knew that if there was enough rainfall, the ground where they beat or trampled seeds to remove the inedible hulls would, after a while, become green with a new growth of that same grass. Seeing their stray seeds sprouting, people tried spreading some of the fattest seeds on the ground in hopes of growing more of the same.

Farming worked only if the people came back to the same place to harvest the crop (often an ancestor of modern wheat), or if they stayed put. But when they had a crop to wait around for — the promise of food — it was easier for them to stop there instead of wandering as nomads. Agricultural villages sprang up.

Something ironic happened in North Africa over those thousands of years when the agricultural lifestyle was taking hold. The weather slowly changed: It rained less. Grasslands and forest gave way to sand. After a long time, fewer seeds sprouted and fewer sprouts matured — not year-by-year but over many, many generations. Villages rose and fell without people being aware of what was happening. In fact, the process is still going on. The Sahara (Arabic for *desert*) still pushes southward, and pushes people farther south. But south isn't the only direction people fled. At least 4,000 years ago and probably much earlier, folks were gathering up the kids (and the goats, too, assuming they'd caught onto that crazy, new, domestic-animal trend), and heading into Asia and the Middle East. In northeastern Africa, they crowded into a thin sliver of land with a terrific source of water — the Nile.

Perils of power

From the time Egypt became one nation, Egypt's increasingly powerful, ever-richer king also underwent a transformation. More than a man, the pharaoh was a living god.

Being a god wasn't as great as it sounds, though, at least not at first. Early kings of unified Egypt had to prove themselves fit to stay on top. A king who failed a rigorous annual physical challenge was considered no longer able to provide for the state and so was killed by priests in ritual sacrifice.

Understandably, considering who made the rules, this practice disappeared by about 2650 BC. Yet letting an *unfit* king die rather than treat him for disease remained customary. That way a healthier god could take his place.

Assembling Egypt

Villages sprang up in the Nile Valley as early as 5000 BC. A thousand years later, people in the valley already buried their dead with meticulous care and orna-mentation, a trend that led to big things, such as Egypt's pyramids. Villages and towns became cities that eventually came together into larger civilizations until the long valley held just two nations — Upper Egypt and Lower Egypt. Then around 3100 BC, a great king named Menes (also known as Narmer, although that may have been the name of a slightly later king) united the nations and built a capital at Memphis. (No, Menes never went by the name *Elvis*. This was a different kind of king, and this was the original Memphis.)

Egypt was a major player among early civilizations, and I tell you more about it — not just in the following section, where I talk about the Kush civilization — but also in parts of this chapter concerning the birth of writing, the Hittites, Alexander the Great, and the Greeks.

Farther up the Nile (or farther down in Africa, if you look at a map), where the Sudan is today, another culture developed in Upper Nubia, or Kush. Influenced by Egypt's culture, the Kushites built pyramid-shaped tombs in the Egyptian style. Egypt actually ruled the Kushites from 2000 to 1600 BC and again from 1500 to 900 BC. Later, in the eighth century BC, the Kushites turned on their northern neighbors and brought down Egypt's ruling dynasty, ruling over Egypt until about 671 BC.

Giving way as new civilizations rise

To the people who lived in early civilizations, their cities must have seemed incredibly modern — so superior to rural villages and nomadic tribes (plenty of which still wandered the hinterlands), and also incredibly powerful and secure. Along with urban civilizations grew armies. (See Chapter 15 to find out about early warfare.) Yet the early civilizations, like every civilization since, faltered, splintered, succumbed, or evolved as political and military fortunes rose and fell.

Babylon grew from a prosperous city-state into an empire around 1894 BC as King Sumuabum conquered surrounding Mesopotamian cities and villages. His successor, Hammurabi, extended Babylon's lands from the Persian Gulf to parts of Assyria before he died in 1750 BC. (See the "Inventing Writing" section for info about Hammurabi's role as a lawgiver). Babylon's first empire (there was another, a millennium later, and I talk about it later in this section) lasted almost 300 years, until 1595 BC, when a fierce neighboring people, the Hittites, conquered Babylon's lands, including the city itself.

The Hittite Empire, at its peak, spread from Anatolia (a mountainous part of today's Turkish Asia Minor) and encompassed territory equal to modern England and France put together. Marauders (possibly an obscure bunch called the Sea People) smashed and burned Hittite cities so thoroughly that eventually nobody remembered who had left carvings such as the twin lions flanking what must have been a grand ceremonial entrance shown in Figure 3-1. It took nineteenth- and twentieth-century archeologists to rediscover these once-mighty people. (In Chapter 1, I talk about archeological discoveries of lost cities in Turkey.)

Based in Anatolia, the Hittites were major rivals, and later major allies, of Egypt. For all the many centuries that the Mesopotamian civilizations grew and changed, through the rise and fall of Babylon's empire, Egypt weathered dynastic shifts and accumulated wealth and power down by the Nile. The two ancient superpowers, the Hittites and the Egyptians, pitted their armies against each other at the Battle of Kadesh in Northern Syria in 1275 BC. A few decades later they were at peace. Pharaoh Rameses II married a daughter of Hittite King Hattusilis III.

The Assyrians, common enemies of the Hittites and Egyptians, eventually ruled Mesopotamia too, which was unfortunate for Babylon. The Assyrians appear to have been a bloodthirsty lot, at least judging from the decorations on their palace walls, carvings depicting war, war, war, hunting, and war — complete with scenes of Assyrians beheading enemies. In Assyrian writings, kings boasted about how many captives they crucified, impaled, and skinned alive.

Babylon emerged as the center of a new empire in the late seventh century BC, after the Chaldeans, a Semitic people (related to Arabs and Jews) based themselves in the ancient city and conquered lands stretching to the Mediterranean. This was the empire ruled by Nebuchadnezzar II (605 to 562 BC), whose conquest of Jerusalem you can find in Chapter 19. Babylonia as an empire fell in the Persian conquest of 539 to 538 BC, but the city of Babylon remained an urban center even in 323 BC, the year that Alexander the Great died there.

Figure 3-1:
Stone lions, carved by the Hittites, guard a civilization that collapsed about 1200 BC.

© Archivo Iconografico, S.A./CORBIS

Building cities along rivers to the east

Early civilization was by no means limited to the lands around the Mediterranean. Just as the Tigris, Euphrates, and Nile Rivers gave rise to cities, so the upper Indus River, in lands now divided between Pakistan and northwest India, and the Yellow River in China provided environments for villages to grow into cities.

Plumbing the mysteries of ancient Indus Valley sites

The cities on the Indus, including sites in modern Pakistan at places such as Harappa and Moenjo-Daro, surprised archeologists who found them for a couple of reasons. First, as with the Hittite cities, nobody remembered that the Indus River cities ever existed — the identity of the people who built and lived in the cities is still unknown. Second, these startlingly modern communities of 2500 BC had streets laid out in a grid of rectangles, like New York City. Houses in Moenjo-Daro (many were expansive mansions) boasted bathrooms and toilets, with drains feeding into municipal sewers.

No one can decipher the writings left at Moenjo-Daro and the other cities of the Indus civilization. Not yet, anyway. That leaves many questions unanswered. At its height, this culture probably covered an area bigger than Mesopotamia and Egypt put together. Moenjo-Daro was rebuilt and rebuilt again, over what some scientists think were centuries of geologic change that plugged up the Indus, changed its course, and put successive layers of houses under water. Others say earthquakes and massive flooding ended the Indus civilization around 1700 BC.

If the people who lived on the Indus River are ancestors of later cultures on the Indian subcontinent, there's no evidence of that. Nomadic, herding tribes from the Iranian plateau arrived in northwestern India around 1700 BC. The tribes didn't build cities or houses with drains, but these nomads did bring an Indo-European language (distant ancestor of English and most other European tongues, as well as many in Asia) and the roots of what became Indian religion and culture.

Historians often say *Aryan* to mean the people that displaced the Indus River civilization and gave rise to later Indian culture, but *Aryan* is a widely misunderstood word because of the perverse way it was misused in Nazi Germany to mean light-skinned Caucasians. Properly applied, *Aryan* refers strictly to speakers of long-ago Indo-European languages and has nothing to do with ethnicity or physical type.

India's Aryans (if you'll excuse the word) observed a strict class (or *varna*) system that preceded the long-lived Indian caste society, and the Aryan's religious tradition, centered on the *Vedas,* or sacred books, grew into early Hinduism. Buddhism later grew from the teachings of Siddhartha Gautama. Born a noble in what is now Nepal in about 563 BC, Siddhartha gave up his wealthy life to seek religious enlightenment, eventually spreading his *four noble truths* throughout the Ganges valley. For more about Hinduism and Buddhism, see Chapter 9.

Separating history from myth: China's oldest dynasties

As with Egypt, Mesopotamia, and the Indus Valley cities, a river runs through the beginnings of Chinese civilization — the powerful, unpredictable Yellow River. Around 4000 BC, people started farming (first millet, later rice) along this northernmost of China's major rivers. Chinese legends attribute the nation's political origins to specific, semi-mystical individuals, including a Yellow Emperor of about 2700 BC, three *sage kings* (from 2350 BC), and an Hsia Dynasty that early accounts say lasted until 1766 BC.

Because historians have no proof that the Yellow Emperor, three *sage kings,* or the Hsia Dynasty are anything but legend, they credit the later house of Shang (also called Yin) as the first dynasty to bring together warring Yellow River city-states, in the sixteenth century BC. Some historians caution, however, that the house of Shang used to be considered mere legend too, until archeologists in the 1920s AD found Shang *oracle bones* — bones upon which Shang scribes scratched the dynasty's historical records. Because this evidence showed that the Shang Dynasty was real, cautious historians think that archeologists someday may also prove the earlier leaders really existed.

Pulling prehistory from a brick pile

Harappa — maybe the dominant city of the sophisticated Indus Valley civilization — was a mess when archeologists started picking through it in 1920. Nineteenth-century railroad engineers mined the site for bricks to build a roadbed. The engineers knew the bricks were old — but 4,000 years old? They left the hole in the ground, so local villagers helped themselves to the bricks, too.

In 1922, two years after the scientists at Harappa began to understand what it had been,

an Indian archeologist tackled another mound of brick rubble and river silt 400 miles away. He thought he had found an abandoned Buddhist monastery. Instead, he unearthed the riches of Moenjo-Daro, a virtually untouched ruin of great villas, public baths, and dazzlingly sophisticated sculpture.

Since then, more than 150 Indus Valley sites have been explored — the remains of a civilization that is as fascinating for the way it so thoroughly vanished as for its far-reaching greatness.

Under the Shang, with their capital at Anyang (from 1300 BC), these early Chinese charted the movement of the sun and stars to predict seasons, kept astronomical records to rival those of the Egyptians, and devised a nifty 12-month calendar. The Shang Dynasty lasted until 1027 BC, when it was succeeded by the Zhou (or Chou) Dynasty.

Isolated from Asia Minor and Africa, where the Sumerians and Egyptians, respectively, invented writing (see "Inventing Writing" in this chapter), the Chinese independently developed their own kind of pictograph symbols, which led to great things. The characters that 1920s archeologists found on Shang Dynasty oracle bones are essentially classical Chinese — the roots of the same writing system that China uses today. China's historical writings outshine the records of any other culture in volume, detail, and continuity. For the BC period, China boasts 26 major official dynastic histories (equal in length to about 45 million English words).

Coming of Age in the Americas

Unaware of what humankind was up to in Africa, Asia, and Southern Europe, early Americans nonetheless got around to building cities, too, although they started a little later.

By 2000 BC, though, there were good-sized communities with public buildings in the Andes mountain range of what is now Peru. The people near modern Lima irrigated their farmland and built a stone pyramid at nearby El Paraiso around 1800 BC.

In Peru's northern highlands, the Chavín people started building cities around 1000 BC. Their culture thrived for 500 years, but they didn't leave many clues for the ages: No one knows much about their way of life. (The better-known Incas didn't emerge as a power in South America until many centuries later. See Chapter 7 to find out about the Inca.)

The Chavín may have traded with the Olmec, who had even earlier urban centers, dating from about 1200 BC, in the gulf coast region of southern Mexico and Guatemala. Only the elite — probably priests or a religious nobility — really lived in what were more like towns than cities. The Olmec did leave huge stone heads that may be portraits of their kings — although not very flattering ones. The Olmec also seem to have passed down their culture and social structure to later, more elaborate civilizations, such as the Maya (more on them in Chapter 4).

Inventing Writing

Farming brought cities, although the transformation of human society took a long time, as I explain in other sections of this chapter. Farming also gave rise to other signs of civilization, disciplines such as astronomy and math.

In Egypt, for example, practical scientific and engineering methods arose as ways to keep track of planting seasons. The Nile flooded in predictable annual patterns (easier to anticipate than the floods of the Tigris and Euphrates). Farmers could calculate when the water would rise. They studied the sun and the stars, and over centuries, Egypt developed the most accurate calendar yet — with 365 days in a year. In Mesopotamia, too, practical considerations, such as keeping track of seasons, trade transactions, lawmaking, and the invention of that most-treasured aspect of modern life — large-scale government bureaucracy — gave rise to record keeping. That soon became writing and reading, without which you wouldn't be doing what you're doing right now.

Planning pyramids

Measuring and math came in handy for building Egypt's pyramids — mind-boggling feats of engineering. Herodotus the Greek, a historian of more than 2,400 years ago, found out from his Egyptian contemporaries that 100,000 men worked 20 years on the Great Pyramid at Giza. The Great Pyramid was already more than 2,000 years old at the time that Herodotus heard about the pyramid's labor-intensive construction.

Building pyramids and keeping calendars would both be almost impossible without a way to note things. As the Sumerians had a little earlier, the Egyptians developed their own way of recording information in the form of pictures (*pictographic writing*), which evolved into a kind of writing called *hieroglyphics* (*medu netcher* or "words of the gods" in ancient Egyptian). Then came written stories, recorded history, love poems, and (with a few steps in-between) e-mail spam.

TECHNICAL STUFF

ABCs in BC

When scribes started using symbols to represent pieces of words — first syllables and then individual sounds — alphabetic writing began. At first it was a form of shorthand, although not actually shorter, just easier than the much more cumbersome pictograph style, which required a different symbol for every word. With an alphabet, you can combine fewer symbols to make many words.

In 1999 AD, American Egyptologists found alphabetic writing inscribed in limestone along an ancient road west of the Nile. In a Semitic script that probably originated in the neighborhood of present-day Syria, the inscription dates to the nineteenth century BC, according to the scientists who discovered it. If they are right, their find is the oldest known example of alphabet use. Other scientists (as often happens in such cases) say the inscription is not as old as its discoverers claim.

An important way for the Egyptians to impose order on their world, hieroglyphics also became an important way for much later people to find out about the Egyptians. I tell you about the Rosetta Stone, the modern world's key to deciphering hieroglyphics, in Chapter 23.

Laying down laws and love songs

In Mesopotamia, the Sumerians' pictographs (even earlier than the Egyptians') also evolved into symbols that represented words, syllables, and eventually even phonetic sounds. *Cuneiform,* the Mesopotamian way of writing — with the sharpened end of a reed in wet mud — spread all over the Middle East.

Also like Egyptian hieroglyphs, cuneiform writing opened up new vistas of early history in the nineteenth century AD, when European scholars figured out how to read cuneiform documents such as royal edicts and business letters. Sumerians wrote love songs that, with the right rhythm track, could find a place on today's pop charts.

Cuneiform writings include early codes of laws. Babylonian king Hammurabi in the eighteenth century BC enacted one of the best known. A sample: "If the robber is not caught, the man who has been robbed shall make claim . . . and the town and its governor — shall give back to him everything that he has lost."

Shaping the World Ever After

REMEMBER

In just about every chapter in this book, you find references to Greeks who lived between about 479 and 323 BC and the way their ideas shaped world civilization, leading to modern science, shaping influential schools of philosophy and religion, and setting precedents for democratic government. I talk about these classical Greeks (as they're known) in the previous chapter and I'm about to talk about them here, too.

I explain this apparent obsession with one early civilization above others as I go. But before I get to the Greeks in this section, I need to tell you about their world — ancient, but less ancient than the earliest Mesopotamian and Egyptian civilizations.

By the seventh and sixth centuries BC, the time of the second Babylonian, or Chaldean Empire (earlier in this chapter) and the Persian Empire that succeeded it, the Middle East had been crawling with civilizations great and small for many centuries.

Before the Persians rose up and asserted themselves, the Persians themselves were ruled by another conqueror: the Medes. Famous for crack-shot archery, Medes came from Media. (No, they didn't watch TV all the time. Media was a country in what is today northern Iran.) Mede archers helped the Babylonians defeat the fierce Assyrians in 612 BC.

In 512 BC, Cyrus, a young Persian king from the Achaemenid family, got tired of paying tribute to the king of the Medes, his grandfather. Cyrus gathered up his troops, turned the tables on Gramps, and then he built the Achaemenid Persian Empire that would rule western Asia for two centuries, taking in an area stretching from western India to North Africa and even into eastern Europe. Around 500 BC, one of the empire's greatest kings, Darius I, built a 1,500-mile highway from Susa in Iran to Ephesus in Turkey with stations providing fresh horses on the way for messengers, as did the U.S. Pony Express of the nineteenth century AD.

Also in Turkey, independent-minded people in coastal city-states stood up to the Persians. These were the Ionian Greeks. Originally from Greece, across the Aegean Sea, these Ionians spoke Greek, organized their society along Greek lines, and looked to Greece, not Persia, as their homeland. With support from mainland Greek cities such as Athens, they rebelled against Persian rule in 499 BC. Darius sent an army to punish Athens for helping the revolt, setting off the Persian Wars. Although the Greeks eventually won, bad feelings remained and flared up more than 150 years later, when a leader called Alexander headed Greek forces. (More about Alexander the Great coming up.)

Growing toward Greekness

Long before the Persian Empire, prehistoric cultures grew and flourished in Greece and on the islands of the Aegean Sea, developing into rich and influential societies.

The Minoans had a complex, centrally controlled economy and the bureaucracy to run it on Crete and other islands in this area until about 1450 BC, when Minoan traders suddenly disappeared from Egyptian trade accounts. (For speculation about why, see Chapter 1.) Mycenaeans, living in thirteenth-century-BC Greece, also had a sophisticated government and culture.

Both were predecessors, and possibly ancestors, of those people I keep talking about, the classical Greeks — called *classical,* not because of their taste in music (Mozart wouldn't be born for a long, long time), but because so much of what they thought and said and wrote has survived them. Classical Greek ideas, literature, and architecture — not to mention toga parties and those cool letters on the front of fraternity and sorority houses — are still around in the twenty-first century AD.

By routes direct and indirect, the Greeks — especially their philosophical approach of critically examining the world — spread all over the Mediterranean and then down through history, profoundly influencing successive cultures.

Adapting a society to the lay of the Greek land

Just as the geography of river valleys determined the rise of earlier farming civilizations, the geography of the Aegean Sea, the Greek peninsula, and the surrounding islands helped Greek civilization develop along its distinctive, influential lines.

Sea and mountains cut up the Greek homeland, separating people instead of bringing widespread populations together. Yet Greek growers gathered for trade. From marketplaces, they built cities in isolated mainland valleys and on isolated islands. Greek citizens gathered and lived in these independent cities, and they did something pretty unusual for this stage of history: they talked openly about how the independent city-state *(polis)* should be run.

A *city-state* was simply an independent city, not politically part of a larger country. Many city-states grew into larger political units. Athens, for example, one of the best known and the most influential of the Greek city-states, became capital of an empire in the fifth century BC. The Greeks were great sailors who founded new city-states not just in Greece and on Aegean islands, as shown in Figure 3-2, but eventually all over the Mediterranean Sea. Greeks settled in places as far away as Sicily and southern Italy. These far-flung city-states were a type of colony, in that they preserved and spread Greek language and culture, but they weren't politically colonial. That is, the remote city-states were often as independent as the city-states back in Greece. Just because adventurers from the Greek city-state of Corinth founded a city-state hundreds of miles away, that didn't mean that the new city-state was necessarily a Corinthian possession.

Not only were individual city-states free, so were Greek citizens, whether in Greece, Turkey, or Italy. I mean that they were *relatively* free to an extent unheard of in imperial societies such as Persia's. Most citizens were small farmers, for whom freedom meant they were able to farm and market their crops without interference. Of course, *citizen* was far from a universal status. You had to be a man (never a woman) of Greek parentage and language. (Foreigners who didn't speak Greek, whose languages sounded like so much "bar bar bar" to the Greeks, were dismissed as *barbarians.*)

Yet among the select, the free Greek citizens, the custom of asking questions — about the way the city was run, about the legends of their gods, or about the way nature works — led to exciting advancements. Inquisitiveness brought philosophy and fueled thinking about nature. Mathematics, astronomy, physics, and even biology became issues to theorize about, problems to solve. Could SAT tests be far behind?

Finding strength in common culture

The city-states fought each other, sometimes for ideological reasons. Sparta, famous for single-minded military ferocity, went into the long, exhausting Peloponnesian War of 431 to 404 BC, because Spartans objected to what they saw as imperialism on the part of Athens — especially under the powerful Athenian leader Pericles. Greek city-states put together empires, but the empires were built largely on influence and alliance rather than conquest. Still, Greek soldiers killed other Greek soldiers, and Greeks sacked the cities of other Greeks. Sparta brought down Athens, center of learning and beauty. Thebes tamed Sparta. (I talk about the Greek style of fighting in Chapter 15.)

Yet these Athenians, Spartans, Thebans, and others never forgot that they were Greeks: They spoke the same language, worshiped the same gods, and grew up hearing the epic poems of Homer. (The *Iliad* and the *Odyssey* were a combination holy scripture, *Star Wars* saga, and *World History For Dummies* of the time.) Different city-states got together for athletic competitions (the original Olympics), and when Greeks were threatened by barbarians, as in the wars against the mighty Persian kings Darius I in 490 BC and his son Xerxes I in 480 BC, the city-states worked together, if only temporarily.

Making Alexander great

The Greeks' fierce, contentious independence made them vulnerable later, when a king to their north, Philip of Macedon, decided to muscle in on the city-states. Unlike the Persian Empire, Macedon (today's Republic of Macedonia and the Macedonian region of modern Greece), a poor mountainous country, seemed an unlikely conqueror to the Greeks, who were caught off-guard. Philip set himself up as protector of Greece and formed the cities into a league that — ironically in light of the Greek's general disregard for conquest — helped Philip's son put together the biggest empire yet.

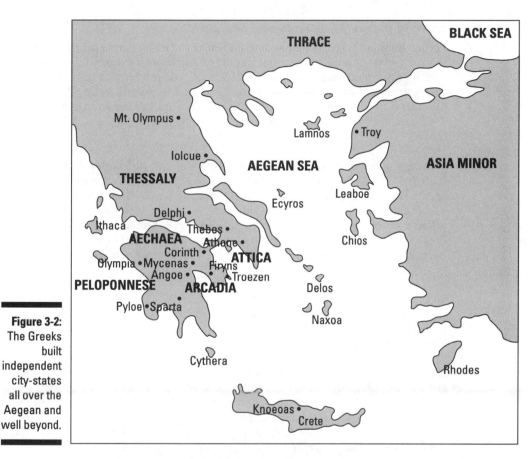

Figure 3-2:
The Greeks
built
independent
city-states
all over the
Aegean and
well beyond.

Philip planned to lead the Greeks against Persia, payback for its invasions of more than a century before. But he was murdered before he could mount the expedition. Some say his wife, Olympias, paid the killer to pave the way for her son, Alexander, to succeed his dad. Nineteen-year-old Alexander, well educated in philosophy (one tutor was the Athenian philosopher Aristotle) and war, joined her in killing other candidates for the throne of Macedon.

The 1955 cinematic epic, *Alexander the Great,* went so far as to portray Alexander (Richard Burton) as an overachiever striking out at father figures. Alexander did quarrel with his dad. He may even have been aware of a plot to kill Philip, and he certainly set out to do what his father planned, better than his father may have accomplished it. But Hollywood psychoanalysis can't explain away Alexander's success.

His power in Macedon secure, the rookie king quickly disabused the Greeks of any notion that they would have an easy time resisting him, in the process nearly destroying Thebes (not to be confused with the ancient Egyptian capital also called Thebes).

Exuding ingenuity, magnetism, and cruelty

Before he died, still a young man in 323 BC, Alexander the Great built an empire beyond the limits of what had been the known world. His career was victory after victory. By the middle of 331 BC, Alexander and his Macedonian-Greek army defeated two great Persian forces, the second led by King Darius III himself. As resourceful as he was brave, Alexander took the island city of Tyre by building a causeway from the mainland, making Tyre an island no more.

Although a brilliant, fearless, and inventive warrior, Alexander didn't do it all by force or ingenuity. The Egyptians, conquered earlier by the Persians, gladly chose Alexander instead, calling him the son of their great god Amun and making him pharaoh. When Alexander marched into Mesopotamia, ancient cities opened their gates to him, and took him as king. When Darius III was out of the way (murdered by his own men), the Persians fell down before Alexander and made him feel almost as if he were a god. He liked that, but his officers didn't.

One night in Persia, after drinking too much wine, Alexander's boyhood friend Cleitus, now one of his most trusted generals, dared to speak up about how Alexander was turning into a Persian. Alexander ran his old buddy through with a spear.

Alexander marched on, beyond the frontiers of Persia, clashing with Afghan tribes, founding numerous cities named after himself, and pushing over the high Himalayas, beyond the Mediterranean–Middle Eastern world. In India, he prevailed against the battle elephants of King Porus. Finally, his troops refused to go farther. Returning as far as Babylon, Alexander died of a fever, probably malaria, at age 32.

Leaving a legacy

Alexander's clout didn't die with him. His followers spent more than two years building an incredibly ornate funeral wagon. As they worked, they kept Alexander's body completely covered with honey (used as a preservative because anything submersed in it was cut off from oxygen, and thus did not decompose or stink). The mourners loaded the imperial casket into the wagon and began a ponderously slow funeral procession toward Macedon, 1,500 miles west, for burial. They never got there, however. Alexander's General Ptolemy, appointed governor of Egypt, diverted the procession to Alexandria, one of the cities the conqueror named for himself. There, the mere possession of Alexander's corpse gave Ptolemy the status to become ruler in his own right. Ptolemy founded Egypt's Ptolemaic Dynasty, which continued until his descendant Cleopatra VII killed herself with a snake in 30 BC.

Alexander may have been the world's first superstar. Everybody knew about him, at least according to the Greek historian Arrian, who wrote a biography of Alexander about 200 years after his death . . . , which states.

> For I myself believe that there was at that time no race of mankind, no city, no single individual to which the name of Alexander had not reached.

And this was before CNN.

One of Alexander's achievements is that he spread that peculiar, infectious Greek way of questioning and thinking about the world. Proud Macedonians, by the way, take exception to the casual way Alexander is sometimes referred to as a Greek. Yet Alexander disseminated Greek attitudes. Alexandria, Egypt, was a center of *Hellenistic* culture, meaning that Greek-influenced ideas and language networked beyond the widespread Greek city-states and lasted into much later eras.

Greek ideas — rationality, democracy, individualism, citizenship, free debate, and the inquiry born of philosophy (a Greek word meaning "love of wisdom," and a topic I explore in Chapter 10) — percolated through other cultures ever after. Philosophy became the cornerstone of science, and the scientific approach became the modern world's primary tool for interpreting reality. In that way, the classical Greeks still exert a powerful influence on twenty-first-century life.

Rounding Out the World

Over the long millennia that the first cities and civilizations were rising and spreading in the Middle East and Asia, many other cultures also took significant strides. Among them

- ✔ **Africa:** In what is now northern Nigeria, the Nok began clearing tropical rain forest for farmland, using iron-bladed axes and hoes, around 600 BC. The Nok were also sculptors, making realistic figurines of terra cotta.

- ✔ **Ireland, Scotland, Denmark, France, and Spain:** Hundreds of years before the first pyramids in Egypt, some people in western Europe built communal graves out of stone and earth. Surviving examples date back to 3500 BC and some good ones remain in Orkney, a group of islands off the coast of Scotland, and at Newgrange, Ireland. Europeans of the late Stone Age also left entire villages built of stone. More spectacular yet are the huge circles and parallel rows of standing stones, called *megaliths* (or big rocks) these people erected. The megaliths probably served as both religious centers and meeting places. Stonehenge, the most famous, was raised in southern England about 2800 BC.

> ✔ **Japan:** People lived in small villages as early as 9000 BC, mostly near the ocean and along rivers, transitioning from a hunter-gatherer lifestyle to agriculture, first growing vegetables and millet. These people were potters, however, and their cord-pattern pots give the period its name, *Jomon.* By the end of the Jomon era, around 300 BC, Japanese potters were showing a broader view of the world as they borrowed Chinese-style decorations. Another Chinese innovation, rice growing, also spread to Japan.

Tracking the Centuries

8000 BC: People live in a walled community at Jericho, a crossroads town at a spring-fed oasis near the Jordan River.

About 5000 BC: Barley and flax farmers dig networks of irrigation canals and build villages along those canals between the Tigris and Euphrates Rivers in what will later be Iraq.

Around 3100 BC: King Menes unites Upper Egypt and Lower Egypt into one kingdom with its capital at Memphis.

2000 BC: Egypt conquers the neighboring Kush culture to the south.

About 1700 BC: Earthquakes and sudden mass flooding may be responsible for ending the sophisticated Indus River Valley civilization.

1200 BC: In southern Mexico and Guatemala, the Olmec people build towns for their priests and religious nobility.

512 BC: Cyrus, a young Persian king from the Achaemenid family, leads troops against his grandfather, king of the Medes.

404 BC: Sparta defeats Athens in the 27-year Peloponnesian War.

323 BC: While staying in Babylon, Alexander the Great comes down with a sudden fever and dies.

1920s AD: Archeologists in China discover ancient writings on bones, proving that the Shang Dynasty of the sixteenth to eleventh centuries BC, until now thought mythical, really existed.

Chapter 4

Not All Roads Led to Rome

*T*he Roman city-state's origins are obscure — lost to history, if not to legend. (See the story of Romulus and Remus later in this chapter.) But Rome's history as it grew into one of the greatest empires the world has ever seen is anything but obscure. Even in twenty books this size, I probably wouldn't be able to tell you everything that's known about the Roman Empire and its people — let alone its pervasive legacy.

Influential Rome left such a history, such a lasting mark on the world, that sometimes it seems as if the Roman Empire was the only great empire of the final century BC and the early centuries AD. But the Roman Empire was far from that. Powerful empires rose and fell in the Middle East and Asia. New empires arose, far away and isolated from the Roman sphere, in China and in the Americas. Imperial expansion dominated much of the world. You can find out about a few of these empires and other civilizations that were contemporaries of the Roman Empire later in this chapter.

Other empires rose and fell and so did Rome's. Also in this chapter, you can find out how Rome grew from a city-state ruled by a king to a democratic empire, and eventually deteriorated into a divided and crumbling political ruin.

Reaching Back to Rome

The Romans weren't the first Christians. Romans fed early Christians to the lions just for the fun of it. Yet the Roman Empire, once it was officially converted to Christianity, promoted, strengthened, and spread that religion in Europe, western Asia, North Africa — everywhere the empire extended. The Church rose to wealth and power under the protection of Roman emperors.

Rome itself became the capital of western Christianity, and remains the seat of the Roman Catholic Church. Yet ironically, by the time Christianity became the official Roman religion, the Roman Empire shifted its energies far away from Rome.

If you get the idea that Roman history contains contradictions, you're right. Rome endured as it did by changing, growing, and reacting. Kings ruled the Roman city-state until the people rose up and threw out their king. Rome became a long-lived republic, and then it was ruled for centuries by emperors. Rome grew into an empire while a republic. In Rome's later years, the Roman Empire was less and less Roman, until what was left became a different empire entirely.

Contradictions? Sure. When an energetic civilization lasts 1,100 years or longer — more than two millennia if you count the eastern or Byzantine branch of the Roman Empire — it's bound to have contradictions. At its height, Rome was too big not to be a mass of contradictions — in administrative style, military policy, and cultural trends. Rome fell apart again and again and still held together. It left no written history of the time before 387 BC, presumably because all the records were lost that year when marauding Celts sacked the city. Yet it bounced back — controlling its region of west-central Italy, Latium, by 338 BC and most of the Italian peninsula by 268 BC, taking over the island of Sicily by 241 BC, and growing steadily for the next 200 years.

If promoting the new religion in the first few centuries AD was all the empire ever did, it still would have a big influence on the whole world ever after. Yet spreading Christianity was only a late manifestation of this incredible civilization.

During the Roman Republic (509 to 39 BC), the former city-state grew into the greatest force in Europe, the dominant empire in the Mediterranean region. After Alexander's death, Rome eventually superceded his heirs and absorbed much of what Alexander amassed — including Macedon and Greece. Rome crushed Carthage in a series of wars and took over the North African city-state's vast wealth and territory.

Rome borrowed freely from other cultures — a pantheon of gods from the Greeks, Athenian-style democracy, metalworking technology from an older Italian culture, the Etruscans. Yet, the Roman civilization did so much with what it borrowed that you can't begin to overestimate its impact, in its own time and ever since. How is Rome's influence felt today? In all kinds of ways. For one, the Roman language, Latin, is the foundation of not just Italian, but also of French, Spanish, Portuguese, and Romanian. Latin also left a deep impression on non-Latin languages, such as English. Even after Latin fell out of everyday use, Latin remained the unifying language of learning, of medicine and science.

Latin was also the unifying language of the Roman Catholic Church, which to Roman and other European Christians before the sixteenth century AD was just the Church — the only church there was. (See Chapter 11 for more on early Christianity.) Even after the Protestant Reformation, and until the middle of the twentieth century, Catholic masses worldwide were always said in Latin. (See Chapter 13 for more on the Reformation and the founding of later Christian churches.)

MILESTONE

The Western Roman Empire was gone in everything but name well before its official demise in **476 AD.** (The eastern branch of Rome, the Byzantine Empire, survived until 1453.) Yet after Rome was no longer an imperial capital, its name loomed so large and for so long in people's minds that it continued to invoke power and an aura of legitimacy. Of course, this was in part because the Church remained headquartered there, but the Church was in Rome because of what Rome was at its political height — the center of the Western World.

The Holy Roman Empire, a much later confederation of European principalities and duchies that changed shapes and allegiances over many centuries, got its Roman name because of the regard that medieval Europeans still had for the concept of Roman power. It started in 800 AD, when Pope Leo III bestowed the new title of Holy Roman Emperor on Charlemagne, king of the Franks and the first ruler since the original Roman Empire's demise to unite most of western Europe under a single rule. Charlemagne's empire, based where France is today, did not long survive him, but the German king Otto I put together a new Holy Roman Empire in 962 AD, the one that hung on until the nineteenth century. (For more on the Holy Roman Empire, see Chapters 5 and 13.) Aside from the pope's blessing, this empire's nominally united German and Austrian lands had little to do with Rome. Still, the name *Roman* smacked of imperial legitimacy.

Whatever it's called, it's still *the* Church

When talking about the Christian Church in its early years, I often refer to it simply as *the Church.* Christianity was a huge cultural force from late Roman times onward. Before the Protestant Reformation of the sixteenth century, the Catholic Church was *the* Christian church in Europe — virtually the only one. It was rarely called the Catholic Church because *catholic* was still an adjective meaning "universal" rather than the name of a religious denomination. (Spelled with a lowercase *c, catholic* still means universal or wide-ranging.) After Rome banned pagan worship, and as the old Norse and Celtic beliefs faded, virtually everybody was a Christian. Catholicism was the universal religion: Everybody was a Catholic, but they didn't think of themselves as Catholics because there was no such thing as a Protestant. Christians always capitalized *the Church* when they meant the network of cathedrals, chapels, priories and so on that looked to the pope in Rome for direction, and so do I in this chapter and in Chapters 9 and 13.

Other Roman terms endured, especially terms for positions of authority. The Russian title *czar* and the later German *kaiser,* both came from the Roman title *caesar.* (Julius Caesar, whose name became an official Roman title, appears later in this chapter and also in Chapter 19). Even the name of a powerful dynastic family, the *Romanovs,* who ruled Russia from 1613 to 1917, referred back to imperial Rome.

Rome's legacy pervades Europe, the Americas, and other places culturally affected by Europeans — a broad swath that takes in the Philippines, South Africa (and most of the rest of the African continent), Australia, and arguably the whole world. Roman influence is so pervasive that you could forget there were other big powers in Roman times, but that would be a large oversight. In this chapter, you can check out some of Rome's contemporaries, other powers that were leaving their marks on different parts of the world during the long ascent and descent of Roman Civilization. If you want to concentrate on Rome, there's more about it later in this chapter.

Building Empires

After Alexander the Great died of a sudden fever in 323 BC, his vast empire almost immediately disintegrated. Without Alexander himself, there was nothing to unite such widespread, dissimilar places as Macedonia, northern India, and Egypt — all among his conquests.

Yet the breakup of Alexander's empire (see more about Alexander the Great in Chapters 3 and 19) brought new empires — not as big, but impressive nonetheless. Several of them were founded by Alexander's former military governors.

Alexander was a conqueror rather than an administrator. As he couldn't personally rule all the lands he won — especially not while conducting further military campaigns — he appointed regional viceroys to govern in his name. These jobs went to some of Alexander's top military commanders.

With Alexander gone, the generals were free to turn their territories — which they had been holding in trust for their boss, Alexander — into personal kingdoms. (See Chapter 3 for the story of Ptolemy, Macedonian governor of conquered Egypt, who used Alexander's funeral procession to found his own Egyptian dynasty.) Although the Roman Empire, the largest and most influential empire to emerge after Alexander, arose first as a city-state, and although the Mediterranean was sprinkled with successful Greek city-states, imperial might was the model for large-scale government in the late centuries of the BC period and the early centuries of the AD period.

Ruling Persia and Parthia

Seleuces was the Macedonian general that Alexander the Great left in charge of conquered Persia (largely what is now Iran) in the 330s BC. The Persian Empire, at its height around 480 BC, was immensely powerful but in decline by the time Alexander added it to his collection of kingdoms. Still, there was a precedent for imperial government in Persia, and Seleuces took advantage of that, bringing Persian officers and Persian regional officials into his government of Macedonians and Greeks, and using his troops to keep order. By such means he successfully transformed himself into a king, no longer a viceroy dependent on Alexander the Great's might to back him up.

Seleuces' descendents, the Seleucid Dynasty, ruled a piece of Asia that stretched from Anatolia (the Asian part of modern Turkey) to Afghanistan. Seleucid rule lasted until a powerful regional rival, the Parthians, conquered Persia in the second century BC.

The rise of the Parthians traces to 250 BC, when the leader Arsaces, from central Asia, founded Parthia in eastern Persia. His descendent, Mithradates I, went on an empire-building campaign of his own between about 160 and 140 BC, assembling lands from the Persian Gulf to the Caspian Sea and eastward into India.

Mithradates' goal was to re-create the Persian Empire ruled over by Darius I more than 300 years earlier. (See Chapter 3 for more about the Persian Empire.) Alexander and his successors displaced Persian culture with Greek — a change called Hellenization because the Greeks called themselves Hellenes. Mithradates reversed Hellenization and revived all things Persian. The Parthian Empire lasted until 224 AD, when a soldier called Ardashir, a member of a noble Persian family called Sassanid, rebelled against the king and killed him. Like the Parthians, the Sassanid Dynasty was Rome's major rival in the East, lasting until the Muslim Arabs conquered Persia in about 642. For more about the Arabs, see the next chapter.

That's a Parthian shot

The Parthians' military success was built, in part, on a simple but effective battle technique. King Mithradates I used mounted archers, who were trained to gallop far forward on the battlefield, shoot an arrow quickly into the opposing forces, then wheel on their horses as if to retreat. But that's when the enemy got a surprise. The Parthians developed the skill of reloading their bows rapidly, turning in the saddle and letting loose another arrow over the horse's galloping rump while heading back to their own lines. It became known as a *Parthian shot*. Much later, after nobody remembered who the Parthians were, the term became the equally descriptive *parting shot*.

India's empires

The political borders within today's India and Pakistan shifted a few times over the centuries between 300 BC and 400 AD, a time that gave rise to both the Indian subcontinent's first united empire — the Mauryan — and India's golden age under the Gupta Dynasty.

Striking back: Chandragupta

In 322 BC, a nobleman named Chandragupta Maurya (sometimes spelled Candra Gupta Maurya) overturned Alexander the Great's Indian conquest, leading a successful revolt against Alexander's governors in the Punjab (modern Pakistan and northwest India). He also seized Magadha, the main state in northeast India and formed them into the biggest Indian political force yet, the Mauryan Empire. Seleucus, the general who became Persia's king after Alexander died, invaded from the west in 305 BC, but Chandragupta beat him off and won a treaty from Seleucus, setting an Indian border along the high Hindu Kush Mountains (an extension of the Himalayan range and the same barrier that Alexander had to cross when he invaded India).

Chandragupta's son and grandson enlarged the empire, especially to the south, but war sickened the grandson, Asoka. After early victories, he became a devout Buddhist, devoted to peace among people and nations. Instead of troops, he sent missionaries to win over Burma and Sri Lanka.

Achieving a golden age

After Asoka died in 238 BC, his successors proved less able to hold the large territory together and the Mauryan Empire declined. An ambitious rival, from the Sunga family, assassinated the last Mauryan king, Birhadratha, in 185 BC, and seized power. The resultant Sunga Dynasty could not prevent the subcontinent from breaking up into a number of independent kingdoms and republics, something like the medieval period that Europe would soon experience.

Then another leader, Chandragupta, united India again, about 600 years after the Mauryans did. The new power grew into the Gupta Empire, achieving great wealth through widespread trade and intelligent government and bringing about the greatest cultural flowering ever to rock India.

Known as Chandragupta I, this conqueror started in the kingdom of Magadha in 320 AD, bringing surrounding kingdoms under his influence by force and persuasion. He revived many of Asoka's principles of humane government. Much as the Romans did, he used local leaders instead of killing or imprisoning them. He propped up regional authorities and made them dependent on his administration. This model for Indian government worked, lasting a long time. Even the British used this model for governing India in the nineteenth century.

Chandragupta had able successors — his son Samudragupta spread the Gupta territory to the north and east. Grandson Chandragupta II, a great patron of the arts, ruled from 376 to 415 AD, spending tax money to promote architecture, painting, and poetry. The Gupta era gave India many glorious temples and palaces, as well as sculpture, music, dance, and poetry.

The Guptas were not without enemies. Huns from Mongolia and northern China battered the northern frontier of India in the fifth century, and in the 480s AD, after the last Gupta king died, they took over the North. For more about the Huns and what they were doing to Europe around the same time, see the next chapter.

Uniting China: Seven into Qin

Seven warring states kept China in turmoil between 485 and 221 BC. Then the king of one of those states, a place known as Qin, emerged as dominant. He united China for the first time by beating his rivals and consolidating their territories into greater Qin, calling himself *qin shi huangdi* or Qin Shihuangdi, meaning "the first emperor of Qin," which suggests that he thought there would be more. He was right. From Qin, which you can also spell as *Chi'in,* came the name *China.*

Qin Shihuangdi got things done. The great Persian road-builder Darius I, an influential guy, may have inspired Qin Shihuangdi. (Darius also inspired the Parthian empire-builder Mithradates, whom you can read about earlier in this chapter. For more on Darius, see Chapter 3.)

Just as Darius built a 1,500-mile highway, Qin Shihuangdi linked the various defensive walls on China's northern border into one Great Wall (which his successors continued to work on until it was more than 2,500 miles long — it's shown in Figure 4-1). He also built roads and canals with a fury. From his northern power base, he conquered southern China. He got rid of feudalism and disarmed nobles, dividing the country into 36 military districts, each with an administrator who reported to the emperor. He was a firm believer in big government, using his clout to reform weights and measures and standardize everything from Chinese script to the length of cart axles.

The emperor also looked after himself and his homeboys, building a palace complex that doubled as a massive barracks, sleeping many thousands. He linked hundreds of lesser palaces by a covered road network. You may conclude that he didn't like to be alone. Perhaps this accounts for what researchers found after they opened his tomb in 1974 — 7,000 warriors sculpted of terra cotta and standing in battle formation as if to protect their king. With painted faces and uniforms, the sculptures still hold real weapons. Terra-cotta drivers man real chariots, hitched to terra-cotta horses.

Figure 4-1:
Qin
Shihuangdi
started
linking
defense
works that
became the
Great Wall.

Hong Kong filmmaker Ching Siu Tung used the pottery army as the premise for his poorly received 1990 adventure-comedy *A Terra Cotta Warrior,* about a Qin guardsman who gets turned into terra cotta, but revives in the 1930s AD to protect the emperor from grave robbers. The warrior also romances a ditsy movie starlet who also happens to be a reincarnated Qin virgin.

The first emperor died in 210 BC, and his dynasty did not last long, yet the family that emerged as rulers only four years later, in 206 BC, was smart enough not to undo the Qin work. Building on his reforms, these rulers, the Han Dynasty, reigned until 220 AD.

Relatively late in the dynasty, during a time called the Eastern Han, the Chinese invented both paper and porcelain, among other important techno-logical advances that flourished under the succeeding Tang Dynasty.

Flourishing empires in the Americas

During the Roman era, empires formed in the Americas. The Mayan culture took shape by about 1 AD in Central America, rising to prominence about 300 AD and enjoying what historians call its Classic Period until about 900 AD, when it went into a long decline.

Sharing with the Maya

In the tropical rainforests on the Yucatan Peninsula, spreading over what is now southern Mexico, Guatemala, northern Belize, and western Honduras, the Maya built on inventions and ideas developed by nearby cultures such as the Olmec (see Chapter 3). The Maya also shared aspects of their culture with the Toltec of northern Mexico, whose great city of Tula, about 40 miles north of present-day Mexico City covered 13 square miles and was home to as many as 60,000 people. (The Toltec predated the Aztecs, who show up in Chapter 7.)

The Maya developed astronomy, a sophisticated calendar, and a writing technique similar to Egyptian hieroglyphics. They built terraced cities in neat rectangular grids, and pyramid temples in ceremonial cities such as Copan, Palenque and Tikal — now ruins for archeologists to study and tourists to climb on.

An elite class of priests and nobles ruled over the majority, who tended fields cleared from the jungle. Modern experts haven't settled on why the Maya ultimately abandoned their cities, although environmental decline may be a factor.

Although Mayan people were widespread and influential through much of Central America and Mexico, there's no evidence that they had any impact on Texas. Movie screenwriter James R. Webb (who wrote 1962's Oscar-winning *How the West Was Won*) fantasized about a party of exiled Mayans who wander north of the Rio Grande in the misbegotten film *Kings of the Sun* (1963). Actor George Chakiris leads the Mayans, exiled from their own lands, as they clash with Chief Black Eagle (Yul Brynner) and his generic Native American tribe. The plot involves the Mayans giving up their religious practice of human sacrifice.

Building in Peru

Farther south, on the south coast of Peru, the Nazca flourished between 200 BC and 500 AD. Their huge-scale earthen etchings, designs that are most visible today from the air, are cited today as evidence of long-ago interplanetary visitors. Archeologists who study the Nazca reject the ancient-astronaut theory as nonsense. The Moche (or sometimes the Mochica, which is also the name of the language they spoke) were more imperial than the neighboring Nazca. Building a large, powerful civilization in fertile river valleys along the north coast of Peru after about 1 AD, the Moche dug neat irrigation canals to irrigate desert land and erected cities.

Although the Maya had hieroglyphics, the Moche were like the Inca (who later succeeded them in South America) in that the Moche had no written language. (You can find out more about the Inca in Chapter 7.)

What is known about the Moche today comes largely from studies of their art and architecture. As in earlier Mesopotamia, the Moche built with mud bricks. Like the Egyptians, the Moche found out how to irrigate and buried their kings in pyramids. (You can find out more about ancient Middle Eastern civilizations in Mesopotamia and Egypt in Chapter 3.) The 525-foot-high Pyramid of the Sun and its near twin, the Pyramid of the Moon are the best-known surviving examples. You can see Moche monuments at the site of the Moche people's capital city from about 200 to 550 AD, also called Moche. It is near today's Trujillo, Peru. The Moche worked in metal — gold and silver jewelry — and left behind beautiful textiles, especially ceramics. Illustrations on the pottery depict a warrior society with distinct social classes, from the king down to the slaves, and a religion that included human sacrifice.

Another agricultural Peruvian culture, the Paracas, rose to its heyday between 500 and 200 BC. Like the Nazca, the Paracas carved giant pictures into the ground along the Pacific coast south of Lima. The Paracas were also great weavers and embroiderers and the Paracas left carefully mummified bodies in underground tombs, provisioned with pottery and textiles.

Rising (And Falling) Rome

From its legendary beginnings to its fractured demise, the Roman civilization had a certain pizzazz that has captured the imagination of not just historians, but everybody fascinated by human achievement, military adventure, political intrigue, and tragedy. Shakespeare was among those drawn to its stories (see more about that coming up in this chapter), and so am I.

What's the attraction? You can look at Rome's long ascent and descent from any number of angles and wonder at the complexity and sophistication, not to mention the cruelty and corruption of this long-lived culture. I hope that in the brief glimpses that follow you can find clues to what fascinates so many about the Roman civilization.

Forming the Roman Republic

Roman legend says that the half-god, half-mortal Romulus, a son of the Greek war god Mars, built the city on the Tiber River in 753 BC and ruled as its first king. The legend also says that a female wolf suckled baby Romulus and his twin brother Remus. Historians tend to disagree, especially about the wolf, and put the founding of Rome a bit later, about 645 BC.

Although he may not have ever tasted wolf's milk or murdered his smart-mouth twin brother, Remus, the legendary Romulus is credited as the first of seven kings who ruled Rome as a city-state (not unlike the Greek city-states around the Mediterranean, which you can find out about in Chapter 3) until 509 BC. That was when King Tarquinius Superbus got on the wrong side of his advisory body of citizen-magistrates, the Roman Senate. (For more about Romulus and Remus, see Chapter 18.)

The Roman Senate kicked out Tarquinius Superbus and set up a republican system of government designed to prevent a tyrant from ever misruling Rome again. Two *consuls,* elected annually, served as administrative executives, under the supervision of the Roman Senate. The republic system worked, bringing the stability that Rome needed as it grew from city-state into empire. And did it grow.

Earning citizenship

Romans lived in a stratified society, organized by class. (See the "Roman class" sidebar in this section.) Opportunities and employment were strictly defined by birth — just as they were in so many other cultures dominated by privileged aristocrats. Yet Roman custom also offered ways to improve your status, or that of your children.

Rome allowed foreigners and slaves to become citizens. It was a highly limited opportunity by modern standards but progressive for its time. Democratic Athens, Greece, (see more about Athens in Chapters 3 and 10) offered no such opportunities for outsiders. Giving the Roman Empire's low-born and conquered people a chance at inclusion in society helped win those people's loyalty to Rome, which added greatly to Rome's growth and resilience.

In a Greek city-state, a slave could be granted freedom, but the best he could hope for was lowly resident-alien status. He was unlikely to develop loyalty to a state that excluded him. (And I do mean *him*. Women couldn't even dream of citizenship.) When war broke out again, the resident alien was unlikely to rally to the cause.

Why so exclusive? Greeks valued *Greekness,* looking down on those who didn't speak their language and worship their gods. But the exclusion was also economic. The city-states of rocky Greece were usually short of resources, especially good farmland. Granting citizenship meant enlarging the number of people with a direct claim on the food supply. Making slaves citizens was too expensive and would also mean enlarging the number of voters, which could cause unwanted power shifts.

In fertile Italy, on the other hand, food was relatively abundant, so shares weren't such an issue. Also, blocks of votes rather than individual votes determined Roman elections. An extra vote in a block had less potential impact. Rome offered slaves the real possibility of earning citizenship, but only the lowest class of citizenship: *plebeian.* Plebeians, however, could hope for their children to rise to a higher class. Further, Rome united other cities to its empire by bringing conquered people into the fold. Roman officers propped up local aristocrats in newly taken provinces, making them dependent on Rome's support. The defeated country's men were enlisted in the next conflict and rewarded with part of the profits from the almost-inevitable conquest: Loyalty was lucrative.

Roman class

Plebeian is a word you still run across. It means a lowly person. In Rome, the plebeian belonged to the second lowest of four classes in society. The lowest was the *slave.* Slaves had no rights at all. Plebeians were a little better off in that they were free, but beyond that they had no clout. Next in the hierarchy were the *equestrians,* or riders. These were rich people — rich men, actually — of a class that rode horses when they were called to fight for Rome. They weren't rich enough to have much power, though. For that, you had to be among the *patricians,* the nobles. Patrician is a word that still gets used, too. Now, as back then, it's applied to people of wealthy families, accustomed to being in authority.

Expanding the empire

By the third century BC, Rome had only one major rival as top dog in the western Mediterranean: the city of Carthage, a big, rich trading port in North Africa.

Before 1000 BC, the Phoenicians sailed out of what is now Lebanon to expand trade opportunities. This led them to found Carthage, in present-day Tunisia, in 814 BC. Around 600 BC, Carthage became so rich and populous that it cast off Phoenician rule.

Carthage and Rome fought three Punic Wars, between 264 and 146 BC. (Punic comes from *Punicus,* a Latin word for Phoenician.) Carthage should have quit while it was ahead. In the first of these wars, Rome won the island of Sicily, its first overseas province. In the second Punic War, from 218 to 201 BC, Carthage lost the rest of its far-flung territories and became a dependent ally of Rome. The alliance, never sweet, soured into the third war, when Rome destroyed Carthage itself.

To the east, Rome fought the Hellenistic kingdoms, those Greek-influenced nations carved out of Alexander's empire. Romans took Macedon, Greece, Asia Minor, and the eastern shore of the Mediterranean, eventually including Judah, founded by the Jewish leader Judas the Maccabee in 168 BC. The Romans sacked Jerusalem in 63 BC, then made it the capital of Roman Judea.

The empire pushed north into Gaul, to the Rhine and the Danube Rivers, growing so big that administering the vast territory became too difficult for the republic, with its unwieldy and often contentious government. Turmoil created opportunity for a military genius named Gaius Julius Caesar.

Crossing the Rubicon

Julius Caesar was a top soldier whose conquests extended the empire, and he was ambitious for himself, too. Rome needed leadership after decades of uneasy peace following a civil war in 88 BC. A former consul, Gaius Marius, won that war, capturing Rome and banishing leaders of an opposition political party before he died in 86 BC, leaving bitterness and a hamstrung government. A dictator, Gaius Marius, emerged in 82 BC, but he retired after a few years and chaos resulted. Quarreling politicians, fighting for power, rendered the Roman Senate useless. In 60 BC, three men formed the First Triumvirate, or *rule by three,* to restore order. The youngest member was Caesar. The next year, grateful Roman citizens elected Caesar *consul,* the top administrative post in the Roman government. A consul was a bit like prime minister, a bit like attorney general.

Caesar's victories in the Gallic Wars (58 to 50 BC), pushed the empire's borders all the way to Europe's Atlantic seaboard. Returning home in 49 BC, he started a civil war by leading his troops across a stream called the Rubicon, boundary of his own province. (*Rubicon* has meant point of no return ever since.) Caesar fought other Roman leaders for the prize of absolute power in battles that continued until 45 BC. His rivals defeated, he took the title "Dictator for Life."

Caesar liked elaborate compliments and formal tributes, making his enemies think he was aiming for not just regal status, but a kind of imperial divinity. Many Romans, upset at what Caesar was doing to their republic, still talked about Tarquinius Superbus, the last Roman king, and how the Roman Senate kicked him out. Two senators, Brutus and Cassius, plotted Caesar's assassination.

England's Shakespeare wrote a terrific play on the subject of Caesar's downfall 1,600 years later. If you ever said "Beware the ides of March" or "Friends, Romans, countrymen, lend me your ears," you quoted from *Julius Caesar.* Director Joseph L. Mankiewicz made a movie version of the play in 1953, with screen sensation Marlon Brando holding his own alongside Shakespearean heavyweights John Gielgud and Lewis Calhern. It's not as much fun as a topflight stage production of the play, and James Mason, as Brutus, seems particularly ill at ease, but the movie could be a lot worse. Don't take *Julius Caesar* for literal truth, though. Shakespeare was a great dramatist but no historian.

Many more years of civil war followed Caesar's assassination. Caesar's cousin and general — Marcus Antonius, or Mark Antony — was in position to emerge with supreme power. But Antony's formidable rival — Caesar's great-nephew and adopted son, Octavian — came out on top in 31 BC with a win over the combined forces of Antony and his wife, the Egyptian Queen Cleopatra, at Actium, off the coast of Greece.

Empowering the emperor

Octavian, now the undisputed ruler of the Roman world, didn't call himself king or emperor, although that's what he was. Instead he took the relatively modest title *principate,* or first citizen. His modesty would have seemed sincere if he hadn't also gotten the Senate to rename him *Augustus,* which means "exalted." Augustus already bore the family name Caesar. Both *Augustus* and *Caesar* became titles handed down to successive Roman emperors.

Augustus cut back the unbridled expansionism of republican days and set territorial limits — the Rhine and Danube Rivers in Europe, the Euphrates River in Asia. The empire was stable. It annexed no territory until taking Britain in 44 AD. In 106 AD, Emperor Trajan added Dacia, where Modern Romania is, and Arabia.

Roaming eastward

Emperors led Rome for hundreds of years more, as dynasties and factions rose and fell, as pressure along the far-flung borders demanded vigilance. (For more on Roman defensive strategies, see Chapter 15.) Cutting back on expansion eased conflict but didn't stop outside incursions.

The hardest pressure was always at the Rhine-Danube frontier. Successive Roman emperors had to concentrate resources there, leading to more administrative focus toward the east. In the third century AD, the Emperor Diocletian built a new eastern capital, Nicomedia, far off in Asia Minor, where the Turkish city of Izmit is now. In 324 AD, the Emperor Constantine put his capital, Constantinople (today's Istanbul, Turkey), in the east, too. He built *New Rome,* as Constantinople was called, at the site of the old city of Byzantium, on the Bosporus, the channel that connects the Black Sea with the Mediterranean. Completing the project in 330 AD, the emperor renamed the city Constantinople.

Constantine was the first Christian emperor, ending a century of persecution against those who followed the new religion. Christians were relatively few until the third century and were largely ignored, but in 235 AD, the Severan Dynasty fell apart and the Roman Empire tumbled into 50 years of chaos. Emperor Decius, looking for scapegoats, began rounding up the increasingly numerous Christians and killing them. His successor, Valerian, did much the same thing. The Goths killed Decius and the Persians captured Valerian, acts the Christians saw as divine retribution. Maybe the emperors thought so too. Romans were highly superstitious and bad luck could convince even an emperor that supernatural forces were against him. Persecution stopped for a while, and Christianity gained many converts.

It took Diocletian, a soldier from Croatia who became emperor in 284 AD, to get government back on line. After accomplishing that, Diocletian started persecuting the Christians again.

How did Diocletian restore order? He split the empire in half, taking the wealthy, healthy eastern half for himself, based at his new capital in Turkey. He tapped the general in charge of Gaul, Maximian, to rule the West. Both had the title *Augustus.* Two more co-rulers, Constantius and Galerius, also military commanders, received the lesser title, *Caesar.* When Constantius died, his son, Constantine, later called Constantine the Great, succeeded him, eventually winning control of the whole empire. The reunification couldn't last, especially considering that Constantine based himself in the east, too. Diocletian's split set a precedent.

Constantine did much more for Christians than stopping the persecution. Starting in 331 AD, he made the Church rich. He seized the treasures of pagan temples and spent them on magnificent new Christian churches from Italy to Turkey to Jerusalem. He handed out huge endowments and authorized Bishops to draw on imperial funds as reparation for the years of persecution. This helped establish the Church as a wealthy institution for many centuries to come. In **391 AD,** Constantine's successor, Theodosius I, added a final touch, prohibiting pagan worship.

One result of the power shift away from Rome was that the Roman Senate was sometimes relegated to the status of a city council. True, Rome was quite a city to be council over. But the power was where the emperor was (or where the emperors were). Rome's western half, less and less an empire, grew more and more vulnerable to invasion by the barbarian tribes from the north — Huns, Vandals, Visigoths, Ostrogoths, and more.

By 400 AD, Theodosius had a senate in Constantinople, and a staff of 2,000 bureaucrats. Also about this time, Roman tax collectors couldn't move about Europe without a military escort. The Visigoths sacked Rome in 410 AD.

Fading into history

With its western territory overrun by barbarians and pirates, the Roman Empire was no longer anything like its former self. In 439 AD, Vandals advanced to Roman North Africa, capturing Roman Carthage. The imperial government in Constantinople stopped speaking Latin and the East's official language became Greek. As the Byzantine Empire, this eastern branch of the Roman Empire would persist for another millennium. For more about that, move on to the next chapter.

Roman administration in the West struggled on until **476 AD,** but without authority. When barbarian leaders closed in on the last emperor to sit on the Roman throne, a poor youngster named Romulus Augustus (a name recalling his great predecessors), they didn't bother to kill him: He wasn't important enough.

Rounding Out the Rest of the World

Over the long stretch of time when the Romans were rising and falling, other cultures around the globe experienced their own changes.

- ✔ **The Aksum:** In northeast Africa, where Ethiopia is now, the Aksum people put together an empire that grew rich after 200 AD by trading with places as far away as India. The Aksum became Christian in the fourth century AD, and spread the new religion to neighboring peoples.

- ✔ **The Celts:** Tribal people with sophisticated metalworking skills but no written language, the Celts kept expanding their European territory from central Europe toward the west. By the fifth century BC, they were dominant in Gaul (modern France), England, Ireland, much of Scotland, and parts of Spain. By the third century BC, the Celts spread through the Balkans. They made beautiful golden jewelry and harness ornaments. In some places, the Celts built large forts atop hills and fought Roman legions as the empire absorbed Europe. Later the Celts clashed with the barbarians that overran their territory through the early centuries AD.

- ✔ **The Japanese:** Discovering how to mine and smelt iron, the Japanese joined the Iron Age sometime in the third century. They also buried emperors and other big shots with their weapons and other valuable possessions in mounds made of stone and earth.

Tracking the Centuries

753 BC: According to legend, this is the year when the half-mortal son of a Greek-Roman war god built the city of Rome.

About 645 BC: According to historians, people from a number of small settlements in west-central Italy establish the city of Rome on a hilly site along the Tiber River.

509 BC: Romans rise up against King Tarquinius Superbus, and drive him into exile. They establish a republic in place of the monarchy.

238 BC: Asoka, emperor of India, dies. His Mauryan Dynasty begins to decline.

221 BC: The First Emperor of Qin unites warring Chinese states.

140 BC: Mithradates I begins a campaign conquest to enlarge the Parthian Empire.

45 BC: Julius Caesar emerges victorious from Roman civil war. He takes the title Dictator for Life.

27 BC: Octavian, great-nephew of the assassinated Caesar, accepts the title *Augustus* (exalted), becoming Rome's first emperor.

324 AD: Roman Emperor Constantine builds his new capital city, Constantinople, in Turkey, far to the east of Rome.

476: Barbarian invaders remove Romulus Augustus, the last Roman emperor of the West, from his throne.

1953: Marlon Brando stars in a movie version of Shakespeare's *Julius Caesar.*

Chapter 5

Transitioning Through the Middle Ages

● ●

In This Chapter

▶ Flexing muscles in Constantinople

▶ Going berserk with barbarians and Vikings

▶ Spreading all over Africa with the Bantu

▶ Uniting Arabs and building empires

▶ Bouncing back in India

● ●

*T*he term *Middle Ages* makes sense if you focus tightly on western Europe, but not so much sense if you consider the world at large. The Middle Ages in western Europe was the period between the collapse of the western Roman Empire (officially 476 AD, although there wasn't much of the empire left to collapse by then) and the Renaissance in the fourteenth century. (You can find much more about the Renaissance in Chapter 12.) That's what the labels Middle Ages and medieval (they mean the same thing) refer to — an age between ages.

Calling them the Middle Ages doesn't mean that nothing happened in western Europe during all that time. There's no such thing as a 900-year span when nothing happened. What it means is that there are two more monumental-seeming eras — the Roman Empire and the Renaissance — on either end of the medieval centuries, which get propped in between. The designation Middle Ages is arbitrary. (Chapter 2 has more about historical labels and why they're nothing to worry about.)

In today's Turkey and a huge surrounding region, history wasn't between two great ages during those years, but smack in the middle of one great age — that of the Byzantine Empire. Other empires peaked in those centuries, too, as India flowered and the Arabs, inspired by their new religion, Islam, conquered vast lands.

In what used to be the western Roman Empire, however, civil authority, what there was of it, became decentralized. Cities weren't as important as they once were. The economy closed in on itself, becoming more agricultural and local, less trade-based and commercial. Authority organized along the complicated rules of feudal loyalty. Instead of depending on imperial hierarchy, local vassals served local lords in return for favor and protection. (The exception was the monolithic Church, extremely powerful and still based in Rome. You can read more about the power of Europe's medieval Church in Chapters 12 and 13.)

The Middle Ages reflected the people who brought them on, the many barbarian groups — Huns, Goths, Avars, and others — whose migrations into Europe and constant raids brought down Rome. The barbarians' descendents remained in post-Roman Europe — blending and clashing among themselves and with the descendents of earlier Europeans. These descendents formed the beginnings of modern nations, standing up to new waves of raiders from the north — the Vikings — and conquerors from the east and south, the Arabs and Moors. The need to stand up to raiders and invaders forced the beginnings of nations. Local lords became willing to join forces, pledging allegiance to a strong king who could bring them together to fend off attackers.

As the barbarians had moved out of Asia, other populations continued to move — and not just into Europe. Wave after wave of a people called the Bantu transformed the African continent over a millennium of southern migrations.

The world that emerged at the end of the Middle Ages was changed from what it was when Rome fell. Maybe the Middle Ages should be called the Transitional Ages.

Becoming Byzantine

Roman Emperor Constantine the Great modeled his eastern branch of the Roman Empire, for that's what the Byzantine Empire began as, on old Imperial Rome — except that the eastern branch was a Christian power, rather than a pagan one, and people spoke Greek, instead of Latin.

Constantine chose the city of Byzantium for his new capital, rebuilding it to fit his concept of a great city and renaming it Constantinople in **330 AD.** By the time the western part of the Roman Empire fell apart in the fifth century, Constantinople (today's Istanbul) was a power center that rivaled old Rome at its height. The Byzantine emperor had even more power than most of his western predecessors and the Byzantine senate evolved as a sprawling, intricate (and notoriously corrupt) bureaucracy.

As a center of government, the Byzantine capital was remarkably stable — an urban seat of vast power, boasting a high level of literacy and wealth, produced by a commercial economy and extensive lands. Changing shape many times, the empire was, in most of those shapes, humongous.

Before he died in 565 AD, Justinian, who became emperor in 537, ruled lands on the north and south shores of the Mediterranean, stretching from southern Spain all the way east to Persia. Trying to reunite east and west into one Christian Empire, Justinian sent his armies to retake many formerly Roman lands in Europe and North Africa. Justinian even recaptured Italy, establishing a western Byzantine capital at Ravenna. Justinian tried, but couldn't reconcile the Eastern and Western branches of the church, which were bitterly divided. (For more about the early Christian Church, see Chapter 11.)

Another high point for the Byzantine Empire came more than 400 years later, when Basil II again stretched Byzantine might from Italy to Iraq.

To last so long as a power center, Constantinople had to endure physically, too. The city's location, on the Bosporus (the channel that links the Mediterranean with the Black Sea), and its heavily fortified walls resisted invasion. Although Constantinople took a beating, the Arabs' four-year siege, which finally ended in 678 AD, failed. (You can read more about Constantinople's strategic advantages in Chapter 16. You can read more about the Arabs, who quickly became a force to be reckoned with, later in this chapter.)

Sharing and Imposing Culture

Trade with the East livened up Italy and then the rest of the West several centuries down the line. By the so-called Middle Ages, the Chinese were already linked through trade with westernmost Asia and easternmost Europe — the Byzantine Empire. From the second century AD, the Chinese carried goods, especially the coveted silk fabric, from central China toward the west along a natural corridor between China's rugged mountains (a route that came to be known as the *Silk Road*), extending their economic influence all the way to the Mediterranean Sea. By the sixth century AD, the Silk Road reached Constantinople.

Bearing with barbarians

The hordes of barbarians battering away at the Roman frontiers for centuries brought cultural crosscurrents, although destructive ones. In a way, the barbarians *created* the Middle Ages, so it may pay to consider who they were.

Revealing obscure origins

To the Romans, a barbarian was an outsider who didn't speak Latin. The word was most often applied, however, to members of tribes such as the Goths and Vandals. Seeking lands to settle and eager for plunder, these migrating, warlike folks were a force in Northern Europe for a very long time before Rome fell and after.

Many came from northern and north-central Asia, in the steppes region, but most were nomadic herders before they turned to raiding. They moved so much that it's difficult to pin down where they started. The Vandals and Alans wandered north of the Black Sea before they came west, as did some of the others, although they may have started wandering somewhere else. Once in Europe they sometimes put down roots in a specific region — the Huns in Hungary for example and the Vandals in Denmark. That didn't mean, however, that the groups stayed put. The Vandals also built Vandalusia, a kingdom in Spain. (Over time, the V fell off and the region is known today as Andalusia.)

When Vandals arrived in Denmark, in Roman times, they met and eventually mingled with people who had been hunting and farming in Scandinavia for thousands of years. The Greek adventurer Pythias of Marseilles, visiting Britain in about 350 BC, wrote that he then traveled across water (perhaps the North Sea) to a place he called Ultima Thule (maybe Norway). There he visited friendly, blond people who threshed their grain indoors to save it from the damp, cold climate.

Whether Pythias's courteous hosts were direct ancestors of later invaders is difficult to say, but it's likely. Before 500 BC, a prolonged warm spell pervaded the far north of Europe. Archeological evidence seems to show that for a while the ancient Scandinavians didn't even have to bother with much clothing. But a gradually cooling climate and difficulty raising food provided the northern tribes with the incentive to come south and prey on Celts and Romans who were enjoying the continent's warmer climes.

The incursions went on for centuries, and tracing them to a colder Scandinavia gives only a small picture (and maybe a distorted picture) of the population movements that defined those hundreds of years.

Related to the Mongols who made China their own, the Huns hailed from Mongolia. Huns rode into Europe in the fourth century AD and settled along the River Danube. From there, their leader Attila launched fifth-century attacks on Gaul (modern France) and Italy. It's amazing how many peoples came out of the east, and how far and fast they came without minivans or superhighways.

Seeking a better life

Until about 550 AD, entire populations were constantly migrating, some for thousands of miles, which wasn't a phenomenon limited to Europe. People migrate: It seems to be part of what human beings are. Migration is a response to economic hardship and to climate changes. When people move, they run into other people. If the ones on the move are warlike and desperate, the encounters get ugly. Many barbarians were poor and looking for a better life. If plunder was a way to a better life, they went for it. No doubt they felt pressures similar to those that would feed the much smaller scale migration of Oklahomans out of the drought-ravaged dust bowl of the United States in the 1930s. (For more on barbarians and their long-term impact, see Chapter 6.)

Traversing Africa with the Bantu

The barbarians weren't the only populations on the move. Bantu people flowed out of today's Nigeria and north-central Africa, beginning in the last century BC and all the way through the first millennium AD. The Bantu, actually a group of related peoples who spoke Bantu languages (the largest group of African languages today), were cereal farmers and metalworkers who mastered iron-smelting technology long before the rest of Africa. Their success led to population growth that in turn forced them to seek new lands. So they took their language and their metalworking technology with them and overwhelmed indigenous populations all the way to the southern tip of the African continent. Most of the people in Africa today are descendents of the Bantu.

Also like the barbarians of Europe, new waves of Bantu continued to move south over successive centuries, overwhelming descendents of earlier waves of Bantu immigrants. In the twelfth century, the Bantu founded the powerful Mwenumatapa Civilization (in today's Zimbabwe), centered in the city of Great Zimbabwe.

Sailing and settling with the Vikings

In Europe, another wave of invasions from the north, beginning around the year 800 AD, profoundly marked the Middle Ages. The people of Norway, Denmark, and Sweden, thriving through agriculture and sea trade, started running out of good farmland. Like northern and eastern people before them, they decided to make new opportunities for themselves. One way to do this was to *go a viking* — adventuring and raiding as far as their sturdy ships could take them, which was very far indeed. With the advantage of good long-boats and experienced navigators, the Vikings raided the coasts of Britain, Ireland, and France — extending their terrifying visits as far as Spain, Morocco, and Italy.

For an engaging, if muddled, depiction of the Viking-Moor confrontation, check out a 1963 film called *The Long Ships*. Richard Widmark leads the Norse and Sidney Poitier heads up the North African contingent. (Kirk Douglas and Tony Curtis did better by the Vikings in the 1958 movie simply titled *The Vikings*.)

The Vikings were opportunists — traders as well as warriors. Like the earlier barbarians, Vikings settled in places they raided. Vikings founded Dublin and Limerick in Ireland, and the Shetland Islands off Scotland remained a Norwegian possession for centuries. In northeast England, the city of York was once a Viking settlement called *Yorvig*. Viking dynasties set up Norse kingdoms in diverse parts of Europe from Sicily to Russia to Normandy, which is a part of France named for the Northmen who came to raid and stayed to settle.

Carrying on through generations

As with the earlier waves of population movement in Europe, the Vikings' prolonged and successive impact echoed across the continent in interesting ways. For example, the Viking leader Hrolfr (or in French, Rollo) founded the dynasty of Norman kings in the duchy (like a kingdom) of Normandy when he conquered that land in 911 AD.

William the Conqueror was Hrolfr's descendent. Yet when he invaded England and claimed the English throne in **1066,** he was battling a land that had only recently been under the rule of Vikings from Denmark.

Edward the Confessor, of Saxon lineage, nominated William's rival, Harold II, for the English throne. Edward, however, gained the throne in 1042 only after a king called Hardicanute, a Dane, failed to leave a successor. Hardicanute's father, Canute (or Cnut) ruled over England, Denmark, and Norway simultaneously. His father, Danish ruler Sweyn Forkbeard, conquered England with Viking raiders in 1013.

Finding and losing the New World

One place Vikings had little impact was North America. Norwegians from Greenland landed in Canada around 1000 AD, but after a few years they lost interest in the new land. The first Norseman to see North America, the trader Bjarni Herjolffson, was trying to get from Iceland (colonized by the Norse in the 860s AD) to recently settled Greenland in the summer of 986 AD. Losing his way in the fog, Herjolffson came to a shoreline, probably Labrador's, which was obviously not where he wanted to go, so he turned around without exploring. About 15 years later, brawny, young Leif Eriksson (son of Erik the Red, who discovered Greenland), bought Herjolffson's boat, rounded up a crew and set out from Greenland to find out more about the new land.

For a short while, parties of Norse explored and even tried settling in the place they called Vinland (probably for the berries they found there, rather than grapes), today's northeastern Newfoundland. They fought with some natives, whom they called Skraelings. Unlike the Spanish explorers who came 500 years later in the south, the Vikings had no firearms, so they had no huge advantage in battle. The newcomers traded with the indigenous people, too, and some Norsemen (and Norse women, too) even built houses and stayed for a while. But they fought among themselves, undermining their chances to thrive. The voyages west from Greenland soon stopped and the Vinland settlements faded into memory.

MILESTONE

Invading England's former invaders

The Anglo-Saxon rulers of England fought wave after wave of invading Vikings, yet Anglo-Saxons were invaders in their own time. Angles, Saxons, and Jutes were among the tribal northerners that the Romans called barbarians. (For why the name of the Germanic tribe called the Angles becomes Anglo in the term Anglo-Saxon, see the sidebar in this chapter called "Angling for a nation's name.")

From northern Europe (Denmark and Germany) they poured into Britain beginning in the 400s AD. The Romans abandoned the island in 410 AD. The newcomers overwhelmed the indigenous Celts, or Britons, and drove some of them west to Cornwall and Wales, north to Scotland, and across the water to Ireland.

The invaders' medieval descendents were *Anglo-Saxons,* as are their descendents today.

For short, and because of the way Saxon leaders exercised power, the Anglo-Saxons of the ninth to eleventh centuries are frequently referred to as just Saxons — especially the Saxon kings, who controlled pieces of Britain for hundreds of years. Challenging Saxon control, for a time, Vikings ruled all of northern England, including Yorkshire. Saxons gained the upper hand in 878 AD when the king of Wessex (or the West Saxon land), Alfred, defeated the Viking ruler Guthrum. He let Guthrum keep the north, called the Danelaw, but Alfred made the Vikings pay him tribute. Saxons ruled for most of the next 200 years, although Vikings reasserted control for a time in the early eleventh century. Alfred is the only English king to be called "the Great."

Even if the Norse had taken a keener interest in North America, their discovery was marred by a number of factors:

- ✔ **The climate changed.** After 1200, the North Atlantic experienced a mini–ice age, which ice-locked ports and closed off Viking settlements in Greenland. No more settlers came and many left.

- ✔ **Trade was less lucrative.** Russian furs flooded the European market and craftsmen clamored for elephant ivory, considered superior to the walrus tusks that the Greenlanders could offer.

- ✔ **Bubonic plague, the Black Death, destroyed Norse Greenland.** When the plague arrived in Greenland in the fourteenth century, it wiped out the small remaining Norse population. Norway and Iceland, both hard-hit by the epidemic, no longer had a reason to send ships so far west.

Planting the Seeds of Nations

In the Middle Ages, the European map looked very little like the familiar borders that you see in a modern atlas. There was no France, no Germany, and no Spain. For convenience's sake, I sometimes refer to these areas by the national names they bear now, but the concept of nationhood was lost on Europe for quite a while after the Roman Empire collapsed.

Yet, in the Middle Ages, people and regions began to join together, to take on identities that would lead to modern nations such as France. The catalyst for this unity came partly from inside, as feudal leaders sought more power. But it got its biggest push from outside, from the very raids and invasions that you can find out about in other parts of this chapter.

When people in Ireland tired of Viking raids, they looked to a king strong enough to bring together regional lords so that they could mount a defense. In France (then called Gaul), the people known as Franks feared invasion by Arabs (the Arabs are later in this chapter) and by fierce Magyar raiders from Hungary. The Franks, like the Irish and other Europeans, looked to somebody who could unite them.

Repelling the raiders

Alfred the Great was the leader who brought Saxons (and Angles and Jutes) together in Briton (you can read more about him in the "Invading England's former invaders" sidebar earlier in this chapter).

Angling for a nation's name

England's Anglo-Saxon rulers were called Anglo-Saxon, just like Anglo-Saxons today, because they descended from Germanic tribes: the Angles and the Saxons. England means the *Angles' Land*. Regions within England also got their names from these people. That's why there's a Wessex (West Saxon Land), Sussex (South Saxon Land), Essex (East Saxon Land), and East Anglia.

People say *Anglo-Saxon* rather than Angle-Saxon because of the influence of Latin on the English language. *Anglo* is a Latinized version of *Angle*, applied when the word (today often used to mean *English*) is put together with the name of another ethnic or national group, as in *an Anglo-Danish business venture* or *the Anglo-Japanese Alliance of 1902*.

French becomes Franco in such combinations, as in a *Franco-American* trade agreement. It gets even crazier when you're talking about the Chinese, because political scientists, historians, and even some journalists cling to an old Greek word for Chinese, then put the Latin ending on it. That's why you might read about a *Sino-Japanese* economic conference.

Modern Americans use *Anglo* without linking it to another word, but usually to refer to Americans who speak English or who are of majority-white background, as opposed to Americans who speak Spanish.

In Ireland, a warrior, Brian Boru, seized power as high king (a king who ruled over lesser kings) and gathered forces strong enough to conquer the Vikings at Clontarf, near Dublin in **1014.** Brian died in that battle, but the Irish won. Ireland, for the first time united under an Irish leader, belonged to the Norse no longer.

Uniting western Europe: Charlemagne pulls it together

The Franks gave rise to the strongest of the new kings, the only one to forge an empire anything like old Rome's. A Germanic people from the Rhine region, The Franks settled in Gaul (roughly identified with modern France) around 400 AD, and in **451 AD** they helped the Romans repel Attila the Hun at Châlons. By 481 AD, the Romans in Gaul no longer had a Roman Empire to back them up. The king of the Franks, Clovis, overthrew them and took possession of all the land between the Somme and the Loire Rivers. Clovis's dynasty, called the Merovingians, gave way to a new Frankish dynasty called the Carolingians in the middle of the eighth century.

The Arab Empire came out of the Middle East in the seventh century, conquering most of North Africa and then extending northward into Spain. (There's more about the Arabs just ahead in this chapter.) In Spain, the Arabs, who were Muslims (followers of the Islamic faith) and their North African comrades, called Moors, beat Visigoth rulers in 711 AD, taking over most of the Iberian Peninsula. (The Visigoths were among the many groups of barbarians who brought down the Roman Empire. Barbarians show up earlier in this chapter.) From their stronghold in Spain, these Moors (as all Spanish Muslims were soon called) pummeled southern Gaul, gaining a real foothold just as the Carolingians came to power later in the eighth century.

In **732 AD,** Islamic forces tried to conquer Gaul. The Carolingian king, Charles Martel, stood up to them and turned them away. If he hadn't, historians say that western Europe would have gone Islamic.

This would have upset Charles Martel's grandson, Charlemagne, a devout Christian. Charlemagne (or Charles the Great) became king of the western Franks in 768 and then, after his brother Carloman died in 771 AD, ruled all the Franks.

Charlemagne wasn't the kind of Christian who thought that the meek inherit the earth. To get the Saxons of Germany (yes, they were related to the Saxons of England) converted to the faith, he fought and subjugated them. Instead of waiting for the Moors to try another invasion, he plunged his forces into Spain and attacked the Amir of Cordoba. He also smashed the kingdom of Lombardy in Northern Italy, among many other conquests that brought most of western Europe under Charlemagne's rule. The extent of his empire at his death is shown in Figure 5-1.

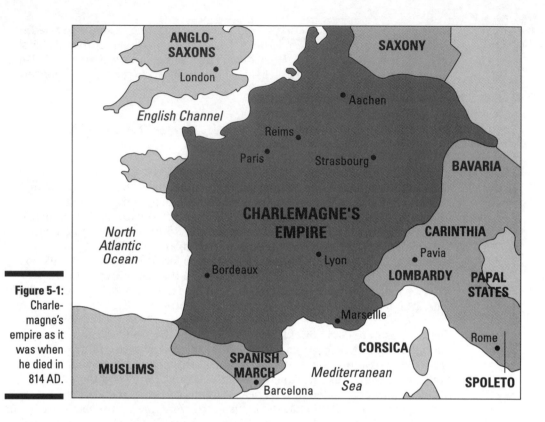

Figure 5-1:
Charle-
magne's
empire as it
was when
he died in
814 AD.

Pope Leo III liked this, especially the part about getting rid of the pesky Lombards. The pope crowned Charlemagne as Carolus Augustus, Emperor of the Romans (or Holy Roman Emperor) in **800 AD,** beginning the strange-yet-enduring European entity, the Holy Roman Empire.

Charlemagne mellowed in his later years. He built churches and promoted education and the arts, along with Christianity. He sponsored improved agri-culture and manufacturing. His stable reign fostered a kind of mini-renaissance, hundreds of years before the big Renaissance. But after Charlemagne died in 814 AD, his empire deteriorated quickly.

Keeping fledgling nations together

Although strong kings rose to patch together diverse, small principalities and duchies (ruled over by princes and dukes, respectively), consolidated power was difficult to keep. The title of king or even emperor didn't guarantee that lesser lords of the feudal system would remain loyal. For example, Otto I (or Otto the Great) of Germany, who became Holy Roman Emperor in 936 AD, also gained the title King of the Lombards in 951 AD, after he rescued Lombardy's Queen Adelaide (imprisoned by a neighboring prince) and married her. Lombardy is in north central Italy and Otto's empire (supposedly *Roman*, although based in Germany), included other Italian lands. Yet even after getting Pope John XII to give him an official coronation as emperor in 962 AD, the German never won Italian support. Italian princes who were officially his *vassals* (meaning they had to pay Otto tribute) fought him at every turn.

Galloping Islamic Fervor

The Arabs are a Semitic people, related to the Hebrews and the old Assyrians and Mesopotamians. Like the Hebrews, they consider themselves descendents of the Biblical patriarch Abraham. Originally farmers in the then-fertile region of what is now Yemen, and also nomads and traders throughout Arabia, they get little mention in history up until the seventh century. Arab states rose and fell. Trade flourished and wealth grew, largely because the Arabs had two substances: frankincense and myrrh, aromatic gum resins refined from the sap of trees (frankincense) and bushes (myrrh). Highly prized for their scent, frankincense and myrrh were as valuable as gold. Think about that next time the clerk at the perfume counter offers you a sample spritz.

The Arabs followed a number of religions, including Greek-style paganism. Judaism gained a foothold, and the new religion, Christianity, won many converts. But that was before an Arab merchant, a fellow called Mohammed, gave up his business so that he could devote himself to contemplating Allah, or the One True God. Things in that part of the world would never be the same.

Religion was volatile during this period — as Buddhism spread east from India to China along silk-trading routes and as Christianity became the one unifying focus all over Europe and other continents. (The Christian faith even spread to the Aksum Empire in northeast Africa.) But perhaps no religion ever had such an immediate and powerful effect as Islam. (For more about religions, see Chapter 9.) Mohammed said the new religion came to him in a vision of the angel Gabriel.

Mohammed became a prophet, but as he gathered followers, he grew into broader earthly roles. Leaders in his native Mecca saw his power grow and kicked him out. In Medina, however, Mohammed became more than a religious leader. He was also lawgiver and judge. Soon Mohammed led a Muslim army out of Medina to conquer Mecca.

Before Mohammed suddenly died in **632 AD,** the Muslims (as he called his followers) had conquered most of Arabia. (See Chapter 18 for more about Mohammed.) His immediate successor, Abu Bakr, finished the job within a couple of years. Then the Muslim Arabs conquered Egypt on the way to expanding westward into Algeria in North Africa, eventually conquering most of Spain and Portugal. Muslims pushed north from Arabia into Iraq and Syria, then west to Persia.

New Islamic dynasties followed, including the Omayyad Dynasty, founded in 661 AD. From its capital at Damascus, in Syria, the Omayyad Dynasty ruled an empire that stretched from Morocco to India. Although factionalism arose within Islam, and disagreements led to power struggles and war, there was remarkable continuity in the Arab world. The Abbasid Dynasty, descended from Mohammed's uncle, succeeded the Omayyads. They moved their capital to Baghdad, in Iraq, and ruled for 500 years.

Rebounding Guptas in India

Islamic armies surged eastward, too. New national and ethnic identities formed around the faith and variations within it. Muslims from Afghanistan conquered much of India in 1100.

Yet before Muslims got there, India experienced another flowering similar to the Mauryan Dynasty of the fourth to second centuries BC. In the previous chapter, you can read about both the Mauryans, the first dynasty to unite most of India, and the Gupta Dynasty, whose stable rule brought an Indian golden age in the arts, architecture, and religion in the mid-fourth to mid-sixth centuries AD.

India is another land where the term *medieval* means little. (See the beginning of this chapter for more about the limitations of the labels *medieval* and *Middle Ages*.) This is despite the fact that Hun attacks on its northern borders eventually caused the Gupta Empire to collapse, just as a western contingent of Huns were among the barbarian people whose attacks brought down Roman authority in Europe, beginning the Middle Ages. As decades passed, the Huns of India became more Indian, adopting local customs and habits.

Assimilating into the general population diffused the Huns' power, and it helped a Gupta leader named Harsha, descendent of the great Gupta kings, reestablish an Indian Empire in 606 AD. Equally good at conquest and administration, and an art-lover like his ancestor Chandragupta II of the Gupta Dynasty, Harsha built a glorious capital city, Kanauj, famous for its magnificent buildings, on the Ganges River. Indian culture, thus fortified, spread to Burma, Cambodia, and Sri Lanka. Indian influence over the region continued as the Chola of southeast India conquered much of the country after 880 AD. Savvy merchants and businesspeople, the Chola built up prosperous trade routes with the Arabs to the West and the Chinese to the east. The Chola governmental style continued the Gupta tradition of allowing local control.

Rounding Out the World

Through the miracle of time-space travel, here's a tiny sampling of happenings elsewhere during Europe's Middle Ages:

- ✔ **The Japanese:** Japan was deeply influenced by China beginning about the fourth century. By 538 AD, that influence took the form of religious conversion as the Japanese court adopted Buddhism and replaced old temples with new. The cultural pendulum began to swing the other way only in the eighth century, as the Chinese-influenced Japanese emperors lost power to a rising warrior class. The warrior leaders, or samurai, organized by clans, fought among themselves, plunging the island into civil war in the twelfth century and giving rise to the imperial office of shogun. Minamoto Yoritomo became shogun in 1192 and used his samurai retainers to impose law and order. Japan was governed this way for centuries. (To read about the Japanese reaction to European traders, see Chapter 7.)

- ✔ **The Khmer:** In Southeast Asia, the Khmer people of Cambodia broke away from foreign influence (Chinese and Indian) as they established their first state, called Funan, on the Mekong River. The later Angkorian Dynasty grew into an empire that built a capital at Angkor and ruled until the fourteenth century.

- ✔ **The Maya:** In Central America, the Maya enjoyed a civilization that lasted from 300 BC to 1500 AD, but what was left after 900 AD was only a shadow of what the civilization was at its height. Great Mayan cities, actually independent city-states, boasted temples, ball courts, and community housing. And Mayans grew much more than corn — they also harvested beans, chiles, other vegetables, cocoa, and tobacco. They domesticated bees as well as ducks and turkeys. More importantly, the Maya were the first people in the Western Hemisphere to use an advanced form of picture writing. Good at mathematics and astronomy, the Maya developed a 365-day calendar. (Find more on the Maya in Chapter 4.)

- ✔ **The Polynesians:** Between 400 and 800 AD, Polynesian people, originally from Southeast Asia, spread across thousands of miles of ocean to virtually every island in the Pacific — Hawaii, Tahiti, and Easter Island among them — proving themselves some of the most skillful and courageous navigators in the world. Then around 1000, when Leif Erikson was checking out the east coast of Canada, a group of Polynesians made it to New Zealand, where they developed the Maori Culture.

- ✔ **The Toltecs:** Farther north than the Maya, the nomadic Toltecs settled down and farmed central Mexico. The Toltecs built the city of Tula. Covering 13 square miles, Tula may have been home to as many as 60,000 people. This was well before the Aztecs rose in the same region. (You can find the Aztecs and the Inca of South America in Chapter 7.)

Tracking the Centuries

330 AD: Roman Emperor Constantine renames his eastern capital, Byzantium (in today's Turkey), making it Constantinople.

538 AD: Japanese adopt Chinese Buddhism.

565 AD: Justinian, Byzantine emperor, rules vast lands stretching west from his capital in Constantinople (today's Istanbul) to encompass much of formerly Roman North Africa and part of Spain and east to Persia.

632 AD: Mohammed, founder of a vigorous new religion, Islam, dies after conquering most of Arabia.

661 AD: The Omayyad Dynasty comes to power over Arab lands, ruling from its capital at Damascus, Syria.

800 AD: Pope Leo III crowns the Frankish king, Charlemagne, with a new, if anachronistic title, Emperor of the Romans. This is the beginning of the Holy Roman Empire.

878 AD: King Alfred of Wessex and his Anglo-Saxon followers defeat the Viking ruler Guthrum, who must then pay tribute to Alfred (later *Alfred the Great*).

911 AD: Viking leader Hrolfr founds a dynasty of Norman (which means the same as Norsemen) kings in Normandy, later a part of France. (Today's French remember Hrolfr by a less phlegmy translation of his name: *Rollo.*)

1000: Leif Eriksson and a party of sailors from Norse Greenland land on the coast of Canada.

1014: Brian Boru, the first high king of Ireland, leads Irish warriors to defeat the Vikings at Clontarf, near Dublin.

1343: Bubonic plague begins its march across Europe, killing one-third of the inhabitants.

1958: Kirk Douglas and Tony Curtis star in *The Vikings*.

Chapter 6

Contending for World Domination

- -

- -

*I*f you were an interplanetary traveler with a life span of say, several thousand earth years, and if you happened to be a betting alien, you may have laid odds, back around the year 1000 AD, that if any culture were to dominate most of the globe, western Europeans, with their messy little kingdoms, duchies, and city-states, would not be that culture. They were too vulnerable to Viking raids, too backward in their agriculture, too dirty, and too distracted by feudal power struggles and confusing divisions between secular and spiritual authority.

No, you'd probably put your money on a culture that had it together. The Arabs, for example, transformed a huge part of the world with amazing zeal and ingenuity in the seventh and eighth centuries.

Then again, you might back the Chinese — arguably the most technologically advanced and best-governed civilization on earth. "Hey, dealer, seven million intergalactic zolars on the Chinese for earth domination by the year 1900, please."

With those smart bets you would have lost. What you failed to take into consideration was that the contender with the greatest desire often wins a contest. The Chinese leaders were justly proud but complacent; sure that no other country had anything they wanted. The Arab Empire fractured into competing sects and contending emirates, united in their Islamic faith but less and less united in international goals.

Betting on the Europeans

Like the Arabs and many other cultures, Europeans fought among themselves, but their competition *also* took the form of a race for riches. Vast wealth, they knew, could be found in trade, especially trade with Asia. Several factors enhanced the European craving for more eastern trade:

- ✔ Some Europeans got a tantalizing preview of Asian luxuries — fine fabrics and spices untasted in the west — with the Crusades, hundreds of years of Christian military expeditions that began against Seljuk-Turk-controlled Palestine in the eleventh century.

- ✔ A vast, Euro-Asian Mongol Empire from the Black Sea to China opened northern trade routes, also bringing eastern goods west.

- ✔ A book about China (*The Travels of Marco Polo*), written by a thirteenth-century commercial traveler from the Italian city-state of Venice, drummed up interest in the far east, a place that sounded too incredible to be real.

- ✔ Finally, oddly enough, a terrible plague in the fourteenth century helped create a market for exotic eastern goods.

Before they could supply that market, the Europeans needed to get around obstacles — cultural and geographical. Europeans needed to find ways to bring cargo from faraway India and fantastic China. The huge Ottoman Empire (ruled by a dynasty of Turks separate from the earlier Seljuks) controlled land routes east. Besides, only sailing ships could carry the volume of merchandise that these European dreamers had in mind, but nobody in Europe knew how to get to East Asia by sea. The Europeans needed sea routes, and the search for those routes brought about a world crisscrossed by new cultural interconnections.

It was becoming an earth that would soon — not in the fifteenth century, which is as far as this chapter goes, but soon after — reward the canny bettor (in the introduction to this chapter) who wagered that Europe would take over the world. In this chapter, I talk about what made Europe eager and *able* to assert itself: One simplistic explanation is that adventurous navigation brought economic heft and military might. (Skip ahead one chapter if you're eager to find out more about Europe's rise.)

Spreading Islam

The Arabs rose to power with incredible swiftness and force in the seventh and early eighth centuries (you can read more about that rise in Chapter 5), inspired by a new religion, Islam, that gave them more than warrior intensity; it also brought education and intellectual advances.

The Abbasid Caliphate, the Muslim dynasty that ruled most of the central Middle East from 750 to 1258 AD, achieved more widespread literacy than any other culture on earth at the time. Mohammed, founder of Islam, left his followers a book, the Koran, as the holy centerpiece of their faith and the guide to proper living. (You can find out more about the roots of Islam in Chapter 9 and read why the Koran is one of the most important documents ever in Chapter 23.) Unlike Christians of the Middle Ages, who left the reading of scripture to churchmen — priests and monks — Muslims stressed that everybody should read the Koran. Good Muslims had to learn to read and the book they learned to read from was the Koran. With this holy book as a primer, the Arabic and Islamic world became a culture of learning and scholarship.

Becoming technologically advanced

The Arabs held onto much of ancient Greek literature, including the Greeks' philosophical, scientific, and mathematical foundations. (See Chapter 10 for Greek philosophy and the roots of science.) They embraced Roman engineering, which had spread to the Middle East during the Roman Empire's height and served the mighty Byzantine Empire of the Middle Ages. (See Chapter 4 for the Roman Empire and Chapter 5 for the Byzantines.) Building on those foundations, the Arabs adapted and refined Roman advances in architecture, such as the dome, adding the delicately distinctive Islamic minaret, one of which is shown in Figure 6-1.

Great astronomers and mathematicians in their own right, the Arabs weren't content to tend the flame of Greek and Roman learning. Continuing to adopt useful new notions such as the number system (from India), the Arabs passed them down as Arabic numerals. (You know: 1, 2, 3, and so on.) That the words *zero* and *algebra* come to English by way of Arabic is no coincidence.

The Arabs were way out ahead of the rest of the world in medicine. For centuries European medical textbooks were Persian collections of Arabic knowledge.

Mastering the Indian Ocean

Arabs, originally from the desert, weren't always the most enthusiastic seafarers. Maybe this had to do with the Arabian Peninsula's lack of protected harbors and navigable rivers — not to mention the scarcity of the wood and resin needed to build ships. But some Arabs did take to the water, becoming some of the world's most advanced sailors, figuring out the tradewinds to master the Indian Ocean before anybody else. Although no Arab made the voyage to test the theory, the great Muslim scientist Al-Biruni speculated as early as the year 1000 that there must be a sea route south of Africa.

Figure 6-1:
The Blue
Mosque
boasts the
distinctive
Middle
Eastern
minaret.

© Yann Arthus-Bertrand/CORBIS

When Portuguese explorer Vasco da Gama found such a route, and arrived in northeastern India's port city of Kozhikode in 1498 — becoming the first European to get to India by sea — he did it with Arab help. (You can find out more about Gama in Chapter 7.) Arab sailors knew the Indian Ocean, especially the arm of that ocean called the Arabian Sea, which was notoriously difficult to navigate and virtually unknown to Europeans. Gama used the best European navigational science of the time to sail around the tip of Africa, but he may not have made it the rest of the way without a stroke of luck. When he docked at Malindi, on the east side of the African continent, Gama hired not just an Arab navigator, but the greatest Arab navigator, Ibn Majid, author of the best Arab nautical directory, to guide him the rest of the way to India. (You can find out more about Ibn Majid in Chapter 20.)

Assembling and disassembling an empire

The late seventh century proved a good time for the Arabs to amass their empire, but they weren't able to hold it together in the ninth and tenth centuries.

Taking advantage of circumstances

Muslim Arabs built on the success of founding prophet Mohammed after his death in 632 AD by completing the conquest of the Arabian Peninsula, then turning their attention to other nearby lands. Circumstances favored the Arab advances because other enemies were bothering both the Byzantine and Sassanid (Syria and Persia) Empires, the region's mightiest powers — making Byzantines and Sassanids distracted and vulnerable.

Those older Middle Eastern powers were busy fighting each other and fending off barbarian invasions. The Sassanids had to worry about Huns hammering away at their frontiers and marauding Avars and Berbers bedeviled the Byzantines. (The Berbers hadn't yet become Islamic themselves, but would later.) The fact that plenty of Byzantine subjects, such as the Egyptians, were fed up with taking orders from Constantinople didn't hurt the Arabs either. (See Chapter 5 and "Excelling in East Asia" in this chapter to find out more about barbarian invasions.)

Growing apart

Islam, and its people, remained an extremely important religious, cultural, and political force as the eleventh century began, but the Arab ascendancy was past its peak. Arabs fought Arabs as early as 656 AD when an Arab civil war resulted in the capital's being moved from Mohammed's power base at Medina (in today's Saudi Arabia) to Damascus (in today's Syria).

In the ninth and tenth centuries, rival *caliphates,* or Islamic kingdoms, arose in Arab North Africa and Spain, breaking the empire into pieces — still united by faith but no longer politically joined.

Although the empire fractured mostly over issues of power and local control, the Islamic world also broke into religious factions. Shiite Muslims, who believed that only Mohammed's descendents could take the religious-political leadership title *imam,* stood apart from Sunni Muslims, the majority, who choose an imam by consensus.

Too big, too diverse, and too multifaceted, Islam was unable to sweep the world again as a single, overwhelming force.

Excelling in East Asia

Great in area and in cultural achievements, China was so far away and so strange sounding that medieval Europeans — those who even heard rumors of such a place — could hardly imagine it. China was a wellspring of technological inventions and economic marvel, and a cultural model for neighboring nations. China's leaders, knowing they had something special, tended to be a bit smug.

Innovating the Chinese way

The 400-year Han Dynasty (actually two dynasties with the same name, separated by a few years of chaos) was a wellspring of innovation and advancement. Chinese scientists invented the compass and the first really accurate grid-based maps, but the Chinese didn't always use their inventions in ways you may think of as obvious. At first, instead of using the compass as a navigational device, the Chinese thought the compass was a dandy tool for making sure that temples were built on the proper, sacred alignment.

Still, these guys were way ahead of their time, especially when you consider that they put efficient rudders on ships back when Romans and barbarians still steered by sticking a big paddle in the water at the back of the boat.

The Han Chinese came up with the crossbow, a serious weapons escalation for its time. They also made the world's first paper, which may not seem like much now, until you consider what the world would have been like without it. (For one thing, you'd be reading this book on *parchment*, which is tanned animal skin.)

Breaching the wall: Invading China

China endured (in a variety of configurations and through successive dynasties) over such a long time that you may think China was invulnerable to enemies, but sometimes China succumbed to invaders.

The Chinese began the Great Wall of China as a string of defensive outposts in the third century BC and over many hundreds of years, added to the wall — a barrier against invaders from Mongolia and Manchuria. But some invaders got past the wall. Around 100 BC, the Xiongnu people challenged the great Han Dynasty. More than a millennium later, in the thirteenth century, a successful Mongol invader breached the wall again. His name was Genghis Khan and his grandson, Kublai Khan, founded China's Yuan Dynasty.

Mongols were another barbarian people, like the Xiongnu. Mongols were also related to the Huns, who invaded both Roman Europe and Gupta India. (You can read about barbarian invaders in Chapters 4 and 5.) These many tribal, nomadic people battered empires everywhere in Asia and Europe, and they built their own empires too.

Genghis (or Chingis) Khan, whose name means "universal chief," built the biggest barbarian empire. He invaded China in 1211 and joined together lands from the Pacific Ocean west to the Black Sea. Before he died in 1227, Genghis Khan split his empire into four parts that he called *khanates*. His Chinese lands made up the easternmost khanate.

Kublai Khan was the first Chinese ruler most Europeans found out about, because the Venetian traveler Marco Polo wrote about living and working in Kublai Khan's court. (More on Marco Polo later in this chapter.) Kublai Khan finished what his grandpa began, making his Mongol capital in Khanbaligh (now Beijing) in 1267 and finally finishing off China's Song (or Sung) Dynasty twelve violent years later.

Innovation didn't stop when the Han Dynasty fell in 221 AD, either. Successive dynasties came up with more ideas. They thought up the stirrup, allowing riders much more control and stability, and giving Chinese horsemen the edge in warfare — for a little while, anyway.

Under the T'ang Dynasty, which took over in 618 AD, China developed beautiful things such as porcelain, and ingenious things such as moveable-type printing, which wouldn't get to Europe for hundreds of years yet. The Chinese invented gunpowder, too, and around 1000, they were already using it in warfare. (See Chapter 16 to find out about military advances such as the crossbow, stirrup, and gunpowder.)

China's economy and agriculture excelled. By the early twentieth century, Chinese peasants were poised on the edge of starvation, but that was after a long decline. In Han times, China's ability to feed its large population stood as a model of self-sufficiency. The climate, especially in the south, allowed two rice crops a year, which fed many mouths, permitting China's growth to outpace that of nearly any other region on earth.

Keeping to itself: Complacent China

Because China had so much that other parts of the world coveted, its leaders rarely cared too much about the world far beyond China.

From the Han Dynasty on, the Chinese believed themselves at the center of the world — at least the part they were interested in. The Chinese were certainly at the cultural center of East Asia, and had a profound influence on language, writing, government, and art from Burma to Korea to Japan.

Trading along the Silk Road

Even if some of their rulers tended toward isolationist policies, Chinese businesspeople certainly traded beyond the Great Wall. From the second century onward, Chinese goods traveled west on the backs of Bactrian camels that trekked the Silk Road (sometimes called the Silk Route). The caravans followed a natural corridor from the north of China through remote central Asia, between the peaks of the Pamir Mountains and through the Taklimakan Desert to Persia (now Iran) and the Mediterranean Sea. Middle Easterners — and some people farther west, as well — came to experience Chinese silk, the finest fabric in the world, along with other luxuries such as spices. (Find out more about the western hunger for eastern goods in the section "Developing a Taste for Chinese.")

The camels carted gold back over the route to China, along with cultural interchange. Christian missionaries from the Nestorian Church, a controversial Christian sect, traveled the Silk Road to spread their faith after the Byzantine Empire exiled them in the fifth century.

Yet the Chinese hungered for little that other cultures offered. Under the early Ming Dynasty — founded by the monk-warrior Chu Yuan-chang in 1368 after he drove out the Mongol rulers of the Yuan Dynasty — China's rulers went so far as to forbid ships from leaving coastal waters. (See the sidebar "Breaching the Wall: Invading China," in this chapter for more about the Mongols and the Yuan Dynasty.)

With long voyages banned, Chinese shipbuilders stopped building big, seagoing vessels.

Sailing with the eunuch admiral

In the early fifteenth century, Emperor Yung Lo turned outward — an unusual posture for a Chinese ruler. Yung Lo sponsored impressive voyages of exploration. Zheng He (sometimes written *Chung Ho* or *Cheng Ho*), a Muslim court eunuch who was also an accomplished sea admiral, commanded the ventures. (Apparently the jobs of eunuch and admiral were not mutually exclusive in those days.)

Zheng sailed seven large, well-financed expeditions, landing in India, navigating the Persian Gulf, and anchoring off East Africa. Zheng He's ships, called *junks,* were larger and faster than Arab and European ships of the time and equipped with sophisticated *bulkheads* (walls between sections of the ship's hold), so that if one part of the ship sprung a leak or caught fire, the damage could be contained and the ship wouldn't sink.

Did the Chinese build on Zheng He's voyages by

- ✔ Expanding trade?
- ✔ Exerting political influence?
- ✔ Expanding military influence?

The answer is none of the above. After Emperor Yung Lo died, the expeditions were curtailed.

The idea was not to subdue other parts of the world anyway. In Chinese thinking, China was not just the best state; it was the *only* sovereign state. The ships were, in part, a peaceful effort to broadcast the message of Chinese superiority. But to Yung Lo's successors, the rest of the world apparently was still not worth the trouble.

Developing a Taste for Chinese

China had what Europe coveted. Along with India and other points east, China was a hot trade destination because of the spices available. (If you think spices are no big deal, imagine what European food tasted like before they had any.)

China had porcelain and luxurious silk; wildly exciting to people who didn't have anything like it. Because it was hard to get, silk was all the more profitable to traders.

The Crusaders sampled these things in Constantinople and Palestine, cultivating a western taste for them. The Moors in Spain, with their eastern ties, had trade-route access to Chinese delights. Genghis Khan's vast Mongol Empire opened more northern trade routes, bringing eastern goods into the German states. Then a Venetian traveler, Marco Polo, went to China and worked for Genghis Khan's grandson, the emperor of China. Polo wrote a book about his adventures.

It all added up to terrific advertising.

Orienting Venice

Marco Polo was from Venice, a city-state of ambitious traders that started as an island refuge from barbarians in the fifth century AD. Venice was part of the Byzantine Empire until the ninth century, and even later, as an independent city-state, the Venetians enjoyed favored trading status with the Byzantines. This eastern connection gave Venice an economic advantage, which its rulers used to build up a neat little Mediterranean Empire, including the Italian cities of Padua, Verona, and Vicenza, along with the islands of Crete and Cypress.

Economically and militarily, Venice was oriented toward Constantinople and Asia. The word *orient,* as a verb, used to mean "to face east."

Although another seafaring Italian city-state, Genoa, gave Venice some stiff competition, Venice dominated Mediterranean trading. The wealth Venetians enjoyed because of their access to the east made the rest of Europe sit up and take notice.

Writing the first best-selling travel book

Marco Polo's dad and uncle were more ambitious than most other traders. Over the Silk Road to China, shippers and wholesalers customarily traded goods, each to the next trader down the way, so that no one trader or camel driver covered the entire, exhausting route.

The Polo family was different. Marco's elders were on their second trip from Italy to the Far East when they invited the teenage Marco to tag along. The trio arrived in Beijing in 1275. According to the book that Marco Polo later wrote, he entered Emperor Kublai Khan's diplomatic service and traveled to other Mongol capitals on official business. (Kublai Khan, though China's emperor, was a Mongol.)

Almost two decades went by. Young Polo, not quite so young anymore, finally left China in 1292 and returned to Venice. But the rival city-states were at war and Polo was captured. He was in a Genoan prison when he wrote, or rather dictated to a fellow prisoner, the story of his fantastic years abroad, *The Travels of Marco Polo.*

Many of his own contemporaries thought he lied, and some modern scholars think they were right — that Polo at least exaggerated. But that doesn't undercut the impact of his descriptions. Polo's book was about such a far-away place that to Europeans at the turn of the fourteenth century it was like a dispatch from outer space. At the very least, Polo's stories spread and fed the perception that China was the trader's mother lode. *The Travels of Marco Polo* was the most influential contemporary book of its time.

Fighting for economic advantage

Venetian success at trade fueled military conflicts — with the rival city-state Genoa and with more remote ckmpetitors. Venice was in there swinging when European Christendom launched the Crusades (see "Crusading" later in this chapter).

Any military campaign against those who controlled access to the Silk Road — whether Turks or Byzantine Christians (western Crusaders sacked Constantinople in 1204) — interested the Venetians, first in line among Europeans who wanted unimpeded access to the profitable thoroughfare.

Venice declined as the major trading power in the Mediterranean only after the naval Battle of Lepanto in 1571 — a fight against the Ottoman Turks, successors to the Byzantines. (There's more about both Turkish empires, Seljuk and Ottoman, in the very next section.)

In the fight against the Ottomans, the Venetians were allied with Rome and Spain in the *Holy League* (created by the pope). Venice won the Battle of Lepanto, but lost its colony Cyprus, and Venice's power slipped.

Arriving in the Mideast: Turks take hold

The Crusades were fought against Turks — not the Ottoman Turks, whose great empire was going to supplant the Byzantine Empire in the fifteenth century, but their predecessors in Middle Eastern empire-building, the Seljuk Turks.

Turks were yet another nomadic and marauding population from interior Asia — the various barbarians that you run into repeatedly in this chapter, as well as in Chapters 4 and 5. Barbarians show up in successive chapters because they kept showing up in successive centuries — riding into lands as diverse and far apart as China and Spain.

Like the China-conquering Mongols, also found elsewhere in this chapter, the Turks called their chiefs by the title *khan*. In the early centuries of the first millennium, Turks were a subject people, paying tribute (sort of like taxation without representation) to another barbarian group, the Juan-Juan, but as the Arab conquests of the seventh and eighth centuries spread the religion Islam, the Turks converted — also adopting the Arab fervor for empire building. (See the section of this chapter about Arabs.)

Taking Jerusalem

The Seljuk, a clan of Turks, rode out of wild north central Asia and into the Middle East, where they took over Jerusalem in the eleventh century. (For more about their conquests, skip forward to the Crusades.)

Seljuk-Turks, like the Mongols, were super horsemen; Seljuk warriors could fire accurate arrows at full gallop while standing in their stirrups. This knack helped them wreak havoc on more established powers as they swept through Afghanistan and Persia in the eleventh century, on their way to Baghdad, a declining capital of an earlier Muslim empire founded by Arabs, and to conquer the Middle East.

Getting around the Ottomans

Turkish empire building reached its height in the fifteenth century when another Turkish clan, the Ottoman Turks, also Islamic, assembled a humongous collection of lands into the Ottoman Empire. Ottoman power lasted until the twentieth century. In its heyday, the empire made significant inroads into Eastern Europe. (Today's animosity between Islamic Bosnians and Christian Serbs is rooted in Ottoman incursions west.)

The Ottoman geographical position between western Europe and the Far-East treasures that European traders lusted after became another motivator for new thinking about how to get from place to place in the widening world. Coupled with Venice's and Genoa's dominance in the Mediterranean, the Turkish presence made other Europeans wonder if they could find their own Silk Roads, perhaps by sea. One sailing ship could carry more cargo than camels could, anyway. The problem was that no one knew how to get from Europe to East Asia by sea.

Necessity, as the saying has it, became the mother of invention. Or maybe it was greed more than necessity. Either way, this hunger to find a new way to get the treasure gave birth to a whole new age of empire — European empires.

The Portuguese, Dutch, Spanish, and English wanted a piece of the Asian market and began exploring as never before. The first to risk a bold western course toward Asia, Christopher Columbus didn't find what he was looking for, but he did bump into the Americas — soon a lucrative market for slaves, who could be used to raise valuable commodities such as tobacco and sugar. (For more about Columbus, skip ahead to the section "Saying hello to Columbus.") Because Europeans were getting familiar with African waters, they knew where to get slaves. The web was growing both wider and thicker, with more and more strands.

Crusading

It seems today that civilization has arrived at its current, global, state of interconnectedness because of air travel and the electronics revolution of the last several decades. Yet today's worldwide connections, as you can tell by skimming through almost any section in this chapter, really started taking shape many centuries back.

Perhaps the earliest events that pointed forcefully toward today's world — still so deeply marked by the European empires of the sixteenth to twentieth centuries — came from much earlier European ventures: the Crusades, hundreds of years of sporadic Christian military campaigns. (For more about the marks left on today's world by Europe's second millennium empires, see the sidebar titled "Putting cultural dominance in perspective" in this chapter. Don't worry. It's not as stuffy as that title makes it sound.)

The Crusades began in **1095,** when diverse Europeans, answering a call from the pope and united in religious zeal (or so they said), tried to *free* the Holy Land, Palestine, from its new Seljuk Turk rulers. (Nobody asked the people living in Palestine if they wanted to be freed.)

These Islamic Turks, who conquered Asia Minor in the eleventh century, whipped the armies of the Byzantine Empire at the battle of Manzikert in 1071, even capturing Emperor Romanus IV Diogenes. They let him go, but Byzantine control of the region was in sad shape.

The Seljuk ascendancy alarmed Christendom (the Christian world) all the way back to Rome, where the last straw for Pope Urban II was the Seljuk takeover of Palestine, including Jerusalem and the holiest shrines of Christianity.

Even worse for the pope were reports that Turks were messing with pilgrims on their way to shrines in the Holy Land. As Muslims, the Seljuk rulers had little reason to protect these Christian travelers, easy pickings for robbers. The pope got so ticked off that in **1095** he called for a war to make Jerusalem safe for Christians again. The Crusades, the answer to his call, may have started out as idealistic religious adventures, but they descended into brutal wars of hatred and greedy opportunism.

Letting misguided zeal inspire them

In 1099, the first official European force to reach Jerusalem massacred most of the people there before setting up four European-ruled and short-lived Latin Kingdoms along the eastern shore of the Mediterranean. The Second Crusade began in 1147 with a slaughter of Jews living in Germany's Rhine Valley as the crusaders surged eastward.

The Fourth Crusade of 1202 to 1204 may have been the ugliest of all. Christian Crusaders sacked Constantinople, a Christian city, then briefly based another Latin Empire there. If the split between the Roman Catholic and Eastern Orthodox churches wasn't already wide enough, this made the division permanent.

Walking with peasants and children

Sadly, the thousands of ordinary Europeans who set out for Palestine full of Christian fervor were the crusaders least likely to survive. They were ignorant. No way were they ready for what they'd face.

The whole mess started with the People's Crusade, a ragtag part of the First Crusade that was led by an itinerant preacher from France, a monk called Peter the Hermit. His followers walked into a Seljuk slaughter. (For more about Peter the Hermit and his colleague Walter the Penniless, see Chapter 19.)

The Children's Crusade of 1212 was the most pitiful. About 50,000 poor kids, and some poor adults, too, walked from France and Germany, under the delusion that they could restore Palestine to Christian control yet again (this had been going on, back and forth, for over a hundred years already). Most of the tots who made it as far as Italy's seaports succeeded only in sailing straight into the Muslim slave markets of North Africa and the Middle East. Few were ever heard from again. Some people say the story about the Pied Piper of Hamelin is based on the Children's Crusade.

Riding with kings

But well-armed nobles and skilled warriors went east too. In 1189, the expeditionary force of the Third Crusade included King Richard I (Lionheart) of England, Emperor Frederick I (Barbarossa) of the Holy Roman Empire, and King Philip II of France. The emperor drowned crossing a stream.

Setting a precedent for conquest

Where did Europeans of the sixteenth through the nineteenth centuries get the nerve to sail all over the world claiming chunks of other continents for their kings back home? You could argue that their attitude hearkens back to

Rome's imperial habits, or that the Europeans, many of barbarian stock (and thus perhaps Asian as much as European), were born to rapacious conquest.

You could, but your argument would be a stretch. More accurately, you could reach back to the Middle Ages, the need to fight off Viking invaders, and how that need led feudal vassals to rally around strong leaders. This trend began to build nations such as Saxon England as it took shape under Alfred the Great. But nation building was a slow process. Europeans didn't think in terms of a political state based on national identity. (For more on the emergence of strong kings such as Alfred and Charlemagne, and the beginnings of nation building, see the previous chapter.)

The Crusades, beginning in the late eleventh century, were just as important because they shaped a European, Christian outlook on the rest of the world and taught westerners to assert themselves beyond Europe. Rulers put their resources toward an imperial venture in a systematic way, setting a precedent for the exercise of power. Christendom became militant, confident of its ability to stomp other parts of the globe. Militant confidence served Europe's nations well several centuries later, after navigators arrived at a reasonably accurate idea of what the globe looked like.

Putting cultural dominance in perspective

Europeans spent several centuries of the second millennium AD venturing out to other parts of the world, subjugating the locals and building empires. The world as you know it — with people speaking English in South Africa and Portuguese in Brazil — still bears innumerable cultural and economic marks of these adventures — many people call them scars.

Other people, some of them historians (although not recently), treated this European ascendancy as if it were inevitable, even right. This short-sighted view is called *Eurocentrism,* and you may think you smell it in this book. A reason for this is that European dominance has been so recent, relatively speaking, and that it continues — with the spread of Western clothing styles, the English language, Western-style economic systems, and American movies. (Although not without some backlash.) This book is partly an account of how

civilization came to this particular point, so it must include the story of how Europeans (and their heirs, such as the United States) accomplished what they did.

Throughout this book, I relate how one culture or another always seems to be coming to the forefront, dominating other peoples for centuries, even a millennium, and asserting itself as superior. I also point out how great civilizations can disappear so thoroughly that nobody remembers them. (For an example, see the Hittites in Chapter 3.) The disappearance of a major civilization seems inconceivable in this age of satellites and computers and the other snazzy gizmos that have transformed commerce and daily life. How could humankind ever forget this great, global society?

But what if it could?

Taking Care of Business

Early in the thirteenth century, Genghis Khan and his Mongol clan conquered a huge swath of Asia stretching from the Pacific Ocean all the way to northeastern Europe above the Black Sea. For part of that century these lands were under one rule. And even after Genghis Khan died, they remained a loose affiliation of allied Mongol powers. (You can read more about Genghis Khan and his conquest of China in the sidebar, "Breaching the wall: Invading China," in this chapter.)

The Mongol Empire cleared northern trade routes between East and West, some of them using the Volga and Dnieper Rivers that feed into the Black Sea and the Caspian Sea of the Middle East, routes used for centuries by Vikings and Slavs. Northern Europeans could take advantage of an eastern trade pipeline that flowed more freely than ever before.

As new goods filtered into northern Europe, towns grew fat. Hamburg on the Elbe River flourished. So did Lubeck on the Baltic Sea. But merchants had a problem. There was no reliable, unified German government, no source of widely recognized order to defend their shipping routes from robbers and pirates.

In 1241, businesspeople in those two towns formed a *hansa* — an association for their mutual protection. Early in the next century that association grew into the Hanseatic League, a commercial confederation of some 70 towns stretching from Flanders (today Belgium and part of Northern France) to Russia. Its interests were purely commercial, but the league performed some governmental functions too. It even went to war in the middle of the fourteenth century when Danish king Waldemar IV tried to mess with its trading. Waldemar proved no match for King Commerce.

Surviving the Black Death

Europeans in the fourteenth century were looking at the world in a new way, seeing far-off places as desirable, worth finding out about, maybe worth acquiring. Yet before Europeans really got out and started taking over that world, there had to be enough personal wealth back home to make a decent-sized market for foreign luxuries. Oddly, it took a horrible disease and mass-scale death for that market to find a foothold.

The *Black Death* (also called the Black Plague), a devastating epidemic of bubonic plague and its variants, probably started in the foothills of Asia's Himalayan mountain range. But in the fourteenth century something happened to make disease spread — perhaps the rise of trade. The disease lived in fleas carried by rats. Where people go, especially people carrying food, so go rats and their parasites.

When a rat died, the fleas jumped to another rat. When no other rat was handy, the fleas tried less desirable hosts. When those hosts were human, the people got terribly sick and most of them died quickly. The blackish bruises that appeared beneath their skin were called *buboes*. That's where the name bubonic plague comes from. (Think of that next time you hear a child call a bruise a "boo-boo.") An even more deadly version of the disease, pneumonic plague, spread through the air from person to person.

Killing relentlessly

In 1333, the plague killed thousands of Chinese. The disease spread west. By 1347, it reached Constantinople, where it was called "The Great Dying," and it continued rapidly west through the Balkans, Italy, France, and Spain. Then year by year, the disease advanced northward. Within a few years the Black Death reached Russia, Scandinavia, and beyond, following the Viking trade routes to Iceland and completely wiping out Norse settlements in Greenland. (For more about the Norse in Greenland, see the previous chapter.)

As many as 25,000,000 people died in Europe. Maybe a third of the people in England fell. Periodic outbreaks followed for centuries after, but the Black Death had an impact even beyond the horror and sorrow and the morbid fascination it inspired. (Many examples of art from this time focus on disease and death.)

Doing the math: Fewer people equals more wealth

Plague so drastically reduced Europe's population that a smaller labor pool changed the economy. Ironically, this improved many Europeans' lives — creating disposable income, which spurred a demand for eastern luxuries and even eastern ideas. (The intellectual and cultural result of this reduction in population and eastward focus was called the Renaissance. You can find out about the Renaissance in Chapter 12).

With so many dead, fewer people were left to work the land. A few workers had the spunk to stand up to the nobles and landowners and point out that they weren't about to give more work for the same money — not when the supply of workers had become smaller and thus more valuable. The most famous of these uprisings was led by Wat Tyler, an English rabble-rouser who got himself killed for his trouble in 1381.

Falling down

The children's rhyme "Ring Around the Rosie" is much older, and much more morbid, than many modern parents realize. It goes back to plague times, when the "rosie" was a rash that appeared as victims first came down with the disease. "Pocket full of posies" refers to the erroneous belief that flower petals were a defense against sickness. The posies did sometimes help with the overwhelming smell of death. "Ashes, ashes," is from the funereal "ashes to ashes, dust to dust." And the final line, "all fall down" originally carried the understanding that few, if any, would get back up again.

Post-plague economics forced some large landholders to split their estates into smaller plots. Instead of remaining tenants who turned over the bulk of their crop to the landlord, some laborers actually began earning pay for their work.

Though there were fewer people overall, more people had land, income, and the potential to buy goods. This stimulated a rise in merchants, craftspeople, and skilled traders who could supply goods. Up until that time, you were either rich or poor, usually poor. Now there was a middle class.

Migrating to and from the Americas

The Arawak and the Carib tribes both came from northern South America. Before 500 AD, some Arawak migrated to the islands later called the West Indies. They farmed peacefully for hundreds of years before the Carib followed.

The Carib weren't much for farming. Warriors and cannibals, the Carib tortured, killed, and ate the men of the tribes they conquered, turning the women into slave wives. Or so the historical record reads. Some people, including Carib descendents, take exception to this depiction, claiming Columbus and his successors made up the whole cannibalism business, creating an excuse for Spaniards to enslave these people.

Around the year 1000, as Vikings poked around the east coast of Canada, the Carib set out on their own sea journeys, from Venezuela or Guyana to the islands. Raiding Arawak villages, the Carib set up a pattern that continued until Europeans arrived with new cultural disruptions. On some islands, the Carib almost wiped out the farmers.

Arriving in the Indies, Columbus probably met some Arawak first and then the more difficult Carib. Full of hope that he was off the coast of East Asia, he called them all Indians. The name stuck.

Saying hello to Columbus

Some people celebrate Columbus; others vilify him, for *discovering* America. But he didn't mean to do it and he died never admitting what he'd done.

Genoa-born and reared at sea, Columbus read the ancient Greeks, particularly the second-century-AD astronomer Ptolemy. A Greek, who lived in Alexandria, Egypt, Ptolemy envisioned the world as a globe. His influential writings, preserved by the literate Arab culture that later ruled Egypt (see the Arabs, earlier in this chapter), came to Europe through Arabic translations.

No scrub, Columbus compiled an impressive resume of voyages, once sailing as far as Iceland, which is a long way from both Italy and Lisbon, Portugal, where Columbus settled early in his seafaring life.

Portugal was a good base for a seafarer because a prince, Henry the Navigator, established Europe's foremost school for navigation, astronomy, and mapmaking there earlier in the fifteenth century. Graduates explored Africa's west coast searching for a way around the continent to the Indies. (You can read more about Portuguese explorers' discovery of a sea route from Europe to India in Chapter 7. Henry the Navigator appears in Chapter 20.)

Trying to reach Beijing

Columbus, working for the Spanish monarchs, sought a sea lane linking Europe and India, but sailed west instead of east, the direction that would occur to most European sailors. This crack navigator boasted a commonsensical grasp of the earth's general shape — even if he did seriously underestimate its circumference. But Columbus never sought new continents and refused, doggedly, to face up to the fact that he did, indeed, find one, the one later called South America.

After his first voyage to the Caribbean, he kept going back there (it was later named after the Carib), not because he loved piña coladas and that calypso rhythm, but because he could not admit that what he'd found was someplace entirely new — to European navigators anyway.

Columbus wanted America to be East Asia, telling himself and anybody who would listen, that these islands were just some obscure part of Indonesia, the *Indies*. If Cuba wasn't part of mainland Asia, which he made his officers swear it was, then he wanted Cuba to be Japan. Who wanted a New World when an old one — China — was the sea trader's big prize?

Smokin'

Among the most puzzling things that Columbus brought back from the West Indies were pungent leaves and seeds of a plant that the Caribbean natives prized. Dried leaves of this kind were among the first presents Native Americans offered the European visitors, who didn't know what to do with them and threw them away. Better for the sailors' lungs that they did, because the leaves were tobacco.

A couple of Columbus's colleagues, Rodrigo de Jerez and Luis de Torres, saw natives in Cuba forming the leaves into the shape of a musket with a palm or corn shuck wrapper, lighting one end on fire, putting the other to their mouths and *drinking* the smoke. Jerez tried it, got hooked, and took the habit back to Spain.

The smoke billowing from his mouth and nose frightened his neighbors and they reported him to the Spanish Inquisition. He spent seven years in prison. And some people think today's anti-smoking laws are extreme.

Tracking the Centuries

618 AD: Tang Dynasty takes control of China, beginning a period of technological innovation that includes the invention of printing and gunpowder.

About 1000: Members of the Carib tribe sail from Venezuela to islands in the Caribbean (as it would later be named, for the Carib). Carib people will still be there when Columbus arrives 500 years later.

1071: Seljuk Turks defeat the Byzantine Empire's army at the battle of Manzikert, capturing Emperor Romanus IV Diogenes.

1147: Christian Crusaders, on their way eastward to liberate Jerusalem from Muslim rule, pause in Germany's Rhine Valley to massacre resident Jews.

1211: Mongol chieftain Genghis Khan invades China, adding Chinese territory to his vast Euro-Asian empire.

1212: About 50,000 poor people, most of them children, walk from France and Germany toward Italy's seaports. They are Crusaders, believing they can free the Holy Land from Muslim rule. Those who do not collapse along the way are sold in the slave markets of North Africa.

1241: Two northern European trading cities, Hamburg and Lubeck, form a *hansa* — an association for mutual protection. It will grow into the Hanseatic League, a commercial and quasi-governmental confederation of some 70 towns.

1275: Marco Polo, a teenage Venetian, arrives in Beijing and takes a job in the diplomatic service of the Chinese emperor.

1347: The Black Death (bubonic plague), on its march across Asia to Europe, reaches Constantinople. The Byzantines call the epidemic *The Great Dying*.

1381: In England, Wat Tyler leads peasants in a revolt against landowners. He dies in the conflict, but the rebellion brings agrarian reforms.

1571: The commercial city-state Venice loses its island colony Cypress to the Ottoman Empire. Without this Adriatic outpost, Venetian trade and influence begins a steep and permanent decline.

Chapter 7

Grabbing the Globe

· ·

In This Chapter

▶ Jostling for position in East India

▶ Slamming the door in Japan

▶ Threatening the old order with Enlightenment ideas

▶ Rebelling Americans and French

· ·

*W*hen European sailors set out looking for new sea routes in the fifteenth and sixteenth centuries, they were in it for the money. Riches beckoned. Some sailors whose voyages changed the circumference of the world:

- ✔ **Christopher Columbus:** A Genoan (from the Italian city-state of Genoa) sailing for Spain, discovered America in **1492** because he was trying to get to Asia — source of lucrative trade goods.

- ✔ **Vasco da Gama:** A Portuguese captain, was also looking for a sea route to Asia as he rounded Africa and sailed East, successfully reaching India in **1498**.

- ✔ **Ferdinand Magellan:** Another Portuguese but also sailing on behalf of Spain, set out for Asia by a different route from Gama's in **1519**, trying to reach the Spice Islands (today's Indonesia).

Magellan, although he died on the voyage, proved that you could get from Europe to Asia by sailing west, as Columbus claimed. (You just had to steer south of the South American mainland first.) Magellan also proved that Europeans could circle the globe. The one surviving ship of his original five rounded Africa from the east and sailed into San Lucar de Barrameda, Spain, in **1522**.

Magellan's achievement was a huge step in navigation, but it was also a symbolic triumph. Europeans could circle the world — by sailing, and soon thereafter, by trade and military conquest. Also in the early sixteenth century, two Spanish generals conquered the two greatest civilizations in the Americas:

- ✔ Hernan Cortés defeated the Aztecs of Mexico in 1521.

- ✔ Francisco Pizarro brought down the Inca Empire of Peru in 1533.

Europeans spoke of a New World, meaning the Americas, but in a sense the entire world was new because the world was suddenly in reach — a ripe plum, ready to be picked. The Spanish and Portuguese, soon joined by other Europeans such as the Dutch, English, and French, picked the plum by trading, conquering, exploiting, bullying, and enslaving. (See Chapter 20 for more on Cortés and Pizarro.)

Between 1500 and 1900, European sea powers brought most of the globe under their influence, but at a price. Almost as soon as Europeans subdued other peoples, those subjects began fighting to break free. This age of empires became an age of revolutions, and not just in the Americas and other colonial lands. The freedom fever spread, and revolution came to Europe, as well.

Sailing South to Get East

For Europeans, 1498 was an even more monumental year than 1492, when "Columbus sailed the ocean blue." Columbus was trying to reach the rich ports of Asia by sea, a major goal for traders and navigators. Gama, sailing for King Manuel I (Manuel the Fortunate) of Portugal, actually did what Columbus failed to do: Find a route to the East.

Gama found a route by sailing south, around the tip of Africa, then up that continent's east coast, through the treacherous waters between the big island of Madagascar and the African mainland and then, with the help of an Arab ship pilot, across the Indian Ocean. The greatest seafaring venture yet, Gama's journey made good on its promise of an economic payoff. (Columbus's mistaken discovery of bewilderingly wild islands had yet to prove economically rewarding.)

Getting a foothold in Indian trade

Vasco da Gama arrived in Kozhikode (sometimes called Calicut), a port city on the Arabian Sea (India's southwest coast), in 1498 eager for Asian spices. But he didn't come well prepared. By custom, the proper way to honor the ruler of Kozhikode, called the *zamorin* — especially if you wanted a favor — was to shower the zamorin with expensive gifts. Gama had little to give the zamorin, and the Indians were not impressed by the trade goods Gama carried. Gama had wash basins, bolts of cloth, hats, beads, and lumps of sugar. These items went over well on the Guinea coast of western Africa, but they were almost laughable in trade-rich Kozhikode.

Gama had to work hard to win a trade agreement from the zamorin, but after three months of appeals, he received approval. Even with his limited trade goods, Gama was able to buy enough spices to impress the folks back home in Lisbon.

Demanding respect

Vasco da Gama's first voyage to India seemed to point the way toward peaceful trade. Before he returned to Kozhikode, however, the tone of east-west relations would turn ugly. Instead of courting the favor of the zamorin on his second trip east, in 1502, Gama used intimidation, achieved through gruesome violence.

Just two of Gama's four ships and 55 of his original crew of 177 survived the first trip to India and back. Those were considered reasonable losses for the time, especially for such a great breakthrough.

King Manuel of Portugal, Gama's sponsor, was pleased. The king sponsored a second expedition, this one led by Pedro Cabral in 1500. On his way down the coast of Africa, Cabral sailed so far west that he discovered Brazil. Cabral claimed it for Portugal, giving King Manuel a piece of the New World, in addition to the route to Asia.

Cabral rounded Africa and continued to Kozhikode, where he built on Gama's work of winning trade privileges, negotiating a full commercial treaty with the zamorin. He also left a small group of Portuguese men in India to gather information for King Manuel.

Although Cabral's mission to India was successful, the men he left in India were murdered. When word of the killings reached Portugal, King Manuel was angry. He thought that Indian officials should have protected his representatives. Manuel wanted to show the Indians that they must respect the Portuguese. He sent Gama on yet another voyage to India in 1502. On this mission to Khozhikode, Gama was heavily armed, and he was not prepared to beg the zamorin for favor, as he had in 1498.

Sailing to India, Gama's ships intercepted an Arab vessel, called a *dhow,* carrying Muslims home from their pilgrimage to Mecca. Gama, demonstrating a new, militant attitude toward easterners, confronted the Arabs and demanded all the treasure aboard. When the Arabs didn't move quickly enough, he ordered his men to board the dhow.

The Portuguese took all the Arabs' money and goods, then used gunpowder to burn the dhow and all the people aboard. One of Gama's crewmen counted "380 men and many women and children."

When he reached Kozhikode, Gama didn't bother with gifts for the zamorin. Gama made no appeals. Instead, Gama demanded that the zamorin surrender and that Muslims, whom he blamed for the killings of the Portuguese that Pedro Cabral left behind, be kicked out of the city. The zamorin stalled and tried to negotiate a peace.

The Portuguese commander's answer to the Kozhikode peace overture was a boat full of human body parts — hands, feet, and heads of Indian traders and fishermen. The Europeans casually swept up victims from the small boats passing in the harbor, put nooses around the men's necks, and hanged them, just for show, before hacking them to pieces. Gama sent the grisly boatload to the zamorin with a message in Arabic, suggesting the ruler use these morsels to cook himself a curry.

This tactic worked. Gama got a cargo of treasure to take back to Lisbon, and he left a permanent naval force of five ships in Calicut's harbor.

Discovering America

Columbus didn't think of himself as a discoverer (see Chapter 20 for more about Columbus and other discoverers) and perhaps you shouldn't either. The whole notion of *discovery* is insulting to the people who already lived in the Americas and had no inkling that they were undiscovered.

Many different kinds of people lived in the Americas before Columbus arrived. Columbus called the people he encountered on Caribbean Islands *Indians* because he thought he was in Asia, so the original people of the Americas have been lumped together under the label *Indians* ever since (although some prefer to be called Native Americans). No matter what you call them, these people were not a single culture. They lived in widely differing climates, made their livings in widely different ways, spoke different languages, and wore different clothes. Even their origins were probably different. (See Chapter 6 for more on the people Columbus first encountered in America.)

Until late in the twentieth century, many scholars thought that all of the pre-Columbian Americans came by way of a land bridge that linked Asia with Alaska between 20,000 and 10,000 years ago. Then archeological finds began to suggest that at least some people were living in the Americas much earlier, maybe well before 30,000 years ago. (Modern human beings arrived in Europe not much more than 40,000 years ago. See Chapter 2 for more about early human migrations.) Based on this archeological evidence, it appears that the earliest Americans may have been many different groups arriving at widely different times.

By the time Europeans came, the Americas — especially Central and South America — had seen civilizations rise and fall. (See Chapters 4 and 5 for more about early American civilizations.) The Spanish arrived in Mexico, Yucatan, and Guatemala in time to see the great Mayan civilization, although it was in deep decline by the sixteenth century. (See Chapter 4 for more about the Maya.)

The Maya flourished until about 900 AD. So by the time the Spaniards first saw the Mayan cities in the sixteenth century, they were long past their glory. Yet they were still impressive, with pyramids almost as big as the Egyptians'. The Spanish probably did not pause to appreciate such Mayan achievements as sophisticated mathematics and astronomy.

To the north of the Maya cities, in the highlands of central Mexico, the Spanish military commander Hernan Cortés in 1519 found a great city, the Aztec capital of Tenochtitlan, that was at its peak, built in the middle of a lake and home to at least 200,000 people. Well-traveled Spanish soldiers said that Tenochtitlan, with its brightly painted pyramids and broad causeways linking the island city to the mainland, was as magnificent as Rome and Constantinople. The Spaniards went on to wreck it, of course, but nobody ever said conquest is pretty.

Although pre-Columbian civilizations boasted great cities and many other accomplishments, they lacked some key advantages that allowed the Spanish to conquer them. Four of the most important were

- **Gunpowder:** Europeans got it from the Chinese, as did the Arabs and the Turks. But a technological advance that had spread all the way across Asia to Europe had not crossed the oceans until the Spaniards brought it with them. (See Chapter 16 for more on gunpowder and firearms.)

- **Iron:** Although several American cultures achieved splendid metalworking by the sixteenth century, none had learned to make iron weapons. Weapons made of iron and *steel* (a mixture of iron and carbon) are harder and more durable than the Indians' weapons.

- **The horse:** There were no horses in the Americas. (See "Calling on Quetzacoatl" for more about the Spaniard's horses. See Chapter 16 for more on the horse's role in warfare.) The closest thing to a horse in any sixteenth-century American culture was the llama, which the Inca of South America used to carry burdens. Nobody would mistake a llama for a war horse.

- **Immunities:** This was probably the biggest disadvantage. Europeans brought diseases that hadn't crossed the ocean before. The Indians had no biological defenses against them. (More about the terrible toll of disease on native peoples in Chapter 8.)

Seeking the eagle with the snake

Before the Aztecs of Mexico rose to power, they were a conquered people, essentially slaves. Legend says they followed a prophecy that told them to build their capital, the great city of Tenochtitlan, where they saw an eagle sitting on a cactus (ouch!) eating a snake. Mexico adopted this image in their national flag, a detail of which is shown in Figure 7-1.

Figure 7-1:
The
Mexican
flag
commemo-
rates a
legend
about the
Aztecs, or
Mexica.

The cactus happened to be on an island in a big lake (now covered over by Mexico City). Other accounts say the Aztecs chose the island as a hideout from their former masters.

Becoming masters

However they came, the Aztecs (also called the *Mexica*), founded Tenochtitlan in about 1345 and began developing military skills so that other people could no longer enslave them. They built temples, roads, an aqueduct, and causeways over the lake. They also built an intricate governmental-religious hierarchy.

By the fifteenth century, the Aztecs were strong enough to turn the tables on their former masters. Aztec Kings Itzacoatl and Montezuma I (or Moctezuma) waged wars of conquest throughout the Valley of Mexico and beyond.

Why fight? One reason was that the Aztec war god, Huitzilopochtli, demanded sacrificial victims. The Aztec religion included the belief that Huitzilopochtli especially relished fresh human hearts, preferably of brave victims. At the dedication of a pyramid in 1489, Aztec priests cut up 20,000 captives. Victims of the Aztecs' wars fed Huitzilopochtli.

Calling on Quetzacoatl

Then in the sixteenth century, things started to go haywire for the Aztec. The people they conquered didn't like having their hearts cut out. Those subject people revolted. King Montezuma II tried to restore order, but he was interrupted when a renegade Spanish explorer, Hernan Cortés, showed up in 1519.

Montezuma II mistook Cortés for the feathered serpent god Quetzacoatl, a god common to the Maya and the Aztec, sometimes represented as a creator. An Aztec myth said that Quetzacoatl argued with another god and left in a snakeskin boat, promising to return. To some Aztecs, including Montezuma II, Cortés' arrival seemed to be that return.

Cortés and his soldiers seemed too strange to be mere men. Aztecs had never seen a horse. To an Aztec, a mounted Spaniard looked like a two-headed beast. When the Spaniard dismounted, they were astonished to see the beast divide itself in two.

The Aztec ruler made nice with Cortés, a very bad mistake. Cortés took Montezuma II hostage for a while, which did not enhance the Aztec king's prestige.

Many of the Aztec's subject people, meanwhile, figured there was a chance Cortés would let them keep their hearts if they backed the newcomer against Montezuma II. Montezuma II died in a 1520 revolt. The next year, the Aztecs' city, Tenochitlan, fell to the Spaniards.

Beating the odds in the Andes

Cortés' conquest of the Aztecs in **1521** inspired another Spanish commander, Francisco Pizarro, to invade the greatest South American civilization — the Inca — a decade later. The invasion he began in 1531 may have been fool-hardy, considering he had only 200 troops to subdue an empire of over a mil-lion people, but it took him only two years, until **1533,** to capture Cuzco, the Inca capital city.

His prize, the Inca Empire, was at its height. Centered in the Andes mountains of Peru and spread over a territory from northern Chile to Equador, the empire encompassed a network of different tribes, all subjugated and admin-istered by one dominant culture.

Following the road to Cuzco

Like the Aztecs to the north, the Inca started as a subject people, under the thumb of previous Peruvian empires. (I talk more about a couple of them, Peru's Nazca and the Moche, in Chapter 4.)

Incas started flexing their muscles in the twelfth century. In the 1430s, a ruler called Pachacuti repelled an invasion by a neighboring people and then went on to increase the size of the Inca Empire until it took in parts of today's Chile, Bolivia, and Ecuador.

By the sixteenth century, Pachacuti's successors controlled more land than any South American people ever ruled before them. Like the Romans (more on them in Chapter 4), the Incas brought the leadership of the conquered into the Inca fold, rewarding those who joined, and making cooperation easier than resistance. Also like the Romans, the Incas were wonderful engineers. Inca stonemasons built fortifications of giant granite blocks fitted so perfectly together that a knife blade still won't penetrate a seam today.

Just as remarkably, especially over such rugged mountains, the Incas maintained a 19,000-mile road system, and the government sent fleet-footed messengers along those roads, with runners stationed every 1½ miles. Using this system, they could send a message 150 miles in a day. The runners kept local leaders connected to Cuzco.

The ruling family held everything together, proving the Incan undoing. All Pizarro had to do was overcome the ruling family and the empire toppled. He accomplished that in 1532, by base trickery.

Accepting the invaders' invitation

In 1532, Pizarro invited the king of the Incas, Atahualpa, to a meeting at Cajamarca, a city away from his capital. Atahualpa accepted.

When the king arrived, along with his enormous royal retinue, Pizarro kidnapped him, surprised his followers and killed several hundred of them. The victims included the king's family members. Atahualpa tried to ransom himself, but Pizarro wanted to use him as a puppet ruler. Atahualpa didn't go along with it, refusing to convert to Christianity. So Pizarro killed the king, too. Then he and his troops marched to Cuzco, Atahualpa's capital city, capturing it in 1533.

The Spanish spent about 30 years beating down revolts through former Inca lands (and fighting among themselves as they fought Indian rebels), but they were fully in control by the 1560s.

Cinematic versions of Pizarro and Altahualpa are the main characters in the 1969 movie *The Royal Hunt of the Sun.* Based on a stage play by Peter Shaffer, the movie provides an interesting discussion of mortality, religion, greed, and culture clash, but for a movie set in the spectacular Andes mountains, it's stingy with visual riches. *Aguirre, Wrath of God*, a 1972 movie by German director Werner Herzog shows how beautiful and ambitious a film about Spanish conquistadors looking for El Dorado (the legendary city of gold) can be.

Circling the Globe

Like Vasco da Gama (read about Gama earlier in this chapter), Ferdinand Magellan was a Portuguese explorer who found a sea route to Asia. Like Christopher Columbus (see Chapter 6 for more about Columbus), Ferdinand

Magellan was a non-Spanish commander of a Spanish flotilla that tried to reach Asia by sailing west from Europe.

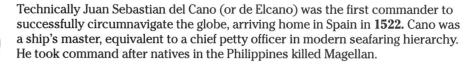

Technically Juan Sebastian del Cano (or de Elcano) was the first commander to successfully circumnavigate the globe, arriving home in Spain in **1522.** Cano was a ship's master, equivalent to a chief petty officer in modern seafaring hierarchy. He took command after natives in the Philippines killed Magellan.

The expedition lost more than its captain. It lost four of its five ships, all of its officers and most of its crew on the eventful voyage that went across the Atlantic, through the straits at the tip of South America (ever after called the Straits of Magellan), across the Pacific Ocean (Magellan named it), through the coveted ports of the Spice Islands (in today's Indonesia), around Africa from the east, and home.

Although he died on the trip, Magellan (whose name in Portuguese was Fernao de Magalhaes) gets credit as the first navigator to circle the globe. He made it as far as the Philippines, and as Magellan may have earlier sailed that far east with Portuguese expeditions, you could say Magellan personally sailed around the world.

The success of his expedition meant that Europeans finally had proof that the Americas were more than just an unexplored part of Asia. The vast ocean to the west of the New World confirmed that it really was a new world, to Europeans, anyway. Further, Magellan proved it was possible to get at Asia from either direction. In 1522, when his one remaining ship and its few sick, emaciated sailors returned to Spain, Asia was still the prize that European traders, and their monarchs, coveted.

Facing Asian empires

Although Europeans were strong and becoming stronger with their worldwide sea routes, they weren't able to immediately grab up huge parts of Asia — the way Spain and Portugal claimed all of South and Central America in the late fifteenth and early sixteenth centuries. The sixteenth century was still a time of huge, powerful Asian empires — or in the case of the Ottoman Empire, of an enormous Asian, African, and European empire.

The Ottoman Empire arose at the end of thirteenth century in northern Anatolia (part of Turkey). Related to the Mongols and other nomads, the Turks, a loosely connected group of nomadic peoples from the interior of central Asia, were organized into dynastic clans, such as the Seljuk Turks, who achieved great power in the Middle East in the eleventh century. European crusaders battled the Seljuk Turks in the First Crusade of 1095. (For more on the nomadic peoples of Central Asia and the Crusades, see Chapter 6.)

The Ottomans, another clan of Turks, captured Constantinople in 1453, ending the Byzantine Empire. (The Ottoman Turks weren't named for a padded footstool; rather the padded ottoman footstool, a Middle Eastern style of furniture, was named after them.)

Like the Seljuk Turks before them, and also like Arabs and other people through western Asia, the Ottoman Turks were Muslims. (See Chapter 5 for more about the rise and spread of Islam.) Also like the Arabs, they fought with the spirit of *jihad* (holy war) to amass an empire that stretched from Budapest in Hungary to Baghdad in Iraq to Aswan on the upper Nile, and also encompassed the Mediterranean Coast of Africa.

Another nomadic people, like the Turks, the Mongols came out of Central Asia to build empires. Their greatest warrior king, Genghis Khan, amassed a huge empire across Asia to northeastern Europe in the thirteenth century. His grandson, Kublai Khan, conquered China and established a dynasty there in **1280.**

The Mongol Empire fell apart in the late thirteenth century, but descendents of Genghis Khan continued to exert power. One of the most famous, Tammerlane (or Timur the Lame) came out of Turkestan to bedevil the Persians and Ottomans in the fourteenth century. Tammerlane's descendent, Babur, who was also of part-Turkish descent, conquered northern India (including today's Pakistan) in 1526, founding the Mogul (also spelled Moghul) Dynasty, based in Delhi and eventually claiming most of the Indian subcontinent, except for the extreme south (where Europeans were just beginning to make their presence felt). Mogul was a variation on Mongol, a reference to Babur's empire-building heritage.

The Mogul Dynasty boasted strong rulers and remarkable stability until the eighteenth century, when struggles within the royal court weakened central authority. The empire began to fragment as provincial rulers, although still officially subject to the Mogul king, claimed more power for themselves. This decline of Mogul rule made gaining more power in India easier for European nations. The British — who established their first Asian trading post at Surat, a port city in western India, on the Gulf of Cambay, in 1612 — abolished the Mogul court 245 years later, in 1857.

European traders moved quickly when the Portuguese opened up the sea route around Africa, in 1498. (See the story of Vasco da Gama's voyages, earlier in this chapter.)

First, the Portuguese built on their success. After they took over Kozhikode, Portuguese traders seized another Indian port, Gao. Sailing on to the Spice Islands (Molucca, in today's Indonesia), they claimed Macao, a narrow peninsula jutting from the coast of China, near Canton.

The Portuguese built fortified outposts from which they could monopolize the spice trade. Commerce paid so well that the Dutch and British couldn't just sit by and watch while Portugal raked in the gold.

Founding East India companies

Eighty London merchants got together in 1599 and formed the East India Company. Elizabeth I granted them a charter in 1600. The Dutch formed their own East India Company in 1602. The French got in on this action with their own East India Company, founded in 1664.

For a short time, the Portuguese enjoyed a trading monopoly as the only European nation with the navigational charts — and the trade contacts — to transport Asian goods by sea. How did the East India companies get around the Portuguese monopoly? Much the way the Portuguese established that monopoly in the first place — by muscling in. After Britain established its first trading station at Surat, India, in 1612, the British moved on to other Indian ports. The British founded Madras, in southeast India, in 1639. Britain's traders built a post at Bombay in 1688 and founded Calcutta, in Bengal, as their Indian headquarters in 1690.

The spice trade proved a high-risk profession. The Dutch took Amboyna, a base in the Moluccas, away from the Portuguese. Then when English merchants tried to trade there, the Dutch put the interlopers to death.

The Dutch captured Jakarta, a city with a fine, protected harbor on the north coast of Java (part of today's Indonesia), in 1619, and renamed it Batavia (after the Batavii, a Celtic tribe in the Netherlands in Roman times). The Dutch East India Company made Batavia its headquarters.

In 1638, the Dutch got another exclusive: They convinced the Japanese to let them take over from the Portuguese as the exclusive European trade representatives in Japan. For the right to stay, the Dutch had to promise not to preach Christianity.

Telling East from West

Why were the British, Dutch, and French trading organizations in Asia called called *East* India Companies? Wasn't India to the east of Europe?

Well, yeah. But now there were those other *Indies* in the west. When Columbus arrived in the Caribbean in 1492 (more about Columbus in Chapter 6, also earlier in this chapter) he wanted desperately for the islands he found there to be part of Asia. He imagined he was somewhere off the coast of China, perhaps in Indonesia. He called the Caribbean islands *Indies*.

After everybody figured out that Columbus was wrong, that the American islands to the west were different from the Asian islands to the east, they distinguished between them by saying *West* Indies and *East* Indies. For a while there, every time you headed out from port you had to specify which Indies you intended to reach.

Distrusting the Westerners in Japan

Japan was always a special case among Asian nations. Isolated by the sea, Japan never succumbed to the invasions of nomadic tribes who roamed the rest of East Asia and rose to power as empire builders (people such as the Mongols, in Chapter 6 and earlier in this chapter). Although its imperial government was structured like China's, since 1192, power was in the hands of a warrior class. Japanese authority was concentrated in the *shogun* — a warlord nominally appointed by the emperor, but in reality, the shogun was far more powerful than the emperor. The shoguns of the Tokugawa family, which ruled from 1603 to 1868, were essentially military dictators over all of Japan.

Tokugawa Ieyasu, the first of the Tokugawa shoguns, gained office in 1603 at the end of a series of messy civil wars. Tokugawa was suspicious of outsiders, especially Europeans. Seeing the Christian missionaries that the Portuguese brought to Japan as a threat, he worried that their influence could undermine the authority of the shogun system. As he had just restored order to the country, he was determined not to see that authority diluted.

Tokugawa Ieyasu passed on his distrust of European Christians to his son and successor as shogun, Tokugawa Hidetada. Hidetada thought that if the Christians gained too many Japanese converts, it would hurt Japan's ability to defend itself against a European invasion. The shogun persecuted Christians more and more severely. In 1622, his officials in Nagasaki crucified 55 missionaries at once.

The next shogun, Tokugawa Iemitsu, threw all missionaries and most traders out of Japan during his reign from 1623 to 1651. He outlawed foreign travel for Japanese and forbade shipbuilders to build the big vessels needed for long-range voyages. Iemitsu even restricted Buddhism. He preferred the Confucian emphasis on loyalty to superiors.

Japan continued to trade with China, Korea, and a small contingent of Dutch, the latter being kept off the mainland most of the time, on an island in Nagasaki Bay. The Togukawa family successfully kept Japan closed off from Western trade until the mid-nineteenth century.

Playing by company rules

The British, shut out of Molucca and Japan, had plenty of other ports to exploit, especially in India. From its headquarters in Calcutta, India, the British East India Company traded in textiles and expanded its influence. It oversaw the administration of trade, but it also governed British subjects in its trading ports and beyond, becoming a quasi-government.

In the mid-eighteenth century, the British East India Company expanded its role to military power, declaring war on the Mogul ruler, Nabob Siraj ud daula. The company took this step after the king, trying to shore up Mogul power against advancing British influence, kicked the East India Company out of Calcutta in 1756.

The East India Company fought back and defeated a coalition of provincial Muslim rulers allied with the king. (The Mogul Dynasty was Islamic.) The British emerged from that war with official rights to collect revenue from the Mogul emperor for the state of Bengal. With that role, the British East India Company became an Indian provincial ruler.

Its power and profits grew alarmingly and so did mismanagement and corruption within the East India Company. Irresponsible speculation in British East India Company stock contributed to a banking crisis in 1772. The British government saw a need to reform the East India Company's charter with a series of laws, beginning with North's Act of 1773. Its provisions included more direct government supervision of East India Company affairs.

An 1857 Indian uprising against British rule — in which Hindu and Muslim rebels massacred British soldiers and the British responded with overwhelming weaponry and mass executions — forced the government in London to reexamine colonial policies again. In 1858, Parliament passed an act requiring the East India Company to hand its powers over to the British crown.

Transitioning from Ming to Manchu

The Ming Dynasty ruled China from 1368 to 1644, a period distinguished by good government, peace, artistic achievements, and prosperity. Ming emperors took an interest in the common people's welfare, going so far as to break up large estates and redistribute them among the poor. Was this some kind of prelude to the much later socialist government that the Chinese established in the twentieth century? Not really, but it *was* forward-looking.

China was also fortunate that when the Ming Dynasty finally crumbled in 1644, a ruling family from the province of Manchuria took over, establishing the long-lived Qing (or Chi'ing) Dynasty, which lasted into the twentieth century. At its height, the Qing Dynasty gave China some of its ablest emperors and most stable administrations ever.

Kangxi, the Qing emperor from 1736 to 1796, molded himself into the image of the ideal Confucian ruler — a benevolent protector of the people. (See Chapter 9 for more on Confucianism, and Chapter 23 for more on Confucius.) Kangxi stressed loyalty, traditional morality, and hard work for the common good — especially in farming.

Adequate food production is the greatest common good in a country growing as fast as China was in the eighteenth century. By 1800, the Chinese population was 300 million, double what it was a century before. Under successive Qing emperors, the Chinese developed fast-maturing varieties of rice so that they could produce multiple harvests within a single growing season.

Dealing opium

The Qing Dynasty traded successfully, even importing foods such as corn and sweet potatoes from the Americas. (With 300 million mouths to feed, why not?) But China was still suspicious of and resistant to most European business overtures, restricting foreign traders to specific ports such as Canton and Shanghai. For most transactions, the Chinese wanted hard currency such as precious metals. The British East India Company had to pay for tea and other Chinese goods with silver. The Brits felt they were getting the short end of this deal, so they looked for something else the Chinese would take in trade. By the nineteenth century they found it — the drug opium, from British-ruled India. More and more Chinese, especially in the south, were smoking opium and becoming addicted, to the point that they were willing to pay in tea, silks, and even in silver that helped to finance British India.

Opium destroyed Chinese lives and damaged the Chinese economy. For both reasons, the Qing emperor sent officials to Canton to burn 20,000 chests of British opium. This kind of thing riles a drug lord even today, and the Brits were mad enough to go to war over it. And they won.

After the first Opium War, 1842's Treaty of Nanjing forced the Chinese to cede the island port of Hong Kong to Britain. Hong Kong remained a British Crown Colony through most of the twentieth century. (In 1997, Britain restored the port city and adjacent territory to China.) Another Opium War followed from 1856 to 1860, with a similar result. China was forced to open more ports to British and other Western traders.

Spreading the Slave Trade

Slavery is evil. You and I know that ownership of human beings by other human beings is among the worst practices ever to blight humankind. Yet much of what is called *civilization* was built on slavery. An economic foundation of ancient cultures including Sumer, Babylon, Egypt, ancient Greece, and Rome, slavery was often considered a reasonably tolerable way of life — preferable to starving anyway.

Perpetuating an evil

The Arabs had little problem with slavery. Neither did the Vikings. Most of Sweden's seacoast is on the Baltic Sea, facing east; so Vikings from that part of Scandinavia sailed eastward. As these Norse adventurers explored harbors, in today's Latvia, Lithuania, and Estonia, they began sailing farther eastward, up inlets and rivers into Russia. In Russia's northern, inland forests they found a source of wealth, tribal people that they captured to sell as slaves.

The slave markets of the Middle East weren't so difficult for Vikings to reach by water. The Vikings simply carried their cargo down a river. The Dnieper runs through today's western Russia, Ukraine, and Belarus on its way to the Black Sea. From there they could sail to Constantinople. Farther east, the Volga flows south into the Caspian Sea, which borders today's Iran. From the Caspian Sea, the Vikings could reach the lucrative slave markets of Baghdad (the capital of Iraq today). When Christian missionaries first ventured into Scandinavia, the Norse captured and sold some of those people too.

Arabs had long dealt in slaves, and had sources besides the Viking traders for captive human beings. Since conquering much of North Africa in the sixth and seventh centuries, the Arabs took slaves from that continent. (Find more about the Arab conquests in Chapter 5.)

African wars, like wars in much of the rest of the world since prehistoric times, often involved one tribe or village capturing people from another tribe or village. As Arab traders penetrated the continent beginning in the sixth century, Africans learned that they could trade their captive enemies to these strangers for valuable goods.

The Arab slave trade created a slave economy in Africa, one that was still in force in the late fifteenth century. When Portuguese navigators began landing at West African ports, they found local slavers willing to sell them laborers. In 1482, Portuguese traders built their first slave-trading outpost in Ghana. By the early sixteenth century, the Portuguese were shipping captives to Portugal and to the Azores Islands in the Atlantic, where Portuguese settlers needed laborers. Within a few years, there would be a new market for these slaves in the Americas, and the Portuguese were poised to supply that market.

Developing a new market

By the middle of the sixteenth century, Spanish settlers on the Caribbean Islands decided they needed a new source of labor. The local Indians, whom they enslaved, had no immunity to diseases from Europe. Many were sick or weak. Too many died.

The Spaniards began importing African slaves, who were less likely to keel over from smallpox. (Smallpox, one of the deadliest diseases among Europeans, and far more deadly to Caribbean Indians, was also widespread in Africa, so African slaves carried natural resistance.) The first African slaves were purchased from Portuguese ships about 1530, beginning a trade that would escalate sharply through the sixteenth and seventeenth centuries, reaching its peak in the eighteenth.

Also in the sixteenth century, the Spanish found that slave labor made cash crops such as sugar, which they could grow on Hispaniola and other Caribbean Islands, highly profitable. They bought more slaves. By 1700, 4,000 slaves arrived in the Spanish-ruled islands every year.

The English, building their first permanent settlement in North America, Jamestown, Virginia, in 1607, didn't wait long to begin importing slaves. The English also had a labor-intensive, profitable crop — tobacco. In 1619 the new Virginians began using African slaves in their tobacco fields.

Portugal brought slaves to Brazil in such numbers that, by 1800, half that big country's people were of African heritage.

Slaving by the numbers

Trafficking in slaves was one of the surest ways to get wealth in the shipping business between 1500 and 1800. Europeans joined Arab traders and local African rulers who could also make fortunes in this ugly business. The Dutch, British, French, and Danish all competed with the Portuguese, building slaving stations in Africa.

In 1713, Spain granted Britain a monopoly to supply its American colonies with 4,800 slaves a year for 30 years. The agreement was called *Asiento de Negros*. Nobody knows how many people were captured and sold, but they numbered perhaps seven million in the eighteenth century alone. One reason the numbers are so hard to come by is that so many died in transit. The appalling conditions aboard slave ships included packing slaves in chains into holds that were only a bit more than three feet high. Many died in the filth, disease, and despair of these holds. Sailors dumped the bodies unceremoniously into the sea. Those who survived were sold at auctions such as the one advertised in Figure 7-2.

Starting Revolutions

Many Europeans who came to the Americas wanted to distance themselves from the countries they came from for one reason or another. Often that reason was economic. The New World offered land to the landless and opportunities to the poor.

Figure 7-2:
African slaves were sold at auctions such as the one advertised here.

> **T**O BE SOLD on board the Ship *Bance-Island*, on tuesday the 6th of *May* next, at *Ashley-Ferry*; a choice cargo of about 250 fine healthy
> **NEGROES,**
> just arrived from the Windward & Rice Coast.
> — The utmost care has already been taken, and shall be continued, to keep them free from the least danger of being infected with the SMALL-POX, no boat having been on board, and all other communication with people from *Charles-Town* prevented.
>
> *Austin, Laurens, & Appleby.*
>
> *N. B.* Full one Half of the above Negroes have had the SMALL-POX in their own Country.

© *Bettmann/CORBIS*

Religion also played a part in making the New World a desirable destination — as it was for the English Puritans who landed in North America in **1620** — the people that Americans remember as the Pilgrims of Massachusetts. In New England, the Puritans could do more than worship according to their own beliefs; they could live and govern themselves by those beliefs, too. England was a little too far away by sailing ship for the mother country to do much hands-on supervision. Other religious refugees followed — Catholics to Maryland, Baptists to Rhode Island, and Quakers to Pennsylvania.

Bringing in the new

The Americas attracted people looking for something new, willing to cast off the old order. In the late eighteenth century, there were two monumental revolutions that threw off the old order: the American Revolution and the French Revolution. It's not surprising that the first broke out in North America.

The American Revolution, beginning in 1776, created the United States of America and spread the idea that colonists could break free of their European rulers. The French Revolution, beginning in 1789, shocked traditionalists even more deeply. The French Revolution revealed that the old order could be completely turned on its head, at least for a while. The French Revolution also confirmed that the old order's head — that is, King Louis XVI's head — could be chopped off and tossed into a bloody basket.

These big events, together with a couple of more peaceable revolutions — agricultural and industrial — made the world a different place all over again.

Playing with dangerous ideas

But first came an intellectual movement, the Enlightenment.

The American and French revolutions grew out of economic and political issues between people and their rulers, but they also grew out of the ideas from a new crop of philosophers. The Englishman John Locke (see more about Locke and the Enlightenment in Chapter 14), born in 1632, was a pioneer in arguing that the authority of government comes from the governed — a big departure from tradition. Locke's outlook was surely marked by the English Civil War of 1642 to 1649, a conflict between supporters of King Charles I and his opponents in Parliament, the Roundheads (named for their close-cropped haircuts). It led to the trial and execution of the English king.

Beheading a country

Ever since 1215, when dissatisfied barons forced the unpopular King John to sign the *Magna Carta* (see Chapter 23 for more about this agreement), English people (especially English nobles) were supposedly guaranteed political and civil liberties. Not everybody considered the agreement binding, of course, especially not Pope Innocent III, who absolved King John from any responsibility to observe it.

The English Civil War wasn't quite the international jolt that the French Revolution would be, but it was shocking. Despite the Renaissance and the Protestant Reformation (see Chapter 12 for the Renaissance and Chapter 13 for the Reformation), which shattered the monolithic authority of the Roman Catholic Church, most people in Europe still agreed with Pope Innocent III that nobody except God (and sometimes the pope) should be able to tell a king what to do.

The Stuart kings, James I (who ruled from 1603 to 1625) and Charles I (king from 1625 to 1649), believed it. Like most people and like all kings, they saw themselves as God's appointees — vice-deity in charge of earthly matters. The Magna Carta, they huffed, was not worth the parchment it was written on. This notion took a serious blow at the culmination of the English Civil War in 1649, when the philosopher Locke was a teenager. Protestant revolutionaries chopped off Charles I's head and set up a *Protectorate* (or republic) led by Oliver Cromwell (more about Cromwell in Chapter 21).

England got its monarchy back in 1660, after Cromwell died and Charles II showed up to mount the throne. (He had been bunking with friends in France.) The *royalists,* supporters of the monarchy, still hopping mad, dug up Cromwell's body and hanged it. Take that! This is the period called the Restoration, because the monarchy was restored.

Trying to forestall unrest in France

The kings of France took some measures to prevent insurrections such as England's in 1649. First, a clever cleric, Cardinal Richelieu (1585 to 1642) set up governmental offices that effectively cut into the power of the French nobles, concentrating the king's authority. Chief minister to Louis XIII, Richelieu suited Louis XIV, who succeeded in 1643, just fine.

The English Civil War began just the year before Louis XIV's coronation, in a clash between Charles and members of Parliament. Louis XIV avoided a potential forum for dissent when he stopped calling the French equivalent of Parliament, the Estates-General, into session.

Like the Stuarts — James and Charles — Louis XIV believed that he, as king, was God's deputy. His spectacularly luxurious palace at Versailles, the show-place of all Europe, reflected this conviction.

But Louis XIV raised taxes to support his free spending and waged an expensive war with Britain from 1701 to 1713. The French people began to grumble and kept grumbling as succeeding kings involved France in more money-draining conflicts, including the War of Austrian Succession from 1740 to 1748 (France sided with Frederick the Great of Prussia) and the Seven Years War from 1756 to 1763, the conflict that Americans call the French and Indian War.

Reasoning reasonably

Ideas such as Locke's — that individual people are free and equal — gained ground in Europe — at least among the educated. In France, the writers François Voltaire and Jean Jacques Rousseau challenged old ideas about the king representing God. The Enlightenment also grew out of scientific thought as men such as Isaac Newton in England and Antoine Lavoisier in France theorized about, discovered, and proved natural laws. Gravity was one of Newton's biggies. (For more about the way philosophy and science intertwined in the seventeenth and eighteenth centuries, see Chapter 14.)

Rebelling Americans

Enlightenment ideas also took hold overseas, where rational science and engineering, including practical agricultural reforms, put people into a rational frame of mind about government. These ideas were natural for the immigrants in North America. As independent-minded as many Americans always were, they had little trouble accepting the ideas that men (although still just white men, according to the ideas of the time) were inherently free and that rulers' authority flowed from the people.

When the British government imposed a series of taxes on the American colonists to pay for the French and Indian War, colonists did not take it kindly. "Where is our voice," they asked. "Who represents our interests in Parliament?" The answer: Nobody.

Among the more creative acts of resistance to British taxes, a bunch of Bostonians dressed up in Native American costume and destroyed the cargoes of several tea ships. Parliament shot back by sending troops and closing Boston harbor. The New Englanders fought the Old Englanders in two Massachusetts villages, Lexington and Concord, in 1775, beginning the American Revolution. A Continental Congress, formed of representatives from 13 British colonies (British Canada did not participate), declared independence from England the next year in a document, the Declaration of Independence, that rings with Enlightenment philosophy. The great shock was that the outnumbered colonists won, but they couldn't have without the French, who supplied money, weapons, and troops to help defeat their longtime enemies, the English.

Erupting France

Enlightenment ideas link the American and French revolutions, but so do economics. Just as England excited unrest by raising taxes to pay for the French and Indian War, so did the French government. And King Louis XVI's administration made the situation worse by stretching French finances even farther to support the American patriots.

Louis XVI's generosity made his government all the more vulnerable to the upheaval that rocked France — eventually spilling over into much of Europe — beginning in **1789** with the French Revolution.

That was the year when Louis XVI called a meeting of the *Estates-General,* the French parliament, which was a bold move, considering that the body hadn't met in more than 150 years. A well-meaning fellow, and smart enough to know that things must change, Louis was trying not to lose his crown, or his head, in the process. Calling the Estates-General was an attempt to get agreement on necessary reforms.

But when he called the Estates-General to session after it had been dormant so long — essentially nonexistent since the mid-seventeenth century — Louis opened a pressure valve. The idea that the king might permit any reform brought forth a flood of pent-up discontent. People were fed up with the privileged class and high taxes.

On **July 14, 1789,** an angry Paris mob stormed the Bastille prison, a symbol of arbitrary injustice, and things didn't settle down for years. The Estates-General, under the leadership of some of its more radical members, became the democratic National Assembly, which issued a Declaration of the Rights of Man, abolishing the constitution and the monarchy in 1792. The new revolutionary government used a French invention, the guillotine, to behead King Louis XVI early the next year.

This wasn't the end of the turmoil, however, not by a long shot. The Reign of Terror followed in 1793 and 1794, a period when a French person could look at somebody cross-eyed and lose a head for it.

Within a decade, in a classic case of pendulum-swing, the neck-chopping excesses of that raging French Revolution provided an opportunity for the first guy who could restore order. He wasn't exactly waiting in the wings — unless you call invading Italy and Egypt waiting in the wings — but when a bold, if short, French military officer called Napoléon returned to France, the revolutionary era gave way to an old-fashioned empire. (You can read more about Napoléon's impact in the next chapter. There's even more about Napoléon in Chapter 19.)

Writing L'Ouverture to freedom

One ironic note about France and its revolution: After folks began throwing around those Enlightenment ideas, the ideas took on a life of their own. François-Dominic Toussaint, a slave in Haiti, was inspired by Enlightenment philosophers as well as by the news from Paris.

Calling himself Toussaint L'Ouverture, he led other slaves against the French authorities in the early 1790s. In 1795, he won control of most of the formerly French-held territory (Haiti occupies about half of the island of Hispaniola). He abolished slavery and in 1801, declared Haiti independent. Napoléon tried to put a stop to this business in 1803 when his forces retook the island nation, captured L'Ouverture, and took him to Paris where he died later that year. The sparks of liberty aren't always that easy to extinguish. Jacques Dessaline soon led the Haitians against the French again and drove them out in 1804. (For more about L'Ouverture, see Chapter 21.)

Ideas imported from Europe took root among people who would use them, over the next century or two, to shake off Europe's hold.

Tracking the Centuries

About 1345: Aztecs establish their great capital city, Tenochtitlan, on an island in the middle of a lake.

1482: Portuguese traders in Ghana build their first African slaving outpost.

1522: One surviving ship of Ferdinand Magellan's expedition to Asia completes the voyage around the world by returning to Spain.

1603: Tokugawa Ieyasu, founder of Japan's anti-European Tokugawa Dynasty, comes into power.

1612: Britain establishes its first trading station in India at Surat.

1619: Dutch traders capture Jakarta, Indonesia, for their Asian headquarters. They rename the port city Batavia.

1649: English Puritans execute King Charles I of England.

1776: Americans declare their independence from Britain.

1789: Angry Parisians storm the Bastille — a prison and symbol of arbitrary injustice.

1801: Rebel slave Toussaint L'Ouverture declares Haitian independence.

1842: China cedes the island port of Hong Kong to Britain in the Treaty of Nanjing.

1997: Britain returns Hong Kong to China.

Chapter 8

Clashing on a Worldwide Scale

*A*s the nineteenth century began, the world headed in two directions at once — defiantly away from European imperialism and headlong into the most imperialist period ever.

After two monumental revolutions — the American rebellion against British rule and the French overthrow of monarchist order — liberation movements rose in overseas colonies, such as the Spanish-ruled lands in Latin America and on the European continent itself. They rolled into the early twentieth century, when reform fervor turned Russia into a new kind of socialist state. (For more about the American and French revolutions see Chapter 7. To find out about philosophies that inspired political revolutions, go to Chapter 14.)

In France, revolutionary fervor faded as Napoléon Bonaparte took over, carving European neighbors into an empire. Britain joined with Prussia, Russia, and other allies to stop ambitious Bonaparte's land-grabs. Yet, Britain, at the same time, amassed more territory. Though it lost North American colonies, Britain expanded and defended an empire that stretched around the world.

Africans, Asians, and other people intent on resisting European control or tossing out their European masters had a difficult job — especially before Europe's powers clashed in cataclysmic twentieth-century conflicts that caught fire through those worldwide empires, drawing in non-European powers, too. World War I and World War II depleted the resources and resolve of colonial powers, forcing them to let go of third-world possessions. Those wars also caused people worldwide to reevaluate warfare and start trying to prevent further conflicts.

Managing Unprecedented Empires

Since the Portuguese sailors Magellan and Gama pioneered sea routes around the world in the late fifteenth century and the early sixteenth century (see Chapter 7), a handful of nations built empires like nothing the world knew before. Both England and France, in 1915, ruled more people in overseas possessions than they did at home. Russia extended its territory east across Asia to the Pacific Ocean. Working in the other direction (east to west) descendents of Europeans in North America expanded their domination all the way to the Pacific's eastern shore.

Battling on multiple fronts

Britain should have beaten the nankeen britches off the upstart American rebels in the 1770s and 1780s. What were *nankeen britches?* Also called *breeches,* they were the khakis of their time — trousers made out of buff-colored cloth from British trading colonies in India — and that's *not* as beside the point as it seems.

At the time of the American Revolution, the British were the greatest sea power of the world and one of the biggest trading powers. They were on their way to amassing an empire that, at its height, would have made Alexander the Great's eyes pop out of his handsome Macedonian head.

The American setback (although the American Revolution wasn't a setback if you were American) could be blamed on just how far-flung and thin-spread the British had become. They were busy in other corners of the globe in the late eighteenth century.

British soldiers fought French forces in West Africa and the West Indies, and British forces faced Dutch forces in India. Spain got into the fight and seized the British colony at Gibraltar. Meanwhile, East India Company forces plunged into the second of four, closely-spaced Mysore Wars against the Muslims who ruled southwest India.

British manpower was so stretched, and Britain's wealth great enough, that Britain resorted to fighting the American war with hired German mercenaries — *Hessians.* (Hesse is a state in Germany.) Well-trained but hardly united behind the British cause, many German soldiers became Americans after the war.

In the larger scheme of world domination, Britain's setback in America — even Britain's inability to bring the Americans to their knees in the War of 1812 — amounted to not all that much. Not compared to all the victories, all the monumental strides the British Empire made in the nineteenth century.

Strides for colonial powers amounted to blows upon many of the world's indigenous peoples. Australia, the last habitable continent to receive Europeans, was home to a British penal colony starting in 1788. Voluntary settlers followed. Many Australian Aborigines, people isolated from most of the world for many thousands of years, met the same fate as natives in the Americas: widespread disease, often fatal.

Without immunities against the Europeans' diseases and no weapons to match the Europeans' guns, the entire native population of Tasmania, the large island off Australia's southern shore, died between 1803, when the British built a penal colony there, and 1876 — a people wiped out in one lifetime — 73 years.

IN THEIR WORDS
"Four score and seven..."

"Wherever the European has trod," wrote the English biologist Charles Darwin in 1836, "death seems to pursue the aboriginal." Darwin was thinking of Australia, the Americas, Polynesia, and Africa. (For more about Darwin, turn to Chapter 23.)

By the early twentieth century, Britain's empire and protected territories included some 400 million people, only 35 million of them in the United Kingdom (which at that time still included what's now the Republic of Ireland). Although other European countries made spectacular gains, Britain was arguably the first global superpower.

Reinventing post-revolutionary France

Circumstances in Europe forced the British to take other challenges more seriously than they did the Americans' colonial breakaway. Another rebellion against a king, the French Revolution (see Chapter 7) changed France radically in 1789, but the governments in Paris and London remained enemies — more bitterly opposed than ever.

British/French rivalry only intensified as Napoléon Bonaparte seized power in France and made much of Europe into his own empire. Conquering Spain, Italy, and the Netherlands, Napoléon tried, in the early nineteenth century, to overtake the entire continent.

Napoléon was so successful in his military conquests and so powerful that some of his most bitter opponents — including Austria and Britain — agreed to peace treaties whose terms were favorable to France. Yet Napoléon was too aggressive for his neighbors to trust him and the peace gave way to more war.

Although he had to abandon the strategy, Napoléon planned an invasion of England in 1805, the same year that Britain's fleet under Lord Admiral Nelson beat the combined French and Spanish Navies at Trafalgar. Napoléon continued to fight Austria, Bavaria, and other neighbors, winning more battles and forcing more short-lived peace agreements that gave economic and territorial concessions to France.

Finally, in 1812, making a serious mistake, Napoléon invaded Russia, marching a force of 500,000 men all the way to Moscow. The outmatched Russians, perhaps aware of what Napoléon was getting into, steadily withdrew, burning what crops and supplies they could not carry, leaving no provisions for the hungry French.

Napoléon realized that although he controlled a huge area of Russia, including its great inland city, he had no way to provision or shelter his troops through the brutal Russian winter, just beginning. This was especially true as Moscow burned. Nobody knows whether the French burned it (if so, a monumental blunder), whether the Russians set fire to Moscow, or whether the fire was an accident. The French were stranded, facing starvation and death from exposure if they couldn't get back to the more moderate climate of western Europe. Thousands froze and starved, their fallen bodies quickly covered by snow as survivors trudged desperately back toward the West.

Anti-Bonapartist European nations — Britain, Austria, Prussia, Russia, Sweden, and more — joined in a series of alliances over Napoléon's years of power. Although these countries' leaders often distrusted each other, they distrusted Napoléon more.

After the disaster of the Russian invasion, Napoléon was vulnerable. His foes invaded France in 1814. Armies led by Alexander I of Russia removed the self-made French emperor from his throne that year. Napoléon's foes exiled him to an island, Elba, in the Mediterranean. But Napoléon wasn't finished. He escaped Elba, seized power in Paris and fought the allies again.

Britain and Prussia, with support from Russia and Austria, finished Napoléon at Waterloo, Belgium, on **June 18, 1815.** (For more about Napoléon, see Chapter 19.)

Another Louis — number XVIII, the former king's brother — took the throne during the Elba exile, but had to skip town when Bonaparte came back. After Waterloo, Louis could don the crown and stay awhile. France was a monarchy again.

What happened to Louis XVII? The son of Louis XVI and Marie Antoinette (and nephew of Louis XVIII) reportedly died in prison without even getting a style of furniture named after him. The fact that he wasn't guillotined led to rumors that he was still alive. A number of imposters claiming to be Louis XVII emerged in the years after the revolution.

Penetrating Africa

Europeans put their figurative foot in Africa's door in the fifteenth century. Portugal was both the first European sea power to sail around Africa and the first to establish a slaving station on the continent's west coast — dealing in human merchandise before 1500. (See Chapter 7 for more about the Atlantic slave trade.)

Other European nations followed the Portuguese into profitable slave trading. Yet it was inevitable that the empire-builders would eventually want more from Africa than just its captive labor. In the nineteenth century, territory-hungry Europeans carved this continent to their south into colonies.

Making gradual inroads

Taking large pieces of African turf took a while because for hundreds of years after the Portuguese began landing at African ports, few outsiders were able to penetrate Africa. Thick jungles, forbidding deserts, and disease-ridden wetlands made overland journeys difficult. Europeans knew as much about Africa beyond Egypt and the Mediterranean in 1760 as their ancestors knew in Roman times — maybe less.

James Bruce and Mungo Park, both from Scotland, began changing that with their expeditions — Bruce in Ethiopia, Park in West Africa — in the late eighteenth century. As more explorers followed, word got out about the vast resources of the interior.

Presuming Dr. Livingstone

In the 1860s, on an African expedition to settle a dispute about the source of the Nile (Europeans weren't sure where the river started), Dr. David Livingstone, a British explorer, medical doctor, missionary, and popular author, disappeared.

Famous for his earlier explorations along the Zambezi River, Livingstone intrigued newspaper readers, who eagerly devoured any report about him. That presented a problem for publishers in Britain and America (where interest in Livingston was also intense) because they had nothing to report.

The editor of *The New York Herald* decided that hiring another explorer, Henry Morton Stanley — who had made his reputation writing dispatches from the American West and the Middle East — to go after Livingstone would be a great gimmick.

After two rough years of searching, Stanley sent back a story reporting what he said when he found the man: "Dr. Livingstone, I presume."

Maybe because the public waited for so long, or because Stanley's greeting was an understated, civilized conclusion to a long search, the phrase struck a nerve. As the only other white man for hundreds of miles, *of course* it was Dr. Livingstone. "Dr. Livingstone, I presume" became a catch phrase, quoted over and over, well into the twentieth century.

Stanley led another expedition into Africa, and his 1878 book *Through the Dark Continent,* was a bestseller. Livingstone, who had not returned on his own because he was too sick, was not so lucky. He died before he could get back to Britain.

Europe's Industrial Revolution (see Chapter 14), which began in the eighteenth century, ate raw materials. Nineteenth-century Europeans realized that they could mine, cut, and grow such resources as minerals, wood, fiber crops, and foodstuffs amid Africa's wilds, empire-building nations began sending large, armed expeditions into Africa to claim rights over one chunk or another of the big, yet-untapped continent.

By the early twentieth century, the African map was a jigsaw puzzle with pieces bearing both African and European names such as French West Africa, Belgian Congo, German South West Africa, British East Africa (Kenya), and Anglo-Egyptian Sudan (British controlled), as shown in Figure 8-1.

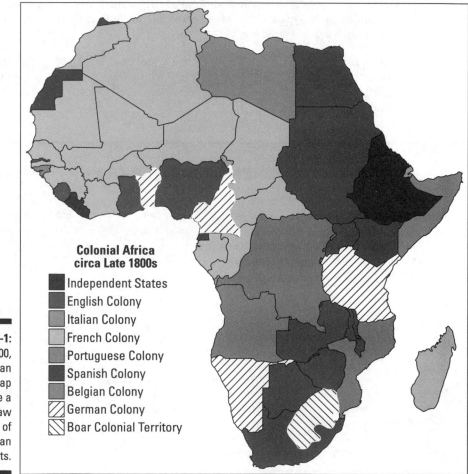

Colonial Africa circa Late 1800s

- Independent States
- English Colony
- Italian Colony
- French Colony
- Portuguese Colony
- Spanish Colony
- Belgian Colony
- German Colony
- Boar Colonial Territory

Figure 8-1: Before 1900, the African map became a jigsaw puzzle of European conquests.

Overwhelming Africa's defenders

African peoples such as the Asante and the Zulu tried to resist the Europeans who took over their lands, but the natives were outgunned.

Samory (or Samir) Ture, the self-appointed emperor of Guinea in West Africa, came to build an Islamic nation in the region of the upper Niger River and had a large and disciplined, if poorly-equipped, army at his command. From 1883, Emperor Ture fought hard, but squeezed between the French and the British, he had little chance. His army was defeated, and he died in exile in Gabon in 1900.

Only one African nation successfully resisted the Europeans. Ethiopia smashed an invading Italian army of 17,000 at the Battle of Adowa in 1896. Ethiopia was the only independent native African nation left.

Holding Out, Striking Back

By the early twentieth century, white Europeans and their descendants ruled so much of the world that it's easier to say what they *hadn't* yet grabbed than to list everything they *had.*

Ethiopia was a black-ruled holdout in Africa. Persia and the Ottoman Empire resisted in the Middle East — although the long-lived Ottoman Empire, based in Istanbul and ruled since the fifteenth century by an Islamic Turkish dynasty, was only a ghost of its mighty former self. In Asia, China stood apart. So did Japan. Beyond that handful, there wasn't much, aside from lesser countries that no European power wanted.

Most of Europe's American colonies had broken free (see more on Latin American revolutions in the next section), but the people who controlled those lands remained largely people of European heritage.

Japan — rushing to adopt Western technological and military advances — was the rare non-European power building an empire.

From 1867, Japan was governed by Emperor Mutsuhito, just a teenager when he succeeded to his father's titular throne. Mutsuhito quickly overthrew the last of Japan's ruling *shoguns* — warlords who had become more powerful than Japan's hereditary emperors. Shoguns ruled the country for 700 years. Matsuhito ended that.

The emperor pushed modernization throughout his long reign, until 1912. He also launched an ambitious, militaristic foreign policy. While many empires of the late nineteenth century and early twentieth century fell back or held steady, the Japanese gained territory from China in the 1890s and from Russia in the Russo-Japanese War of 1904 to 1905, a humiliating defeat for the

Russians because everybody *assumed* Europeans would win these conflicts. In 1932, Japan turned Manchuria, once the homeland of China's Manchu Dynasty, into the Japanese puppet state of Manchukuo.

Turning against Spain

Despite all the eighteenth- and nineteenth-century imperial expansion — and certainly because of it, too — this was also an era of widespread rebellion.

Spain's greatest empire from the time of Christopher Columbus was in the Americas. Claims based on Columbus' explorations in the late fifteenth century brought Spanish colonization to much of southern and western North America, all of Central America, and most of South America.

Rebels challenged Spain's authority in South America starting in the late eighteenth century, while the British were still trying to squash the revolt in their North American colonies.

In Peru in 1780, Jose Gabriel Condorcanqui, a rich man, rallied miners and factory workers — descendents of the Inca — against their Spanish bosses. They attacked Cuzco and La Paz, in neighboring Bolivia (although it wasn't called Bolivia yet).

Condorcanqui, of mixed Spanish-Inca heritage, called himself Tupac Amaru, borrowing the name of a sixteenth-century emperor he claimed was his ancestor. The Spanish caught and tortured him to death and finally crushed the revolt after two years. But more unrest was on the way.

Ascending with O'Higgins

Spanish authority in the Americas really faltered after Napoléon, self-crowned emperor of France and conqueror of Spain, knocked King Ferdinand VII off the throne back in Madrid. In 1808, Napoléon put his own brother, Joseph Bonaparte, on Spain's throne. (Find more about Napoléon and his imperial conquests earlier in this chapter.)

Two years later in Chile, a Spanish captain-general lost his power to a *junta* (a political committee) that, in turn, was replaced by one republican leader and then another, creating continuous confusion. In 1814 (when Ferdinand regained his Spanish throne), royalist troops marched to restore authority in Chile and the military leader who emerged from the republican chaos to fight them was Bernardo O'Higgins. (Now there's a historical name you can remember, even if you forget what he did.) The royalists drove O'Higgins out of Chile, but the fight was not over, as you can see just ahead. (For more about South American revolutionaries, see Chapter 21.)

Breaking away with Bolívar

The situation in South America began to snowball. Simón Bolívar, inspired by the North American patriots and the French revolutionaries, got the idea that the entire chili-pepper-shaped continent needed to break free from Spain. His revolutionaries took over Venezuela in 1816. Then Bolívar beat the Spanish in Columbia, where he became president. He went back to Venezuela when the Spanish tried to recapture it, and drove them out again. Yet Bolívar was far from finished.

Hopping the border with Jose San Martin

Down in Argentina, the Spanish-trained soldier Jose de San Martin led a revolutionary army in that country's fight for independence. Then he joined O'Higgins, who had been driven out of Chile by royalist troops.

Together, they beat Spain, and Chile declared independence in 1818. With O'Higgins in charge as *supreme director* (dictator), San Martin headed to the next spot on the map — Peru.

He won again, declaring Peru independent in 1821. He even stayed on for a bit to lead the new government in Lima. After he retired in 1822, the Peruvians got a good replacement — Simón Bolívar (see the previous section), who drove the remaining Spanish forces out and became dictator in 1824. But Bolívar still wasn't finished overturning Spain's colonial authorities. He moved north and founded Bolivia.

Struggling in Mexico

Mexico's struggle to break free of Spain began only a few decades after the United States had thrown off British rule, but Mexico suffered many setbacks on its way to a stable independent government. Early in the nineteenth century, Spanish authorities arrested two priests, Miguel Hidalgo y Costilla and Jose Maria Morlos y Pavon, for spreading ideas from the French Revolution (see Chapter 7). Both received the death sentence — Hidalgo y Costilla in 1810 and Morlos y Pavon in 1814 — but the revolutionary fever took hold. Augustin de Iturbide broke Mexico free of Spain in 1823, declaring a short-lived Mexican-Guatemalan Empire. The following year, Mexican patriots replaced Iturbide with a constitution based on that of the United States, but they could not secure a stable Mexican government.

The biggest setbacks came in quick succession in the 1830s to the 1860s. Still struggling to find its feet after winning independence from Spain, Mexico lost its northeastern state of Texas to a second-generation independence movement in 1836. Then Mexico lost huge territories in western North America to the United States in the Mexican-American War of 1846 to 1848. For more on the Mexican-American War, see *U.S. History For Dummies* by Steve Wiegand (Hungry Minds, Inc.).

France invaded Mexico in the 1860s. Without bothering to complete the conquest, French Emperor Napoléon III, offered the Mexican throne to Ferdinand Maximilian Joseph, Archduke of Austria, who belonged to the Hapsburg Dynasty of European kings. The Hapsburgs (also called the Habsburgs) conquered Austria in the thirteenth century and emerged as the most prominent and enduring of European royal families from the fifteenth to the twentieth centuries, ruling Spain, the Netherlands, the Holy Roman Empire and more. (See Chapter 13 for the Hapsburg role in the religious wars of the sixteenth century.)

The new Mexican emperor, known as Maximilian, didn't last long. Napoléon III withdrew French troops, leaving Max unable to maintain authority. Mexican General Benito Juarez defeated and captured Maximilian on **May 15, 1867.**

On the whole, Europeans were not hanging onto colonies in the Americas.

Reclaiming Africa for Africans

Africa, although conquered late, did not wait long to get in on this rebellion business. Although their revolt failed, the people of Zimbabwe rebelled against the British in 1896. Africans in Tanzania rose against their German government in 1905, but that movement, too, was crushed. Colonial troops burned crops to create a famine.

The Herero and Nama people of Namibia suffered incredible losses in uprisings against the Germans. The Nama, a cattle-raising people, were reduced from a population of 20,000 to less than half that. Even worse for the Herero, of the estimated 80,000 living in central Namibia before the war, only 15,000 were left in 1911.

This sorrowful struggle finally began to result in self-rule for African nations in the 1950s. In 1948, Riots shook Ghana, then called the Gold Coast. The British government, by that time, woke up to the fact that Britain, its treasury and ambition depleted by World War II, couldn't afford to hang onto its empire. World War II rocked all the Europe-based empires to their foundations (more later in this chapter).

Rising Asians

In the 1820s, the Dutch rulers in Java fought a Javanese prince, Diponegoro, who tried to liberate his island from the foreigners.

The Dutch arrested and exiled him. As it would in so many colonial holdings, Indonesian independence would have to wait until after the turmoil of the World Wars loosened the Europeans' hold.

It's fiction, and perhaps too preoccupied with melodramatic family tensions, but the 1979 film *November 1828,* by Indonesian director Teguh Karya, is an engrossing portrayal of Indonesia's traditional Javan culture and the struggle against colonial rule. You probably won't find it at your local movie rental place, though. If you live in a large city, check out a video store specializing in world cinema. Or see if your local university has a Southeast Asia film collection.

Europeans had to fight to hang onto their economic dominance in other parts of East Asia too. The Chinese went to war against Britain from 1839 to 1842 and again from 1856 to 1860 over the issue of illegal British imports of the drug opium from India to China. (You can read about how this conflict started in Chapter 7.)

Although China lost, and had to allow trading concessions to the British and other European powers as a result, deep-seated resentment lingered.

Ricocheting unrest comes home

Europe didn't shake its own unrest after the French Revolution. The ideas that fueled upheaval in 1789 didn't go away. The French were ready for another revolution in 1848, although this one didn't involve so much head chopping. The French replaced King Louis Phillipe, a champion of the rich, with President Louis Napoléon. You can tell from his name and from his governmental tendencies who Louis Napoléon's uncle was: In 1852, this Louis was crowned Emperor Napoléon III.

What about Napoléon II, you ask? He never got his opportunity. Born in 1811, Napoléon's son was a toddler when hard-line supporters of a Napoleonic dynasty tried to prop him up as an emperor in 1815. The allies who beat his dad at Waterloo discouraged the attempt. Nap Jr. moved to Vienna and stayed out of the way.

France had company in 1848. Many Europeans were miserable — hungry, out of work, and angry. The adjustments of the agricultural and industrial revolutions weren't working out to everybody's benefit. (See Chapter 14 for more about economic changes in nineteenth-century Europe.) In 1848 and 1849, rebellious blowups battered the continent. Revolutionary movements broke out in Austria and Hungary and many of the German and Italian states.

Revolts also rocked Ireland, Switzerland, and Denmark. The revolutionaries failed to overthrow their governments, but the people made themselves heard. Change was in the air. Austria and Hungary finally got rid of serfdom, a medieval form of forced labor. (See the section about Russia, just ahead in this chapter, for more on serfs.) Most of Europe — especially western Europe — headed toward democracy, but there would be big trauma on the way.

Revolting in Russia

The pressures that erupted into the 1848 revolutions in Europe were much the same as the pressures that brought about revolution in Russia a half-century later. In 1905, Russian troops fired on Russian people. The targets were workers marching in the streets of St. Petersburg, trying to win higher wages and shorter hours in the factories.

Shooting at them didn't work. The demonstrators went on strike, and strikes spread from St. Petersburg to other Russian cities. Then the rebellion spread to rural revolts against landlords.

Standing apart up north

Russia had long been a special case among European nations — partly because it was so remote, so much of it northern and inland. Founded by Swedish Vikings who headed east instead of west or south, as Norwegians and Danes had, the Russian nation began forming in the ninth century. (See Chapters 5 and 6 for more about Vikings.)

As in Poland, the indigenous population was largely Slavs, a people of obscure origin who had somehow withstood centuries of Huns, Goths, Avars, and other barbarians rumbling past on their way into Europe. (See Chapter 6 for more about these invasions.)

In social, economic, and technological progress, Russia lagged behind countries to the west. To a Russian, even a Russian of the highest rank, the western European level of craftsmanship and skill — in fields from shipbuilding to architecture, from weaponry to printing — seemed remarkably advanced. Peter I, who became sole ruler of Russia in 1696, spent two years traveling in places such as England, France, and the German states, learning about a wide variety of industries. When he returned, he brought teachers with him. He was determined to drag Russians into the eighteenth century, kicking and screaming if necessary. He dragged many of them literally kicking and screaming, because the six-foot-seven Peter beat them with a stick if they argued with him. (For more about Peter the Great, see Chapters 2 and 21.)

Yet despite modernizations, Russia still stood apart — mired in the past — as the nineteenth century changed the rest of Europe. For example, as many European nations abolished the old feudal system of serfdom, Russia went the other way, and made even more people into serfs.

Serfs were not little blue cartoon characters (those are Smurfs), but people at the bottom rung of society who had no rights. About the only way they differed from slaves is that their masters, under feudal rules, owed them protection.

Serfdom disappeared from England in the Middle Ages, but continued in many lands on the European continent. France formally abolished the institution with its Revolution of 1789. In Austria and Hungary, serfdom endured until 1848. Russia was last with this reform, finally freeing its serfs in 1861. (Smurfdom, sadly, continues in many regions of the world.)

Rushin' toward rebellion

Perhaps it's not surprising that revolutionary unrest hit Russia hard and went to extremes.

After serfdom was abolished, you'd think Russian peasants might be happy, but an unfair land settlement left many former serfs and their descendants without enough soil to grow adequate food. Ironically, better medical care made the situation worse. Toward the close of the nineteenth century, fewer peasants died of diseases, which left more mouths to feed.

High taxes also fueled unrest. Urban professionals and nobles didn't like paying for their government to build an expensive fleet of warships, just to see the Japanese sink the ships during the Russo-Japanese War of 1904 and 1905. (If you're interested in why it's called the *Russo-Japanese* War, rather than the *Russian*-Japanese War, you can find out in Chapter 5, where I talk about *Anglo-Saxon* and similar terms.)

Unrest locked up the country. In 1905, rebels elected representatives to the St. Petersburg Soviet of Workers' Deputies, a council to coordinate strikes and demonstrations. Other *soviets,* or councils, soon formed across Russia. In October of that year, Czar Nicholas II agreed to reforms, including the creation of a Russian parliament, the *Duma.*

By giving unhappy Russians a legislative body, Nicholas hoped to provide a safety valve to ease political dissatisfaction — a place for society to air its grievances, if not actually achieve solutions. But the Duma was doomed from the beginning. On the left, socialist groups boycotted the Duma. On the right, reactionaries in Nicholas' court fought the Duma's efforts to reform tax and agrarian policies. The czar's advisors convinced Nicholas to dissolve the legislature every time they didn't like its direction. Between 1905 and 1912, he dissolved the Duma three times in a row.

In 1917, after five million Russian soldiers died in World War I, Nicholas faced widespread and dangerous unrest. Again, he ordered a disobedient Duma to dissolve itself. This time, the legislators refused his order.

Taking power: The Soviet Union

The Duma wasn't in session when Nicholas abdicated, but a broad coalition of representatives — liberals, social democrats, and agrarian socialists — formed a provisional government, setting up headquarters in the czar's Winter Palace. The provisional government held elections for a Constituent Assembly — a representative body to draft a constitution. But before the body met, extremists from the Russian Social Democratic Party seized power by force.

Led by Vladimir Ilyitch Lenin, just returned from wartime exile in Germany, the extremists called themselves *Bolsheviks,* which means *majority,* even though they were a minority. They captured the palace in October 1917. Lenin allowed the Constituent Assembly to convene in January 1918, but then he used soldiers to break it up.

Lenin and his Red Army fought counter-revolutionaries over the next few years, but Russia — renamed the Union of Soviet Socialist Republics (or the Soviet Union, for short) was going to be a very different beast for most of the twentieth century.

Inspired by the writings of the nineteenth-century German economic philosopher, Karl Marx, Lenin set up a government based on national ownership. Farms and factories belonged to the government. Everybody worked for the government (or, nominally, for "the people"). For the first time ever, leaders seeking to overthrow and replace all existing society with communism's new economic model ran a great national power. (For more about Lenin, see Chapter 21.)

Progress for the people?

As Lenin's successor, Josef Stalin, later proved, a Leninist-Marxist system could bring about rapid industrialization, turning Russia into one of the two greatest economic and military powers in the world by the middle of the twentieth century. But on his way toward economic gains, Stalin left many millions of people dead. His agricultural reforms, violent collectivization of family farms, caused widespread starvation. Stalin unleashed his secret police, killing millions of peasants and small landholders who tried to keep the grain they grew (to eat or to drive up the price to a level that would reward them for their work).

In the 1930s, Stalin brutally eliminated any colleague he perceived as a rival for his power — staging show trials and executions of many men who had stood beside him in 1917 — many of his closest peers through Lenin's regime. The USSR's most revered Bolshevik veterans were forced to confess to unlikely crimes, then sentenced to death by firing squad or a term in a prison camp from which they would never return. Between 1934 and 1938, hundreds of thousands of lesser officials also disappeared — victims of Stalin's purges.

Nobody knows exactly how many millions of people Stalin killed and imprisoned. Estimates range as high as "tens of millions" dead.

Returning Russia

In economic ruin by 1991, the Soviet Union, stretched by military spending (see the Cold War, coming up in this chapter) fell apart. A new Russian Republic then emerged, among other, now-independent former Soviet republics. Struggling to recover and control other parts of the former USSR, Russia fought against an Islamic independence movement in Chechnya, a region between the Black and Caspian Seas.

Accelerating Toward the Present

As you get closer to modern times, you find that human civilization — in its ever-quickening progression from isolated tribes toward a global, interconnected society — became more tightly crisscrossed with interconnections than ever before. The strands of this net between peoples and places grew in number and each connection got faster. Technological innovation contributed as people used new machines — born of the Industrial Revolution (see Chapter 14 for more about the Industrial Revolution) to make distances less . . . well, less distancing.

Getting somewhere in a hurry

Ever since the discovery of new sea routes in the fifteenth and sixteenth centuries, oceans brought continents together rather than separating them. With the harnessing of steam power in the eighteenth century, ships covered those distances quickly, or at least at a steadier, more reliable pace. After the steam engine got wheels, a land transportation revolution quickly followed.

Steaming into port

The steam engine, first used to pump water out of coal and tin mines, became a primary engine of the Industrial Revolution. (See Chapter 14 for the Industrial Revolution of the eighteenth and nineteenth centuries.) This coal-fired power source was adapted to drive boats successfully early in the nineteenth century.

Robert Fulton, an American, built a functional steamship, the *Claremont,* in 1807. Around the same time, England's Patrick Bell built a similar boat. At first, steam was considered useful mainly for river and canal travel, but by the 1830s steamships were already taking trans-oceanic voyages. Shippers, no longer relying on favorable winds, could keep to schedules as never before. International commerce boomed. Steam, rather than sail, soon inter-linked vast empires such as Britain's.

By the 1880s, steam engines powered virtually every kind of vessel — warship, cargo carrier, passenger liner. Steam-driven navies featured battleships that could be more heavily armed and more heavily armored than any in history. (For more about technological advances in modern warfare, see Chapter 17.)

Steam engines became so reliable that ships finally stopped carrying sails at all. The sailor's craft, once all about canvas, rope, and pulleys, became an occupation concerned with boilers, pistons, and coal fire.

Working on the railroads

Richard Trevithick, a British engineer, put a steam engine on wheels in 1804 and made it run on rails. (Mining wagons pulled by animals had long run on iron rails). In 1825, England saw its first commercial railway — the Stockton and Darlington. By 1851, there were rail networks in 17 other countries. By the end of the century Russia had built a railroad across Siberia.

In the United States, people who had spent arduous months crossing the continent to California in wagons could retrace the journey in a week, rumbling along in rail passenger cars.

Rail travel revolutionized commerce, transporting goods more quickly than ever before. It opened up vast inland areas — once too isolated for large-scale settlement — to trade, commercial agriculture, and city building as brand-new communities grew up along rail lines.

Driving innovations

The steam engine uses heat from a fire to create steam, which then drives a piston to create power. The fire is not in the cylinder that houses the piston, but outside, making the steam engine an *external-combustion* engine. The early success of this technology inspired some dreamers to wonder if it would be possible to build an engine that contains the fire itself within the cylinder — an *internal-combustion* engine. In Switzerland, Isaac de Rivaz (or Rivas) built such an engine in 1804, and used it to push a cart across a room.

Rivaz's machine, however, was not practical. For one thing, his engine burned a mixture of purified hydrogen and air, which had to be injected manually with every pump of the cylinder. Rivaz also had to kick open an exhaust valve over and over.

Other inventors, among them Samuel Brown of England and Jean-Joseph-Etienne Lenoir improved on Rivaz' crude design through the middle of the nineteenth century.

To efficiently ignite fuel within a closed cylinder, inventors had to find a way to mix the fuel with air. No fuel will burn without oxygen. To fill this need, they found that a flammable liquid that could be delivered into the cylinder as an even more flammable vapor or mist was best. Refined petroleum oil, in forms such as gasoline and diesel fuel, became the recognized choice.

Because the internal-combustion engine was so much lighter than the steam engine, requiring no cumbersome boiler and no firebox, it seemed particularly well-suited for powering vehicles light enough to travel on roads built for horse-drawn traffic, rather than on the rails required for heavy steam locomotives.

By the 1880s in Germany, engineer Gottlieb Daimler was using an internal-combustion engine to power an efficient motor car. (The word *car* began as a short version of *carriage*.) He began building and marketing these vehicles, leading to one of the twentieth century's biggest and most world-changing industries.

Large-scale automobile manufacture took off in **1908** when American Henry Ford (1863 to 1947) began using an assembly-line factory in Michigan to make cars cheap enough that middle-class people could afford them. From that time on, automobiles changed people's lifestyles. The machines encouraged massive road building and changed the shape of cities as workers — suddenly mobile — relocated their families from central cities to suburban neighborhoods.

Taking to the air

A couple of bicycle mechanics from Ohio, Orville Wright and his little brother Wilbur, flew an airplane for the first time in 1903. Commercially built aircraft followed almost immediately, with passenger travel right behind it. Places formerly days apart, even by the fastest train or car, were now separated by hours — fewer hours as passenger jets came on the scene after World War II.

Sending word

By the middle of the nineteenth century, it was possible to send messages over wires by electric current. This change — the telegraph — amounted to a communications revolution in itself, but it was only the beginning of a wired-up world.

Stringing cables

Samuel Finley Breese Morse, an American artist and inventor, came up with the first practical, wide-scale application for electromagnetic impulses when he invented Morse code in 1837. Seven years later he sent an instantaneous message, "What hath God wrought!" over a telegraph line strung from Baltimore to Washington, D.C.

What did he mean by that? It was a reverent expression of wonder. For its time, the telegraph was incredibly newfangled — far slicker than an ISDN Internet hookup is today. Cables quickly crisscrossed industrialized countries in Western Europe and North America, then spread to more remote parts of the world.

Talking on the phone

Alexander Graham Bell, a speech and hearing therapist, put his interest in sound and communication together with telegraphic technology (see the previous section about the telegraph) to build an experimental telephone in 1876.

Bell, an immigrant from Scotland to the United States, built and marketed the devices, founding the Bell Telephone Company. By the early twentieth century, the phone, no longer a novelty, became an everyday convenience.

Sending radio waves

At the end of the nineteenth century, the Italian-born inventor Gugliemo Marconi demonstrated that radio waves could be used to send signals without wires. Doubters thought that radio waves couldn't travel distances far enough to make them useful. Marconi, who lived and worked in England, proved them wrong by sending a Morse code signal (see the preceding "Stringing cables" section) nine miles across the Bristol Channel. In 1901, he sent a signal much farther — across the Atlantic Ocean from Cornwall (on the southwestern tip of the main island of Britain), to Newfoundland, Canada. Marconi won the Nobel Prize for physics in 1909.

By adding voice-signal technology developed for the telephone by Bell (earlier in this section) and by American inventor Thomas Edison for his innovative phonograph, engineers turned radio communication into a voice-transmission system for ship-to-ship communication, airplane-to-ground communication, and for many other practical links.

Radio also became an entertainment medium; businesspeople saw it as a way to publicize their products. Advertisers began sponsoring music, news, drama, and comedy programs as affordable receivers allowed more and more people to tune in. People over vast distances joined as a common audience for this new experience.

Radio gave birth to TV. In the 1920s, inventors in the United States came up with devices for sending electronic pictures using radio waves. Philo T. Farnsworth invented an electronic picture scanning system in 1922. Vladimir K. Zworkin followed with the television camera and picture tube in 1923.

By the middle of the twentieth century, these devices brought huge and growing audiences a form of instantaneous mass togetherness beyond any precedent in history.

Surfing the 'Net

In 1969, engineers working for the U.S. Defense Department linked four computers together so that the machines could exchange information. Gradually, more computers were hooked up to this network.

Around the same time, more and more government and university programmers and researchers found that sending messages from computer to computer was a good way to trade information. Data began flowing, although the use of this network was largely limited to people who were adept at computer programming.

As computer use spread, and as new personal computers — designed for use by people who weren't computer specialists — put the machines on more and more desks, the growing network became a communications phenomenon. When U.S. universities hooked their *supercomputers* (super-large and super-fast in their capacity to store and process data) together in the 1980s, the Internet as it's known today began to take shape. Commercial services started offering Internet access to businesses and homes, over ordinary telephone lines.

Physicist Tim Berners-Lee invented *hypertext markup language (HTML),* a way for non-specialist Internet users to display their data in everyday language, pictures, and sound, so that other computer users could access them over the Internet. In 1991, Berners-Lee put his creation, the World Wide Web, on the Internet. The World Wide Web quickly became the fastest growing part of the Internet, a place for businesses, political parties, activists, service organizations, and ordinary individuals to air information and exchange views. As with the telegraph, radio, and the telephone (and as with the printing press of the fifteenth century), people became more tightly interconnected than ever before.

Advancing the Methods of Fighting

Although steamships, railroads, and the telegraph — the advances you can find out about earlier in this chapter — bridged distances for commerce and peaceful communication, they also provided advantages for admirals and generals planning attacks and invasions. (To find out more about how technology changed war in the nineteenth and twentieth centuries, skip ahead to Chapter 17.)

Even if you're just casually skimming through this part of the book (and by all means, feel free to skim), you may notice how European nations that had the rest of the world in a bear hug by the year 1900 seemed to fight an awful lot of wars — both with other parts of the world and particularly between themselves.

War was the way to secure and keep empires from ancient times, long before the ruthless Portuguese sailor Vasco da Gama sent a boatload of body parts to the ruler of Kozhikode (India) in the late fifteenth century. (You'll find Gama in Chapter 7.) But with the rise of Europe's new, global empires of the nineteenth and early twentieth centuries, and all the advances in travel and communication, wars tended more than ever to spill over from one part of the world to another.

An early example of what was coming, the Seven Years War had multiple fronts in India, Europe (where Prussia, Hanover, Austria, and Russia sided with Britain, and Spain with France), and America (the French and Indian War). The trend only got worse — lots worse. Anybody who was alive in the twentieth century remembers what it led to — a couple of whoppers known as World War I and World War II.

Weapons advances, such as the more accurate, easier-to-load rifles used in the Crimean War of the mid-nineteenth century, kept right on advancing until, by 1945, one airplane, carrying one bomb, could destroy a major city and kill most of the people in it. Even that wasn't enough. Soon nations had the ability to push a single button and launch a missile attack capable of wiping out civilization on the planet (more about modern wars and weaponry in Chapter 17).

Redefining war: World War I

At the time, nobody gave *The Great War* a number, because they weren't planning to have another. One was quite enough, thanks.

Later called World War I, this conflict proved uglier, bigger, longer, more widespread, and more brutal than many people realized a war could be. From 1914 to 1918, a line of infantry soldiers stretching across northern France and Belgium faced each other month after month, year after year, hunkered down in muddy, rat-infested, soul-killing trenches only a few hundred yards apart.

Mechanized as no war before, World War I took to the skies as airplanes dropped bombs and fought the first ever air to air battles. World War I brought about submarine warfare. German U-boats (the "u" stood for underwater) sank enemy warships and neutralized transports without warning. Troops moved by trucks and armored personnel carriers. Guns were bigger, faster-firing, longer-range, and more numerous than those of any war before. And now there were so-called advances such as crippling mustard gas. Modern chemical warfare had arrived.

Precipitating events and attitudes

You may have heard that the war started when a Serbian terrorist shot an Austro-Hungarian archduke in Sarajevo, Bosnia, in 1914. It's true but much more complicated than that.

For one thing, the Serbians were angry with the Austro-Hungarian Empire (yes, it was a combination Austria and Hungary) for annexing Bosnia (even though Bosnia still technically belonged to the Ottoman Empire, which was weakened by its own internal revolt). The Austro-Hungarians worried about the Serbs potentially uniting all the Slavs in southeastern Europe, which could threaten the Hungarian part of their empire. Russia was mad at Austro-Hungary too. The Russians saw that part of Europe, the Balkans, as their sphere of influence — especially Slavic Serbia.

Russia didn't declare war but mobilized troops. That was enough for the Germans, allies of the Austro-Hungarian Empire, to declare war on both Russia and its ally France. The Germans cut through neutral Belgium on the way to attack the French.

Britain had no formal quarrel with Germany, but relations between the two countries were strained by an undeclared race between them for naval superiority. Starting in the 1890s, Wilhelm II, the German emperor, or *kaiser,* aggressively built more and bigger ships. Many British thought he wanted a bigger Navy than Britain's, the largest and most powerful in the world. The British government responded by stepping up its own shipbuilding. Some British also feared Wilhelm as a rival for colonial power abroad.

German troops crossing into Belgium in 1914 solidified anti-German feeling in Britain. The German incursion violated international law, giving the British an excuse to mobilize troops.

Adding combatants to the war

The war grew bigger as Japan and Serbia jumped in on the side of the *Entente,* or Allies (Britain, France, and Russia). Later in the war, Portugal and Romania also lined up on the side of the Allies. The Ottoman Empire cast its lot with the *Central Powers* (Germany and Austro-Hungary), then Italy joined the Allies.

The United States joined the Allied side in 1917 after Germany's submarine blockade of Great Britain began sinking neutral ships. By war's end, even China formally joined the fight on the Allied side.

Reacting against the carnage

If you looked at the earlier section of this chapter about Russia, you know that World War I helped create the Soviet Union. But World War I changed more than Russia. Four empires — the Russian, the Ottoman, the German, and the Austro-Hungarian — collapsed in that war.

Besides rearranging the map (and the changes were felt even in sub-Saharan Africa, where Germany lost its colonies), the Great War brought famine, collapsed economies, and demonstrated to a shocked public that war — which so many still thought of as an opportunity for gain, or at least for glory — had become largely a disaster.

The war ground up and spit out entire towns, villages, and even countries. Even people not directly hit by the Great War realized by the time it was *over, over there* (to quote a popular American song of the time) that maybe war wasn't so great, after all. This was not the glorious warfare of patriotic songs, but a horrible blight.

A leader in this line of thinking was Woodrow Wilson, a former Princeton University professor turned politician. As president of the United States, Wilson worked on the terms of peace in Europe, making sure the peace process included the League of Nations — an international body created for preventing future wars.

The League of Nations, established by the Treaty of Versailles in **1919,** helped Europe rebuild after the war. Fifty-three nations joined by 1923, including Britain, France, Italy, and Japan.

Unfortunately, the League of Nations didn't work, especially not for Wilson. The U.S. Senate refused to approve Wilson's terms or let the United States join the League of Nations. Wilson suffered a nervous collapse trying to drum up public support to make the senators change their minds. Wilson spent the rest of his term, until 1921, as an invalid.

Although Germany joined the League in 1926, it withdrew, along with ally Japan, in 1933. Italy withdrew three years later. The organization subsequently proved helpless to stop German, Italian, and Japanese expansionism. By the late 1930s, Europe and the world were in for another big one.

Nobody before him ever tried regulating international life the way Wilson envisioned. So maybe his brainchild was bound to fail. But the League of Nations was a step toward something new.

Returning to conflict: World War II

The Second World War's seeds came from the first one — from the discontent and hardship, in the festering resentment in Germany, unhappy with the terms of the Versailles Treaty.

Germans especially didn't like a *war guilt clause* that blamed everything on Germany. Germans hated losing territories — Alsace-Lorraine to France, the Rhineland as a demilitarized zone, most of the overseas colonial holdings to various other empires. Cash reparations — fixed at 6,500,000 British pounds — proved impossibly high for the war-ravaged country.

Breaking the treaty: Hitler moves his troops

Adolf Hitler — an ultra-nationalist political party boss who had become chancellor, then dictator of Germany (even though he was Austrian) — secretly rearmed the country in the 1930s and then started moving his troops in direct violation of the Versailles Treaty.

Hitler occupied the Rhineland (so much for a demilitarized zone), annexed Austria, and headed for Czechoslovakia. He considered himself within his rights going against the Czechs, because he worked out a deal with the governments of Italy, France, and particularly Great Britain, to extend Germany's power in Czechoslovakia.

Hitler thought that the German-speaking people in the Sudetenland region, which was awarded to Czechoslovakia after World War I, belonged instead to his government, the *Third Reich*. Italian dictator Benito Mussolini, whose post-World War I rise was not unlike Hitler's, arranged the meeting in Munich at which Hitler, British Prime Minister Neville Chamberlain — bending over backwards to avoid conflict with Germany — Mussolini, and French Prime Minister Edouard Deladier carved up Czechoslovakia, without consulting the Czechs.

Hitler also signed the Nazi-Soviet Pact with Josef Stalin, Lenin's successor in Moscow. (There's more about both Lenin and Stalin earlier in this chapter.) After the Sudetenland, the Nazis plunged into Poland, with the idea of dividing that country with the Soviet Union. (For more about Hitler, turn to Chapter 19.)

Choosing sides

Germany's 1939 invasion of Poland proved too much even for peace-seeking Chamberlain. London didn't want another war, especially not a war against formidable Germany, but the British woke up to the reality that there was no avoiding it. Britain declared war that year.

Germany took Denmark, parts of Norway, Belgium, the Netherlands, and three-fifths of France. Hungary, Romania, Bulgaria, and Slovakia got behind the Nazis and took over Yugoslavia and Greece. Strongman Benito Mussolini brought Italy into the war from the first — on the German side. Japan sided with Germany and Italy. When Japan attacked the U.S. fleet in Hawaii in 1941, the United States was still officially neutral, although leaning toward Britain. After the attack, the Americans declared war on Japan and its Axis allies. The Soviets, originally on Germany's side, were forced to switch allegiances abruptly when Hitler violated his pact with Stalin and sent an invasion toward Moscow. As with World War I, the conflict spread and spread.

Assessing the war's damage

Ending in two atomic blasts, World War II killed 15 million military personnel — two million of them Soviet prisoners of war. As many as seven million of the 35 million civilians killed were Jewish victims of organized anti-Semite mass murders and concentration camps in Germany and Eastern Europe.

The weapons grew faster, deadlier, and bigger than those in the last war — especially missile launchers and aircraft, which became big enough to drop massive bombs. Bombs from both sides devastated many European cities.

The Allied bombing of Dresden in 1945 killed 80,000 civilians in a night. That was the work of hundreds of bombers, but later that year, on **August 6, 1945,** an American plane dropped a single bomb on Hiroshima, Japan, demolishing everything in a four-mile radius of where it went off. That atomic blast, and a second atomic bomb dropped on Nagasaki a few days later, remain the only nuclear weapons ever used on people. (See Chapter 22 for more about the bombings.) The war ended soon after.

Redrawing the map

World War II rearranged the map of Europe, as World War I did almost three decades earlier. Among the more dramatic changes after World War II, Germany emerged as two nations — one aligned with the United States and other Western powers, the other a satellite of the Soviet Union. (Earlier in this Chapter, you can find out how World War I drastically changed the European map.)

The war also brought profound changes to Asia and Africa, largely because of the way it drained power and money from the remaining European colonial powers. Britain, on the winning side but nearly ruined, had neither the resources nor the will to keep or defend its remaining overseas holdings.

The years after World War II were big on independence movements. You can find out more about some of them earlier in this chapter. Britain left India in 1947. France tried for almost two decades to hang onto Algeria, but finally let go in 1962.

China, at war with Japan from 1937 until 1945 (Japan surrendered on that front, too), promptly plunged right back into a civil war between Nationalist and Communist parties. The Communists won, and under the Marxist leader Mao Zedong, the ancient civilization became the People's Republic of China on **October 1, 1949.**

Hot and Cold Running Conflicts

The years after World War II weren't peaceful. But they didn't erupt into World War III either (cross your fingers). For much of the time after World War II, the major world powers were preoccupied with a game of nuclear standoff.

The major powers, by the way, turned out to be the United States and the Soviet Union. The United States expected to enjoy its nuclear monopoly for 20 years or more, but the Soviets surprised everyone by developing their own atomic bomb in 1949. Allies on the winning side of World War II, the nations became bitter rivals very soon afterward.

Soviet foreign policy, reflecting Josef Stalin's viciously paranoid behavior toward any rival — real or imagined, internal or abroad (see more about Stalin in "Progress for the people?" earlier in this chapter) — became increasingly exclusionary and closed off. Soviet goals included maintaining control over satellite communist states, several set up in Soviet-controlled Eastern Europe in the wake of World War II, while keeping out foreign cultural and economic influences.

The United States emerged as leader of the West — meaning western Europe, the Western Hemisphere, and developed nations anywhere that resisted communism and promoted (or at least permitted) the private pursuit of profit in their trade policies.

Daring each other to blink

With their nuclear arsenals, the Soviet Union and United States engaged in a Cold War. It amounted to a diplomatic, cultural, political, and military standoff.

In diplomatic and military terms, the Cold War took the form of each side daring the other to fire the first nuclear shot. Both nations built more and more, bigger and bigger missiles and warheads. Missiles became capable of delivering a nuclear bomb from a Nebraska wheat field into downtown Moscow. Both nations developed the ludicrously tragic ability to blow up the Earth several times over. (I go into more detail about nuclear weapons and the Cold War in Chapter 17.)

This madness was tempered a little with a Nuclear Test Ban Treaty in 1963, numerous arms talks, and even arms reduction agreements, but the two nations basically kept their guns pointed at each other's heads until one, the economically ruined Soviet Union, blinked — or in this case, fell apart. Along the way, several other countries built nuclear arsenals — China prominent among them.

Returning to arms

Meanwhile, many regional wars raged. Among them, the United States was embarrassed in a futile attempt to keep Vietnam, a former French colony (and before that, a sometime Chinese vassal state) in Southeast Asia, from going communist. The Soviets squandered a lot of resources and international good will fighting Muslim rebels in Afghanistan.

When Israel, a new Jewish state, was established in 1948 in what was British-ruled Palestine, surrounding Arab nations joined Palestinian Arabs in opposing it. (For more about the founding of modern Israel, see Chapter 9.) The disagreement turned violent many times, with wars in 1956, 1967, 1973, and 1982. Also in the region, Iraq fought Iran. Then Iraq invaded Kuwait and a U.S.-led international force turned it back.

Horrible intertribal violence broke out in Africa. Terrorist bombings threaten people on every continent. Clearly, humanity has not come close to achieving a world without war.

Erasing Borders?

So what happened to Woodrow Wilson's splendid, post-World War I idea of a League of Nations (see "Reacting against the carnage" earlier), dedicated to preserving international peace and security by promoting disarmament and intent on preventing or quickly settling international disputes?

Wilson's idea is still around. The term *United Nations* emerged during World War II, when 26 Allied nations pledged themselves to continue the fight against the Axis Powers (Germany, Italy, Japan, and so on). After the war, 51 countries signed a charter creating the United Nations as a permanent organization (see Figure 8-2). The League of Nations then turned its functions over to the new UN.

The charter defines the UN as a world community of independent sovereign states. It says that by preserving this community, the UN will protect international peace — if necessary by taking collective action against war or against forces that threaten war.

By the late 1990s, the UN's membership total was up to 185 nations — many of them former colonies that won independence from European masters.

The UN has many sub-organizations and functions, not to mention critics. Some people see the UN as a plot to undermine the sovereignty of individual nations. The UN was less than effective in many of its attempts to keep international conflicts from turning into wars. But it has scored some moderate successes. As it was with the League of Nations, this business of internationalism is still new to humankind.

Figure 8-2:
Some see
the United
Nations as a
plot to
undermine
individual
nations'
sovereignty.

© David Turnley/CORBIS

The United Nations may be beside the point as transportation and communication continue to accelerate. The world keeps shrinking and political borders may even blur. Western European nations, for example, spent the last decades of the twentieth century forging themselves into a unified economic force — even sharing a currency. International trade agreements are transforming global business, sparking fierce debates.

With communications satellites and the Internet, every place is simultaneously in touch with every place else. United Nations or not, national sovereignty may come to mean less and less as cultural intermingling speeds up. Civilization, whatever that funny word means, may finally become truly global.

So, will that be a good thing?

Tracking the Centuries

1788: Britain establishes a penal colony in Australia.

1808: Napoléon puts his brother, Joseph Bonaparte, on Spain's throne in place of King Ferdinand VII.

1810: Spanish authorities in Mexico sentence a priest, Miguel Hidalgo y Costilla, to death for spreading the ideas of the French Revolution.

1837: Samuel Finley Breese Morse, an American, invents Morse code.

1848 and 1849: Revolutionary movements sweep Europe, erupting in France, Austria, Hungary, and many of the German and Italian states.

1890s: Germany's Kaiser Wilhelm II begins an aggressive shipbuilding campaign, prompting the British — determined to maintain their status as the world's top naval power — to step up shipbuilding as well.

1914: In Sarajevo, Bosnia, a Serbian terrorist assassinates Archduke Francis Ferdinand, heir apparent to the throne of the Austro-Hungarian Empire, triggering World War I.

1939: Germany invades Poland, beginning World War II.

1991: Tim Berners-Lee makes his creation, the World Wide Web, available on the Internet. It quickly becomes the fastest-growing part of the Internet.

1991: The government of the Union of Soviet Socialist Republics collapses. Russia reemerges as an independent sovereign state.

Part III
Mind, Soul, Heart

In this part...

You can glimpse ways that thoughts, ideas, and feelings — and how people express and explore them — shaped history.

Religion and philosophy drove human societies long before the first cities arose. Religious differences sparked wars both ancient and modern. Spiritual fervor built empires. Much of history's greatest art expresses religious feeling. And the whiz-bang technological marvels that made the past 100 years so distinct from all the centuries that came before grew out of a scientific tradition founded in Greek philosophy more than 2,400 years ago — an effort to understand how the world's parts fit together and the place of human beings among them.

Trying to figure out reality — basic to religion and philosophy — led to writing down history. Looking back at the past is part of the impulse to make sense of it all.

Chapter 9

Believing and Believers

· ·

In This Chapter

▶ Recognizing the role of religion in history

▶ Placing gods at the center of creation — or not

▶ Seeing the world in spiritual terms

▶ Identifying the world's major religions

· ·

*W*hat does religion have to do with history? Just about everything. Religious belief has united societies and ripped them apart. Religion probably played a large and forceful role in creating civilization (see Chapter 3). Religious belief has also been a primary cause of wars, revolutions, explorations, and migrations. Conquerors attack in the name of religion. It shapes societies, because people act on what they believe.

Many civilizations were built around religious belief. For thousands of years, societies raised their rulers to divine status or thought of their royalty as human descendents of gods or mortal representatives of gods. Egyptians, at least as long ago as 2950 BC, considered their kings deities. Alexander the Great (356 to 323 BC) declared himself a god. Rome bestowed divinity on Augustus (27 BC to 14 AD), its first emperor (see Chapter 4). And in South America, the Incas of the fifteenth century AD worshipped their king as *Sapa Inca,* or Son of the Sun.

About 250 years ago, many Christians still thought that absolute monarchy was the right way for a godly society to be organized. (For more about *divine right of kings*, see Chapters 7, 11, and 14.) They believed God wanted the world run that way.

Separation of church and state may be a dandy concept for governing a diverse society such as the modern United States, but it doesn't apply when you're trying to understand why the Egyptians built the pyramids or why Europeans launched the Crusades.

To understand religion's impact on civilization, first consider what religion is and where it may come from. In this chapter, I discuss the variety of forms a religion can take, introduce you to major religions around the world, explain how each arose, and illustrate some ways that each influenced social or political life.

A disclaimer

This chapter is dangerous. For many people, religion is at the core of everything. It's the ultimate database for determining right from wrong, good from evil, how to live in the world, and how to prepare for a world yet to come.

If religion holds this level of importance for you, I assure you that nothing in the following pages is meant to challenge, undermine, or insult your beliefs. But I do try to examine each religion in this chapter objectively, which means I don't give one belief system preference over another. If the prospect of seeing your religion set side-by-side with other systems of belief — looked at as pieces of human history — bothers you in any way, I encourage you to skip this chapter. Or you can just skip any part that you suspect may offend you.

Further cautions: If you find that I don't adequately explain the complex system of belief that is your religion, you're surely right. If I leave out your religion, apologies. In either case, I mean no disrespect. I don't intend this chapter to be a complete guide to *any* religion, and neither is it a comprehensive catalogue.

Major religions have the most followers and play the biggest role in history. In this chapter, I present basic definitions, then I give you some brief sketches of the world's major religions, arranged in a rough chronology (the origins of some religions, such as Shinto, are too obscure to pin a date on).

Defining Religion

No single definition could sum up the traditions, practices, and ideas lumped together under the general category *religion*. The word *religion* refers to publicly shared beliefs, privately held convictions, and ways that people express their faith. Worshipful customs such as regular churchgoing and daily prayer are part of it. So are dietary rules (as when Muslims fast for Ramadan) and modes of dress (such as an Orthodox Jew's skullcap, called a *yarmulke*). It also refers to rituals, from the simple lighting of a candle to human sacrifice. (The Aztecs, for example, used to slaughter thousands of captives at a time to feed their war god's blood lust.)

Divining the role of god (s)

Most major religions are based on belief in a god or in multiple gods, but not all. Buddhism, for example, does not require a belief in gods, but rather concerns reincarnation and freeing the self from desire. Even where the belief in gods became a part of Buddhism, the gods are not central to the religion.

Creation stories

Whether the inspiration was divine or earthly, early people told stories in an effort to understand nature's workings and explain how the world and its inhabitants got here in the first place. Cultures everywhere have different ways of accounting for the beginning of the world. Folklorists call these stories *creation myths*. Somebody probably told the first one not long after language evolved (see Chapter 2 for the beginnings of language).

In the Ancient Egyptian religion, for example, the creation story starts with a watery chaos called Nun, from which the sun god (Atum, or in his later manifestation, the hawk-headed Re) rose to bring forth air (Shu) and moisture (Tefnut), twin deities who combined to create earth (Geb) and sky (Nut). Geb and Nut produced other gods.

Religions that require a belief in a god or gods — such as Judaism, Christianity, and Islam — are called *theistic* religions. Specifically, these three religions are *monotheistic,* meaning they are built on belief in a single all-powerful god. Other religions are *polytheistic,* embracing multiple gods. The religion of ancient Greece was polytheistic. So was the Germanic-Norse religion that preceded Christianity in Northern Europe.

Worshipping a supreme god

Many religions recognize a father god, or supreme god. (See the sidebar "Creation stories" for an example of a main god who brought forth other gods.) Some religions feature a sky god that reigns above all others. Others focus on an earth god or goddess. In the old Germanic, or Norse, religion practiced in much of Europe before Christianity displaced it about a thousand years ago, Odin (or Wodin) was the father god and the ruler of Valhalla (a supernatural drinking hall for dead warriors).

The Greeks' Zeus was a father god. In some later forms of Greek religion, Zeus became so supreme, so powerful, that he was worshipped as virtually the only god. Note that the Greek word *Zeus* resembles the Latin *Deus,* for the almighty Christian God.

Taking a step beyond the father god ruling other gods, *monotheistic* (one-god) religions center on a single *true God,* forsaking other, *false* gods. The second of the Ten Commandments, central to Judaism and Christianity, is "Thou shalt have no other gods before me." The first part of the *shahada,* the Islamic profession of faith, is "There is no god but God."

Monotheistic religions often originate with, or are reinvigorated, or reinvented by an individual prophet who claims a direct relationship with God. Judaism, Christianity, and Islam all trace their roots to Abraham (also called

Abram or Ibrahim). Sometime after 2000 BC, this patriarch moved his clan from the Mesopotamian city of Ur (today's Iraq, see Chapter 3) to the promised land of Canaan (roughly today's Israel).

Later leaders such as Moses, the lawgiver of Judaism and Christianity, and Mohammed the Prophet, founder of Islam, are in the tradition of Abraham. (See Chapter 18 for more about both men.)

Not all monotheistic visionaries fall into this Judaic-Christian-Islamic tradition, but religious ideas travel. In the fourteenth century BC, King Akhenaton of Egypt imposed monotheistic worship of the sun-disc god, Aton (or Atum), in place of traditional Egyptian polytheism. After his death, his successors went back to the old ways. Some people wonder if there was a link between this Egyptian fling with monotheism and other monotheistic movements, particularly Judaism.

Worshipping many gods

Many religions are *polytheistic:* The cultures that follow them worship a group of divine figures. Greek polytheism, probably the best known polytheistic religion, features lustful, flawed, human-like gods such as the great god-king Zeus (often depicted as a buff old guy with a big, fluffy beard) and his daughter Athena, the goddess of wisdom. Although the Greek religion arose separately from Egyptian polytheism, it adopted some Egyptian gods, such as the mysterious Isis.

The Romans adopted Greek polytheism, combining it with early Roman beliefs such as the worship of ancestors. (Many early religions required reverence for ancestors.) Rome renamed the gods. For example, *Zeus* became *Jupiter,* and *Athena* became *Minerva.*

Together, the characters in Greek-Roman theology are called the *pantheon.* Long after they were worshipped, the gods in the pantheon are still widely known as literary characters. The gods figure in the Greek poet Homer's epic poems (see Chapter 1). Because Homer told stories that were at least partly true, his poems are not just literature, but a source for rare early history about a real war between ancient Greeks and Trojans. So these gods are mixed into that early history, creating a dilemma for historians trying to winnow the facts from the myths.

Playwrights in the ancient world, poets of the European Renaissance, and later writers often based works on Greek and Roman myths and Homer's stories. Hollywood screenwriters still use these stories. Two syndicated TV series of the 1990s — *Hercules* and *Xena, Warrior Princess* — used a glitzy, twisted version of the Greek-Roman pantheon, with characters very loosely based on the myths.

The Disney people took their shot at the pantheon in 1997's animated cartoon *Hercules,* and missed. The breezy irreverence for cultural and classical sources that made *Aladdin* and *Mulan* entertaining (if less than educational) add up to a giant bore in this sanitized story of the demigod strongman. Even James Woods's creepy vocal performance as *Hades,* lord of the underworld, fails to pep it up.

Projecting will on the physical world

Some thinkers wonder if the human tendency to project personalities on inanimate objects, especially among long-ago people eager to explain natural phenomena, may have brought about a form of religion called *animism.*

In my living room, there is a small painting on a plaster disk, showing an easy chair and a TV set. You see the chair from behind, with a spiky, yellow hairdo showing above the backrest. The person in the chair faces the TV, which appears with its screen full of jagged lines of static. "The TV god is very angry today," reads a caption at the bottom. A creation of North Carolina artist Darcy Szeremi, this painting — a stylized picture of an ordinary inconvenience — is not a shrine or an icon. My family does not worship a TV god (not if I can help it). The caption is a wry comment on the way that people sometimes think about the physical world, especially when it refuses to behave the way they want it to.

When my wife was a girl, her father drove a Dodge sedan that he named Brunhilde, after a Valkyrie — a mythical figure from the old Norse-Germanic religion. He called that car "she" and my wife continues to use the feminine (and now politically incorrect) pronoun when reminiscing about that car.

Did my wife, a journalist, and her father, a scientist, ever really think of Brunhilde as anything more than a machine? Not on a rational level, certainly. Yet human beings are often irrational. Who hasn't named a car or some other possession? Who hasn't thought, or said in frustration, that some inanimate object "wants" or "doesn't want" to do something? (A nail "wants" to bend rather than be pounded straight into the board; a jar lid "doesn't want" to come loose; the lawn mower engine "doesn't want" to start.)

It doesn't mean you really attribute a will, let alone a soul, to the car, the nail, the jar lid, or the mower. Even if you did, you probably wouldn't worship these objects (unless the car is really expensive). Yet these instances illustrate the human habit of thinking about the world as if it were filled with personalities whose whims shape everyday life.

Seeking understanding through spirit

Prehistoric life was tough. The human ability to see cause and effect was a great survival tool, but it also raised questions. Early people saw patterns in herd migrations and the changing seasons. They recognized how vulnerable they were to forces beyond their control, such as floods and storms. Who wouldn't want to understand what made such things happen, to appease nature, to seek fate's favor?

Animism, occurring in cultures all over the world (from Native American to pre-Islamic Arab), is based on the idea that rocks, trees, and animals have souls and that these spirits influence events.

Some late-nineteenth-century scholars — including the anthropologist Edward Taylor (1832 to 1917) — argued that animism was the earliest form of religion, and that other forms of religion sprang from it. More recent anthropologists reject Taylor's view as too simplistic. (That's too bad for people like me, who like to keep things simple.)

Connecting animals to deities

Simplistic or not, animism probably did give rise to the more discriminating practice of *totemism,* in which a particular animal or plant bears special significance for a clan or tribe. Some Australian Aborigine tribes have the kangaroo as a totem. The pioneering French sociologist Emile Durkheim (1858 to 1917) saw totems as a key part of primitive religions.

Ancient Egypt's religion (see Chapter 3) seems to have arisen from tribal beliefs that a certain animal represented a certain god. As Egyptian society developed, villages and regions considered specific gods — shown in paintings and carvings with human bodies and animal heads — their own. The animal was not the god, but sacred to the god. For example, the hawk was sacred to the Sun-god Re and the sky god Horus.

Analyzing the religious impulse

Scholarship sometimes looks at religions as purely human-made phenomena. Anthropologists, archeologists, and psychologists trace the religious impulse to the human need to understand or to the societal need for authority — for an unassailable source of agreed-upon rules. Such theories rarely credit religious beliefs and customs as coming from a supernatural or transcendent truth.

Most religious people, on the other hand, would argue strongly that the god or gods they worship (or the transcendental reality they seek) existed before humans occupied the earth and will exist after humankind is gone. Religion, to most who embrace it, is a way to connect with and pay tribute to a power (or *the* power) greater than earthly existence.

Distinguishing philosophy from religion

Drawing a line between religions and philosophies, ways of explaining and coming to terms with existence (see Chapter 10), is sometimes difficult. For example, the ancient Chinese philosopher widely known as Confucius (his name was really Kung Ch'iu or Kung Futzu) taught a system of ethics based in responsible behavior and loyalty to family and society. He didn't advocate any particular religious creed, yet after his death in 479 BC, his teachings became the basis for a religious cult that lasted until modern times. Confucianism even became a state-sponsored religion in China. Japanese leaders embraced it too, sometimes promoting Confucianism over the indigenous Japanese religion, Shinto.

Yet basic Confucianism has little if any spiritual concern with a world beyond this one, a concern that plays a significant role in most religions. Sometimes Confucianism is considered a religion, and other times it's not.

Some scholars even argue that *Marxism* — the basis of communism — is in many ways a religion, rather than just a political or economic philosophy (see Chapters 8 and 14). It calls for devotion and commitment from its followers, much as religions do.

Judaism

The roots of both Christianity and Islam are in early Judaism, which arose sometime after 2000 BC. The God of Abraham revealed himself to his chosen people through a series of prophets. His word is contained in the Hebrew Bible (Christians call it the Old Testament), especially in the first five books, the *Torah*. The Torah contains hundreds of commandments, including the central Ten Commandments delivered from God by the prophet Moses (see Chapter 18).

Awaiting a messiah

Jews believe in Hebrew law, that the human condition can be improved, and that a *Messiah* (Hebrew for *anointed one*) will someday bring about a state of earthly paradise.

Modern Judaism contains groups that differ in the ways they interpret the Torah. Orthodox Jews view the Torah and its commandments as absolutely binding. Conservative Jews observe the Torah but allow for changes to accommodate modern life. Reform Jews concentrate mostly on the ethical content of the Torah rather than the specific laws it contains.

Maintaining Jewish nationalism

The tribal descendents of Abraham united under King Saul in the eleventh century BC to create the kingdom of Israel, which split in the late tenth century BC into the separate kingdoms of Israel and Judah (sometimes called Judaea). The land and its people later fell under others' rule — notably that of the Seleucid Dynasty (after Alexander the Great's conquests — see Chapter 3), the Syrians, the Romans, the Byzantine Empire, and the Seljuk Turks.

Through a long history, much of it chronicled in the scriptures, Jews remained distinct from other people of the region, such as the Canaanites. Jews also spread through other parts of the world, notably Europe. Jews were often the targets of anti-Semitic persecution by Christians.

Anti-Semitism culminated in the 1930s and 1940s when the Nazi government of Germany rounded up millions of Jews (along with Gypsies, homosexuals, and other "undesirables"), shipped them to concentration camps, and systematically killed them.

The belief that God promised Israel to Abraham, and that God restored the homeland to Moses' followers after their slavery in Egypt, has had a powerful influence on international relations, especially in the Middle East. The struggle to regain, keep, and control this homeland became part of the religion. The feast of Hanukkah, for example, commemorates the Jews' rededication of the temple at Jerusalem after a victory over the Syrians in 165 BC.

The hilltop fortress Masada, where 400 Jewish revolutionaries committed suicide rather than surrender to the Romans in **73 AD,** is an important symbol of Jewish solidarity.

The modern Zionist movement, starting in the late nineteenth century, was an effort to return far-flung Jewish populations to the homeland. Beginning in 1917, Britain encouraged Jewish immigration to Palestine. After World War II, the British government referred the issue to the United Nations (see Chapter 8), which carved Israel's territory out of what was British-controlled Palestine, against the wishes of Palestinians (both Muslim and Christian.) As a modern nation, Israel declared its independence in 1948.

Director Otto Preminger's *Exodus,* filmed in 1960, was adapted from Leon Uris's best-selling novel about the founding of modern Israel and its first immigrants. It tells the intertwining stories of an Israeli freedom fighter and an American nurse who meet as passengers aboard a ship called *The Exodus,* carrying Jewish survivors of the Nazi Holocaust to Palestine. The movie skips over moral issues in favor of action and romance.

By partitioning Palestine in 1948, the United Nations assured a chain of resentments and hatred that has brought a series of wars to the Middle East and many terrorist attacks on Israel and its citizens through the second half of the twentieth century. U.S. support for Israel contributed to intense enmity by some Islamic nations, such as Iran, toward the United States and its Western allies.

Hinduism

Around 1700 to 1500 BC, nomads from the Iranian plateau filtered into India, bringing with them a culture and language that produced a profound effect on that part of the world ever since.

The religion practiced by the nomads became the roots of Hinduism. Hindus believe that living beings are reincarnated repeatedly and that the form you take in the next life is directly related to the positive or negative quality of your actions in this life (your *karma*). Hindu sacred scriptures, the Veda, dating from about 1500 BC, contain hymns, chants, and monastic doctrine. While Hinduism's polytheism supports numerous Hindu gods, chief among them are the trinity of Brahma the creator, Vishnu the preserver, and Shiva the destroyer, shown in Figure 9-1.

Figure 9-1: Shiva is one of three central Hindu gods, along with Brahma and Vishnu.

© Historical Picture Archive/CORBIS

Traditional Hindu belief separates Indian society into castes, with priests, rulers, and warriors at the top and farmers and laborers at the bottom. Under the caste system, marriage outside your own caste is forbidden. Many modern Hindus have rejected the concept of caste, but it still colors social interaction among Hindus. Sects within the religion practice a wide range of rituals and hold diverse beliefs.

There are 780 million followers of Hinduism worldwide; most are in India, where the religion survived many challenges. The Emperor Asoka established Buddhism as India's state religion in the third century BC, and Buddhism gained ground — although many people may have taken up Buddhist practices in addition to Hinduism, rather than in place of the older religion. After Asoka, Hindu beliefs rebounded and spread, withstanding the period from 1526 to 1857, when Muslims ruled most of India as the Mogul Empire. (See Chapter 4 for more about Asoka.)

Religious disagreement often escalates into violent conflict in India — always a diverse land of many languages and ways of life. For example, a Hindu extremist assassinated the nationalist leader Mahatma Gandhi (see Chapter 2) in 1948, because Gandhi was trying to stop Hindu-Muslim conflict in the Indian state of Bengal.

Sometimes India's religious conflicts have grown into interregional and even international disputes. For example, the country of Pakistan was carved out of India in 1947 as a separate homeland for the Muslim minority. Since then, the two nations fought wars over territory — wars with their roots in the cultural-religious difference.

Buddhism

Siddhartha Gautama, a prince from southern Nepal, achieved enlightenment in the late sixth century BC by meditation in the tradition of Hinduism, already well established in the region (see Hinduism, earlier in this chapter). He gathered a community of monks to carry on his teachings, built on the law of karma, a concept adapted from Hindu belief, and on the *Four Noble Truths*.

The law of karma says that good and evil deeds result in appropriate reward or punishment in this life or in a succession of rebirths on a path toward *Nirvana*, or "the blowing out of the fires of all desires." The Four Noble Truths are

- ✔ Existence is a realm of suffering.
- ✔ Desire, and belief in the importance of one's self, causes suffering.
- ✔ Achievement of Nirvana ends suffering.
- ✔ Nirvana is attained only by meditation and following the righteous path in action, thought, and attitude.

Buddhism has two main traditions. The first, *Theravada,* follows the strict, narrow teachings of the early Buddhist writings. In the more-liberal second, *Mahayana,* salvation is easier to attain. Other schools include Zen Buddhism, Lamaism, Tendai, Nichiren, and Soka Gakkai.

In the third century BC, the Indian king Asoka made Buddhism his official state religion. He adopted a policy of *dharma* (principles of right life), and stopped waging war. This is a rare instance of a religious principle overcoming dynastic ambition. Buddhism has not always had such a calming influence on the politically ambitious. The fourteenth-century AD Chinese emperor Chu Yuan-chang started out as a Buddhist monk, but he fought his way to power and used brutal violence to discourage dissent.

Christianity

Early in the first century AD, a carpenter called Jesus of Nazareth traveled through the Roman vassal state of Judaea (today's Israel) teaching a philosophy of mercy and God's redeeming love. His sermons and his apparent ability to heal the sick made him so popular that local leaders thought he threatened their authority and arranged to have him nailed to a wooden cross — the painful Roman method for executing criminals.

Christians believe that three days after he died, Jesus left his tomb and after revealing himself to his followers, he rose bodily, straight into heaven. He is considered the Messiah, as promised in the Hebrew Bible (which Christians call the Old Testament).

Jesus is also seen as both God's son and God in human form — an idea hammered out in early theological debates within the Church (see Chapter 11). To Christians, his death is an act of God's love, to save believers from eternal condemnation in Hell. Jesus was bestowed the title *Christ,* from the Greek for *savior.*

MOVIE

Fantasizing on faith

In 1988's *The Last Temptation of Christ,* Jesus contemplates the lure of normal, mortal life. Willem Dafoe plays the title character in this adaptation of a novel by Nikos Kazantzakis.

The film depicts a Christ so fully human that human trivialities such as pain and sexuality threaten to distract him from his purpose. An angel shows Jesus, already on the cross, a vision of an earthly existence as a husband and father, giving him the choice of rejecting his own godhood.

Kazantzakis's concept, interpreted by director Martin Scorsese, offended many Christians. Protesters marched outside cinemas where the movie was shown. Some theaters refused to book it.

Four of Jesus' twelve disciples, who were called *the Apostles,* wrote down his words and deeds in the Gospels, which make up a major part of the New Testament. The Old Testament and the New Testament together comprise the Christian Bible.

At first considered a heretic sect of Judaism, Christianity grew into one of the most powerful religious, philosophical, and political influences in history.

The Roman Catholic Church

One of the Apostles, St. Peter (originally Simon or Simeon), organized Christian believers into the early Church. That is, he seems to have; historical accounts say little about Peter's life and work. St. Paul, an early Jewish convert who is also considered an Apostle, preached extensively among *gentiles* (non-Jews), including Romans. (You can read more about St. Paul in Chapter 20.)

The Catholic Church credits Peter as the first bishop of Rome, where legend says the Romans crucified him in about 64 AD. The Church came to be based in Rome, where the successive popes (from the Latin *papa,* meaning *dad*) have been honored as Peter's successors and the representative of God on earth.

Becoming "the" Church

Until the Protestant Reformation (discussed later in this chapter and in Chapter 13), the Roman Catholic Church was just *the Church* — at least in Europe. Spelled with a lowercase "c," *catholic* means universal or wide-ranging. The Roman Catholic Church was everybody's church.

Roman Catholic doctrine (see Chapter 11) centers on the Holy Trinity, in which one God takes the form of three *persons*: God the Father, God the Son (Jesus), and God the Holy Spirit. Catholics also honor Jesus' mother, St. Mary, believed to have been a virgin when she miraculously gave birth. (*Saints* are human beings whose exemplary lives bring about God's miracles and whose virtue, as confirmed by the Church, accords them blessed status.)

Although several Roman emperors persecuted Christians, Emperor Constantine the Great (you can find him in Chapter 4) did an about-face in the fourth century AD and not only ordered the toleration of Christianity, but made the Church both wealthy and powerful.

Being a unifying force

After the fall of the Western Roman Empire in the fifth century AD (see Chapters 4 and 5), the Church remained the main civilizing, unifying force in Europe, also called *Christendom.*

Kings claimed their authority as a right granted by the Christian God. The pope was a political, as well as a spiritual, leader. Pope Leo III (later St. Leo) crowned the Frankish king Charlemagne as Emperor of the West (or Holy Roman Emperor) in 800 AD.

Pope Urban II's clout began the Crusades when he called for the liberation of the Holy Lands (today's Israel) from Turkish control in 1095 (see Chapter 6).

Facing dissent and departures

Not everybody agreed, however, on whether a king answered directly to God or to the pope. This brought centuries of power struggles. In twelfth-century England, this disagreement led Henry II's soldiers to murder the Archbishop of Canterbury — a public relations disaster for the king. King Henry denied ordering the hit, but he had complained about the archbishop, Thomas à Becket, who was also his former chancellor. The king wished aloud to be rid of the "turbulent priest."

Sometimes disputes arose about who was rightfully pope. When the Holy Roman Emperor Frederick I disagreed with the choice of Orlando (or Roland) Bandinelli to become Pope Alexander III in 1159, Fred simply appointed his own alternative. Then he appointed another and another — the *anti-popes*. Victor IV, Paschal III, Calistus III, and Innocent III all called themselves pope, but Rome replied, "You aren't either the *real* pope, so there."

Power struggles between the Church and national rulers fueled the Protestant Reformation of the sixteenth century (discussed later in this chapter and in Chapter 13).

The Reformation brought Protestant versus Catholic military struggles, the biggest being the Thirty Years War. It started in 1618 when Protestants in Bohemia, part of the Holy Roman Empire, tried to appoint a Protestant king. Spain plunged into that war on the Catholic side. But as if to show that religious wars are often about things other than religion, Catholic France joined the fight on the Protestant side. (The French were nervous about the Hapsburg family, Catholics who ruled both Spain and the Holy Roman Empire, getting too powerful.)

Some nominally Protestant-Catholic conflicts raged much later. One especially bitter struggle centered on whether Northern Ireland, where the majority of people are Protestant, should remain a part of Great Britain or join the Republic of Ireland, a Catholic democracy.

Instigating the Inquisition

Before a German priest called Martin Luther touched off the Reformation in 1517, Church officials tried to deal with the widespread and growing perception among Europeans that priests and monks had become corrupt, lazy, and arrogant. Some cardinals and bishops tried to root out unfit priests. The reform efforts had little success, except in Spain — a country that faced different challenges than most of Europe and came up with a more extreme solution.

The Moors, who were Muslim, ruled Spain for hundreds of years. Christians took over the last of Spain's Muslim kingdoms in 1492, the same year that Christopher Columbus set sail. Many Jews lived in Spain too. The Moors were more tolerant toward Jews than European Christians were, so Jews liked it there.

With the Moors out of power, however, Muslims and Jews were stuck. They could get out of the country, adopt Christianity, or possibly be killed. Many converted, but they were tepid Christians at best. Many hated the Church and everything it stood for, practicing their own religions in secret.

Spanish Christians worried that these *new* Christians would revolt if Moors from North Africa or Muslim Turks from the east attacked. Church officials worried about the new Christians' resentment undermining priestly authority.

To alleviate these fears, the monarchs Ferdinand and Isabella (see Chapter 18) started the *Spanish Inquisition,* a campaign to root out, expose, and punish heresy.

The Spanish Inquisition gained a reputation for thoroughness, even-handedness (commoners, nobles, and churchmen were all vulnerable), and unspeakable cruelty. Operating in secret, using anonymous informers and making arrests by night, the Inquisition employed solitary confinement and torture to force confessions.

Sentencing was public, however, involving a gaudy ceremony called an *auto-da-fé,* with prisoners dressed in special gowns called *sanbenitos.* Punishments ranged from fines to flogging to forced labor as an oarsman in a galley ship.

These tactics and punishments weren't unusual for the time. The Inquisition was less cruel than many civil courts, prohibiting torture that did permanent physical damage, and requiring that a physician be present. Convicts burnt at the stake had to be dead first, usually strangled.

Still, the Inquisition was feared. Foreign sailors dreaded an arrest in Spain for smuggling or piracy, certain that they would be turned over to the Inquisition. They spread stories about its horrors.

Meantime, the Church in Spain tightened up. Lazy and corrupt priests, monks, and even bishops got the heave-ho. By the time the Reformation arrived, Spain was not fertile ground for northern ideas. The Inquisition made short work of the few people tempted by Protestantism. And just to make sure, the Inquisition kept out ideas they considered dangerous by banning foreign books and prohibiting Spaniards from attending foreign universities. It worked. Lutheran and Calvinist ideas never gained ground on the Iberian Peninsula.

Maintaining continuity

The Church remained a major civil influence in solidly Catholic countries and their territories in the sixteenth century and remains powerful in many such countries today. Priests, who were among the first Spaniards in many parts of the New World (see Chapters 7 and 8), built missions and converted the Indians, establishing Catholicism as the majority religion through most of Latin America.

The Catholic Church still exerts political influence. Its laws have long influenced civil law, especially on moral issues such as divorce and birth control, in Catholic countries, such as Italy and Ireland.

Some dealings in political affairs, however, are contrary to Vatican policy. In the twentieth century, the Roman Catholic Church rebuked South American priests for teaching liberation theology and taking part in popular political movements.

The Eastern Orthodox Church

Constantine the Great made Christianity the state religion of the Roman Empire, but he built his new, Christian, imperial capital far to the east of Rome, at Byzantium (today's Istanbul). This new city (named for its founder as Constantinople) was a center of Christianity in its own right, especially after the western Roman Empire collapsed.

Rome's Church had less and less influence over the Eastern faithful between the fifth and the eleventh centuries. And when Roman Catholic crusaders sacked Orthodox Christian Constantinople in 1204, it showed how alienated from one another the two branches of Christianity had become. (For more about the Crusades, see Chapter 7.)

The Eastern Orthodox Church evolved into a communion of self-governing churches centered in Eastern Europe, Greece, Ukraine, Russia, Georgia, and the Middle East. They honor the primacy of the patriarch of Constantinople, but they don't hold him supreme, as Roman Catholics do the pope.

Orthodox doctrine looks to the scriptures as the source Christian truth and rejects points of doctrine developed by Church fathers in Rome. Much of the estrangement between the Eastern and Roman churches began in disagreements over basic questions about the nature of God and the relationship between Jesus and God the Father (see Chapter 11).

Orthodox worship places particular emphasis on the Holy Spirit within the Trinity (see *Roman Catholicism* earlier in the chapter). Orthodox faithful also use icons in their churches, usually paintings of a holy figure such as Jesus or a saint.

The Orthodox Church suffered a serious blow in 1453 when the Ottoman Turks conquered Constantinople. The city became Islamic and its name was changed to Istanbul. The Turks turned its magnificent domed church, Hagia Sophia, into a mosque. Now it's a museum.

Grand Prince Vladimir established the Russian Orthodox Church in 988 AD. It remained Russia's state religion until the Revolution of 1917 (see Chapter 8). Communist officials restricted worship and persecuted worshippers through most of the twentieth century, but the church endured and began to rebuild itself after the Soviet Union collapsed in 1991.

Relations between the Orthodox churches (which have 218 million members worldwide) and Roman Catholicism finally improved in the later decades of the twentieth century.

The Protestant churches

Protestant is a broad and imprecise term applied to a wide range of churches, most of them offshoots of the Roman Catholic Church or earlier Protestant churches. Unlike Catholics, Protestants don't look to the pope as the ultimate authority on issues of faith.

The word *Protestant* is related in meaning to *protester*. At first, *Protestant* applied to a group of sixteenth-century German princes siding with the breakaway priest Martin Luther. These princes protested efforts by other German leaders to force them and their subjects back into the Roman church's fold.

The whole Protestant Reformation started with an individual act of protest. Luther, a university professor as well as a priest, didn't like the Archbishop of Mainz (in Germany) raising money by sending a friar around to cities and towns selling indulgences. An *indulgence* was a sort of pass that Christians could buy to get themselves into Heaven without so much suffering.

If you think that's a gross oversimplification of what an indulgence was, you're right, and you can find more about indulgences (simplified a little less grossly) in Chapter 13. The point is, however, that Luther thought it was wrong. He wrote almost 100 reasons why he disagreed with the archbishop and the friar and stuck the paper to the door of the church in Wittenburg on **October 31, 1517.** The list is called the 95 Theses (arguments), and its posting is considered the start of the Reformation.

The Reformation soon involved Frederick, the Elector of Saxony (who started the University of Wittenberg and thus was Professor Luther's protective boss) and Charles V, the Holy Roman Emperor. The Reformation would quickly touch other kings, nobles, churchmen, and commoners in ways that Luther never could have imagined.

Even England, a country where the king was so fiercely anti-Lutheran that the pope named him *Defender of the Faith,* became Protestant as that same king (Henry VIII) named himself head of a church that no longer answered to Rome.

A few of the major Protestant denominations are Lutheran (of course), Baptist, Church of Christ, Church of England and its American spin-off the Episcopalian Church, the Reformed Church (an ideological descendant of the French moral reformer John Calvin — see Chapter 13), Methodist, Presbyterian, and Quaker. Many of those denominations have subgroups, such as the Southern Baptists and the Evangelical Lutheran Church in America (ELCA).

Protestant churches are prominent social forces. In twentieth-century U.S. politics, for example, fundamentalist denominations went so far as to endorse candidates and lobby on social and moral issues. Ironically, these Protestants sometimes find that their closest ideological allies — especially on issues such as legalized abortion (which they oppose) — are Catholics.

Shinto

Shinto arose as a form of nature worship in the interior forests of Japan long before writing was introduced to that country in the fifth century AD. Just how long before, nobody knows. To distinguish Shinto from Buddhism, the faith became known as *Shinto* or *the way of the spirits* only in the eighth century.

Shinto ceremonies often take the form of appeals for benevolence and protection from many spirits of nature, called *kami.* Shintoists pay tribute to the kami at shrines and hold festivals in their honor.

After Buddhism spread to Japan in the sixth century AD, Shinto took on some features of the new religion. Also, in the eighth century, a state Shintoism arose. In State Shintoism, the imperial family is believed to have divine origins. Obedience to the emperor became a religious duty.

Confucian ethics — especially frugality, loyalty, and incorruptibility — melded with Shinto ideas in the development of *bushido,* or *the way of the warrior.* This philosophy, practiced by the powerful warrior gentry, or *samurai* class, contributed to the rule of Japan by *shoguns* (military rulers) from the twelfth to the nineteenth centuries (see Chapter 5). Bushido also had a strong influence on the stoic officer class of the Japanese army through the Second World War.

Shinto lost its official status after Japan surrendered to the Allies in 1945, but its worshippers persist, numbering nearly three million in the 1990s. Honoring their ancestors and celebrating the kami, adherents are supposed to be pure and sincere and are expected to enjoy life.

Islam

Exploding out of Arabia in the seventh century and early eighth century AD, Islam was at once a spiritual, political, and military movement. You can read in Chapters 5 and 18 about Mohammed (often written Muhammad or any of several other spellings), founder of the faith, and how he grew from a religious visionary to a lawgiver, judge, military general, and ruler before his death in 632 AD.

The Five Pillars

Islam means *submission to God.* Followers worship through the Five Pillars:

1. The *shahada,* or profession of faith: "There is no god but God, and Mohammed is his Prophet."

2. Formal prayer, the *salat,* performed five times a day while facing Mecca.

3. *Zakat,* purification achieved through sharing wealth by giving alms.

4. *Saum,* fasting during the holy month of Ramadan.

5. *Hajj*, the pilgrimage to Mecca (Mohammed's birthplace, now the capital of the Hejaz region of Saudi Arabia).

Going beyond Mecca and Medina

Rising out of Mecca, where Mohammed, then a merchant, received the holy vision that commanded him to preach "the true religion," Islam spread quickly during Mohammed's lifetime. When officials there threw Mohammed out, he built a power base in Medina, 200 miles north of Mecca. He later returned and took Mecca by force.

In the 1976 movie *Al-Risalah* (also released as *The Message* and *Mohammad, Messenger of God*), the early Muslims are portrayed as a persecuted minority that emerges victorious. Made in Lebanon, the movie features an international cast led by Anthony Quinn and Michael Ansara. The film doesn't depict the prophet himself, but has other characters address the camera when talking to him. This odd device makes the audience see things from Mohammed's viewpoint.

Mohammed's followers united most of the Arabic-speaking peoples behind this new faith in only a few decades, but there was some resistance and backlash from Arab tribes that initially accepted and then renounced Islam. This resulted in *Jihad,* or holy war, to restore the faith by force.

That Jihad built huge momentum over the century after the Prophet's death, sweeping far beyond the traditional Arab lands. Muslims believe that individuals, societies, and governments should all be obedient to the will of God set forth in the Koran. The Muslim warriors who waged Jihad were sure that if they died honorably while fighting for Allah they would get into paradise right away. That gave them a fervor that was hard to defend against, especially as the Persian and Byzantine Empires were in decline.

The conquests led to an Arab Empire that, at its height, stretched from Spain to the Indus Valley in northwest India. (See Chapter 5 for more about the Arab conquests.)

The Arab Empire later splintered into smaller caliphates, or Islamic kingdoms and empires. Although Arab political unity disintegrated, Islamic beliefs and law maintained a cultural unity among Muslim countries.

Early on, Muslims were rather tolerant toward other religions, especially Judaism and Christianity, because of the kinship between the three religions. (Muslims see Mohammed as the ultimate Prophet in a line of God's prophets that began with Abraham, continued through Moses, and included Jesus.) In Syria and Egypt, the Arab conquerors let Christians and Jews keep their faiths as *dimmi,* or protected peoples, although the *dimmi* had to pay a tax for the privilege.

Clashing cultures

Enmity between the Islamic, Jewish, and Christian faiths developed over centuries. The Crusades, which began in the eleventh century as European Christian attacks on the Islamic Seljuk Turk rulers of Palestine, left bad feelings. So did territorial clashes as Christians struggled to take Spain away from its Muslim rulers, the Moors. The Ottoman Turks, also Muslim, clashed for centuries with Christians over territory in Eastern Europe.

Turks were among many non-Arab peoples who embraced Islam, which also spread among non-Arab people in Africa, East Asia, and Southeast Asia. Indonesia is the most populous of the predominantly Muslim countries today. It has also been the site of violent clashes between Muslim and Christian groups.

As Islam spread, sects arose. The two largest groups within the faith are the Sunni Muslims, who are the vast majority, and the Shiite Muslims.

Much of the fractious politics of the region called the Balkans, in southeastern Europe, results from religious differences. In one late twentieth-century flare-up, Serbian (mostly Orthodox Christian) troops drove Albanian (mostly sSunni Muslim) civilians from their homes, killing many in the process and briefly depopulating much of the province of Kosovo.

Muslim-Jewish enmity caught fire in modern times after the United Nations carved up Palestine to create the new nation of Israel in 1948, displacing natives (both Muslim and Christian) and outraging the Arab world. (See *Judaism* earlier in the chapter.)

Islamic fervor has also fed rebellions against the Soviet Union in Afghanistan and against post-Soviet Russia in Chechnya. Pan-Islamic activists, who believe that Muslim identity overrides national borders, have aided these rebellions.

The Sunnis believe that correct religious guidance derives from the teachings or *sunna* of Mohammed. They recognize the first four *caliphs* (spiritual leaders) of the Arab Empire as Mohammed's legitimate successors. They also believe that just government can be established on the basis of correct Islamic practice.

The Shiites, about 10 percent of Muslims, believe that only descendents of Mohammed's family are the legitimate leaders of the faith. They recognize only the line of Ali, the fourth caliph and nephew and son-in-law of Mohammed, as the prophet's legitimate successors.

Among the subgroups of Shiites, the Imamis are the largest. Found in Iran, where Shiism is the state religion, the Imamis believe in twelve *imams,* charismatic leaders who were infallible sources of spiritual and worldly guidance. Since the last of these imams disappeared in the ninth century, the Imamis believe that holy men called ayatollahs are in charge until the twelfth *imam* returns.

Often referred to as fundamentalist Muslims, the Shiites brought about the Iranian Revolution of 1978 and 1979. Opposed to what they saw as its Western decadence, Iranians overturned the government of their monarch, Shah Mohammad Reza Pahlavi, while he was in the United States for medical treatment. Demanding that he be returned to face punishment, the revolutionaries occupied the U.S. Embassy in Iran and held many of its staff hostage for over a year.

The enmity of some Islamic extremists toward what they term Western decadence, toward Israel, and toward the policies of the United States and it allies in the Middle East took the form of terrorist attacks in the late twentieth century, including bombings of commercial airliners.

The extremists are an infinitesimally small, if attention-getting, fraction of the 1.1 billion Muslims worldwide.

The Sikhs

Founded around 1500 AD, Sikhism combines aspects of Hinduism and Islam into what is called the religion of the gurus. Sikhs seek union with God through worship and service. The Guru Nanak, Hindu by birth and upbringing, was an Indian seeker of spiritual truth who gathered his followers in Kartarpur, Punjab.

Nanak wanted to unite Islam with the ancient Brahmanism that was part of the Indian Hindu tradition. He also held *pantheistic* beliefs, which means he thought God and the universe are one — an idea found in Hinduism and some sects of Buddhism.

In the doctrine of Sikhism, as laid out in the Adi-Granth, its sacred scripture, God is the true guru. He has spoken to humanity though 10 historical gurus, the first being Nanak. The last of these died in 1708, leaving the Sikh community at large to serve as guru.

Sikh teachings are closely related to Punjab identity. Sikhs fought fiercely in two closely spaced wars between 1845 and 1849 to prevent British conquest of the region in Northwest India. The British won, but Sikh pride endured.

Modern Punjab is partitioned between India and Pakistan on religious grounds, with a Muslim majority in Pakistani Punjab and a population that is 60 percent Sikh in Indian Punjab, where there remains significant support for Sikh independence.

Tracking the Centuries

1700 to 1500 BC: Nomads from the Iranian plateau arrive in India, bringing with them the roots of Hindu religious belief.

Eleventh century BC: Tribes descended from the patriarch Abraham unite under King Saul to create the kingdom of Israel.

Third century BC: Asoka, king of India, makes Buddhism his official state religion. He adopts a policy of *dharma* (principles of right life), and stops conducting wars of conquest against neighboring countries.

About 33 AD: Roman authorities, at request of local Jewish leaders, arrest Jesus of Nazareth. He is sentenced to death and nailed to a cross where he hangs until pronounced dead.

313 AD: Roman co-emperors Constantine (Emperor of the West) and Licinius (Emperor of the East) jointly issue the Edict of Milan, recognizing Christianity and extending tolerance to its followers.

About 610 AD: The Prophet Mohammed (or Muhammad) begins teaching "submission to God," or Islam.

About 1500: In Kartarpur, Punjab, the Guru Nanak seeks to unite ancient brahmanism, part of the Hindu tradition, with Islam. He founds the Sikh religion.

October 31, 1517: Martin Luther, a German priest and university professor, nails his 95 Theses against the clerical practice of selling indulgences (forgiveness of sins) to a church door.

1948: The United Nations carves a new Jewish homeland, the modern nation of Israel, out of what was British-controlled Palestine.

Chapter 10

Sharing a Love of Wisdom

*P*hilosophy often gets dismissed as mind games — idle speculations cooked up by eccentrics with overactive imaginations. If that's all philosophy were, you wouldn't have to take it into account when considering history. But philosophy keeps bumping into history by getting into religion, politics, and government and influencing how people conduct their lives. Therefore, it's important to look at philosophy and where it comes from.

Traditionally, philosophy is thought to come from the ancient Greeks, although they probably picked up on earlier cultures' philosophical traditions. Wherever they got their inspiration, the Greeks — a culture of talkers — made the most of it.

Asking the Big Questions

Philosophy can sound wild, especially when you ponder what the guys trying to practice it over 2,500 years ago had to say. But they were doing the best they could with the knowledge and tools they had. And most of what they wrote has been lost, which makes it difficult for history to give them a fair shake.

For example, Thales, who was born about 625 BC, said the world floated on water. He also seemed to think that everything was made of water. Actually, he just could have been impressed by how much water there was: "Wow," he may have remarked, "there sure is a lot of water."

What Thales was talking about isn't clear. No complete texts of philosophical works from that far back survive. However, it seems that Thales and the philosophers following him — proposing such things as air and fire and the infinite as the basis of all matter — were thinking about a reality based on observable phenomena.

What exactly do philosophers do? They tackle the big questions:

- What is the world?
- Who am I?
- What am I doing here?
- Does reality consist of what people see and experience?
- If not, what is reality?

And the biggest question of all:

What does it mean?

Founding science in philosophy

Scientists have answered many questions *empirically* — based on physical evidence. But before modern scientific methods, scientists were philosophers: They asked questions and thought about possible answers.

In Greece almost 3,000 years ago, few tools were available for conducting scientific experiments. Thales couldn't take samples of water, marble, fingernail clippings, and olive oil and run tests that would show him that they *weren't* really all forms of the same thing.

Testing a theory but blowing the methodology

Anaximenes, who came along a bit later than Thales (Anaximenes died around 500 BC) did conduct experiments. They were flawed experiments, but they had an inkling of scientific method about them.

Anaximenes thought everything was made of air — that air could transform by compression or expansion into other matter. He decided clouds were made of condensed air on its way to becoming more condensed. At a certain point, it would become so condensed that it would turn into water. His theory was wrong but not entirely unreasonable.

Anaximenes took this idea further, of course. Even more tightly compressed air, he thought, became mud, earth, and stone — in that order. Fire, Anaximenes said, was extremely rarified air.

He thought he had good proof for his theory in that when you purse your lips tightly and blow, a compressed stream of air comes out cold. If you open your mouth wide and breathe out, the air — now rarified rather than condensed — feels hot. Presumably, by extension, if you could open your mouth really, really wide, you could breath out fire.

Diverging disciplines

As thinkers figured out more and better ways to test, prove, or disprove their theories about the physical world, sciences split off from philosophy. Philosophers continued to ask questions about the nature of being (called *metaphysics*), ethics, and morals — questions that couldn't be satisfactorily answered by experiments.

Yet despite this split, philosophy and science overlapped in many ways. Until the 1840s, scientists were called *natural philosophers*.

Mixing philosophy and religion

Just as philosophy and science intermingled, so did philosophy and religion — as they still do. What do I mean by *religion?* It often means much the same as philosophy — a way of understanding reality. Religion includes publicly shared beliefs, private convictions, and ways that people express faith. The Greek religion focused on a group of gods, the *pantheon,* who behaved much as human beings do, but in a supernatural realm that interacted with and affected mortal affairs. You can find out more about religion in Chapter 9.

Early philosophers apparently weren't content with taking creation myths and Greek *polytheism* (the worship of many gods) at face value. However, that doesn't mean they rejected religion.

One early Greek philosopher, Pythagoras (about 560 to 480 BC), founded a religious community and preached about the transmigration of souls. His followers said he was the son of the god Apollo and that he could appear in two places at once.

Xenophanes, a philosopher born around 580 BC, opposed *anthropomorphic* gods (gods who look and act like people) and polytheism, yet he described a god that he called "the greatest amongst gods and men." Parmenides, a philosopher of the early fifth century BC, wrote a poem called *Truth*, which begins "Listen to me, you souls of darkness/ Because I have spoken with the goddess. . . . " The *truth* still flowed from the divine. Legend says that Empedocles, who thought the universe was made of four elements (fire, air, water, and earth), claimed to be a god himself. To prove it, he jumped into a live volcano (and was never seen again).

Greeks, and later Romans, kept worshipping the gods of their pantheon for century after century while philosophical arguments rose, fell out of favor, and rose again. Plotinus, a Greek from Egypt who moved to Rome in 224 AD, mixed religion and popular myths together with the philosophy of Plato (discussed later in this chapter). Plato, who lived 500 years before Plotinus, said that the world as people experience it is made of imperfect, temporary reflections of perfect, eternal *Ideas,* or forms. Plotinus also stirred in bits from Aristotle, the Stoics (more about them soon), and the Pythagorians and came up with Neoplatonism, a school of thought that flourished for a millennium and came back in new Christian forms in the fourteenth and fifteenth centuries. This philosophy took many forms through Roman times, into the Middle Ages, and beyond the Renaissance.

Neoplatonism looked to a perfect reality beyond the imperfect earthly realm of mortals. This perfect reality was sometimes identified with the Roman gods, and later with the Christian God. Some forms of the philosophy saw the ideal reality as completely separate from its blurry reflection — the world that people inhabit. In other forms of Neo-Platonic thought, the everyday world was linked as in a seamless chain to God's perfect being — with each link representing a level of remove from God. Later yet, Neoplatonism took a turn in which the real world *reflected* God's perfect light, and thus was holy in itself. You can find out about some of these permutations of Neoplatonism in Chapters 11 and 12.

Tracing Philosophy's Roots

Greeks coined the term *philosophy,* but they weren't the first to ask basic questions. Supernatural creation stories (see Chapter 9) addressed some of the same things that the first philosophers wondered about: What is the world made of? What are the sun and moon? How about the stars? What is humankind's place in nature? Philosophy arose among the Greeks less than 3,000 years ago, yet complex sophisticated civilizations existed long before that (see Chapters 1 and 3).

Some scholars argue that the Greeks built on a tradition of inquiry that came from the ancient Hindus. In the sixth century BC, an Indian philosopher known as Ajita of the Hair Blanket (catchy name, huh?) said the world consisted of four elements: earth, air, fire, and water. More than a century later, a Greek named Empedocles said the same thing. Usually, Empedocles gets credit for thinking up this idea on his own, but nobody knows whether a philosophical predecessor influenced him. In the fifth century BC, the Greek Leucippus argued that the world is made up of tiny particles, or atoms. But Pakudha Kacchayana, an Indian of the sixth century BC, walked that path first.

Sumer and Babylon, both in Mesopotamia, had traditions of literacy that long predated the Greeks (see Chapter 3). Persia did as well. Some scholars point to Africa as the original source of intellectual inquiry. The problem with these claims is that there's no proof. Clues, however, indicate that Greek philosophy benefited from cultural crosscurrents. For example, the first Greek philosophers didn't live in Greece.

Living on the Edge(s) of Greek Society

Greeks were colonizers. As they sailed around the Aegean Sea and beyond, in the wider Mediterranean, they liked to settle and establish city-states like the ones back home. Their colonies produced the Greeks' earliest hotshot thinkers.

Pythagoras was born on an island off the coast of Turkey and moved to Italy. Thales, his student Anaximander, and the younger Anaximenes are called the *Milesians* or the *Ionians,* because they lived in Miletus, a city-state in Greek Asia. (That part of the world — in present-day Turkey — was called *Ionia*.) Xenophanes lived in Colophon, near present-day Izmir, Turkey.

Drawing inspiration from other cultures

You may think of the Greeks of the fifth century BC as an early culture. But they looked back on an honored past embodied in the works of their poets — especially Homer. Greeks held a traditional regard for wisdom (their word for it was *sophia*) and for skill with words. They also had a tradition of considering what is right and moral and questioning how society should function.

Greeks living on the frontiers of their culture may have found their traditions stimulated by the scholarship of other cultures. For example, Babylonians studied the stars and planets for centuries. (They thought stars and planets were gods, but that didn't invalidate their calculations.) Some historians say that when the Greeks got their hands on Babylonian astronomy and started talking about the stars as natural phenomena rather than supernatural personalities, *science* began.

Writings from Persia and probably Egypt — considerations of natural phenomena such as tides and stars and human inventions, such as mathematics — circulated among the learned in Greek society.

Traveling broadens the mind

Thales (fascinated by water) made at least one visit to Egypt and came up with a way to measure the height of the Great Pyramid, shown in Figure 10-1. Standing next to the pyramid as the sun rose in the sky, he watched his shadow. When his shadow exactly matched his own height, he hurried to

Figure 10-1:
Thales
reportedly
came up
with a
method for
measuring
the Great
Pyramid.

© Larry Lee Photography/CORBIS

mark the length of the pyramid's shadow. By measuring the shadow, he determined the pyramid's height. Was this novel thinking on Thales' part, or did an Egyptian surveyor teach it to him?

Living where they did, Thales and his progeny could have seen Indian poetry or accessed Sumerian texts. Could these guys have just taken older, Eastern or African ways of looking at the world and talked them up among their fellow Greeks? Nobody knows for sure, so they get credit as original thinkers.

Examining Eastern Philosophies

China developed philosophical traditions around the same time that the Greeks were creating a name for themselves in the field. Chinese philosophies had a widespread impact throughout East Asia.

Confucius and Lao-tzu, China's most famous early philosophers, were roughly contemporary with Anaximenes of Miletus. However, there's no evidence that their teachings influenced the Greeks. The teachings of both men grew into traditions that are now considered religious as much as philosophical. Confucians stress the importance of cultural heritage, family, and society. Taoists look to the natural world and its underlying path, or *way,* as the route to peace.

Also in China, the *School of Names* liked to twist concepts around and play with paradoxes. This group of philosophers theorized that if you took a stick and cut it in half every day you would never use it all up, because half of any length, no matter how short, is still not zero. This thinking corresponded with the ideas of a fifth-century BC Greek, Zeno of Elea, who said that to run any distance you must first run half that distance. To run that half-distance you must first run one-quarter the total distance. But first you must run one-eighth the distance. Carried to extreme, such an argument could *prove* that you could never run the entire distance.

Another major Chinese tradition, *legalism,* concerned a ruler's need to bring forth laws, to set out rewards and punishments, and to build the kingdom's power against its rivals — practical, governmental philosophy.

Leading to (and from) Socrates

People who study philosophy draw a line between Eastern traditions and the Greeks. Scholars also draw a line within the Greek tradition — a line that falls right at Socrates, who lived from 469 to 399 BC. Like all such lines, it's arbitrary, but Socrates really did change things.

Socrates began something that his student Plato and Plato's student Aristotle continued: a tradition founded in a personal understanding of what is true and what is right.

Unlike the Ionians and other colonial philosophers, Socrates, shown in Figure 10-2, lived smack dab in the middle of Greek culture — in the great city-state of Athens at its cultural, economic, and military peak.

Building a tradition of seeking answers

The philosophers who came before Socrates — men such as Pythagoras, Thales, and Anaximenes — are often lumped together as the *pre-Socratics.* You can find a few of their ideas — such as Thales' thoughts about water — at the beginning of this chapter. Many pre-Socratic ideas seem weird, even from the perspective of later Greek philosophers who wrote about them.

For example, Anaximander of Miletus thought that the earth was shaped like a cylinder and that gigantic, tire-shaped rings full of fire surrounded it. The firelight shone out of various holes of different sizes, which people on earth saw as stars, the moon, and the sun. Anaximander also thought that the first human embryos grew inside fish-like creatures. (He didn't eat fish.)

Figure 10-2: Socrates's reputation as a philosopher rests mainly on what Plato wrote about him.

Heraclitus, who lived in Ephesus (present-day Turkey) in the early fifth century BC, thought all things are made of fire. He also said that the soul runs around inside the human body the way a spider patrols its web.

The importance of the pre-Socratic philosophers was that they started a tradition of observing, thinking, and questioning that would reject Anaximander's fish embryos and Heraclitus's spider-like soul. But it would hang onto their insistence on trying to understand.

Emerging as the leading city-state

Greeks who lived in Miletus or other parts of Asia Minor weren't carefree, even if their theories suggest that they were. They were on chancy political turf: Persian territory. The Persian Empire controlled that part of the world since the middle of the sixth century BC.

In Ionia, where the early philosophers lived, Greeks rebelled in 500 and 499 BC, but Persia's King Darius crushed the rebellion. Then he decided to teach a lesson to mainland Greeks who had supported the rebellion.

Persia attacked Greece, bringing about the Persian Wars, which lasted from 490 to 449 BC. Over that time, the sometimes-fractious Greek city-states put their resources together and won (see Chapter 3). Athens emerged as the leader of a federation of city-states, including those in Ionia. Called the *Delian League,* it amounted to a far-flung Athenian empire.

Arguing the importance of persuasion

By 460 BC, Athens was a democracy, the culmination of hard-won government reforms that began in the late sixth century BC. Athenians chose jurists and even magistrates by lottery. All the citizens — a class restricted to free, Athenian (as opposed to slave or foreign-born) men (no women) — were eligible to sit in the popular Assembly, the city-state's main lawmaking body. It became important for young men to learn how to speak persuasively.

For that, Athens needed teachers. Itinerant instructors came to be known as the *sophists* — men skilled in rhetoric and legal argument. Mostly concerned with teaching privileged youngsters how to plead their cases, sophists were criticized as more concerned with winning arguments than with truth. *Sophistry* became known as the art of constructing arguments that sound good, despite their flaws.

But some genuine philosophers emerged from among the sophists, paving the way for Socrates by engaging in thoughtful, persuasive dialogues. Many Athenians considered Socrates another sophist. The comic playwright Aristophanes made fun of sophists in general and Socrates in particular in his play *The Clouds,* which depicts the philosopher walking around with his head literally in the clouds.

Living and thinking in a heady time

After the Persian wars, a thinker from Turkey named Anaxagoras moved to the city-state. He talked philosophy with Pericles, the Athenian leader, who became his friend and supporter.

Pericles, who built Athens into a monumental city with architecture to fit its new status as imperial capital, also hobnobbed with the new Athenian playwrights such as Sophocles and Aeschylus, men who were inventing the Western theater. The playwright Euripides studied with Anaxagoras. This was a heady time to live in Athens.

His friendship with Pericles helped make Anaxagoras a VIP around town. Not that the philosopher's ideas weren't intriguing on their own: He propounded a kind of proto-Big Bang theory that sounds like modern astrophysics. In Anaxagoras's version, everything started out packed inside an infinitely small pebble-like unit that began to spin and expand, throwing out all matter into an ever-expanding universe. He also envisioned an *infinite Mind* (not unlike a single god), separate from and governing all matter.

Some of what Anaxagoras said was controversial, especially ideas about the sun that contradicted religious orthodoxy. Eventually the philosopher found himself banished. (Athenian citizens voted every year on whom they wanted to *ostracize,* a word that to them included physical banishment.) Before he left town, Anaxagoras may have taught Socrates.

Another war, this one pitting Athens against the Greek city-state Sparta (which had grown tired of being in Athens's shadow), lasted from 431 to 404 BC. Early in this conflict, called the Peloponnesian War, Pericles died of a plague. Sickness and lack of leadership in Athens helped the Spartans win (see Chapter 3), and Athens changed dramatically.

Thinking for himself: Socrates's legacy

Already in his late 30s when the Peloponnesian War broke out, Socrates served bravely in the Athenian infantry. Later in the war he sat as a member of the Assembly when that lawmaking body judged some Athenian generals accused of abandoning warriors after a victorious sea battle. The lost warriors fell overboard in a sea so stormy that the generals decided to let the high winds blow them home, instead of fighting their way back to seek unlikely survivors. The generals arrived expecting to be hailed as heroes but were tossed in the clink instead.

All but one Assembly member voted for conviction. The holdout was Socrates. Why? For one thing, the law said the generals had to be tried as individuals, not in a group. Everybody else conveniently overlooked this. Socrates was not one to follow the herd.

Socrates made up his own mind and saw it as the individual's responsibility to determine virtue from vice and to act on the resulting knowledge, without regard for consequences.

Glimpsing Socrates through Plato's writings

Socrates didn't write about his philosophy. His reputation rests on what other people, especially his student Plato, wrote about him.

Plato depicted Socrates as intent on convincing his fellow Athenians to re-examine their ideas about right and wrong. Plato's writings describe Socrates using a technique that's been called the *Socratic method* ever since: Socrates asks the person he is talking to for a definition of a broad concept (such as *piety* or *justice*) and then tries to get the person to contradict himself with his answer.

What Socrates seems to have believed can be summed up in a quote attributed to him: "There is only one good, knowledge, and one evil, ignorance."

Viewing Socrates as the scapegoat

Socrates was a critic. He lived to question, to pick apart assumptions. During the Peloponnesian War, Athenians' assumptions that they were the best among Greek city-states and the certain winner of the war fell apart — just like the city walls that the Spartans pulled down when they finally won.

When Athens went looking for a scapegoat after losing the war, its eyes fell on the man who had questioned (and thus undermined) their earlier ideas about Athenian supremacy. Socrates was charged with *impiety* — disrespecting the state religion — and with corrupting the young.

He could have apologized. He could have promised to shut up. He could have saved his own life. But that wasn't Socrates's style. He preferred to drink hemlock — Athens' method of execution — rather than abandon his principles.

Socrates's insistence on making up his own mind, based on his own under-standing of what is good, made him a new kind of hero — not a warrior but a man of conviction.

Building on Socrates: Plato and Aristotle

Before Socrates, Athens became a great imperial capital. While Socrates was alive, the city lost its imperial greatness. But after Socrates's death, Athens rebuilt itself as a center of learning. Plato, after traveling widely, returned to Athens to set up a school (at nearby Academia) that would train generations of thinkers.

Tracing Plato's influence

Plato developed doctrines — including a theory about the immortality of the soul — that would wield incredible influence over philosophers who followed him. The Englishman Alfred North Whitehead, who taught and wrote in the late nineteenth and early twentieth centuries, described the entire tradition of European philosophy as "footnotes to Plato."

Advancing the theory of Ideas

Perhaps the best-known tenet of Platonism is the theory of *Ideas* or Forms. Plato thought that elements of the material world — such as a table, a man, or an acorn — were imperfect reflections or *shadows* of eternal, perfect ideas — such as the idea of a table, a man, or an acorn.

In his book *The Republic,* Plato described an ideal political state that brings forth philosopher kings, trained at the highest levels of knowledge.

Recognizing Aristotle's advancements

Plato is often seen as the inventor of idealism, while Aristotle, his student, is seen as a hands-on realist. Aristotle was a naturalist, an ahead-of-his-time marine biologist who gathered knowledge from studying the real world.

Aristotle could be down-to-earth about seemingly universal matters. When he made his famous statement "Man is by nature a political animal," Aristotle was probably just observing that human beings are more like bees, who live in relation to one another, than like cats, who hunt alone. His ideal state, unlike that in Plato's *Republic,* was based on the Greek city-state, with traditions such as family and even slavery intact. Aristotle wrote about ethics, morality, politics, and much more, often refining Plato's ideas rather than overturning them. This makes sense, considering Aristotle was Plato's student for 20 years. He had opinions on matters from the nature of being (the word *metaphysics* comes from the title of one of his works) to earning interest by lending money (he opposed it).

Alexander and After

If it weren't for Aristotle, and for a rather special student of his, history may have taken a very different course.

Socrates taught Plato, who taught Aristotle, who taught Alexander the Great, who conquered the world. Okay, not really the world. But Alexander conquered such a large and wide-ranging territory that it *seemed* like the whole world to the people of his time (see Chapter 3).

Alexander was never a philosopher, but he did collect samples of exotic plants and animals while on his empire-building campaigns. He sent them back to Aristotle so that his old tutor could study them. The philosopher and the emperor later grew apart, especially after Alexander proclaimed himself a god. (If you value your philosophy professor's good opinion, don't claim personal divinity.)

The philosophical schools founded by Plato and Aristotle didn't build Alexander's empire, but the thinking they nurtured was at the center of what became the dominant culture of the Mediterranean.

Influencing everyday life: Hellenistic philosophies

The period after Alexander's conquests is labeled the *Hellenistic Age* (Greeks called themselves *Hellenes*) because *Hellenistic* (Greek-like) philosophies spread and remained influential through the height of the Roman Empire.

Some of these philosophies had names still recognized today — not just in the philosophy department's faculty lounge, but in everyday life. You may call somebody a *cynic* or *stoic*. You may find yourself *skeptical* as you read this sentence. Perhaps you are an *epicure*. These terms, applied to people behaving or thinking in certain ways, emerged from the philosophies of the Hellenistic Age — from the heirs of Plato and Aristotle.

Pleasing yourself: Hedonism

The pleasure principle has been around at least since the fourth century BC, when Aristippus, who studied under Socrates, decided that the sensation of pleasure is the only good. His followers, though they practiced hedonism, were called *Cyrenaics,* after Cyrene in Africa (Aristippus's birthplace).

They were *so* extreme in their if-it-feels-good-do-it approach that they didn't allow for anticipation or reminiscence. Pleasures future and past, they thought, have no present value.

Hedonism is not often clearly articulated as a philosophy — at least not by its adherents — because it's not much fun to articulate a philosophy. As a practice, hedonism sometimes figured in social movements, as with the widespread relaxation of social mores in the United States and Western Europe in the 1960s and 1970s.

Looking at original Cynicism

If you think everybody's trying to con you, you may have a reputation as a cynic, but that wasn't what cynicism used to be. (No, I'm *not* trying to con you about this.) Antisthenes, a friend of Socrates, started *Cynicism,* which was essentially about getting back to nature, ignoring social conventions, and living simply.

Antisthenes's follower and colleague, Diogenes of Sinope, really got into *asceticism* — shunning civilization's pleasures and sleeping in a tub. Legend says he walked around Athens in broad daylight, carrying a lantern, and saying he was searching for an honest man. It was probably a commentary on the artificiality of life in the city.

Yet the idea stuck that the cynics thought honesty was hard to come by, so *cynicism* became a word for distrusting everybody and everything.

Indulging in Epicureanism

The meaning of *epicure* evolved too. Nowadays, an *epicure* (or Epicurean) is somebody who indulges appetites. But Epicurus, who founded the movement in the early third century BC, believed in moderation.

Epicurus was concerned with logic and physics. He was an *atomist,* advancing theories of earlier philosophers about a universe composed of tiny particles that they called atoms.

His name, however, became attached to his teachings about ethics, and then to gross distortions of those teachings. He thought the chief *goods* were peace of mind and freedom from pain. He called that *pleasure*.

Epicurus saw excessive desire as an enemy of pleasure, not something to be indulged. His idea of pleasure got mixed up with other people's grosser ideas, and the result is Epicureanism that would have appalled Epicurus. Epicureanism flourished in Hellenistic Rome from about 320 BC to 200 AD.

Standing together in Stoicism

Around 300 BC, a group of philosophical types gathered every day where Zeno of Citium taught, at, the painted colonnade in downtown Athens. The words for painted colonnade were *Stoa poikile,* so these folks were called the Stoics.

Zeno's students shared a vision of the world as a benevolent, organic whole. If people see evil, it's because they don't see or know the entire thing. The Stoics thought, as Socrates had, that human virtue is based in knowledge: The more you know, the more you see the good.

Like Aristotle, the Stoics saw reason as an underlying principle of nature. They thought individuals should live in harmony with nature. The most famous part of Stoic philosophy is a bit about how pleasure, pain, and even death aren't really relevant to true happiness and that all these things should be borne with equanimity.

Stoicism spread to Rome, where it competed for followers with Epicureanism and skepticism. The Stoics believed in a brotherhood of humans. That made it the philosophy of Roman republicans who opposed a return to monarchy.

Doubting the world: Skepticism

A *skeptic* is somebody who habitually doubts, especially somebody who questions accepted assumptions. There was an element of skepticism in the way Socrates rooted out contradictions in conventional wisdom.

Skepticism as a philosophical tradition, however, goes deeper than that, casting doubt on the possibility of any human knowledge. The way its founder, Pyrrho (360 to 270 BC), looked at it, everybody is clueless. The best thing to do is suspend judgment and stay calm. Skepticism had adherents in Rome.

Putting philosophy to practical use

If you get the impression that Greeks after Alexander the Great didn't do anything but philosophize; remember that much of what came under the broad heading philosophy (Greek for *love of wisdom*) had practical applications. Geometry, for example, came in handy for surveying and building.

Incredible buildings went up during the Hellenistic Age. Among them was a fantastic marble lighthouse in the harbor of Alexandria, Egypt. Alexandria became a center of Greek-style learning. The library there held 700,000 volumes.

The librarian in charge of that great storehouse of information was a Greek named Eratosthenes, who was also a geographer. He worked out a formula for measuring the circumference of the Earth, measuring shadows in Syene, Egypt and in Alexandria at the same time — at noon on the summer solstice. Then he used the difference between the shadows, multiplied by the distance between the two cities, to calculate the planet's size. Another Greek at Alexandria reportedly built some kind of steam engine, although nobody knew what to use it for. That thread of knowledge would be picked up in England quite a few centuries later (see Chapter 14).

Tracking the Centuries

May 28, 585 BC: The sun darkens in an eclipse, accurately predicted by the philosopher Thales of Miletus.

Sixth century BC: Indian philosopher Ajita of the Hair Blanket says the world consists of four elements: earth, air, fire, and water.

500 BC: Greeks in Ionia (today's Turkey) rebel against Persian rule.

430 BC: According to legend, philosopher Empedocles demonstrates his own immortality by jumping into the volcanic crater atop Mount Etna.

449 BC: Athens emerges victorious from Persian Wars as leader of a federation of city-states, the *Delian League*.

423 BC: In his comedy *The Clouds,* playwright Aristophanes makes fun of Socrates, depicting him with his head literally in the clouds.

399 BC: Condemned to death for his teachings, the imprisoned Socrates drinks the poison hemlock, surrounded by his followers.

387 BC: Plato returns to Athens to found a school of philosophy.

384 BC: Aristotle is born in Macedon, the son of the king's physician.

300 BC: Zeno of Citium teaches philosophy every day at the painted colonnade, or *Stoa poikile*, in central Athens.

About 255 BC: Eratosthenes becomes librarian at Alexandria, Egypt, in charge of the largest storehouse of knowledge in the world.

Chapter 11

Being Christian, Thinking Greek

*A*t a casual glance, Christianity and the philosophies that pre-Christian Greeks developed don't seem as if they have much to do with each other. Jesus, after all, was a Jew. His followers saw him as the messiah promised by the Hebrew scriptures. They consider him both the Son of God and that God in human form — a *monotheistic* God.

The Greek philosophers came from a *polytheistic* tradition. (To find out about polytheistic religions, see Chapter 9. For more on the Greek philosophers, see Chapter 10.) They were seemingly without connection to the Christian message. Yet their philosophies didn't go away when Christianity came in. If anything, those old philosophies became more important than ever.

Greek thought — especially the lines of thought founded by Plato and Aristotle — worked right to the center of Christian religious contemplations and right to the center of the way European society was organized. This habit of reaching back to the pre-Christian thinkers continued right up to the Renaissance, then accelerated considerably.

 Why am I telling you more about Christianity and Greek philosophy? Because the world that you and I live in, here in the early twenty-first century, is still a product of the way Europeans and European descendents (as in Americans) threw their military and economic weight around in the sixteenth through the twentieth centuries. They threw their spiritual certainty around, too, with missionary zeal.

What is called *globalization* (from McDonald's hamburgers in Beijing to worldwide online stock trading) follows European imperialism. Looking at forces that shaped the way Europeans thought and behaved helps me understand how the world got this way. Christianity, liberally laced with the traditions of Greek philosophy, is among the biggest of those forces.

Elaborating on The Great Chain of Being

What Greek ideas hung around into Christian times? How about the one that came to be known as *The Great Chain of Being,* a way of ordering reality that owes its basics to the tradition of Platonic thought (see Chapter 10). The Great Chain of Being was central to the way most Christians looked at the world in medieval and Renaissance times.

The Great Chain is an organization chart of existence — with the richest, most complex grade of existence at the top and the humblest at the bottom. Everything can be ranked by its relative distance from the ultimate, or ideal, reality. This Platonic notion adapted well to Christianity, with God at the top of the chain. Everybody and everything had a station on the chain — each above and below certain other links in the chain.

The chain lent itself to the certainty that kings were closer to God than lesser nobles, who were closer to God than commoners were. *Serfs,* who were virtual slaves, could be comfortably tucked at the bottom of Christian humanity without worry. Yet even serfs got to be above animals and other life forms. Worms and fleas and such were *waaay* down there. Thus, differences between levels of human society and between biological species were the same thing — part of the proper, godly order.

The Great Chain of Being was rigidly conservative, nailing society's institutions — especially class distinctions — in place. The Great Chain went hand in hand with the notion of the *divine right of kings,* under which doctrine a monarch's authority came from God and a kingdom's obedience to its sovereign reflected Christendom's obedience to the Almighty. To defy the state was to defy God on high.

Kings and would-be kings disagreed all the time, of course, about who was God's rightful candidate. Sometimes churchmen got into these arguments, too. (You can find several of their clashes mentioned in other chapters of this book, notably Chapters 6 and 12.) But the overarching principle hung on through the Middle Ages and beyond.

How did Christianity get mixed up with this brand of Platonism? How did Platonism and Christianity blend so well? It started very early on.

Interpreting Theology

Based on Jesus' teachings about God's forgiveness and on the miracle of the Resurrection of Christ (see Chapter 9), Christianity gave rise to two millennia worth of painstaking interpretation and fierce, often violent, disputes that have even grown into wars.

Divergent ideas aren't unusual in religion. Most beliefs evolve that way, with variations on their central themes emerging and breaking off from the central religion. Yet in the case of Christianity, circumstances contributed to especially early and wide-ranging interpretations.

Stacking scripture upon scripture

One reason Christianity was so open to various interpretations is that it is a religion built on another religion, embracing the writings of the original — Jewish — tradition as its own.

The Holy Scripture consists of the much-older Jewish Bible (the Old Testament) with the newer, Christian, first century AD writings (the New Testament). From the get-go, Christians had to make decisions about how to reconcile this wealth of literature. What did these incredibly rich writings — often seemingly contradictory from one book to another and from Old to New Testaments — really mean?

By necessity, Church fathers based their teachings on interpretations — not always agreed upon among themselves — of God's will. For example, although Christians revere the Hebrew scriptures, they never followed many Hebrew laws. Judaism's dietary restrictions and ritual circumcision were not part of the new religion. Saint Paul, a Jewish rabbi before his conversion, brought the gospel message to many *gentiles* (non-Jews) in the first century AD. He taught that Christians could disregard these Hebrew requirements.

Replacing Homer with the Bible

Another reason why furious interpretations and counter-interpretations marked Christianity from the beginning: Look at the places where Christianity sprang up. Christianity filtered through a world marked by *Hellenistic* (Greek-like) traditions, by the Greek teachings that followed Socrates, Plato, Aristotle, and Alexander the Great's empire. (You can find out more about the Greek tradition of thought in Chapter 10.)

Early centers of the Church included Alexandria, Egypt, which was a capital of Greek scholarship, and Rome, where so many Hellenistic philosophies rubbed up against one another for a long time. The New Testament was written in Greek and Jesus himself came to be known by a Greek word meaning messiah: *Christ.*

As Greek thought shifted to Christian thought, the Bible took the place of Homer's poems and the Greek–Roman pantheon as a general context for philosophical questioning.

By *the Greek–Roman pantheon,* I mean the many gods such as Zeus (the father god), Athena (goddess of wisdom), Apollo (god of the sun), Adonis (god of nature's regeneration) and Dionysus (god of wine and celebration). Greeks worshipped these human-like, yet supernatural personalities and credited them with influencing nature and human lives. The Greek gods were characters in Homer's poems and in many other stories (today called *myths*) that all Greeks knew. (Romans, who worshipped many of the same gods by different names, knew the stories, too.) When Greeks talked about abstract concepts such as *good* they relied on phrases such as "pleasing to the gods." They used stories about the gods to illustrate points of philosophy.

The intellectual energy from all the Greek-based philosophies of the Hellenistic Age seemed to funnel into Christian philosophy. Philosophical thought became the province of *theologians* — people trying to figure out, or at least interpret, God. In the part of the world that embraced Christianity, scholarly priests absorbed and redefined the ideas of the Greeks, channeling those ideas into beliefs about how the Church and the world should be arranged.

Establishing Jesus' Divinity

Constantine the Great — along with his co-emperor Licinius — issued the *Edict of Milan,* which ordered toleration of Christians, in **313 AD.** Only 12 years later, after Constantine had defeated and killed Licinius to become sole Roman emperor, he called together the top bishops of the newly liberated Christian Church. The churchmen met at Nicaea, a town near Constantine's new Christian capital of Constantinople to hammer out important issues. (See Chapter 5 for more about Constantine's founding of Constantinople.)

How important were those issues? Well, the bishops wanted to work out an official policy about Jesus' divinity: Just how divine was he? In the early centuries of the Church, some priests taught that Jesus, as the Son of God, was subordinate to his father, the Hebrew God. Others thought that Jesus was essentially a mortal, God's greatest prophet, but not divine in himself. The bishops disagreed with these ideas and drew up the *Nicene Creed,* which said that Jesus was God the Son — in essence, the same as God the Father.

The issue wasn't settled easily, however. (It remains a point of departure for some sects even today.) Disagreement over whether Jesus and God the Father were *the same* or *similar* separated Christians in Rome from those in Constantinople. And the question of how to regard the third part of the Christian Trinity — the Holy Spirit — was a sore spot between the Western and Eastern branches of the Church, a major cause of their eventual split from one another (more about the split in Chapters 5 and 9).

Inquiring into Augustine's ideas

The most influential early interpretations of proper Christian thought came from Saint Augustine, a North African who followed Platonic philosophy and the religion of Manicheism before he was baptized as a Christian in 387 AD.

Augustine became a priest and was appointed the Bishop of Hippo (a city in what is today Algeria).

Divining the mind of God

Some of Augustine's early writings adapted Plato's ideas to Christianity. Plato (turn to Chapter 10 for more on him) thought that everything you can see and experience is an imperfect reflection of a perfect, eternal *Form* or *Idea*. In other words, there is an *Idea* of a table and an *Idea* of a woman, apart from and superior to all actual tables and all actual women. In Augustine's version of Plato's philosophy, these eternal Ideas reside inside a mind — the mind of God.

Condoning righteous killing

Augustine's teachings affected history powerfully and directly. One example: Although some early Christians were strict pacifists and interpreted the biblical command "Thou shalt not kill" quite literally, Augustine wrote that war is not wrong if it is conducted on divine authority. He also taught that it was okay to carry out the death penalty in accordance with the laws of the state.

A just, Christian society had the authority to kill people. This opened the moral and ethical door wide, considering that there aren't many societies whose leaders would admit to being unjust.

Tracing two paths to salvation

What does the title of a television sitcom have to do with Christian philosophy? The title *Will and Grace* may just be a joke on a TV producer's liberal arts education, but even that reflects how deeply philosophical arguments came into the workings of the world.

Will (as in free will) and Grace (as in God's grace alone) are two possible paths to salvation in competing Christian philosophies. They reflect a debate that began in the writings of Saint Augustine.

Adapting Augustine's ideas

Unlike just about anybody on television these days, Augustine rejected sexual pleasure and things of the flesh. He seems to have picked up this aversion during a youthful fling with Manicheism, which was founded in Persia (today's Iran) in the third century AD.

Manicheism taught that the material world represents the powers of darkness, which have invaded the realm of light. An ascetic and puritanical religion, Manicheism seems to have marked Augustine profoundly, even though he roundly denounced it when he converted to Christianity. Especially as he got older, he became firmly convinced that the whole human race had somehow taken part in the sin of Adam and Eve.

In the Bible story of man's creation, Adam, enticed by Eve, disobeys God's order not to eat the fruit of the Tree of Knowledge. God drives Adam and Eve from the Garden of Eden for this.

Here's where Augustine started interpreting: Everybody descended from Adam, he believed, inherited that original sin of disobedience. That's everybody — except God in human form, meaning the immaculately conceived Jesus. The only thing that can save any human soul is God's grace. Further, God awards that grace (and this is the tricky part) without regard for individual merit. That is, you can't earn your way into heaven. Prayer and good deeds won't do it. Salvation or damnation is decided beforehand. You have no free will. You can't even hope to understand grace. God is beyond understanding.

As you may imagine, Augustine's *predestination* proved controversial. Many who rejected his doctrine preferred the view that God gave human beings *free will* — a mind and the ability to make up that mind — and with that freedom comes the responsibility to embrace God.

Predestination has been interpreted and argued over in endless ways since Augustine. Some versions embrace *fatalism,* the idea that the future is just as unchangeable as the past. Not all versions of predestination go that far, nor are all versions restricted to Christian thought.

In Islam, a person cannot oppose God's will, but can accept or reject God. If you reject God, you face dire consequences. Much of Christianity took philosophical routes not far from this one.

Promoting other views on predestination

Some leaders of the Protestant Reformation (find more on this movement in Chapter 13) embraced predestination. The Frenchman John Calvin, a major force in shaping Protestantism, was especially Augustinian. His version of predestination, *theological determinism,* asserts that people can't influence God in the matter of who is saved and who isn't. Predestination remains a belief of some Protestant denominations.

In most branches of Christianity that preach a form of predestination, believers are supposed to be good — that is, to do God's will — out of faith, love, and devotion. But they're not supposed to behave virtuously just because they're angling for a heavenly payoff or out of fear of eternal punishment. Yet without the spiritual equivalent of a carrot or stick, keeping some people on the narrow path is impossible, so some moralists consider predestination a lousy motivator.

Including the Ideas of Aquinas

The way Augustine looked at religion (see the preceding section), you couldn't understand anything without first believing in God. The last thing you want to try is to arrive at belief by way of understanding. Yet scholarship, the quest for understanding, survived.

Yes, there was *too* such a thing as medieval scholarship. Okay, so this scholarship had strict boundaries, involving mostly churchmen and a few effete nobles. Yet it mattered.

Promoting education and scholasticism

The idea of medieval times as *dark ages* where everybody in Europe was sunk in ignorance fails to account for the fact that universities are a medieval invention. The University of Bologna was the first, in the tenth century. Then there was the University of Paris in the twelfth century and Oxford in the thirteenth.

Scholasticism was the intellectual tradition at these universities. Saint Anselm, an archbishop of Canterbury (in England) at the turn of the twelfth century and a scholastic himself, described scholasticism as "faith seeking understanding." With that orientation, working out ideas using Greek philosophy was considered okay.

For early churchmen, Aristotle's line of reasoning caused more trouble than Plato's. At least in Augustine's faith-based brand of Christian Platonism, you didn't have to see and touch and feel objects (things your senses perceive) to tell you about the truth. Those things, by definition, were not true. They may be *reflections* of the truth, but the truth was in the *Idea,* which flowed from God.

In Aristotle's way of looking at the world, however, you can work your way *up* to understanding, even to understanding ultimate truth, using your senses and reason. This puts much more responsibility on the sinful human being. Scholasticism, however, embraced this Aristotelian way of doing things after an Italian priest named Thomas Aquinas (later Saint Thomas Aquinas) brought Aristotle into the Church.

Coming back to Aristotle

Aquinas wasn't the first medieval European scholar to be drawn to Aristotle. An important predecessor — not a Christian, but a Muslim — was Ibn Rushd, who became known to Latin-speaking European scholars as Averroës. He was a twelfth-century Islamic judge and physician who lived and worked both in Moorish Spain and in North Africa.

His writings contemplating Aristotle found their way to a German with the unwieldy name Albertus, Graf von Bollstädt. (*Graf von* means "count of.") Also a churchman, he started applying Averroës' arguments to Christian faith. Albertus passed on his interest in Aristotle to his pupil, Thomas Aquinas.

Supporting faith with logic

Aquinas wrote the major works that hooked Aristotelian reasoning into the Church, where it eventually became official Catholic doctrine. Aquinas even used Aristotle's logic to *prove* the existence of God.

How did he do that? Here's an example of his logic:

> [W]hat is in motion must be put in motion by another. If that by which it is put in motion be itself put in motion, then this also must needs be put in motion by another, and that by another again. But this cannot go on to infinity, because then there would be no first mover, and consequently, no other mover. . . . Therefore it is necessary to arrive at a first mover, put in motion by no other; and this everyone understands to be God.

Arguments such as that one fired scholastics with a passion for using their minds to get at big questions. The Christian universities became places where scholars pursued logic and rhetoric, debating the nature of being (within boundaries).

Embracing Humanism and More

Embracing the human intellect as a tool to confirm faith contributed to big movements in world history — such as the Renaissance (which you can read about in the next chapter). The focus on intellect also led to a rediscovery of classical (that is, Greek and Roman) science, which led Europeans to scientific and navigational advances. That, in turn, helped make possible the voyages of exploration that I talk about in Chapter 7. The reliance on rational thought wasn't a linear path, however. Not at all. You can point to scholasticism as a root of something called *humanism,* which focuses on the relationship between God and humans. Yet humanistic thinking arose as a *backlash against* the scholastics — a reaction to the abstract concerns of medieval scholarship — all that logic and analysis and such.

Nothing secular about it

Nowadays, *humanism* usually comes after the word *secular. Secular humanism* is often criticized as an anti-religious philosophy. But late medieval and Renaissance humanism was a Christian religious movement. Humanists asked: What is humankind's place in God's plan?

Does this mean that the humanists broke with all those centuries of reaching back to Greek philosophy? Not at all. Early humanism is identified with Neoplatonism (which I tell you about in Chapter 10). Humanism didn't embrace Augustine's brand of Platonism, however. Augustine didn't trust the things of the world, which he saw as false reflections of the perfect reality (God). Living in this false, material world, human beings couldn't understand God.

Humanistic Neoplatonism looked at things the other way around, seeing human beings as not just made by God, but as expressions of godliness. Giovanni, Conte Pico della Mirandola (from Mirandola, Italy) was a Renaissance philosopher who probably expressed it best. In his view, all the universe — stars, trees, dogs, sausages, and human beings, especially human beings — reflected God. (Read more about Pico in Chapter 12.) With this in mind, humans could be understood as perfect expressions of the ultimate truth. You were a small version of God's universe — a microcosm.

Not only could a human being seek God, a human being could *find* God within the individual soul. You could look inside your finite self and find infinity.

Tracing Humanism's impact

The concept that humans have the ability to find God had everything to do with what happened in Renaissance art, theology, philosophy, science, and even politics. If everything that human beings can think and create, including pre-Christian art and science, reflects God, the door to exploration opens all the way. As you can see in Chapter 12, the Renaissance brought major scientific discoveries, giving rise to the Enlightenment, a rational-humanist philosophical movement, which, in turn, brought forth modern democratic theory.

All of the Christian theology and philosophy mentioned in this chapter flowed from Greek ways of thinking. And at every stage through these Christian times, philosophical movements reached back to the Greeks and Romans for their ideological underpinnings.

Tracking the Centuries

325 AD: Christian bishops gather near Constantinople (in today's Turkey) to hammer out basic theological principals.

354 AD: Aurelius Augustinius, later known as Saint Augustine, is born in the Roman-ruled community of Numidia, North Africa.

387 AD: Augustine becomes a Christian, accepting baptism on Easter Sunday.

1180s: Ibn Rushd, an Islamic judge and physician in Moorish Spain, writes interpretations of the Greek philosopher Aristotle.

1273: In his book *Summa Theologica,* Thomas Aquinas shows Aristotle's thoughts to be compatible with Christian doctrine.

1879: The Roman Catholic Church adopts the writings of Saint Thomas Aquinas as official Catholic philosophy.

2000: The title of a popular television sitcom, *Will and Grace,* reflects a medieval theological debate over possible ways to achieve salvation.

Chapter 12

Awakening to the Renaissance

· ·

In This Chapter

▶ Bringing books out of the ivory tower

▶ Spurring a scientific revolution

▶ Pursuing perfection for God's glory

▶ Warring for control of Italy's greatness

· ·

*T*o many people, the word *Renaissance* means art, especially Italian art. If you're one of those people, good. Keep thinking art. Keep thinking Italy.

You can look at Renaissance art — the result of a creative explosion that began in early fifteenth-century Italy — and understand not just why the artists saw and depicted the world differently than their predecessors did, but why their vision reflected the world at large.

Renaissance art embodied ideas about the place of humankind in God's universe, reflecting a significant shift in the perception of what being human means. Because of this shift, striving to make the very best of mortal minds and bodies became important. The new thinking said that you could strive to be your best, and *should* do so, while enhancing, rather than imperiling, your immortal soul.

Even the Protestant Reformation (see Chapter 13), when all those European Christians broke away from the Roman Catholic Church, becomes easier to grasp if you look at the paintings and sculptures of Masaccio and Michelangelo first.

Never heard of Masaccio? Don't worry. I discuss him — and other Renaissance supermen — in this chapter.

Realizing the Reach of the Renaissance

By focusing on Renaissance artists, you may wonder, don't I risk missing the scope of the Renaissance? Wasn't it about so much more?

Yes, it was. The Renaissance was about philosophy and religion. It was also about literature, architecture, technology, science, music, political theory, and . . . just about everything imaginable. The Renaissance was about more than I can possibly do justice to in this chapter. So why mention art? If you're interested in history, it's convenient that the intellectual, spiritual, and even commercial trends of the Renaissance are all reflected in its creative works. A defining worldview (and don't worry, I'll explain what that worldview was in just a few paragraphs) shows up in the art, so the paintings and sculpture can help you understand what made this era tick.

Didn't the Renaissance spread outside of Italy, all over Europe? Right again. One reason it's hard to put dates on the Renaissance is that it was gradual. Different aspects of it hit different parts of Europe at different times — from the fourteenth to the sixteenth centuries, and maybe beyond.

The Renaissance spread far beyond Europe as explorers, responding to the same economic and cultural influences that stimulated artists back in Italy, landed in the New World and found sea routes from Europe to Asia in the late fifteenth century.

One root of all this change was more individual wealth. More Europeans could afford to buy foreign trade goods. And (here I go oversimplifying again) that came about in part because there were fewer Europeans, at least temporarily. The bubonic plague (see Chapter 6) killed so many people that those who survived had more resources, more land, even more money. The value of their work increased because of the scarcity of workers.

Are you still thinking art and Italy? Good, because I'm getting closer.

Redefining the Human Role

Chapter 11, which discusses Christian philosophies through medieval times, ends with a focus on *humanism* — a philosophy that concentrates on God's relationship with humanity. This philosophy was a big deal during the Renaissance (and has been important for most of the time since it appeared), because Christian writers started to depict human beings not just as God's creations, but as symbolic of God — little embodiments of divinity. Among the earliest writers to reflect this view were the Italian poets Francesco Petrarcha (1304 to 1374), known as Petrarch, and Giovanni Boccaccio (1313 to 1375).

Florence in flower

This Italian-based shift in thinking got a boost when the Florentine chancellor, Coluccio Salutati (1331 to 1406), started promoting his city-state's status as the intellectual capital of Europe. In 1396, he invited Manuel Chrysoloras, a scholar from Constantinople, to teach Greek in Florence. Many more eastern scholars came west, bringing with them Greek learning and philosophical traditions, after Constantinople fell to the Ottoman Turks in 1453.

The status connected with scholarship wasn't lost on another Florentine leader, the financier, statesman, and philanthropist Cosimo de' Medici (1389 to 1464). He was a patron of Florence's Platonic Academy (founded by Salutati), where scholars such as Marsilio Ficino (1433 to 1499) and the philosopher Giovanni, Conte Pico della Mirandola (1463 to 1494) worked to reconcile Christianity with newly rediscovered ideas from Greek and Roman philosophy.

In this effort, Pico della Mirandola mixed Greek and Roman Stoicism (a philosophy that saw the world as a benevolent, organic whole, as you can read about in Chapter 10), material from the Jewish Kabbala (or *Kabbalah*, a philosophical and literary tradition rooted in a mystic striving to know the unknowable secrets of existence), and Islamic sources into his Christian humanism. He thought all people's intellectual and creative endeavors were part of the same thing: God.

Spreading the word

The Platonic Academy in Florence and other schools like it drew students from far away, and their influence spread humanism all over Europe.

An example: John Colet (1467 to 1519) came from Oxford, England, to Florence. When he returned to England and became a priest, he shared Florentine teachings with prominent Englishmen and the famous Dutch scholar Desiderius Erasmus (1466 to 1536), who lived in England. Erasmus wrote criticisms of the Church that anticipated the Protestant Reformation, which I discuss in Chapter 13.

Promoting human potential

Why did this philosophy pack such a wallop? Well, Pico della Mirandola — who best expressed what the early Renaissance was about — wrote that the human being is a perfect expression of the ultimate truth. As a human, he argued, you are a tiny reflection of God's enormous universe — a microcosm. This may seem less-than-adventurous reasoning today, or even old-fashioned, but it was an enormous change from the way medieval Christians thought about themselves.

Under the influence of St. Augustine, medieval Christian thinking held that humankind was false, flawed, corrupted, forever marked by Adam's sin, and unable to play any active role in winning redemption. (See Chapter 11 for details.)

Humanism changed that, making it okay within a Christian context to celebrate human beauty and creativity in ways that nobody in Europe had since Roman times.

Reclaiming the ancients

Because intellect and creativity now reflected God's greatness, all of the classical poets and playwrights whose works were ignored, lost, or both through medieval times could be reclaimed and inducted into the Godliness Hall of Fame (figuratively speaking). Roman playwrights such as Seneca (who wrote comedies) became fit subjects for study and emulation.

Renaissance writers took ideas from Rome and Greece and put new life into them. The word *renaissance* means rebirth or reawakening. Renaissance scholars woke up to old books that had been kept in monastery libraries — books that monks copied by hand from still older books.

Chrysoloras, the Greek who came from Constantinople to teach in Florence, contributed to this trend. He encouraged his students to start collecting ancient Greek manuscripts. (There were no Pokemon cards, so they thought this would be fun.)

Well-heeled Florentines even started traveling to Greece to look for books. They came back with literary treasures and began amassing the first private (rather than Church-kept) libraries since the Roman Empire.

Presenting the printing press

And then, in Mainz, Germany, along came the right technology at a crucial time. Johann Gutenberg, who started as a goldsmith, devised a way to print books and pamphlets using movable type. He made a little metal cast of each letter (his goldsmith skills came in handy), and then arranged the letters, clamped them firmly into place, coated them with ink, and printed as many identical pages of type as he liked before rearranging the letters and printing copies of the second page, then the third, and on and on.

Fifteenth-century printing wasn't as easy as clicking a Print icon, but it was much easier and faster than what medieval monks were doing: painstakingly lettering every word on every page by hand. Until Gutenberg's advance, books were high craft, each a precious, one-of-a-kind artifact. Now they could be mass-produced.

Printing the Gutenberg Bible

Gutenberg and his financial backer Johann Fust built their press around **1450.** The Gutenberg Bible, the first mass-produced book, came off that press (or a successor to it) around **1455.** (Actually, Fust and his son-in-law, Peter Schöffer, completed the Gutenberg Bible after Gutenberg went bankrupt. Unable to repay Fust, the printer had to hand over his innovative press.)

Books were suddenly more numerous and cheaper, so more people could afford them. This meant that more people learned to read.

Reading other early publications

At first, printing was called *the German art.* But technology never respects borders. A wealthy merchant named William Caxton learned the new process in Cologne and took it to England around 1473. (Caxton's first publications included a history of the Trojan War and a collection of sayings of the philosophers.)

In Venice, the scholar Aldo Manuzio (born in 1450 and also known by his Latin name, Aldus Manutius) picked up Gutenberg's craft and printed easy-to-read, easy-to-carry editions of Greek and Latin classics at affordable prices. Imagine the change from going to a musty abbey and heaving open a hand-lettered volume so valuable that it was chained to the library shelf, to carrying a book in your pocket.

Having an impact on Church authority

Because the pre-Christian authors were now considered reflections of God's glory, there was a reason to read, admire, and even copy them — doing so didn't put your faith in jeopardy. But in a subtle and gradual way, the pre-Christian books undermined the Church's authority, anyway. Through medieval times, the Church held the monopoly on wisdom. Now other, older, diverse voices were influencing people throughout Europe as literacy flourished.

This was one of the ways that the Renaissance led to the Reformation.

Uniting Flesh and Soul

Are you still thinking Italian art? Good, because it's time to glance toward Michelangelo's *David,* shown in Figure 12-1, which the Renaissance artist sculpted in Florence at the beginning of the sixteenth century. This white marble statue depicts a perfect, exquisitely rendered male form — lean, muscular, graceful, and nude. David is a sculpture of the hunkiest young man that probably anybody in Italy could imagine — sexy in the extreme but also a representation of a sacred subject: David, the great biblical war hero and Hebrew king, the earthly ancestor of Jesus.

Michelangelo's masterpiece is flesh and spirit rolled into one. Sex and scripture. Earthly and godly. Flesh, according to the philosophy of humanism, *is* spirit. (Not all Christians were comfortable with this convergence, which is another factor that contributed to the Protestant Reformation.)

Figure 12-1:
Michel-
angelo's
David, a
holy hunk.

© David Lees/CORBIS

Inspiring Michelangelo

Of course, Michelangelo (1475 to 1564), whose style may be considered the height of Renaissance sculpture, didn't think up his approach all by himself.

Pioneers such as the painter Masaccio inspired Michelangelo. Born in Florence in 1401, the painter was born Tommaso di Giovanni di Simone Guidi, but called himself Masaccio. He painted biblical scenes of unprecedented drama and sensual richness, exploring the human form in ways that may have seemed sinful a century before. His fleshy, dramatic approach changed sacred art, even though he died at 27.

The sculptor Donatello (originally Donato di Betto Bardi) was another pioneer and inspiration. Born around 1386, also in Florence, he was the first artist since classical times to make statues that were independent works of art rather than parts of a building. He fashioned an anatomically impressive David too — one made of bronze.

Donatello was one of the early Renaissance artists to rediscover mathematical perspective, along with Filippo Brunelleschi (1377 to 1446), who moved on from sculpture to architecture. In art, perspective is any method used to achieve the illusion of three-dimensional depth. The ancient Greeks, who were interested in geometry and optics, noticed how objects appear smaller the farther away they are from the person looking at them. What's mathematical about that? An artist with a feel for geometry can give the impression of distance in a drawing or painting by working as if on a grid of lines (merely imagined, or painted over in the finished work) that seem to project from a point of convergence on the horizon — the vanishing point. (Imagine staring at a straight two-lane highway that you can see all the way to the horizon on a level plain.) Brunelleschi came up with this *one-point system* about 1420.

Living in the material world

Because Renaissance thinking held that the human form was a reflection of God and the material world was an aspect of the divine, concentrating on all the angles and curves, all the contours and colors of the physical world became positively holy. Artists wanted paintings and sculpture to be lifelike, to reflect reality — albeit an idealized reality.

To that end, artists branched out. Artist Leonardo da Vinci (1452 to 1519) was also a human anatomist, botanist, engineer, architect, and many other things. His knowledge of the physical world informed his art. He and other painters and sculptors ushered in new ways of thinking about the physical world and how its pieces interact. Leonardo even drew diagrams of flying machines, though he never built them.

Painting a picture of Genesis

Michelangelo is the guy you may picture lying on his back on top of a scaffold, painting the ceiling of the Sistine Chapel. In 1965, director Carol Reed made a movie about this little project. Called *The Agony and the Ecstasy*, it features Charlton Heston as Michelangelo and Rex Harrison as the pope, who stares up at him while he paints. There's some good dialogue between the two, assuming you can buy Heston as the artist, but the movie has to work too hard to come up with a love affair and battle scenes to flesh out the action.

Leonardo's work in engineering and perspective stimulated and intersected with the work of a new breed of architects and mathematical theoreticians — some of them much more practical minded than he was. While the artist was sketching flying machines, some other Italian engineers built on ancient mathematical disciplines to improve weapons and fortifications.

Returning to Science

The Renaissance planted the seeds of a scientific revolution that took off after 1600 with discoveries made by people, such as the astronomer Galileo and the physicist Isaac Newton. (See Chapter 14 for more on both men.)

Shifting the center of the universe

Copernicus, a Polish-born, Italian-educated churchman, took a big step toward the scientific revolution in **1543,** when he published his theories about how the earth and planets move in relation to the sun. Copernicus said that the sun, not the Earth, was the center around which the universe revolved.

Copernicus delayed releasing his findings for a long time, knowing they would disturb and anger some people. He was right about the reaction. His sun-centered universe, along with the notion that the earth spins on its axis, upset other astronomers and other churchmen. (Copernicus was a *canon*, a member of a cathedral order.)

To claim that God would place His creation on a spinning ball that revolved around another heavenly body struck many people as preposterous, not to mention heretical. The Catholic Church banned Copernicus's book, *The Revolution of the Heavenly Spheres,* in 1616 and didn't lift the ban until 1835.

Studying the human anatomy

While Leonardo's interest in engineering stimulated and was part of a revival of mathematical theory and classical architecture, his anatomical studies came just as the field of medicine began to catch the Renaissance spirit.

Medieval *physic* (as doctoring was called) was based on a theory that the body contained four fluids: blood, yellow bile, black bile, and phlegm. Called the *humors,* their balance was considered essential to good health. People today still sometimes refer to *good humor,* which is a reference back to this theory (although a Good Humor Bar wouldn't be nearly as appetizing if it made you think of bile).

At the turn of the fourteenth century, Pope Boniface VIII prohibited the dissection of human cadavers. The idea that human flesh reflected God created conflicted ideas about cutting into and studying it. The pope's decree interrupted the work of doctors who thought that there was more to learn about the body than this humors business.

Some maverick researchers conducted dissections in secret. By 1543, this science was out in public again with the publication of *Seven Books on the Structure of the Human Body,* a breakthrough work by Andreas Vesalius, a professor of surgery and anatomy at the University of Padua. His successor there, Matteo Realdo Columbo (who was born around 1516) figured out heart-lung circulation, a phenomenon that Michael Servetus of Spain discovered independently. Their work led to the Englishman William Harvey's discovery of the circulation of the blood throughout the body in the following century.

This new focus on the body resulted in medical breakthroughs:

- Girolamo Fracastoro, who practiced medicine at Naples after 1495, came up with a theory about microscopic contagion, which was based on his work with syphilis, typhus, and tuberculosis patients.

- In Bologna, Gaspare Tagliacozzi (1545 to 1599) pioneered plastic surgery in the late sixteenth century when he transplanted skin from his patients' arms to repair noses eaten away by syphilis.

Until these guys came along, surgery was something that barbers did. The anatomist and French Army surgeon Ambroise Paré (1510 to 1590) helped change that. Among his advances, he was the first to tie off arteries after an amputation. Until Paré, cauterizing a blood vessel with a hot iron was the accepted way to close off the vessel.

Being All That You Could Be

You could think about what happened in the Renaissance as a kind of philosophical-intellectual feedback loop.

A *feedback loop,* as anybody who was ever in a rock band knows, happens when the microphone or electric guitar picks up part of the output signal from a nearby amplifier or speaker. The mike or guitar then sends that sound back to the amp, where it is made louder, so that it creates louder interference, which is amplified again and then goes through the loop over and over — all at the speed of electric current. Within a second or two you have a shrill, incredibly loud shriek that causes everybody but really hardcore heavy metal fans to hold their hands over their ears and scream for mercy.

The noises that the Renaissance made were more pleasant and varied than that. So were the ideas and the works of art. But the Renaissance movement fed itself, and fed on itself, because humanism made it not just okay but actually *virtuous* to both contemplate and pursue human achievement.

Achievements — intellectual, artistic, physical — amplified and gave glory to the reflection of God. The pursuit of human perfection fed an appreciation for human perfection that in turn spurred even more pursuit of human perfection.

Striving for perfection

Everybody had a responsibility to become as perfect as possible. Everybody was supposed to develop all the powers given by God. Long before the U.S. Army began urging young people to "Be all that you can be," this was the motto of a new-style individual, the *Renaissance man*.

In this pursuit of human potential, artists studied math, architecture, engineering, and even literature. Long before the world thought in terms of *interdisciplinary,* all of these subjects sort of ran together.

Renaissance man sounds sexist today, and it was. There's no pretending otherwise. Although human beings — male and female — could be exalted, males were thought to have the godly gifts most worth developing.

Many people think Leonardo was the ultimate Renaissance man: engineer, artist, inventor, and so on. There were others — many others — including the sculptor-architect Brunelleschi, who was also a goldsmith. The Spanish medical researcher Servetus was a theologian. Michelangelo, a great painter and greater sculptor, was a poet too. See the "What a man" sidebar for another example.

What a man!

One of the most wide-ranging Renaissance men was the Genoan architect Leon Battista Alberti (1404 to 1472), an artist, poet, physicist, mathematician, and philosopher, as well as one of the finest musicians of his day (he played the organ) and an astonishing athlete.

He claimed that he could leap, with his feet together, between the heads of two men standing shoulder-to-shoulder without touching them. Who said white men can't jump?

His arm would have made him a fortune today as a pro baseball pitcher or football quarterback. Alberti surprised people by throwing an apple over the highest roof in Genoa, and he could chuck the javelin farther than anybody who challenged him. He was also a crack archer.

Hate him already? Me too, especially after I read that he was always in a good mood — cheerful, unflappable, and uncomplaining, even in terrible weather.

Stocking up on self-help books

Because making the best of what God gave you was so important, self-improvement became a hot topic during the Renaissance.

The best-selling book of 1528, *The Courtier* by Count Baldassare Castiglione, spelled out rules for what a gentleman ought to be. Among the most desirable qualities: You should be good at everything, but you shouldn't look like you're trying too hard. Even your manners should be easy and natural — unfailingly good, but not formally polished. *The Courtier* was sixteenth-century cool.

Castiglione thought that being a *courtier,* one of those nobles who hangs around the castle and waits on the prince or king, was one of the most important things anybody can do. Today, you may look back on courtiers as hangers-on and "yes" men, and many of them probably were. But Castiglione saw the courtier's job as both advising the prince and setting a good example for him. Even if the prince was a slobbering clod, the good manners and wisdom of exemplary courtiers were supposed to rub off on him.

If being a courtier was an important job, ruler was more important. Nicolo Machiavelli wrote the most notorious how-to book of the Renaissance, a little volume called *The Prince.* This 1513 publication was and remains controversial, because the book seems to advocate an amoral pragmatism, a way of operating that came to be called *Machiavellian.*

Machiavelli may be remembered as an advocate or as simply the best, most honest reporter of another aspect of all this focus on human achievement. On the more ear-punishing fringes of rock music, feedback becomes an instrument in itself. Within the Renaissance focus on humanity, sometimes the chase for human perfection could turn to a selfish pursuit of human glory, personal wealth, and especially political power.

In Machiavelli's view, a ruler's end justified his means. If a prince is successful, he is right. "Cruelties inflicted immediately to secure one's position are well inflicted (if one may speak well of ill)," he wrote.

To be feared is more important than being loved, the author claimed. As for honesty, a prince should keep his word as long as it's useful to do so.

Machiavelli's critics call him evil. His defenders say that he was telling it like it was, sharing what he learned as a Florentine official and diplomat. Machiavelli himself placed his work well within the framework of Christian humanism, as he understood it.

"God is not willing to do everything," he wrote, "and thus take away our free will and that share of glory, which belongs to us."

Writing for the Masses

With the spread of printing, language changed. Regional tongues such as French, English, and Italian took on a new vitality and authority. More and more writers began using these instead of Latin to write poetry and plays (see the "Who killed Latin?" sidebar). The old prejudice that educated people shouldn't write in the *vernacular* (common) language faded.

Even before the Renaissance, the poet Dante Alighieri (born in 1265) wrote his *Divine Comedy* and other works in Italian. London's Geoffrey Chaucer (born in 1343), who traveled in Italy and read works by Boccaccio, wrote in English.

Creating new classics

Writing in the vernacular really caught on as printers realized there was a commercial market for it. William Caxton, who brought printing to England, achieved a bestseller when he published Chaucer's comic *Canterbury Tales*.

Many of the new books written in everyday language, given time, proved just as *classic* as the old Latin and Greek books:

- Castigliano wrote *The Courtier* in Italian. (See "Stocking up on self-help books" earlier in this chapter.)
- François Rabelais, a physician and humanist, wrote controversial sixteenth-century satires in French.
- In the late sixteenth and early seventeenth centuries, William Shakespeare cranked out plays for the popular theater (and the popular press) in English.
- Shakespeare's contemporary, Miguel de Cervantes, wrote *The Adventures of Don Quixote* in Spanish.

Staging dramas with classical roots

Shakespeare brought Renaissance drama to its peak, but he built on a tradition that began in the late thirteenth century when the Italian Albertino Mussato began writing comedies in the style of Seneca, a Roman. In addition to *The Prince* and other work in political science, Machiavelli wrote stage comedies after the classical style. The most famous to survive is called *The Mandrake,* which he wrote in 1518.

Shakespeare's plays show how thoroughly the new scholarship permeated European society. Full of references to Greek and Roman gods, his plots were sometimes drawn from Roman plays and even, as with *Julius Caesar* and

Antony and Cleopatra, from Roman history. Even some of Shakespeare's plays set in his own time take place in Italian cities that gave rise to the Renaissance.

Packing Something to Read aboard Ship

Europe's growing literacy — rooted in a return to ancient classics and powered by the invention of printing — influenced matters much more down-to-earth than poems and plays. (See "Returning to Science," earlier in this chapter). The ancients also wrote serious books about geography and navigation, and they drew maps that preserved what Greek and Phoenician navigators learned about seas and landmasses. Greek and Phoenician navigators were the greatest travelers of their times. (See Chapter 4 for more about Phoenicians, their North African city Carthage, and its seafaring empire.) Europeans of the Renaissance read those books too.

Who killed Latin?

Latin is a dead language. But did you know that it lived long after the fall of the Roman Empire? Only when Renaissance scholars tried to *save* Latin did the language ossify into the sterile tongue it's been ever since.

Latin — the language of Rome, from everyday people to government, business, and scholarship — helped hold the Roman Empire together as long as it existed. And after the Rome-based western empire declined, Latin hung on in western Europe. (The eastern, Byzantine Empire spoke Greek.)

Educated people all over western Europe continued to communicate in Latin. All the courses and debates at medieval universities were conducted in Latin. The universality of Latin was really cool if you were a professor, because whether you were from Ireland or Italy, you could be just as much at home in a German classroom as a colleague from Cologne. That applied to students too. You didn't have to understand French to study in Paris.

As living languages do, Latin kept growing and changing. Grammatical uses shifted. Sentence structure became a little simpler here and a bit rougher there.

Then in the Renaissance, scholars began reading Latin from texts that were 1,500 years old and realized how different their Latin was from the language of the great Roman rhetorician, Cicero.

With their newfound appreciation of pre-Christian classics, these scholars saw Cicero's Latin as the original, uncorrupted language: the right stuff. So they worked hard on setting the clock back on their own scholarly language, making strict rules of grammar and usage and enforcing them as an important part of a *classical education.*

Schoolboys all over Christendom conjugated Latin verbs, which may have been a good tool for building disciplined young minds, but it was the beginning of the end for Latin. Losing its flexibility, Latin no longer lived, the way ever-changing English, for example, lives today.

It took centuries, but Latin eventually fell out of use, even in most areas of scholarship.

Fifteenth- and sixteenth-century advances in navigation and cartography (mapmaking), like other intellectual advances of the time, had their roots in the relevant Greek and Roman texts. Explorers such as Christopher Columbus and Vasco da Gama (more about them in Chapter 20) started with an atlas designed by the Egyptian-Greek astronomer Ptolemy (90 to 170 AD) and then radically redrew it. Their discoveries about the shape and size of the world went hand in hand with the theories of Copernicus (earlier in this chapter) and his heirs: Johannes Kepler and Galileo. (Both astronomers are in Chapter 14.)

Fighting for Power in Europe

All the cross-pollination of the Renaissance — with scholars and their ideas traveling from city to city, country to country — suggests a climate of political harmony throughout Europe. It wasn't that way. The Renaissance was a time of many borders and lots of political powers vying for dominance of one another.

Battling for control of Italian city-states

Italy, the heart of the Renaissance, was nothing like the modern nation it is now. Italy was a hodgepodge of city-states, kind of like ancient Greece had been (see Chapter 9).

Some of these city-states, such as intellectually rich Florence, were wealthy trade centers. Their rulers, people such as the Medicis (see "Florence in flower" earlier in this chapter), a family that got rich in banking, hired the sculptors, painters, architects, and writers that made their renaissance *the* Renaissance.

Italian rulers also competed with each other for influence and territory. Just as the bankers and traders who marked this age kept financial agents in other cities to look after their interests, so the rulers (some of them also bankers and traders) placed political agents to watch out for them in competing capitals. This is how modern diplomacy was born.

The Italian states also hired mercenary soldiers, or *condottieri*. Moving as a unit — a military leader and his men — provided armed support to anybody who paid. Some were foreigners. An Englishman, John Hawkwood, and his men, the White Company, were among the fiercest. Some mercenaries were lords of Italian cities themselves. The Montefeltro family, rulers of Urbino, financed their municipal budget by hiring out as *condottieri*.

In his book *The Prince*, Machiavelli argued that a successful ruler needs to use cleverness and trickery. Italian princes, overseeing a heady time, valued brainpower over brute strength. But sometimes they outsmarted themselves.

In 1494, Duke Ludovico Sforza of Milan invited the French to help him defeat Naples. Since the French king, Charles VIII, had a claim on the throne of Naples (these families intermarried and seldom agreed whose turn it was to rule), the French accepted.

The French army easily routed Naples' smaller force. But then Sforza and his Italian co-conspirators, including some from the island of Sicily, turned on their northern allies and forced the French to high-tail it over the Alps.

Boy, were those French angry. Sforza's trick humiliated them and the French wanted revenge. They also had a taste of Italian wealth, and they wanted that too. After Charles VIII died, Louis XII succeeded him. Charles was known as "the Affable." Nobody called Louis affable. Also believing that he had a claim on Milan's throne, the French king mounted another invasion force. This time, the target was Ludovico Sforza.

Milan was not ready. The French overwhelmed the city, captured Sforza and threw him in prison, where he died. He wasn't so clever after all.

Things got worse for Italy — a lot worse. Remember those Sicilians who helped Sforza drive the French away in 1494? Their king was Ferdinand, who also ruled Aragon, one of the largest kingdoms in Spain, which was coming together as a united land. (His wife and joint-ruler, Isabella, was queen of Castille. See Chapter 18 for more on them.) Ferdinand had a claim to Naples as well. And like the French, he had noticed how rich, and how politically divided, Italy was.

The Holy Roman Emperor, Maximilian, wanted in on this action. The Holy Roman Empire, as I note in other chapters, wasn't really Roman. It started out French, under Charlemagne, but for a long time it was mostly German and Austrian. Yet Maximilian had hereditary "Roman" claims on northern Italy. Since he and Ferdinand were inlaws (two of Max's kids were married to two of Ferdie's), the Emperor sided with Spain.

This meant war, actually a series of wars. Spaniards and Imperialists fought to get the French out of Italy. Various Italian states fought on one side, then the other.

Spilling outside of Italy's borders

The Italian Wars melded into more wars that spilled out into other parts of Europe (see Chapter 13). Charles I, becoming co-ruler of Spain in 1517 (along with his mother), won election as Emperor Charles V of the Holy Roman Empire two years later. This made the French nervous, because the Hapsburg Empire was now on either side of them.

The election of Charles was not democratic, by the way. Just as the Holy Roman Empire was not Roman, it wasn't really an empire either. The Holy Roman Empire was a conglomeration of states, some of which were practically kingdoms. The electors, powerful princes who enjoyed the hereditary right to choose each new emperor, ruled seven of them. They elected Charles.

Being picked by the electors wasn't always a vote of confidence. Sometimes they chose rulers that they thought they could manipulate. Charles, however, had considerable success taking charge. He wrested Milan away from his French rival, Francis I (successor to Louis VII). Charles' Spanish troops even took Francis prisoner. Charles got Naples, and the other Italian states knew not to mess with him.

Yet that didn't settle things. The Italian Wars melded into a long Hapsburg-versus-France enmity that lasted until the middle of the eighteenth century.

Before he retired to a Spanish monastery in 1556, the embattled Charles found it necessary to split his empire back into two parts — Spanish and Austrian — to make it less unwieldy and easier to defend. If this reminds you of something that the Roman emperors did more than a thousand years before Charles's time, good for you. If not, you can read about that in Chapter 4.

By the time Charles called it quits, other things in Europe had changed profoundly, partly as a result of the financial strains of prolonged wars. Taxes rose. Princes were forced to borrow money, enriching new generations of bankers — and sometimes bankrupting the bankers when the princes defaulted on loans. Then came this big thing called the Protestant Reformation. (I devote Chapter 13 to the Reformation.)

An irony of the Renaissance is that the place where it began, Italy, ended this era in such disarray and decline. While Spain, Portugal, England, Holland, and other powers were starting worldwide empires, becoming richer and more powerful, the once-mighty Italian city-states remained divided and dominated. Foreigners ruled several of them.

Renaissance buildings and sculptures, once symbols of a thriving, ahead-of-its-time movement, became tourist attractions, which they remain today. The symbols of a vital present and a promising future turned into artifacts of yet another glorious past.

Tracking the Centuries

1360s: Geoffrey Chaucer, an English diplomat and poet, travels to Italy and meets the writer Boccaccio.

1396: Coluccio Salutati, chancellor of Florence, invites Manuel Chrysoloras, a scholar from Constantinople, to teach Greek to Italian students eager to probe ancient writings.

About 1420: The artist Filippo Brunelleschi invents the *one-point* system for giving perspective, the illusion of depth, to paintings and drawings.

1453: Constantinople falls to the Ottoman Turks. Many scholars of the Byzantine Empire flee west to Italy.

About 1455: Johann Fust and his son-in-law Peter Schöffer publish the Gutenberg Bible, the first mass-produced book. Gutenberg, unable to repay a loan to backer Fust, had to surrender his revolutionary press.

About 1473: William Caxton returns to London from Cologne, where he learned "the German art" of printing, and goes into the publishing business with a book about the Trojan war and a volume of sayings of the ancient philosophers.

1519: Charles I of Spain wins election as Emperor Charles V of the Holy Roman Empire. The French, who are between Spain and the Holy Roman Empire, do not find this a reassuring development.

1528: In his book *The Courtier,* Count Baldassare Castiglione spells out rules for gentlemanly behavior. He says you should be good at everything, but you shouldn't look like you're trying too hard.

1543: Andreas Vesalius, anatomy professor at the University of Padua, publishes seven *Books on the Structure of the Human Body.*

1556: The Emperor Charles V of the Holy Roman Empire retires to a monastery in Spain.

1835: The Roman Catholic Church lifts its 219-year ban on Copernicus's book, *The Revolution of the Heavenly Spheres.*

Chapter 13

Making a Break: The Reformation

*S*tarting with a disagreement over faith and turning political almost immediately, the Protestant Reformation provoked war and even revolution. It rearranged Europe's power structure. In its wake, the Holy Roman Empire was nearly ruined. And Spain, that most unshakeable of Catholic countries (see Chapter 9), fell into decline.

In this chapter, I guide you through causes and effects of this religious revolution, which spread beyond Europe and eventually around the world.

Cracks in the Monopoly

To understand how the Reformation began, it helps to consider how ready some people were to turn on the Church — for reasons that often had little or nothing to do with the question of how to get into heaven. As in so many conflicts, the reasons included:

- **Money:** Many nobles (and commoners, too) thought that the Church had too much of it and demanded too much of theirs.

- **Land and other property:** Regional and national rulers thought the Church possessed and controlled too much of it.

- **Power and autonomy:** Local rulers, especially in Germany, wanted to wrest more control away from the Pope and the Holy Roman emperor.

Losing authority

How vulnerable for a shake-up was the Church in the early sixteenth century? In Chapter 12, I point out ways that Renaissance trends undercut the Church's authority.

For one, the pre-Christian authors (those ancient Greek and Greek-style philosophers that I keep harping about) became part of Christendom during the Renaissance. These classical authors were now seen as manifestations of God's glory, but their voices and views were diverse and contradictory. Where once there was one supreme source of wisdom — the Church — now wisdom came in a variety of flavors.

The Church even lost its monopoly on interpreting scripture. The first mass-produced book was the Bible and printers quickly saw how newly literate Europeans wanted to read in their own languages, instead of in Latin or Greek. Scholars started translating the Bible into *vernacular* (common) languages. Desiderius Erasmus, the most famous scholar of the time, was a prolific translator of scripture.

Satirizing the Church

Erasmus, who was from the Netherlands and lived in England, also wrote original works, saying things that many people agreed with but that few stated as eloquently. In 1509, he ridiculed silly, lazy, and incompetent churchmen in a popular satire called *The Praise of Folly*. Erasmus wasn't anti-church, but he thought the Church could be run better.

The Church was a huge, international bureaucracy with layers upon layers of officials. (Remember that virtually every Christian in Western Europe at this time — almost everybody — belonged to one church, the one based in Rome. That's why it was called *the Church* with a capital "C." The word *Catholic*, which means "universal," was part of its name, but there was no reason to say "Catholic," because there were no Protestants — yet.) Like bureaucrats anywhere, some Church officials were inefficient and lazy. Some were dishonest. Imagine how much worse your state's Department of Motor Vehicles would be if rude, slow clerks claimed divine authority. (What's that? They already do?)

People complained for centuries about this. There was a widespread feeling that churchmen had it too easy. Folks thought too many priests were hypocrites for telling the rest of society what to do while living in sin themselves. Erasmus knew about such resentment firsthand, because he started life in Rotterdam as the illegitimate son of a priest.

Some bishops — at a higher level of the priesthood, yet still sworn to celibacy — kept mistresses and then used Church influence to get advantages for their out-of-wedlock offspring. Even popes begot children. Pope

Alexander VI, who served from 1492 to 1503, had many mistresses and many kids. Even Pope Clement VII, who precipitated a separate branch of the Reformation in England by refusing to annul the marriage of King Henry VIII to Catherine of Aragon (coming up in this chapter), reportedly fathered a son.

Alexander, Clement, and Pope Leo X (who became pope in 1513 and was pope when the Reformation began four years later) were all privileged men from wealthy families who received cushy Church positions by virtue of their connections. Leo began life as Giovanni de Medici, of the powerful Medici family that controlled the city-state of Florence. Leo nearly wiped out the Vatican treasury with his extravagant lifestyle

Leo pampered himself with the Church's money, but he also spent it on Renaissance glories. He speeded up construction of St. Peter's Basilica in Rome, a landmark of the period's architecture, and he enlarged the Vatican library. But many Christians, especially in Northern Europe, were not impressed. They were tired of seeing their hard-earned coins carted off to Rome to pay for sculptures and painted ceilings. "What good do those things do us?" asked the Germans and the Swiss.

I don't want to give the impression that all priests (or monks, bishops, cardinals, and popes) were hypocritical or corrupt. Many, and probably most, led devout lives of worship, service to others, and self sacrifice. Those honest churchmen resented the bad reputation that followed their corrupt brothers, rubbing off on the Church at large. One of those was the German priest and university professor Martin Luther (more about him later in this chapter.) Church officials promised reforms, and some really tried to clean things up, but abuses persisted.

Erasmus wasn't the first to mock or criticize churchmen. John Wycliffe, an English priest and theologian, anticipated the Reformation by more than a century when, in the 1370s, he began attacking the worldliness of the Church, arguing for limited papal authority over government matters, and insisting that churchmen who fell into mortal sin must forfeit their authority. But Erasmus's international prominence (he was widely read), and the timing of *The Praise of Folly* directly paved the way for a widespread public criticism of Church abuses — one that followed his book by less than a decade. It's been said that Erasmus laid the egg, and Martin Luther hatched it.

Luther Challenges the System

Many of history's great changes can be traced to a visionary: who did what it took to make a dream come true. Martin Luther wasn't one of those. He didn't set out to trigger religious revolt, let alone unleash international tensions. But that's what he did.

Luther — a monk, priest, and theology professor at Wittenberg University — pondered the individual's relationship to God. His thoughts on that topic interacted with other forces building in Europe in the early sixteenth century, starting a movement that profoundly changed the world even beyond Europe and America (a continent most Europeans had not yet heard of when the Reformation began). Yet it all began with a rather small gesture — a one-man protest.

Luther possessed deep moral conviction, powerful faith, and incredibly stubborn resolve, but if he had known that he was going to split the Church six ways to Sunday, he might not have tacked his protest literature on the door of a Wittenberg church on **Oct. 31, 1517**.

What protest literature? It was called the Ninety-five Theses (which means 95 arguments) and was a list of Luther's objections to the way that Church leaders in his neck of Europe (Germany) sold indulgences, a kind of official forgiveness for sins.

Selling salvation

An indulgence was a grant of forgiveness, issued either to a living person or to someone who had died and whose soul was believed to be in purgatory (a sort of anteroom in which sinners must be cleansed before entering heaven).

You can think of an indulgence like this: Say you do a good deed. Your reward is that God doesn't make you suffer so much for your bad deeds, so you get into heaven a little easier. Now, say you *need* a good deed to earn this consideration. Doesn't giving the Church money count as a good deed?

But what if your brother died before he could build up his spiritual credits? Not a problem. You, his surviving relative, can give money to the church by purchasing an indulgence, then transfer your credit to bro, getting him off the hook in the afterlife.

Okay, so that's a simplistic explanation of the concept, which also involves a sort of bank account of godly merit, built up through the good works of Jesus and the saints. The important thing is that the practice of selling indulgences led to an impression among common people that they could buy an express, one-way ticket to heaven.

Peddling to pay the pope

Luther was ticked off in particular at a Dominican friar called Tetzel, who traveled around peddling indulgences. (The word *friar* meant "brother," and it was used for men who were members of certain religious orders, such as the Dominicans.)

Tetzel came into a village or city and gathered a crowd, much as a snake-oil salesman did in a frontier American town three centuries later. Imagine him hawking indulgences as if they were the latest things in patent medicines for your soul.

Why did he do it? Well, Tetzel was not, as it may seem, an entrepreneur. He was a deputy sent out by the newly appointed Archbishop of Mainz.

Another Church practice that bred widespread skepticism was this: Anybody appointed to a high ecclesiastical office, such as archbishop, had to pay fees to the pope as a sort of recompense for the appointment. In 1514, when this archbishop got his job, Pope Leo X was spending a lot of money in Rome — especially on the building of St. Peter's Basilica. Leo set a high fee.

The new Archbishop of Mainz lacked ready cash. So he borrowed from an Augsburg family called Fuggers. (No remarks, please.) Powerful banking families, another Renaissance phenomenon that started in Italy, had risen in northern Europe by this time. (The Welser family, also of Augsburg, was the other big banking force in Germany.)

Now the archbishop needed to repay the Fuggers. To help, the pope gave him an easy way to raise funds. He made the archbishop regional distributor for holy indulgences. Tetzel was the archbishop's shill.

Insisting on faith

If you wanted to rub Martin Luther the wrong way, you couldn't come up with a better method than mass-marketing indulgences. Luther, a theology teacher, for years had thought hard about the correct path to heaven. What did God expect of a Christian?

He decided that God was merciful. As Luther saw it, you must honestly believe. Belief, rather than good works, was the key. In some ways, Luther reflected the Renaissance philosophy of humanism (see Chapter 12). He saw a direct relationship between the individual mortal and God. But in other ways, Luther returned to St. Augustine's idea that good works on earth won't earn you entrance to heaven (see Chapter 11). You had to rely on God's grace.

Luther thought that a good Christian would do good works — go to church, pray, and be kind to others — as a result of belief, not as a way to escape punishment or win reward. How much you paid to an itinerant salesman monk didn't count at all toward eternal bliss.

In his theses, Luther condemned the indulgence campaign as exploitation, and he slammed the corrupt clerical bureaucracy. But he didn't mean to raise a call for mass rebellion. As a scholar, he observed a tradition that had grown up in the medieval universities. Professors argued points of religion — that's what they did.

Luther thought that Tetzel was wrong, so he challenged anybody who supported Tetzel to a debate. He did this on October 31, or All Hallows Evening (the night before November 1, All Souls Day), but this was no trick-or-treat prank. By pinning his theses to the door of the church, Luther issued a public challenge.

A Precarious Empire

Besides the writings of Erasmus and a general unhappiness with the Church, there were other reasons why Europe, and especially Germany, stood ready to erupt early in the sixteenth century. (Keep in mind that Germany wasn't really Germany yet; that wouldn't happen for centuries. It was the Holy Roman Empire, a messy conglomeration of semi-independent states where Germany and Austria are today.)

It had been a long time since the Holy Roman Empire embodied the vision held by the pope when he crowned Charlemagne Emperor of the West in 800 AD. The emperor was supposed to serve as the pope's partner and chief protector of the Church (see Chapters 5, 11, and 12.) But popes and emperors quarreled often and bitterly.

Searching for sources of cash

When Luther posted his theses, the emperor was Maximilian I, who ruled from 1493 to 1519. In Chapter 12, I discuss how Max hooked up with Spain to attack the French in Italy. A big reason for that excursion was that the emperor, like everybody else in this story, needed money.

Max enjoyed spending his dough on art. He also liked hunting, processions, flashy clothes, and armor — the perks of being the emperor. Beyond that, he had expensive plans to strengthen the empire. (Even money couldn't help him there, however, as long as the individual German princes, whose land made up the empire, held power in their own hands. They were getting stronger and turning their states into little nations.)

Max was so strapped for cash sometimes that he couldn't pay his soldiers, or *landsknechts*. This made it hard for him to keep an army. Sometimes the landsknechts hired themselves out as mercenary units, even to the emperor's enemies. Some even resorted to robbery and extortion.

Fighting crime and inflation

Times were hard for other Germans, too. With no strong national government to keep order, and with the line between knight and robber blurred, merchants had to pay protection money or hire their own muscle just to transport goods safely. The high cost of shipping contributed to inflation. Prices rose, not just in Germany, but all over Europe.

The situation was more complex than this (isn't everything?), but the inflation also was tied to an increase in population. In Chapters 6 and 12, I mention that a decrease in the number of people in Europe (caused by the bubonic plague) helped bring about the Renaissance, because plague survivors and their children had more material wealth to go around.

Good times bred more people, however, and by the sixteenth century, the population burgeoned. People needed work, food, clothing, and shelter, but now there wasn't enough for everybody. So things cost more, despite the fact that nobody had more money to pay. The price of a loaf of bread, for example, just about quadrupled between 1500 and 1600.

Cash-strapped landlords put the squeeze on peasants, to get more work for less. People were poor, overworked, overtaxed, hungry, and nervous.

Setting the stage for dissent

All of these factors help explain why Luther's protest became more than a theological discussion. People took the *Ninety-five Theses* as a rallying cry against the Church and its high-handedness. Some who agreed with the priest copied Luther's arguments, took them to printing shops, and sent copies all over Germany and beyond. Luther was suddenly famous.

Luther's action still wouldn't have had quite the impact it did, however, if rulers hadn't also been ready to challenge the Church. Some German princes were as edgy as their subjects were. They sought to limit the emperor's meddling in their kingdoms, and they were even more resistant to the pope sticking his nose where they thought it didn't belong.

Seven German princes called the *electors* got to choose the emperor (see Chapter 12). One of them — Frederick, Prince Elector of Saxony — backed Luther in the religious dispute that broke out after 1517. Frederick didn't necessarily agree with Luther, but since Frederick had founded the University of Wittenberg not many years before, he had a stake in protecting his faculty member, the overnight celebrity.

Standing Up to the Emperor

When Luther really needed a friend, Prince Freddie @ known as Frederick the Wise — came through for him. It happened shortly after the Emperor Charles V, who succeeded his grandfather Maximilian I in 1519, tried to make Luther change what he had said about indulgences and the Church.

Charles made his challenge in 1521 at the Diet of Worms (which wasn't nearly as disgusting as it sounds). In the Holy Roman Empire, the word *diet* had nothing to do with Jenny Craig. A *diet,* from the medieval Latin *dieta* (meaning "a day's work"), was an all-day meeting — a day in court, or in this case, the Imperial Assembly. The name *Worms* referred to a city, rather than a mess of tubular, dirt-dwelling animals. (Worms is on the Rhine River near Mannheim, Germany.) At the Diet of Worms, Emperor Charles V (who was also the king of Spain) met with the empire's princes and with churchmen, including Luther.

Although nobody asked him to ingest squirmy, legless invertebrates, Luther gagged anyway — at the suggestion he give ground.

Oh, he thought about it. When the emperor tells you to change your tune, you have to at least think about it. Luther turned it over and over before he came back the next morning with his answer.

Luther faced up to the emperor, the princes, and the bishops and said, "Here I stand. I can do no other. God help me. Amen."

At least, that's how the story goes. There's some doubt whether he ever really said that, but it's too good a quote to throw away (so here I quote it, I can do no other). Whether those were his exact words or not (and, come to think of it, he didn't even speak English), they sum up what Luther meant.

Here I sit

Martin Luther may not have eaten worms, but he probably could have used a change of diet. The reformer suffered from chronic constipation and is said to have done some of his best praying while in the squatting position.

This historical aside probably interests you only if you have an adolescent fascination with the scatological. It certainly doesn't sound like a worthy subject for a movie. Yet in the 1973 bomb *Luther,* star Stacy Keach strains to make it work.

The story doesn't limit itself to Luther's irregularity, but neither does it do a good job of dramatizing his struggle. The script is adapted from a 1960s play by Britain's original "angry young man," John Osborne, who also wrote *Look Back in Anger* and *The Entertainer.* For this one, the creative pipeline got plugged up on the way to the screen.

Gaining a Following

Martin Luther, now an outlaw, headed home to Wittenberg to prepare for his arrest and a probable death sentence. But on the way, he disappeared. It turned out that Prince Frederick's men kidnapped him. The prince elector locked Luther up for his own protection.

In the castle of Wartburg, Prince Freddy gave Luther a study where he could work. And work he did. Instead of taking back his theses, he noisily attacked other beliefs of the church. Realizing the power of the printing press, Luther published his ideas — among them his claims that priests were not the big deal they thought they were. You could get into heaven without one, Luther said. It was *cut-out-the-middle-man* spirituality. Luther said that Christians should read the Bible for themselves. He translated his own user-friendly German version. He wrote both words and music for hymns such as "A Mighty Fortress is Our God" — the theme song of the Reformation.

A pamphlet he published in 1520, *To the Christian Nobility of the German Nations* — addressing the ruling class of the Holy Roman Empire — was especially popular. Some nobles, scholars, and other people who agreed with Luther's writings began to think of themselves as his followers. Just a few years after the Ninety-Five Theses, some Christians began to call themselves "Lutherans."

The princes, especially the less devout among them, tended to like Luther's argument that they had a duty to put the Church back in its place. In those times of inflation, a reasoned excuse for confiscating the Church's wealth appealed to free-spending aristocrats.

If a powerful noble or merchant became a Lutheran, it often meant that his followers, people who depended on him for their livings, became Lutheran too — by persuasion or coercion.

Losing control

Anti-Church sentiment, once unleashed, flew out of control. A bunch of knights attacked the Archbishop of Trier in 1522, trying to oust him in the name of Luther. (Luther had nothing to do with it.) Other discontents, former Catholic priests and self-appointed preachers, used Luther's rebellion as a jumping-off point, a cue that let them spread radical ideas far beyond Luther's. They said nobles and the rich should embrace the poor and share the wealth. Luther was *much* too conservative to have taught such a thing. There was so much pent-up discontent that the extreme ideas took hold and spread.

Unrest turned to violence in 1524 as the Peasants' War ripped through central and southwestern Germany and into Austria. "Hey," said Luther. "This wasn't supposed to happen." (My own loose translation.) He thought people who twisted his teachings were even more wicked than churchmen who sold indulgences. He wrote a scathing pamphlet with the title *Against the Murdering, Thieving Hordes of the Peasants.*

Luther urged the princes to crush the rebels. The princes complied (as they would have without Luther's encouragement). Here was some work for those soldier-for-hire landsknechts. Thousands of peasants died in battle, with more captured and put to death.

Choosing sides

After the Peasants' War nastiness was settled, the princes tried to sort out what to do about Lutheranism. Several sided with Luther. After all, he had sided with them. More to the point, Lutheranism offered freedom to rule with less interference from Emperor Charles and none from the pope. Some Lutheran partisans formally broke religious ties with Rome and set up their own Lutheran churches. Other princes stuck with Rome. They tried to force the Lutheran princes to change their minds.

This was when the Lutheran rulers got to be known as *Protestants,* because they protested their peers' attempts to force them back into the old Church. In 1531, they formed a mutual protection alliance, the *Schmalkald League.* Their relations with Paul III (who became pope in 1534) and Emperor Charles further deteriorated.

The Empire Strikes Back

Charles V's resources were strained, for reasons I discuss in Chapter 12. He was fighting in Italy and taking care of his lands in Spain. He had a major rivalry with the French. He didn't want to fight the Protestant princes. He wanted to settle the issue with diplomacy.

Finally despairing of that option, the emperor marched an army into Germany in 1546, the same year Luther died. Thus began the first of the Religious Wars of the sixteenth century.

Savoring a bitter victory

In 1547, at the Battle of Mühlberg, Charles walloped the Lutherans. Yet Protestants wouldn't get behind him. In the Treaty of Passeau, ending the war in 1552, Charles offered to make changes in the Catholic Church if they would support him. (Pope Paul III was actually working on reforms, the Counter-Reformation.) The Protestants stood fast.

Even more frustrating for the emperor: Some princes who had been loyal to him during the war started to worry that, with the Protestants defeated, he was getting too powerful. They turned on him and drove him out of Germany.

Achieving compromise

Finally, Charles had little choice but to recognize Protestantism. The *Religious Peace of Augsburg* said that each prince in the empire could decide what would be the official church in his own kingdom or duchy. The princes and the emperor signed it in 1555. The Augsburg agreement was not a move toward a stronger or more united empire — quite the opposite. But it kept the confederation from falling completely apart.

However, religious war in the Holy Roman Empire was not over. It would erupt again in the next century with the Thirty Years' War. (See the section on Calvinism and its aftermath, later in this chapter.)

Spreading Across Europe

Kings outside Germany reformed their churches, too. Lutheranism spread into the Scandinavian countries. Variants took hold throughout Northern Europe. Ultimately, the Reformation didn't create just one new church; it created many (see Chapter 9).

As in Germany, some rulers agreed with Luther's religious convictions, while others saw the growing Reformation as a great excuse to confiscate church wealth. The king of England was one who certainly did not agree with Luther, yet he was strong-willed and took opportunities as he found them.

The Church of England

England was primed for religious reform, although perhaps not in the same way Germany had been. Papal taxes stirred widespread resentment. The dissident priest John Wycliffe (earlier in this chapter) had set the stage, even winning the support of England's royal family with his arguments about Church abuses in the fourteenth century. Wycliffe also organized the first English translation of the Bible. Desiderius Erasmus, (also earlier in this chapter) author of the satire on Church abuses, *The Praise of Folly,* lived in England in the early sixteenth century.

But after the Reformation had begun, especially once it turned violent, Erasmus rejected it. He wanted orderly reform, not revolution. Erasmus's friend Sir Thomas More represented King Henry VIII in Parliamentary arguments against Lutheranism in 1523.

Henry VIII's call for divorce

England's king, Henry VIII, was vociferously anti-Luther. Henry issued writings condemning the German rebel priest. A grateful Pope Leo X rewarded Henry with the title Defender of the Faith.

Relations between Rome and London soured, however, when Henry decided that he needed to dump his wife, Catherine of Aragon, shown in Figure 13-1. Note that she was "of Aragon," and a daughter of Ferdinand and Isabella, the Catholic monarchs whose marriage united a large chunk of Spain (see Chapter 18).

Figure 13-1:
To be rid of wife Catherine of Aragon, Henry VIII cut England's ties with the pope.

© Bettmann/CORBIS

Catherine was also the aunt of Charles V, who was both Holy Roman Emperor and (as Charles I) king of Spain. All these circumstances gave her a certain pull with the pope.

Henry had gotten engaged to Catherine when he was only 11; she was already the widow of his elder brother, Arthur. She had borne Henry five children, but only one — a daughter, Mary — had survived. Henry wanted a son to be his heir.

Until Arthur died, Henry wasn't the crown prince. He'd actually been educated to become a churchman — maybe an archbishop. So he knew a bit about religious law. And he thought that he knew a lot. He decided his lack of a son was God's punishment for having married his brother's widow. He presented that as reason enough for the pope to rule that his marriage to Catherine had never been proper to begin with. Under Church rules, annulment was the only path to legal divorce.

Leo's successor, Pope Clement VII, wasn't buying it. Maybe the Emperor Charles, Catherine's nephew, carried more weight in Rome than Henry did. Or maybe Leo knew Henry's *other* reason for wanting a divorce: Anne Boleyn, the king's mistress.

A frustrated monarch

Henry's *chancellor*, or chief advisor, was a churchman, Cardinal Thomas Wolsey, formerly Archbishop of York. Wolsey had aspirations to be pope, so he supposedly knew his way around Church politics.

Henry gave Wolsey the specific job of getting Pope Clement to give in on the divorce question, so that Henry could make Anne his queen.

When Wolsey failed, the king impeached him and seized his property. Henry exiled Wolsey and then decided to execute him, but Wolsey died in 1530, before the king could get him back to the chopping block in London.

Henry tried to hit the pope in the pocketbook. He arranged for Parliament to pass laws cutting English fees and offerings paid to Rome. Actually, one of his advisors, a fellow called Thomas Cromwell, came up with this clever idea. If Parliament cut the payments, Cromwell told the king, Henry could pin the blame on the members.

Clement still didn't budge, so in 1533, Henry married Anne Boleyn anyway. He had an old buddy, Thomas Cranmer, Archbishop of Canterbury, perform the ceremony. (What was Cranmer going to do? Say no to the king? You could lose your head for that.)

Catherine, having never seen the movie *The First Wives Club,* lived out her days quietly in a convent. She died in 1536. Clement hadn't given permission to the king to marry again and, when the deal was done, he didn't offer forgiveness. Paul III, who became pope in 1534, excommunicated the king of England.

Breaking ties with Rome

Henry made a big move, telling Parliament in **1534** to declare the king Supreme Head of the Church in England. With that, England — like the duchies of those Protestant German princes Henry so eloquently disagreed with — broke away from Rome. Henry still said he wasn't siding with the

Lutherans. If he found a Lutheran in England, he dutifully ordered the heretic burned at the stake. He wasn't changing religions, said Henry, just correcting the pope's boo-boo.

He did add a few Protestant touches to the Church of England, however. For example, he had English translations of the Bible installed in the churches. It was an English church now, after all.

Paying the penalty for disloyalty

Henry also had no mercy for Catholics. Never mind that he had been one until recently. Disloyalty would not be tolerated.

Anybody still loyal to Rome was beheaded or *drawn and quartered*. (Drawing and quartering was a gruesome form of dismemberment practiced on living individuals.) Remember Erasmus's friend Sir Thomas More, who helped the king attack Protestantism? More, a churchman who became chancellor in Wolsey's place, refused to swear obedience to the king's church. Henry ordered More decapitated.

Only one English bishop, John Fisher of Rochester, publicly opposed the new church. Henry had Fisher killed, too. Is there any wonder more people didn't speak up?

The king did stir opposition with his next step. On the advice of More's replacement, the crafty Thomas Cromwell, the king confiscated all the monasteries and convents.

I wouldn't want the job as Henry's chancellor, would you? Not after the last two received death sentences for crossing the boss. But apparently Cromwell was smart enough to hold his own. And Henry liked the way he thought.

Staging (then filming) a crisis of conscience

Faith and conscience prevented Sir Thomas More from endorsing Henry VIII's supremacy over the Church of England. To renounce the pope's supremacy, More believed, would be wrong in the eyes of God. More wouldn't give in to save his life.

His dramatic, tragic standoff with Henry inspired playwright Robert Bolt's stage play *A Man for All Seasons*. Director Fred Zinnemann adapted it for a 1966 movie, starring Paul Scofield as More, Robert Shaw as Henry, Leo McKern (TV's

Rumpole of the Bailey) as Thomas Cromwell, and Orson Welles, who steals the show in his cameo as Cardinal Wolsey.

Sincere to a fault, the movie doesn't quite do justice to the story, or to Bolt's play. You can find Zinnemann's *A Man for All Seasons* on video. You may also run across Charlton Heston's admirable, remade-for-TV *Man for All Seasons* from the late 1980s. But seeing a well-acted stage revival of the play is the best way to enjoy this stimulating moral drama.

Cromwell pointed out to Henry that he could present the confiscation of Church property as a reform measure. Those monks and friars and nuns weren't doing their jobs, so out they go. What Henry really wanted was the monastery lands and treasures — centuries' worth of offerings that pilgrims had given the monks.

What happened to the monasteries and convents and their lands? Henry sold most of them because he suddenly needed a lot of money. In Chapter 12, I mention that Charles V and Francis I of France were always fighting. When the two of them made peace and started acting threateningly toward England, Henry decided to boost defense spending.

Nobles bought the former abbeys and priories and turned them into private estates. Now, as any tourist can tell you, they're some of the stateliest (or at least the oldest) among the stately homes of England.

Making the Pilgrimage of Grace

Up in northern England, especially Yorkshire, some people came to the defense of the monks. They thought Henry was taking too much power for himself, so in 1536, they marched south. Called the *Pilgrimage of Grace,* it must have looked more like an invasion force.

Astoundingly, Henry was able to talk these armed marchers into going home. He blamed all the problems on Cromwell. Then he ordered his guards to overtake the homeward-bound Yorkshire rebels and kill as many of them as they could in the ugliest, most conspicuous ways possible. He ordered pieces of their hacked-apart bodies set out in all the towns where the rebels had lived, to serve as warnings to anybody else who might think about marching on the king.

Realizing Henry's legacy

The Catholic Defender of the Faith had made England a capital of Protestantism, although there would be turmoil over this issue for many decades to come. And what did Henry get for it?

Well, he did get to marry Anne Boleyn, but she never gave him the son he wanted (only another daughter, who turned out to be Queen Elizabeth I). Henry had Anne beheaded and went on to four more wives, only one of which, Jane Seymour, gave him a son, the sickly Edward VI.

Edward ruled for only a few years. As a devout Protestant, he brought some Reformation ideas into the English Church but they were largely erased by his half-sister and successor, Mary (Catherine's daughter), who re-instituted Catholicism during her brief reign in the 1550s. It took Henry's other daughter, Elizabeth — one of England's greatest monarchs — to bring back the Church of England and make it stick. Wouldn't her daddy have been proud?

Along Comes Calvin

Luther wasn't the last word in church reformers. Also in the sixteenth century, a young fellow from France moved to Switzerland and shared Protestant teachings that resulted in widespread changes. His name was John Calvin.

Reforming the Swiss church

The Reformation in Switzerland started about the same time it did in Germany, and in much the same way. A priest named Huldreich Zwingli opposed the selling of indulgences in 1518.

As in Germany, fighting broke out over the reform movement. Zwingli, unlike Luther, was in the thick of it; he died in battle near Kappel, Switzerland in 1531. Like the Holy Roman Empire, Switzerland was a confederation of smaller states (the Swiss called them *cantons*). It became another area where Protestantism won official recognition, meaning that the rulers of the cantons were allowed to decide which brand of Christianity to follow.

Establishing Puritanism

Calvin was a brilliant classics scholar at the University of Paris when the Reformation began. He was steeped in Greek and Roman philosophy as well as Christian theology. (Those Greeks keep popping up, don't they?) His thinking reached back to St. Augustine's Christian version of Platonic thought, built on the idea that humanity is a false and corrupt shadow of God's perfect Idea. Like Augustine, he thought people are bad and have been so ever since Adam and Eve sinned.

But Calvin agreed with Luther that God is merciful. Instead of condemning everybody to Hell, God chooses to save some.

This type of thinking put Calvin at odds with his peers in France. University scholars in Paris had no patience for Reformation ideas, so Calvin left and headed for Switzerland. Before long, he got an invitation to teach reform theology in Geneva. His ideas became the basis of what's called *Calvinism* or *Puritanism.* Calvin set them down in an influential 1536 book called *Institutes of the Christian Religion.*

Calvin went much farther than Luther in embracing predestination. Although Calvin supported Luther's idea that good works alone cannot win salvation, he dissented regarding the importance of faith in securing a place in heaven. Calvin thought that God decided each person's salvation or damnation at the beginning of creation. Nothing you do or believe influences whether you will be saved or damned.

But predestination did not mean that you could do anything you wanted, according to Calvin. In fact, Calvin taught that in order to live a godly life, you must be vigilant and strict. It wasn't to win God's favor or reap a reward. Calvin's God did not bargain. But if you believed, you had the opportunity and obligation to act on that belief.

His followers had to watch for every sort of sin, and they had to be ready to cast the unworthy out of their church. Geneva, once a wide-open party town, became a place where you could be punished for singing a dirty song or even wearing clothes that were too colorful.

If you crossed the Reformed church, you could be exiled or tortured to death. The Puritans disapproved of feasts. They banned dancing. They thought the theater sinful. They believed in hard work, thrift, and honesty. By exercising these values, some Calvinists became wealthy.

Calvin's ideas were so strict that more liberal Genevans initially resisted and even threw him out of town. But Calvin returned, and by the time he died in 1564, Geneva was considered Calvin's town, a Puritan town. His critics called him "the Pope of Geneva."

Puritanism soon became influential in other parts of the world as well, as the following sections illustrate.

Causing turmoil in France

Because Calvin came from France, it seems right that his teachings returned there. Ministers from Geneva spread the word, but as had happened in the Holy Roman Empire and in Switzerland, some French nobles broke with Catholicism for reasons that were more political than religious. They clashed with Catholic rivals. The conflict erupted into armed violence in 1562, with intermittent fighting taking the form of nine separate French Wars of Religion over the next 36 years.

The French royal family saw the French Calvinists, or *Huguenots*, as a threat. The Huguenots suffered severe persecution. King Henry II, who came to power in 1547, wanted to kill every Protestant in France and the Netherlands. His sons Charles IV and Henry III continued this policy. Before he became king, Henry III was among the soldiers who slaughtered 50,000 Huguenots at the Massacre of St. Bartholomew in 1572.

It wasn't until Henry IV gained France's throne in 1598 that the country settled down. Henry IV had been a Calvinist, but he had to become Catholic before he could rule. He still liked the Huguenots, however, and he gave them forts where they could fend off attacks.

Sparking rebellion in Holland

Calvinism caught on in the northern Netherlands, called Holland. This did not sit well with the king of Spain, Phillip II, who also ruled that country (inherited from his dad, Holy Roman Emperor Charles V).

While the southern Netherlands remained Catholic and Spanish, the Calvinist north broke free in 1608, becoming the United Provinces.

The Calvinist teachings of hard work and thrift helped push the Dutch to successes in navigation and trade. They excelled as merchants and colonists through the seventeenth century.

Weakening the Holy Roman Empire

By 1618, both Protestantism and Catholicism had changed. Militant Calvinism infused the Lutheran movement. Catholicism, through a reform movement called the Counter-Reformation, had managed to reinvigorate itself.

Catholics and Protestants clashed again in the last big religious war of the Reformation, the Thirty Years' War. It broke out after the Protestants in Bohemia tried to appoint a Protestant king in place of the Catholic emperor of the Holy Roman Empire.

Emperor Mathias sent forces to oppose the Bohemian Protestants. German Catholic states waded in behind the empire. Protestant states backed the Bohemians. Spain, still ruled by Hapsburg cousins of the emperor, sent soldiers to help him, and the Catholics got the upper hand.

But then in marched the Swedes on the Protestant side, commanded by King Gustavus Adolphus. The Protestants were on top now, until Gustavus died in battle. Then the Catholics were poised for victory — except that one more country was about to enter the war.

It was Catholic France. Did this mean the end for the Protestants? Well, not exactly. You see, France under Louis XIII and his top government minister Cardinal Richelieu (that's right, a high official of the Roman Catholic Church) got into this conflict on the *Protestant* side.

Richelieu's interest was France's security. He mobilized against the Hapsburg family — rulers of the Holy Roman Empire and Spain — to keep them from getting too powerful. (See how "religious" this war was?)

French troops helped secure the Peace of Westphalia, ending the war in 1648. Germany, after decades of fighting, was an economic wreck. Spain was bankrupt. Fighting the Reformation sent it into a long decline.

In retrospect, everybody may have done much better to let the Bohemians have their Protestant king.

Embattling England

As Calvinist teachings caught on in England, some people there wanted to make Puritanism part of the Church of England. This movement eventually led to the English Civil War in 1642, the execution of King Charles I, and the establishment of the *Protectorate* — a government of the Puritans and by the Puritans (see Chapter 7).

Spreading to Scotland

John Knox, born in Scotland in 1523, was a Catholic priest who became a Lutheran and, during the time that he spent in Geneva, came under Calvin's influence.

Knox founded the Church of Scotland in 1560. The Scottish Calvinists, called *Presbyterians,* organized their worship and religious authority after the Swiss model, but they faced a powerful critic in King James VI. He hated Puritanism and installed bishops in the Scottish church. James VI became King James I of England in 1603, and thus the head of the Church of England (see Chapter 18).

Emigrating to America

The Pilgrims who came from England to North America aboard the Mayflower, landing at Cape Cod Bay, Massachusetts in **1620**, were strict Puritans, seeking the freedom to observe their Calvinist beliefs.

Considered founders of American society, their highly moralistic brand of Christianity — not unlike the rigorous Calvinism practiced in Calvin's Geneva (earlier in this chapter) — shaped social attitudes and civil policy for centuries.

New England Puritans earned notoriety for labeling certain women as witches and persecuting and killing them. This practice wasn't exclusive to America or Puritans or even Protestants. Catholics burned witches through medieval times. The judgmental strictures of Calvinism, however, tended to encourage this kind of thing. Scottish Presbyterians were also especially strident in their witch hunts.

Tracking the Centuries

1509: Desiderius Erasmus publishes his satire on Church corruption, *The Praise of Folly.*

October 31, 1517: Martin Luther nails his Ninety-five Theses, a protest against Church abuses, to a church door in Wittenberg, Saxony.

1524: The Peasants' War, a rebellion of the poor against nobles, rips through central and southwestern Germany and into Austria.

1534: The English Parliament, at the order of Henry VIII, declares the king Supreme Head of the Church in England, superceding the authority of the pope.

1536: French-Swiss religious leader John Calvin publishes his influential book *Institutes of the Christian Religion,* setting down the tenets of Calvinism.

1555: The Religious Peace of Augsburg grants each prince in the Holy Roman Empire the right to decide the official church affiliation of his own kingdom or duchy.

1572: The future King Henry III of France is among soldiers who slaughter 50,000 Huguenots (French Protestants) at the Massacre of St. Bartholomew in 1572.

1608: The Protestant northern region of the Netherlands (Holland) breaks free of Catholic Spanish rule and becomes the United Provinces.

1620: English Puritans, seeking religious freedom, arrive in Massachusetts.

1648: The Peace of Westphalia ends the Thirty Years War.

Chapter 14

Opening Up to Science and Enlightenment

Science and engineering shape everything in today's society — not just super-fast computers and global positioning screens in cars. I mean everything. For centuries, human beings have used scientific inquiry, method, and invention to remake the world.

Every scientific advance traces back to an idea. Yet because so much of science's incredible yield is right here where you can touch it, use it, and curse at it (especially when your computer crashes), how all this hardware and software owes its distant origins to philosophers is easy to overlook. Just as easy to forget: How philosophy owes huge areas of modern thought to science.

Mingling Science and Philosophy

The electric light you use to read and the computerized publishing process that produced this book are obvious examples of how science touches you. But so is your shirt. It may be made of a synthetic fiber, a product of chemistry. Even if it's made of a natural fiber such as cotton, consider that the fiber comes from a plant that was almost certainly grown by scientific methods and harvested with machines powered by internal combustion engines — more science and engineering. Then the fabric was woven mechanically, on electric-powered looms and probably colored with chemical dye. Yet more science.

What you eat, how you travel, what you do for a living, and the way you spend your leisure time — are almost certainly all marked in some way by scientific discoveries and inventions, new and old.

Where did all this inventiveness come from — besides the marvelous human mind? Modern scientific and engineering creativity grew from a tradition that traces back to the ancient Greek philosophers, a tradition of asking questions about the world and how it works. (See Chapter 10 for more about the Greek philosophers and the beginnings of science.)

Things really got cooking when the Renaissance (see Chapter 12), an economic and intellectual movement that reached back to Greek and Roman scholarship, brought forth a Scientific Revolution in the seventeenth century. That led to the Industrial Revolution in the eighteenth century. Discoveries and inventions — and the habits of thought they inspire — have been revolving madly ever since. Science shaped technology, which shaped industry, which shaped economies, which shaped society at large.

The Scientific Revolution, born of philosophy, also brought forth new ways of thinking. Rationalism and empiricism, influential ways of looking at the world, came out of scientific perspectives. The Enlightenment of the eighteenth century, also called the Age of Reason, had its roots in science. Ideas given birth during this age fueled the American and French revolutions (find more on revolutions in Chapter 8).

The scientific and engineering applications that created the Industrial Revolution changed the way people made their livings, bringing hardship to many and fantastic rewards for a canny (or lucky) few. Social changes — child labor, slums, and newly wealthy industrialists — influenced philosophy and inspired the new field of economics.

Starting a Scientific Revolution

From a sharpened stick to a campfire to those flaked stone blades that early humans taught themselves to make, all the way up to silicon chip microcircuits, humans have this drive to come up with useful tools. (Find out about early human advances in Chapter 2.) So even without the Greek philosophers and their followers, people may have devised some of the modern wonders you take for granted every day.

But as it happened, Renaissance scholars — European guys steeped in old Greek ideas — were the ones who kick-started scientific inquiry and headed humanity toward this modern, scientific world.

Gazing at the heavens: Astronomy

Among the most influential scientists were astronomers.

The Renaissance spirit (see Chapter 12), as embodied in Poland's Copernicus, brought about new theories concerning the Earth's place in relation to the sun and planets. Copernicus's theories challenged the medieval beliefs (founded on the work of Aristotle and the Greek-Egyptian astronomer Ptolemy) that Earth was the center of the universe and that the stars were eternal and fixed in place.

Brahe sees a comet

Other philosophers around this time were carefully noting the night sky. A Dane (born in what was then Danish Sweden) named Tycho Brahe (1546 to 1501) pioneered modern astronomy, even though he had no telescope, by painstaking measurements and multiple observations.

Brahe was from a noble family, and he won the sponsorship of the Danish crown, including an island, Hven, and money to build his observatory there. Brahe had the wealth, the instruments (such as navigator's sextants for measuring the positions of stars), and the staff to explore the skies as nobody before him had ever done.

Among his discoveries, he realized in 1572 that a nova, or exploding star, was farther away than the planets. As something new in the sky, the nova wasn't supposed to be among the stars, because the stars were considered eternal. Later, in 1577, he realized that a comet was farther away than the moon. This, too, upset conventional assumptions about how the sky was arranged. The comet's distance and movement especially clashed with a long-held idea about transparent spheres that supposedly carried the planets around the earth.

Brahe was daring enough to conclude that if the comet could move through them, perhaps the spheres did not exist. Perhaps the planets moved independently. This began astronomy's shift from geometry (tracing the curves and relationships of the spheres) to physics (trying to understand the motion of independent heavenly bodies).

Brahe could not embrace one daring idea of Copernicus's — that the earth moves. Besides overturning Aristotle's cosmology, a moving earth challenged the Lutheran Brahe's religious sensibility.

Brahe fell back on an old proof for a fixed, immobile earth: If you shoot an arrow straight up on a windless day, it falls straight down, landing at the spot where you fired it. If the Earth spun, Brahe and many others thought, the arrow would land at a different place because the Earth would have revolved under it. (This was about a century before Isaac Newton, coming up later in this chapter, figured out a thing or two about how gravity works.)

Further, Brahe couldn't detect the *parallax,* a movement in the positions of the stars, that would show him that the ground from which he observed them was a moving platform. The idea that they were so far away that his instruments couldn't detect this movement made no sense to him. The entire universe, he thought, was only about 14,000 times as large as Earth.

All of these things illustrate how difficult sloughing off old prejudices was for science. Even Tycho Brahe, a starwatcher from the time he was a teenager, the guy with the best instruments and the best information yet gathered, couldn't get past some of his essentially non-scientific ideas about how the universe must work.

Kepler charts planets

After Brahe died, his assistant and scientific heir, the German Johannes Kepler (1571 to 1630), took Brahe's copious data and applied it to support Copernicus's theories.

Kepler — who couldn't see well and had limited use of his hands (both the result of severe smallpox when he was a toddler) — nonetheless came up with laws of planetary motion that are the basis for study of the solar system since his time. The first of these laws is something you probably ran across in elementary school: Each planet travels an elliptical orbit with the sun at one focus.

Galileo's telescope

Meanwhile, an Italian math teacher, Galileo Galilei (1564 to 1642), came up with a fresh and exciting way to check out the stars by using cutting-edge technology. Only recently developed and considered a tool for gathering military intelligence, the telescope turned out to work even better for expanding scientific intelligence.

Galileo (best known by his first name) saw heavenly visions nobody saw before. He saw mountains on the moon and that Jupiter had moons of its own. In 1610, Galileo reported his findings in a book, *Sidereal Messenger* (*sidereal,* from a Latin word for star, means "pertaining to constellations or stars").

Galileo also saw, as nobody could before him, just how right Copernicus was. Many heavenly bodies clearly did not orbit the earth.

He published these findings in 1632, a move that got him in trouble with Church authorities. Rome's branch of the Inquisition — not as notorious as the Spanish Inquisition (covered in Chapter 9), but also fiercely conservative — forced him to recant and sentenced the then-69-year-old Galileo to live the rest of his life under house arrest.

Galileo, in true Renaissance fashion (find more on the Renaissance in Chapter 12), was much more than an astronomer. He was also an artist, musician, engineer, and mathematician.

Galileo's work in physics paved the way for England's brilliant Isaac Newton, born the year Galileo died. Perhaps the best-known physical principle that Galileo established is that weight does not determine the rate at which an object falls. In other words, if you discount factors such as wind resistance, a bowling ball and a soccer ball fall at the same speed. Legend says Galileo established this principle by dropping balls off the Leaning Tower of Pisa, but that's not so. His experiment involved timing balls of equal size but unequal weights rolling down an incline. Galileo approached his work with careful observation, experimentation, and mathematics. In his wake, science came to depend increasingly on unbiased inquiry. That is, you tried to come at a question without prejudice, to base any conclusion on hard evidence or a solid mathematical model.

Advancing scientific method

All kinds of discoveries came from people following Galileo's example — in physics, mathematics, anatomy, astronomy, and more.

An English nobleman, statesman, and philosopher, Francis Bacon (1561 to 1626) did a good job of putting his ideas into words. He argued in favor of *induction* — working from observed or demonstrated specifics to a general principal. Bacon's certainty that nature could be understood and even controlled became the orthodoxy of *natural philosophy.*

Another Englishman, the genius physicist and mathematician Isaac Newton came along a bit later (he lived from 1642 to 1727). Newton is also cited as establishing scientific method, although he's more famous for establishing things such as the Law of Gravity (a legend started by his niece says an apple falling from a tree inspired him), among other useful physical laws. He also invented calculus.

Newton applied his work with gravity to Kepler's laws of planetary motion. All the fellows mentioned in this chapter built on each other's work. Although the Internet didn't exist back then, the printing press (see Chapter 12) made keeping up with one another much easier for scholars. Among many advances from this time:

- England's **William Harvey** (1678 to 1757): a Renaissance man who studied at Padua, Italy, discovered the circulation of the blood.

- **Carl Linne** (1707 to 1778): known by his Latin name, Linnaeus, classified the plant and animal kingdoms for the first time.

- **Robert Bakewell** (1725 to 1795): explored scientific methods for breeding bigger, stronger farm animals.

Waking Up to the Enlightenment

In "Rules of Reasoning in Philosophy," an essay included in his 1687 book *Principia,* Newton wrote:

> We are to admit no more causes of natural things than such as are both true and sufficient to explain their appearances.

This approach toward exploring the world — objectively, without prejudice — was also a foundation for a branch of philosophy called *empiricism,* the idea that knowledge is based on experience, derived from the senses.

Along with rationalism, a contrasting way of seeking truth based in inherent reason rather than experience, empiricism signaled more than a growing openness to new ideas. These and related philosophies, together called the Enlightenment, rearranged conventional thinking, then politics and government, in earthshaking ways.

Experiencing empiricism

John Locke (1602 to 1704), an English medical doctor and philosopher, introduced empiricism in his 1689 *Essay Concerning Human Understanding*. He and his empiricist heirs — among them the Scotsman David Hume (1711 to 1776) — took the natural sciences as their model for all knowledge.

Locke's work was tremendously important to philosophy, but he had just as big an influence on political thought, especially with his idea that authority derives solely from the consent of the governed.

If you contrast that with older notions about the divine right of kings (see Chapter 7), you can see how Locke's idea led to political upheaval. Locke's work influenced the men who set the American Revolution in motion. Some French guys that you can read about in just a few paragraphs were on a similar wavelength.

Living a "nasty, brutish, short" life

Not every philosophy rooted in scientific thinking seemed pointed toward popular revolt. Thomas Hobbes (1588 to 1679) was an Englishman who took an intellectual route from mathematics to political theory, a path that led him to advocate absolute monarchy.

The Oxford-educated, well-traveled Hobbes became interested, rather late in life, in why people allowed themselves to be ruled and in what would be the best government. In 1651, he wrote his famous work *Leviathan*. (Although the word means "sea monster" and sometimes refers to a whale, Hobbes applied it to the powerful state, or commonwealth.)

Hobbes argued that each person is self-interested and thus the people collectively cannot be trusted to govern society. Perhaps the most often quoted thing he wrote was a description of what human life was, or would be, without strong authority to keep everybody in line:

> During the time men live without a common power to keep them all in awe, they are in that condition called war . . . as if of every man against every man. . . . The notions of right and wrong, justice and injustice have there no place. . . . No arts; no letters; no society; and which is worst of all, continual fear, and danger of violent death: and the life of man, solitary, poor, nasty, brutish, and short.

The "solitary, poor, nasty, brutish, and short" part drew much attention, especially "nasty, brutish, and short." (No, it's not a description of Hobbes, although I could think of some people it fits.) I did a simple search for just those three words on the Internet and found many references to the phrase. Among them, I learned that *Nasty, Brutish, and Short* is the name of a rock band in England.

For all his distrust of human nature, Hobbes was interested in justice and he did advocate that people band together so that the monarch would hear their concerns. He even coined the term "voice of the people."

Reasoning to rationalism

Rationalism, another seventeenth-century philosophy, chose reason, rather than observation (the senses) as the basis for knowledge.

That way of thinking traces to René Descartes (1596 to 1650), the French mathematician who invented analytical, or Cartesian (for Decartes) geometry. (Cartesian geometry uses algebra to solve geometric problems, in case you were wondering who to blame for that.)

Descartes believed reason could be based on knowledge that just exists — independent of sense-experience. (Think of the way mathematical principals seem to exist on a plane separate from everyday reality.)

Descartes decided that the only thing beyond doubt was his own thinking. This resulted in one of the most memorable quotes in all philosophy: "I think, therefore I am."

Rationalism grew into a political movement, too, based in Paris and embodied in a group of writers including the poet Voltaire (1694 to 1798) and Swiss-born essayist Jean Jacques Rousseau (1712 to 1778).

Expanding to the Encyclopedists

In the 1770s, Voltaire and other leading thinkers, led by the critic Denis Diderot (1713 to 1784), published *Encyclopèdie,* a collection of social and political writing. *Encyclopèdie* used reason to attack France's old order, the *ancien régime*.

The Encyclopedists were intensely interested in the American Revolution, which broke out in the same decade that they were collaborating. The interest was mutual. Many of America's rebels were Enlightenment thinkers — especially Thomas Jefferson, who wrote the Declaration of Independence. Signed in 1776, it contained phrases such as "We hold these truths to be self-evident" (rationalism) and "certain unalienable Rights" (which sounds inspired by Locke and Rousseau).

Jean Jacques Rousseau's works — especially his 1755 *Discourse on the Origin and Foundations of Inequality Amongst Men,* which emphasized the natural goodness of human beings, and 1762's *The Social Contract* — had a big influence on political thinking of the time. *The Social Contract* introduced the slogan, "Liberty, Equality, Fraternity," battle cry of the French Revolution in 1789 (see Chapter 7).

Engineering the Industrial Revolution

Some thinkers were more interested in solving practical problems in the material world. If physical reality was not just knowable but controllable, as Francis Bacon thought, then it fell to engineers to devise ways to control it.

One of these, England's Jethro Tull (1674 to 1741) invented the seed drill (which hardly seems a good reason for a 1970s folk-rock band to steal his name). The seed drill, unlike the flute (featured instrument in the Jethro Tull band), allowed crops to be planted more quickly, in neat rows that you could weed between. Crop production rose.

England's Thomas Savery thought along practical lines, too. In 1698, he patented a device that used steam pressure to pump water out of tin and coal mines. With the help of blacksmith Thomas Newcomen, he improved his device until he had a commercially feasible steam engine. Its primary use remained pumping water, but using the steam engine to turn grinding wheels, as in a flourmill, occurred to other, equally practical folks.

In the second half of the eighteenth century, Thomas Hargreaves, an illiterate carpenter in Nottingham, England, built a machine that put several spindles on a frame to spin several threads at once — making possible a production volume far beyond that of the spinning wheel. He patented his _spinning jenny_ (as he named it, after his wife), in 1768. In the next year, Richard Arkwright came out with a similar device that was powered by a water wheel — as grindstones in mills often were.

For centuries, women had spun thread and yarn by hand, and woven textiles on hand looms. These were cottage industries, carried out in cottages, people's homes. Arkwright's machine and others were too big, too expensive, and too complex for people to use at home. There wasn't even such a thing as online tech support back then.

Businessmen put up large buildings where several of Arkwright's water frames could be set up in one huge room and hired laborers to operate them. This process got bigger, faster, and more powerful in 1779 when Samuel Crompton came up with the _spinning mule_ (named after his brother-in-law — no, just kidding). The water-powered _mule_ could spin up to 1,000 threads at a time and it could also be rigged to a newfangled steam engine.

Large-scale industrialization was off and running. Scotland's James Watt perfected the steam engine in 1790 and more and richer investors got behind this new factory system. Mass production of goods created a need for better ways to transport them, and the raw materials that manufacturing required. Industrialization led to widespread networks of canals. Then some bright inventors figured out how to make the steam engine mobile. That meant railroads and steamships (which I cover in Chapter 8), and, as you well know, innovations ever since.

Dealing with the social fallout

The Industrial Revolution was just as profound a change as any political upheaval. It killed cottage industries, and separated home from workplace, forcing people to move to the cities for jobs. England, and then other countries, became urban as never before.

It wasn't just established cities like London that were growing like weeds. Brand new towns sprung up around mills, mines, and factories.

These social changes, although they created wealth for factory owners and employment for thousands of people, caused serious problems too. Countryfolk who relocated for factory jobs found themselves in small, crowded houses with inadequate ventilation and sanitation. Most of these neighborhoods rapidly deteriorated into miserable industrial slums.

Factory owners had absolute control. Remember that Europe's population had grown rapidly through the Renaissance. This meant that labor was plentiful and cheap. Workers had no leverage, and worked under conditions you wouldn't put up with: A workday was a hard 12 hours or more, factories ran six days a week, and so did workers.

Many of the new machines didn't require a man's strength. Power looms and spinning machines could be run by women and children, many of whom had little choice but to work those long hours — for less pay than men got. Figure 14-1 shows one such worker.

There was also a new, urgent need for coal and iron. Coal fired the steam engines. And in the 1850s, an engineer called Henry Bessemer came up with a cheap way to make steel — a hardened mixture of iron and carbon. Now steel mills rose. Mining boomed.

Figure 14-1:
Children often tended the machines of the Industrial Revolution.

© CORBIS

In the mines, even little kids did grueling physical labor, such as pulling heavy coal wagons along tracks deep under the ground, through tunnels too small for even a donkey to work easily. For all the work there was to do, poverty was cruel. You took the job on the factory owner's terms or your family starved.

Such conditions inspired new lines of social philosophy — the most influential developed by the German Karl Marx, who is coming up a little later in this chapter.

Raging against the machines: Luddite uprising

Legend says that in 1782 (or by some accounts, 1779) a laborer in Leicestershire, England, Ned Ludd, destroyed some machinery used to make stockings. Ludd blamed the machines for putting local hand-knitters out of work.

Ludd's name came up in 1812, when workers in Nottingham rioted, attacking and destroying power looms. The rioters saw the new machinery as the source of their misery. These people were called the Ludds, or _Luddites,_ after the man who supposedly inspired them. The authorities rounded them up, trying them altogether in London. Many were hanged; others deported to Australia.

Ever since, people who blame or fear technology have been called Luddites. The word saw resurgence in the late twentieth century with the dawning of the computer age.

Marketing Economics

Just as philosophy gave rise to individual scientific disciplines, it also split off into other branches of philosophical thought. In the eighteenth century, economics became a discipline in itself.

Playing the money game with Adam Smith

Adam Smith, a Scot born in 1723, used his professorships in logic and moral philosophy at Glasgow University to study how markets work and such things as division of labor.

Smith traveled to Paris and met with some of the same philosophers mentioned earlier in this chapter — the ones who were transforming French political thought. He found himself in tune with Francois Quesnay, who opposed tariffs and other government intervention in international trade. Smith's ideas could be made to fit into the French Encyclopedists' notion of an inherent, just, social order.

Smith believed that if government left the marketplace alone, individuals pursuing selfish economic ends would be led, as if by an *invisible hand* to benefit society as a whole. Of course, it hasn't always worked out that way; especially not when you take into account the squalor and poverty that accompanied the Industrial Revolution.

Yet, over the long-term, Smith's ideas about economic freedom, which he presented in his 1776 book *An Inquiry into the Nature and Causes of the Wealth of Nations,* were enormously influential in the development of modern economic theory and continue to be cited today.

Developing capitalism and Marxism

Smith's theories support free-market capitalism, although Smith never called it that. Another classical economist (in the field of scholarship Smith founded) invented the word *capitalism,* one who saw capitalists — those who owned the means of production — as oppressors.

Karl Marx was born in Trier, Germany, in 1818, and grew up seeing the effects of industrialization. He was attracted by the ideas of Georg Friederich Wilhelm Hegel (1770 to 1831).

Hegel, an idealist, developed his own brand of *dialectic,* a philosophical technique for inquiry. Dialectic traces back to fifth-century BC Athens and the philosopher Socrates, who pretended he didn't know the answers to questions he asked, all the while using those questions to coax truths out of the people who answered him. Hegel's dialectic involved putting forth something as true (thesis), denying it (antithesis), and then combining the two (synthesis) to arrive at a greater truth.

Unlike Hegel, Marx came to believe that everything is composed exclusively of physical bits within time and space. In other words, he was a materialist. Forms of materialist philosophy go back to another Greek, Epicurus. Marx nonetheless applied Hegel's dialectic as he worked toward his own theories about economics and class struggle. (You can find about Socrates and Epicurus in Chapter 10.)

Marx saw *capitalism* — his word for the Industrial Revolution's economic system, dominated by factory owners and mine masters — as a primitive societal stage just above feudalism. Capitalism was a plateau on the way toward socialism and ultimately, what he thought of as an ideal arrangement, *communism.*

In his major work, 1867's *Das Kapital,* he described the state as an instrument of class rule, supporting private capital and suppressing the masses. In contrast to Smith's theories about economic freedom benefiting society as a whole, Marx looked at the realities of the Industrial Revolution and argued that the need to earn a profit forces wages down to a subsistence minimum.

Marx said capitalist societies are unstable, defined by contradictions. Because the need for profit keeps wages down, workers can't achieve purchasing power to acquire goods that the economy produces. (He failed to anticipate the letter that starts: "Dear Mr. Marx: Congratulations! You have been pre-approved for a Citibank VISA account.")

Capitalism's inherent tendency toward booms and slumps, Marx said, would worsen until it incited a working class revolution. He argued that the working class, or *proletariat,* would grab the reigns of the state and establish a people's dictatorship.

Marx also argued that because an industrial economy was capable of producing enough for everybody, there was no *need* for social strata. Communal ownership, he thought, would bring the abolition of social class. A classless society would lead to the withering away of the state, resulting in communism.

Marx and his collaborator, Friederich Engels (1820 to 1895), envisioned this taking place in Germany and then spreading through the rest of industrialized Europe. The last place they figured their economic theories would click in was the rural empire of Russia.

Yet with a little reworking by Vladimir Lenin (more on him in Chapter 8), Russia became the starting place. This experiment in Marxism, the Union of Soviet Socialist Republics, didn't work out quite as Marx and Engels predicted. The state eventually fell away all right, in 1991, but largely because the USSR was bankrupt and had lost its political credibility. The USSR was replaced by another state, today's Russia.

Still, Marxism, which also took hold in various forms adapted to China, Cuba, Vietnam, North Korea, and a few other outposts, was a major influence on the twentieth century — although Marx may not have recognized many of the interpretations of his ideas.

Many nations in the twentieth century, including those of western Europe, have developed forms of democratic socialism — influenced by Marx but not chained to his ideas.

In general, the experience of the twentieth century shows that allowing people to pursue wealth brings a more robust and resilient economy — driven by incentive. Putting everything under government ownership tended to breed economic stagnation. Even China, the largest Marxist nation, reintroduced capitalist elements to its economy at the end of the twentieth century.

Tracking the Centuries

1543: The Polish astronomer Copernicus publishes his theory that the sun is at the center of the universe.

1560: Tycho Brahe, a teenager in Denmark, sees a partial solar eclipse and decides to devote himself to astronomy.

1564: Galileo Galilei, son of a music teacher, is born in Pisa, Italy.

1610: After aiming a new invention, the telescope, at the night sky, Galileo reports his findings in his book, *Sidereal Messenger.* His most startling observation: Copernicus was right; planets do not orbit Earth.

1687: Isaac Newton's greatest book, *Principia,* establishes the basic laws of physics, including his famous third law of motion: "For every action there is an equal and opposite reaction."

1768: Thomas Hargreaves invents a machine that can spin several threads at once, the *spinning jenny.*

1770s: In Paris, Denis Diderot collects the works of his fellow thinkers and writers, including Voltaire, into *Encyclopèdie,* an anthology attacking France's old order.

1776: In *An Inquiry into the Nature and Causes of the Wealth of Nations,* Adam Smith argues that if government left the marketplace alone, individuals pursuing selfish economic ends would be led, as if by an *invisible hand,* to benefit society as a whole.

1812: Workers in Nottingham, England riot, destroying power looms. They call themselves Luddites, after Ned Ludd, an earlier rebel against factory machines.

1867: In the book *Das Kapital,* Karl Marx describes the state as an instrument of class rule, supporting private capital and suppressing the masses.

Part IV
War

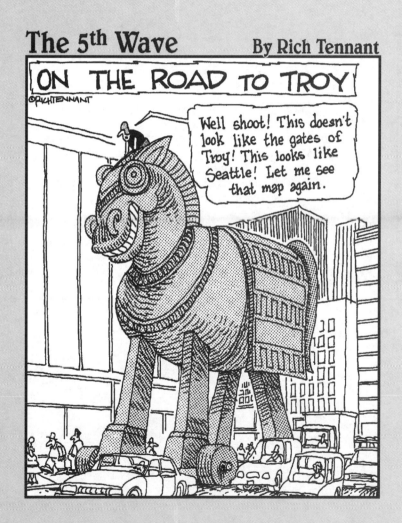

In this part. . .

War, sad to say, is inseparable from human history. War and the ability and willingness to wage war drives societies and nations — a fact I chronicle throughout this book. Military might is important — often tragically important. People fight wars over boundaries, resources, ethnic differences, religious disagreements, and political alliances — among too many other causes.

In this part, you can find out about the origins of war, how warfare has changed over many millennia, and how those changes shaped the world. You can also glimpse latter-day movements to end international aggression.

Chapter 15

Hurling Sticks and Stones

*W*ithout warfare, the human story would be very different, maybe unrecognizable. War stories are among the earliest and most influential folklore and literature. (See Chapter 3 for a glance at the *Iliad*.) For millennia, everybody knew who fought the Trojan War and how it turned out: The Greeks won.

Cultures in every corner of the world worshipped war gods and defined themselves by military conquest. By looking at how early wars were fought, you can get an idea of what set this violent species on the path toward smart missiles, stealth aircraft, and neutron bombs.

Fighting as an Ancient Way of Life

When outsiders first stumbled across the interior valleys of New Guinea in the 1930s, they found village after village of stone-age farmers who looked on the people of the other villages around them as eternal enemies, or potential enemies. Revenge wars, their root causes lost in time, were the overwhelming rule.

In the late 1970s, anthropologist Carol Ember reported that 64 percent of remaining hunter-gatherer societies in the world at the time fought a war at least every two years. War was rare or absent in only 10 percent of groups studied. In the 1980s, another anthropologist, K.E. Otterbein, turned up even more dismaying results. Studying both hunter-gatherer and primitive farming peoples, he found that 92 percent waged war.

> ## Not the only ones
>
> Scientists say humankind is not the only war-making species. What other animal indulges in such mass violence? For one, humanity's closest genetic cousin, the chimpanzee. Researchers have seen bands of male chimps, all from one group, raiding another band. If they can, they kill all the other group's males and gain mating privileges with the females.
>
> Jane Goodall, the most famous researcher to study chimps, said, "If they had firearms and had been taught to use them, I suspect they would have used them to kill." This and other evidence causes biologists such as Michael P. Ghiglieri of the University of Northern Arizona to believe that human beings didn't invent war at all. Rather, war is a part of pre-human behavior.

Archeologists note how often ancient human skulls appear to have received violent, bone-breaking blows — as if from clubs or axes. The evidence suggests that ancient times were violent times, and that people have always fought wars, or at least armed skirmishes.

Raising Armies

Cave people made war, but war didn't get organized on a large scale until civilization did. Armies arose among early civilizations in the Middle East (see Chapter 3), as did formations, such as the column and the line, and classic military strategy, such as the *flanking maneuver* — going around the side of the enemy line.

Sometime after 10,000 BC, the bow and sling both joined the warrior's arsenal. Like the earlier spear and ax, these surely doubled as hunting tools, but they changed the way wars were fought. The simple wooden bow with its string of animal gut could propel a stone-tipped arrow farther than a football field is long.

Made of a leather pad with two thin straps attached, the *sling* had even more range. The *slinger* put a rock or a solid, baked clay projectile into the pad, swung it around his head by the straps and then let one of the straps go, sending the missile flying. The Bible hero David felled the Philistine giant Goliath with a sling. Stone carvings from the tenth century BC show Mesopotamian soldiers (from what is now Iraq) using the weapon.

Keeping out attackers

Ancient cities had defensive walls, perhaps to keep out predatory animals, but most prehistorians who study defensive walls think they were built to protect against attackers. Jericho (see Chapter 3), perhaps the oldest town that left substantial ruins, was distinguished by a defensive ditch around the community, a stone wall, and a tower with an inside stairway. Towers let you see the attacking force while it's still far away. From the top, you can rain down projectiles.

Another ancient ruin, the town of Catal Huyuk in central Turkey, is made up of mostly windowless, doorless houses — again, probably designed for security against attackers. Under siege, residents of those houses could pull up their ladders, drop the ladder and themselves through their rooftop hatches, close the hatch and sit out the attack.

Defenses evolved wherever people clashed, which was just about anywhere people lived. European villagers as long as 4,000 years ago built hill forts ringed by earthen ramparts. By 220 BC, the Chinese put up the first parts of the Great Wall to protect against northern nomads. Eventually the Great Wall stretched 2,550 miles. When European explorers arrived in New Zealand in the eighteenth century AD they found Maori warriors in timber forts atop steep coastal cliffs.

Escalating weapons technology: Using metal

As defenses evolved, so did weapons. A big leap came with metal blades and points. A mummified man from about 3300 BC, found in Europe's Alps, carried a copper ax. Copper is a soft metal, however, and that limits its usefulness. By 3000 BC, Middle Eastern metalsmiths were mixing it with tin to form the harder metal bronze.

Bronze made tough cutting blades and piercing points. You could also pound bronze into helmets, shields, and armor. Bronze battle-axes and swords became standard. Iron — even harder — followed by about 1500 BC.

Riding into battle: Hooves and wheels

Around 300 BC in Mesopotamia, armies used wheeled wagons to transport fighters. The people of Sumer, perhaps the first great urban civilization, fashioned heavy, clumsy vehicles, with four solid wooden wheels. Donkeys — notoriously balky — pulled them. So did plodding oxen. (*Oxen*, the plural of *ox*, means cows or bulls, usually castrated, used for pulling.)

After about 1800 BC, armies preferred horsepower. They hitched horses to two-wheeled chariots, faster and lighter than the wagons, but still big. Unlike the racing chariots in the 1959 movie *Ben Hur* (set in early first-century AD

Rome), these earlier chariots carried several men — warriors, javelin throwers, and a driver. The Assyrians, whose civilization arose from the city-state of Assur, on the upper Tigris River, made especially good use of chariots.

Bristling Assyrian Arsenals

Around the Middle East, the Sumerians, Egyptians, Babylonians, and Hittites were military powers in an ebb and flow of early martial power. But other, lesser-known peoples — Hurrians, Mitannians, Kassites, Elamites, and Amorites — fielded armed forces, too.

The Assyrians, who I tell you more about in Chapter 3, grew particularly warlike. Perhaps Assyrian aggression began with defense. In the eleventh century BC, waves of nomadic northern invaders beat the Assyrian kingdom down to an area only 50 by 100 miles along the Tigris River in northern Mesopotamia. But at the end of the next century, Assyrian warriors began to overrun other societies until they ruled an empire 1,000 miles from border to border, stretching from Egypt to the Caucasus (between the Black Sea and the Caspian Sea).

Assembling the units

At their height, the Assyrians could field an army of 100,000. But they also relied on specialized units: quick-moving, lightly armored infantry and slower, but heavily armored infantry; warriors with spears, others with bows, and more with slings, pikes, and swords; and war chariots.

Perhaps most impressive, the Assyrians had engineering units. Advance corps blazed trails and laid roads for supply wagons. When the army needed to cross a river, engineers built a pontoon bridge — much as it was done for millennia afterwards.

What could ancient Assyrians use for pontoons? How about inflated animal skins? Log or reed boats lashed together could also float a roadway.

Assyrians also pioneered ways to get past a city's defenses. They built *siege engines* — towers on wheels or sometimes on pontoons that could be moved right up next to a city's walls. Siege engines were made of timber frames, covered with layers of tough cowhide that could fend off arrows. Attackers could stay inside until the engine was in place, then climb up the inside, emerge on top, and go over the wall.

Sometimes Assyrian engineers went down instead of up — digging under a city's wall, and shoring up their tunnel with wooden beams, as miners do a shaft. Once under the wall, the engineers would set the tunnel supports on fire and then turn around and run for daylight. The supports burned up. The tunnel collapsed and the wall above, literally undermined, crumbled. Soldiers advanced through the gap.

Other methods included building a ramp of dirt and rubble to scale the wall.

Wreaking havoc

Atrocities — such as the wholesale slaughter of a city's residents or the mass deportation of entire populations — are among the worst aspects of modern war, but slaughter and deportation are anything but modern and the Assyrians did both. In one instance, they deported 27,000 Jews — the Lost Tribes who disappeared from history — to eastern Syria. The Assyrians used captives as forced labor, which sometimes made taking prisoners more economical than killing everybody.

The Assyrians finally fell from power at the end of the seventh century BC, when neighbors united against them, but that didn't mean Assyrian military methods were lost. The Persians built their own vast empire with war tactics inherited from the Assyrians. (You can find more about the Persians ahead in this chapter.)

Farming and Fighting Together in Greece

Like the ancient Greeks' way of governing (which you can read about in Chapter 3) and the Greek way of thinking (see Chapter 10), a Greek style of warfare grew out of the geography of mainland Greece and its agricultural economy.

Greek soldiers of the sixth and fifth centuries BC were largely small landholders, family farmers who made their livings from fields scraped out of rocky hillsides. Because these farmers — whose landholder status made them members of a privileged middle class, the citizenry — were determined to maintain control of their property and their communities, they volunteered as *hoplites,* heavily armored foot soldiers. Military service for no pay was the mark of full membership in the community.

Every Greek citizen who could afford the equipment — a bronze breastplate, a helmet with a fashionable horsehair crest, a short iron sword, leg protectors called *greaves,* and the most essential item, a nine-foot-long spear —

joined up. The hoplites took their name from one other piece of equipment: the heavy wooden shield they carried by its double handle. They slid one loop over the left forearm to the elbow, and grasped the other loop, at the rim of the shield, in the left hand.

Soldiering shoulder to shoulder

The heavy hoplite weaponry fit the way Greeks fought, in a tight, porcupine-like formation called the phalanx. It grew out of conflicts between competing city-states.

In formal disputes, usually over farmland, the two sides decided the issue through an afternoon's worth of armored columns facing each other on cleared fields, each side trying to bulldoze the other to a resolution.

When you hear somebody describe any group of aggressive people — say, reporters covering a big story — as a *phalanx*, remember that the original phalanxes were much deadlier (if perhaps less obnoxious than modern reporters). Your spear, when you were in battle formation, stuck out beyond the guy in the rank in front of you.

Hoplites fought shoulder to shoulder. They couldn't see well because of their helmets and they couldn't move quickly because of the heavy gear. What the hoplites could do was advance behind those shields that each held to protect the bearer's shield side and his neighbor's weapon side. The Greek historian Xenophon put this interdependence in its agricultural context:

> Farming teaches a person to help others. In fighting enemies, just as in working the earth, each person needs the help of others.

When two Greek phalanxes clashed, one would break through the other. The disrupted phalanx became ineffective because its helmet-blinded, armor-encumbered members were likely to become confused and fight each other. That happened at the Battle of Delium in 424 BC, when the Spartans broke through the Athenian line and the separated Athenians grabbed their swords and commenced hacking at anything that moved, including their comrades.

Standing up to the Persians

In time, the phalanx proved effective against other cultures' military formations, including quicker moving light infantry (foot soldiers without such heavy gear) and even attackers on horseback.

Hoplites passed their biggest test in 490 BC, when King Darius I of Persia invaded mainland Greece. Athenian and allied hoplites, outnumbered two to one, confronted the Persians at Marathon.

Persians organized their armies along lines developed by the Assyrians (earlier in this chapter), with horses, archers, swordsmen, engineers — the whole, coordinated, multi-tiered shebang. To Darius's forces, this bunch of spear-carrying soldiers who looked like shields with stubby bronze legs, promised easy pickings. But the Greeks would not fall back. When a hoplite stumbled, the hoplite in the rank behind him stepped over him and shored up the advance. The Greeks pushed forward until their flanks — the far ends of their line — overwhelmed the most vulnerable part of the Persian forces and then folded the Persians in toward the middle. At that point, Darius's army wisely turned around and high-tailed it for their boats.

The outnumbered Greeks beat the Persians again 11 years later at Platea. The Greek phalanx made heavy infantry *the* essential force of its time. (More about that later in this chapter.) For centuries, commanders saw cavalry and archers as support for well-armored foot soldiers.

Facing Macedonian ferocity

When the Greeks finally fell to a foreign force it wasn't the mighty Persians but a strongman king to the north of Greece, Philip of Macedon, applying his own version of the phalanx.

Imagine Clint Eastwood at his most squinty, his most unmercifully flinty, in the role of Philip, a hard guy. Phil put cavalry behind his infantry, each rider armed with a *xyston,* a 12-foot-long lance with a foot-long iron point at both ends. The cavalry's job was twofold:

- To support the foot soldiers
- To kill any man among them who turned and ran

Macedon arranged its infantry in a phalanx, but made crucial improvements. Philip's soldiers strapped a small, round shield that wasn't so heavy (or as much protection) as the bigger hoplite shield, to the left shoulder, leaving both hands free to wield a long pike called a *sarissa,* like the cavalry xyston but with a special metal spike on its butt end. A soldier could plant the spike in the ground and then impale a charging horseman with the business end.

The sarissa was so long that the weapons carried by the soldiers in the fifth rank of the Macedonian phalanx, extended beyond the first rank. (See Figure 15-1.)

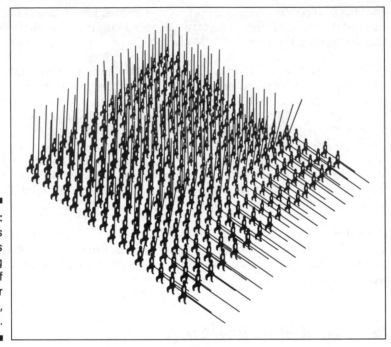

Figure 15-1:
Macedon's
phalanx was
a marching
hedgehog of
muscular
men, wood,
and metal.

Macedon's army also took the best of Assyrian-Persian weaponry and tactics. Phil deployed archers, javelin throwers, and slingers. As the Assyrians had, he made conquered armies part of his own force and told them to use their own weapons and formations to support his. Philip also employed Assyrian-style combat engineers and his inventors improved the siege engine, adding a drawbridge to the top, and many platforms for archers to stand on. This new siege engine didn't have to be right up next to the target city's wall. If you came fairly close, you could let down the drawbridge and cross it onto the battlements.

Even more inventive than that, Macedon's engineers built a catapult that unleashed the tension of wound animal hair or sinew to hurl a large rock 1,000 feet.

Philip's approach to warfare spurred the successes of his son, Alexander the Great (I tell you about Alex in Chapters 3 and 19). Alex took the conquered Greeks with him as he turned tables on the Persians, thoroughly defeated them, and marched through Mesopotamia and beyond to grab part of India. Alex's troops weren't even fazed by the Indians' ultimate weapon — armored battle elephants.

Making War the Roman Way

The Latins, shepherds who built a city on the Tiber River in what is now Italy, were among many Mediterranean people who admired and imitated the way the Greeks fought.

At the end of the sixth century BC, Latins organized themselves into a Greek-style phalanx and challenged their northern overlords, Etruscans. The Latins won, and their city, Rome, became the center of a new culture built on military prowess.

Marching in three ranks

The Latin shepherds became the Romans, who soon found that the phalanx, nifty as it was for fighting the Etruscans — another Greek-influenced people — wasn't perfect for fighting less-advanced neighboring tribes.

Greeks developed the phalanx on farmland — battle*fields*. The Romans found that their tribal neighbors weren't interested in marching formation-to-formation on a cleared hillside. Faster moving than the shield-carrying Romans, a gaggle of tribesmen could come around the flank or hide behind trees and dart out in a raid.

Even the Greeks eventually found the traditional phalanx less and less effective — especially as their armed forces evolved, in the later decades of classical Greece, from neighborly bands of farmer-citizen-soldiers to a mix of citizens and resident aliens, some of whom were paid mercenaries. A shoulder-to-shoulder, soldier-to-soldier style didn't work so well when you weren't quite sure about the guy next to you.

Needing their own, more flexible military style, the Romans came up with the *legion* in the fourth century BC.

The legion was made up of three lines of foot soldiers. Only the third line carried traditional spears. The first two lines carried a variation on the theme — a javelin (or *pilum*) designed for throwing and boasting a cool technological advance: The head was designed to bend and break off, making the javelin useless to the enemy once it struck its mark. The bent spearhead also tended to stick in an opponent's shield or armor.

The Roman legion worked like this:

- **Hastati:** The first line, made up of young guys, threw their javelins, then drew their swords and charged. If they had to fall back, they scrambled for a position behind the second rank.

✔ **Principes:** The more experienced second rank also threw, then charged. If they, too, found they had to fall back, they got behind the third rank, the *triarii*.

✔ **Triarii:** These steady old hands stood fast in a solid defensive line to let the other guys retreat in safety. But Rome's battles rarely came to that. The legion usually won.

Even when Rome didn't win, the other side suffered. In 280 BC, Pyrrhus, king of Epirus, defeated troops led by the Roman Consul Laevinus (*consul* was top administrative post in the Roman republic). Both sides suffered horrible losses. After the dust cleared, 15,000 lay dead. Pyrrhus said:

> If we win another battle against the Romans, we shall be completely ruined.

Like the Greek phalanx, the legion began as a citizen corps. Most soldiers came from the small landholder class, and just about every man served. Each citizen (as in Greece, women weren't citizens) between 17 and 45 had to devote 10 years to military service. A leader had to prove himself in battle before he could win political office. Failure at soldiering was failure, period.

Recruiting a standing force

Despite successes — and because of them — Roman commanders realized by the year 100 BC that they needed to change the empire's military. Battling foes from Germany to Africa to the Black Sea, the Roman Empire grew so fast that its republican legions of citizen-soldiers couldn't keep up. Troops posted far away on those frontiers couldn't come home and tend their property after a few months' campaign.

Besides that, the prosperity that came of Rome's expansions, and the resulting boost in trade, made the wealthy patrician class in Rome even wealthier. Rich guys were amassing big estates — cultivated not by citizen-farmer-soldiers, the small landholders who traditionally manned the legions, but by slaves. Slaves were exempt from military service.

Rome started struggling to fill the legions' ranks. Recruiters began conveniently overlooking the property ownership requirement for service. Commanders turned to the urban poor to fill out their rosters, but things just weren't the same. These new guys didn't have the same stake in the empire. They were harder to discipline.

Gaius Marius, a lowborn soldier who rose to the political office of consul, figured the time had arrived for Rome to ditch the old civil militia idea and officially make the army a full-time, professional gig.

The professional army worked. The military became an attractive career choice and a means of upward mobility. There was a downside, however. Instead of the citizen-soldiers' loyalty to Rome, the new pros were loyal to their commanders first. The republic became vulnerable to civil wars. A military leader whose troops are more loyal to him than to the government may fancy himself a dictator or emperor. Rome became an empire with the coronation of Augustus in 31 BC (see Chapter 18).

Diversifying the legion

The coronation of Augustus wasn't the end of the citizen soldier. Roman strategy in the later centuries of the western Roman Empire (the eastern Roman Empire became the Byzantine Empire) involved much defensive work — holding fortified outposts and cities against barbarian attack. Resident defenders were important in that work.

How warlike were the tribes that hammered away at Rome's borders? The Langobard people were named after their weapon: *Langobard* means "long axe." Saxons took their name not from a sexy-sounding musical instrument (invented in the nineteenth century) but from a machete-like knife, a *sax*. Imagine a modern nation called the Thermonuclear Missiles.

In Chapter 4, I talk about the waves of people who came down through Europe, each clashing with the previous residents, some settling and becoming defenders against later waves. The Roman Empire's task of standing up to these assaults took plenty of personnel. Residents in places such as Gaul (now France) pitched in to defend their towns. The old idea that warriors fought better in defense of their own land came back.

When Attila the Hun (find more on Attila in Chapter 19) invaded Gaul in 451, he and his fearsome allies spent months trying to break down the defenses of walled cities. They ran out of food and had no forage left for their horses. While Attila hammered away at the city of Orleans, the army of Roman General Aetius, Germanic soldiers raised mostly in Gaul, attacked and pursued the Huns to Châlons. There the Huns turned and fought, but they were too depleted to prevail. (Note, however, that it took Roman cavalry to beat Attila.)

Returning to riders

Military strategists considered cavalry secondary to infantry for centuries. But after the murderous Huns had swept into Europe on horseback, terrorizing everyone with their swift fury, war strategists woke up again to the importance of speed.

By the sixth century AD, Rome no longer ruled western Europe, but the eastern branch of its empire, based in Constantinople, endured. There, swift-riding horse units patrolled the vast borders of the Byzantine Empire (more about the Byzantine Empire in Chapter 5), backed up by lightly armored archers who could move more quickly than the heavy infantry that were the backbone of traditional Roman and Greek forces. The old-style shield-carriers now operated mostly as garrison defense.

Tracking the Centuries

About 10,000 BC: The bow and the sling become part of the warrior's arsenal.

Tenth century BC: Assyrian warriors overrun neighboring peoples, building an empire stretching from Egypt to the mountains between the Caspian and Black seas.

424 BC: Spartans break through the Athenian line at the Battle of Delium. The disoriented troops from Athens drop their spears, grab their swords and begin hacking indiscriminately, wounding many of their own.

409 BC: Although badly outnumbered, Athenians and their allies defeat King Darius I's invading Persian forces at Marathon.

451 AD: In Gaul (today's France), Aetius, a Roman general commanding Germanic troops, drives Attila the Hun away from his siege on Orleans. Then he pursues the Huns and defeats them at Châlons.

1980s: Among hunter-gatherer societies and primitive farming people studied by anthropologist K.E. Otterbein, 92 percent waged war.

Chapter 16

Advancing the Technology of War

- -

In This Chapter

▶ Standing in stirrups, cavalry can fight more effectively

▶ Donning metal suits, knights fend off armors and lances

▶ Flying sparks from fireworks become firearms

▶ Bringing down the Byzantine Empire with big guns

- -

Since before the spear, warfare has always stimulated technology. Assyrian military engineers, Macedonian weapons inventors, and Roman fortification builders were the techies of their respective times.

It's hard to imagine anybody coming up with a horrific substance such as *Greek fire,* a highly combustible liquid that long predated twentieth-century napalm, except as a weapon. And metalworking seems to have fed on the needs of weapons-makers and armorers. But inventions spur warfare, too.

More than a millennium ago, two dandy little innovations from Asia, gunpowder and the stirrup, enabled and demanded many adjustments in how wars were fought, and even how war was perceived:

 ✓ **Gunpowder:** The Chinese mixed up the first batch in the ninth century AD, although they didn't try to blow anybody up with it until a while later.

 ✓ **The stirrup:** Far less flashy (pun intended) but exceedingly practical, the low-tech stirrup — that thing that you put your foot into to climb onto and ride a horse — became part of a Chinese horse soldier's gear in the fourth century AD.

Reinventing the Cavalry

Gunpowder and the stirrup filtered west through Asia to Europe, after the fall of Rome's western empire, but the simpler stirrup came first. It coincided with a reemphasis on speed and mobility that I talk about at the end of the previous chapter. Horseback warfare gained greater importance in medieval

times, and it took diverse forms ranging from the lightly armed Arab conqueror on his small, fast-turning steed to the steel-plated European knight on
his ponderous, metal-clad charger.

Standing tall and staying astride with stirrups

Stirrups make it vastly easier for a rider to stay balanced while swinging a
sword, aiming an arrow, and especially while wheeling around in a strategic
maneuver. That, in turn, allows the violence-prone equestrian to wield bigger
weapons with better control. Europe's armor-clad age of chivalry would have
been unthinkable without stirrups. A couple of thirteenth and fourteenth century styles are shown in Figure 16-1.

Figure 16-1:
Front and
side views
of the
stirrup, a
techno-
logical
innovation
that
changed
warfare.

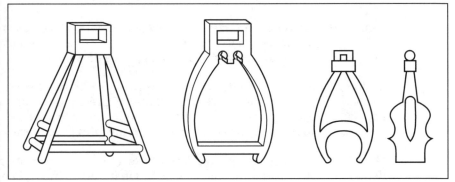

Imagine a rider encased in a pounded-steel suit, bracing a long, heavy lance
with one arm, trying to use his metal-shielded thighs and buttocks to grip the
undulating flanks and back of a galloping steed. It wouldn't work. But give
that same knight two hanging platforms, one for each foot, so he can lift and
center his weight and the heavy armor and lance become formidable instead
of cumbersome.

The stirrup originated either in China or in central Asia, among the nomadic
tribes and clans that are often labeled *barbarians*.

Raiding as a way of life on horseback

Chinese soldiers started using the stirrup around the fourth century AD, but
the hard-riding Asian nomads called Avars probably had the invention as
early as the first century BC. Their riders' feet were tucked into stirrups

when the Avars stormed into Eastern Europe in 568 AD, taking Danube Valley lands away from the Byzantine Empire.

Avars and other barbarian peoples used the stirrup while attacking towns and cities to get what they wanted — valuable trade goods, food, money, and sometimes even control of a region or an empire. (You can find out more about barbarian raiders and conquerors in Chapters 5 and 6.) Raiding became a way of life for some nomadic tribes from interior Asia's steppes. Because these herders and hunters had little to offer in trade to settled farmers and towns-folk, such as the Chinese, they resorted to getting things they wanted by force.

Raiding is best performed quickly. You make the hit, then put plenty of ground between yourself and your target. Horsemanship gave raiders an edge and the stirrup sharpened it.

Guarding Byzantine borders

The rich Byzantine Empire (see Chapter 5) was a prime target of raiders. That's why fast horse patrols served best to guard its borders. Stirrups, probably copied from the Avars, gave the Byzantine patrols an advantage over western Europeans, who didn't have the technology yet. This superiority, coupled with the use of a commissariat — a support organization that made sure cavalrymen and foot soldiers had enough to eat, even during long sieges — made the Byzantine Empire extremely difficult for outsiders to penetrate. Constantinople, the Byzantine capital, needed every advantage in the seventh and eighth centuries as its troops faced a new and persistent foe, the Arabs. (See Chapter 5.)

The Arabs used stirrups, too, on relatively small, quick horses. More than great riders, the Arabs focused spiritual enthusiasm to help them spread throughout the Middle East, eastward into India, and westward across North Africa and Spain. (See Chapters 5 and 9.)

Yet Constantinople withstood the Arabs. The Byzantine capital (today it's Istanbul, Turkey) enjoyed a terrific strategic position, sitting on a point of high land jutting into the sea. Unable to take the capital on horseback, the Arabs tried ships in the eighth century, mounting a naval blockade, which may have succeeded, except for Greek fire.

A military secret, Greek fire may have been mostly naphtha, refined from coal oil that seeped to the surface from underground deposits. Whatever Greek fire was, it ignited on impact and it floated.

The Byzantines catapulted clay pots full of Greek fire onto the decks of enemy ships, setting them aflame. Even if the pot missed, the pots' contents burned atop the water. Sometimes the Byzantines squirted Greek fire out of hand-powered pumps. After losing too many ships, the Arabs called off the blockade.

Moors challenge

Arabs may not have brought down Constantinople, but their light cavalry strategy worked just about everywhere else. (*Light cavalry* refers to lightly armored horse units that emphasize speed.) In 711 AD, Muslim Arabs conquered Spain, which remained in Muslim control long after the great Arab Empire broke up into regional Islamic kingdoms.

The Muslims in Spain, who advanced from North Africa, quickly came to be called Moors. (Find more on the Moors in Chapter 5.) Christians living a little north of them, especially the Franks, didn't like them as neighbors.

Ruling what was Gaul (now it's France and much of Germany), the Franks were old-style barbarian ground fighters, but disciplined and willing to adapt. When quick-riding Moors raided his borders, the Frankish king knew he needed more speed. His solution: build up his cavalry.

Ironically, to defeat the invading Moors at Poitiers in 732 AD, that king, Charles Martel, ordered his horsemen down on their feet. Facing the attacking riders with shields and spears, the Franks stood fast and successfully repelled the Moors.

Yet despite that return to infantry tactics, this battle marked the beginning of the age of chivalry, a time when the armored knight dominated European warfare.

Chivalry

The words *chivalry* and *chivalric* are related to the French *chevaux* (horse) and to other horse-based words, such as *cavalier* and the Spanish *caballero*. These words show how people of the Middle Ages associated nobility, gentility, and courage with mounted warriors.

This era, like so many before it and since, glorified violence. People thought of fighting skills as a mark of civilization. Jean Froissart, a fourteenth-century French chronicler, wrote,

Gentle Knights were born to fight, and war ennobles everyone who engages in it without fear or cowardice.

Ennobling or not, war costs money and it became extremely expensive to outfit an armored, mounted knight. Charles Martel helped his riders pay for their gear by taking land from the medieval Church (see Chapters 9 and 11 to learn more about the Roman Catholic Church in medieval society) and giving it to the warrior-nobles. Under feudalism (which you can find out about in Chapter 5), a landlord profited from his tenant farmers' harvests.

Charlemagne, a slightly later Frankish king and the first to unite a big piece of Europe after the Romans fell, accomplished that unification with his cavalry. (Find more on him in Chapter 6.)

Fending Off Deadly Weapons with Armor

A culture of chivalry lasted for hundreds of years in Europe. In movies, this armor-clad culture is associated with the legendary King Arthur, who may not have existed at all (see Chapter 18). If he did exist, Arthur may have led Celtic Britons against invading Saxons in the sixth century AD, but certainly not in plate-metal armor. Plate armor didn't come into fashion until 800 years later, in the fourteenth century.

Interlocking metal rings: Chain mail

Before plate armor, knights wore chain mail; before chain mail, they wore scale armor, a defense against arrows since Assyrian times (in the previous chapter). Scale armor, like a lizard's scales, used small metal plates sewn into overlapping rows on a leather vest. Chain mail was a bit more ingenious — interlocking metal rings made into a doublet, or close-fitting jacket. The Crusaders wore mail as they rode east to *liberate* the Holy Land from Muslim control. (See Chapter 6.)

Chain mail became obsolete only as archers got better bows — bows that could send an arrow through chain mail.

Putting more power into the archer's bow

The crossbow was yet another Chinese invention, and an ancient one at that, dating back to the fourth century BC. European archers rediscovered the crossbow's deadly power in the tenth century AD.

A short, extremely stiff bow was mounted on a stock with a mechanism for cranking back the bowstring and holding it there, at a higher tension than a man could achieve by pulling the string back manually. You loosed the arrow with a finger-lever, or trigger.

The crossbow shot short bolts, often made of metal, that flew hard and penetrated surfaces that an arrow from a conventional bow could not. The Normans who conquered England in 1066 used the crossbow.

Pope Urban II condemned the crossbow in 1096 as "hateful to God." In 1139, the Church banned the crossbow for use against Christians. (When it came to pagans such as the Saracens, a name for Turks and other Muslims, it was okay.)

Some century

The name of the Hundred Years' War suggests ten solid decades of constant battle. Actually, it wasn't one war but a series of back and forth conflicts from the 1330s to the 1450s.

In 1337, Philip IV of France snatched Aquitaine from Edward III of England. Edward invaded France. The next century included many battles and raids. But there were also truces, including a 28-year peace after Richard II of England married the daughter of Charles VI of France in 1396.

France eventually won, largely because England — weakened by an internal struggle, the Wars of the Roses — gave up trying to conquer its neighbor across the English Channel.

Charging behind the lance

Although Crusaders used the crossbow, there seemed something less than honorable about it. Chivalric values centered on personal combat. When there wasn't a war to fight, knights rode against each other in fierce and often deadly *jousts*.

The lance — a long, pointed weapon that a jousting knight tucked under his arm — delivered incredible force. Increasingly metal-clad riders balanced on their stirrups and braced against high-backed saddles as they used this variation on the ancient spear to try knocking each other off their horses. Heavier armor kept them from being pierced through.

Mock battles let knights win status and stay sharp for the real thing, but the mock battles were *real,* themselves. At a 1241 tournament in Neuss, Germany, about 80 men and boys died in the *games.*

Marrying precision to power: The longbow

The English longbow, a refinement on ancient Welsh technology, became the latest thing in weaponry during the fourteenth century. Both precise and powerful in the hands of a skilled archer, the longbow gave knights another reason to wear solid metal armor.

The crossbow was powerful, but its accuracy and range were limited, and it took too long to load. An English longbow could do damage at 750 feet and you could reload rapidly. Only a skilled archer could use a longbow well, however, so England required yeomen to practice marksmanship. (Yeomen were small landowners, who served, when needed, as soldiers — as small farmers had in ancient Greece and Rome. See previous chapter.)

In 1346, at the Battle of Crécy (in the Hundred Years' War between France and England), English archers with longbows brought down wave after wave of

French. France lost more than 1,500 knights that day and 10,000 foot soldiers. England lost only two knights and fewer than 200 overall.

In the short term, Crécy led the French and other European knights to strap themselves inside heavier suits of armor. Nobody knew then that armored knights were on the way out. Guns were coming. A century later, firearms outshot and outpierced any bow yet invented.

Adding Firepower with Gunpowder

Between the twelfth and the eighteenth centuries, guns spread from China to western Asia, to Europe, and then around the world. They advanced from primitive experiments to precision technology. Warriors were forced to revise their strategies, sometimes adapting ancient battle formations to the new weaponry, while defenders had to find new ways to fortify outposts and cities.

Lighting the fire of discovery

Light a fire on a patch of dirt that has sulfur in it and you get a sizzling, popping reaction. Somebody whose name is lost to history noticed this a long time ago in China, an observation that led other Chinese to experiment with putting concentrated sulfur together with charcoal. By the ninth century AD, another genius added potassium nitrate crystals (saltpeter). Burn that mixture and you get sparkly effects that made a nice backdrop to formal ceremonies. Taoist monks played with these chemicals until they had fireworks.

Over time, pyrotechnicians (fireworks makers) also realized that their mixture, gunpowder, could make stuff fly — dangerous stuff. Soldiers noticed this, too. By the twelfth century, the armies of the Sung Dynasty added metal grenades to their arsenal. China pioneered fragmentation bombs, whose casings shattered into deadly shrapnel. Within another hundred years, Chinese factories made hundreds of military rockets and bombs, some filled with poisons, such as arsenic, that released on impact. Others were packed with tar and oil, designed to start fires. The Chinese also built early guns, metal barrels packed with gunpowder, which shot out a rock or a metal ball.

Spreading explosive news

News spread west along the ancient trade route, the Silk Road. (See Chapter 5.) The Arabs got primitive firearms by the late thirteenth century. In 1267, the recipe for gunpowder turned up in Europe, in the hands of English scientist Roger Bacon.

Less than a century later, European armies began using crude cannons. Archers with longbows, not their innovative comrades who were trying out noisy, stinky little *firepots,* decided the battle of Crécy, mentioned earlier in this chapter, but the primitive cannon was a sign of things to come. The early European cannon was called a firepot because it was pot-shaped. It propelled an arrow (yes, an arrow) with impressive force, but little reliability, and no accuracy. Craftsmen who until then made church bells were the earliest European gunmakers. Often they melted down bells to make cannons. Soon the gunmakers found out that a tubular barrel worked better, and that it should propel a metal shot. You could knock down a castle gate that way, or level a house.

Bringing in the big guns

By the early sixteenth century, the Italian writer Niccolo Machiavelli observed, "No wall exists, however thick, that artillery cannot destroy in a few days."

Guns were already big, although some of the biggest didn't work so well. In the early fifteenth century some weighed 1,500 pounds and discharged balls 30 inches in diameter. How did anybody back then make a cast-metal barrel that big? At first, it wasn't cast, but pieced together out of forged iron staves, like the curved boards used to form a pickle barrel. Iron hoops held the staves together — temporarily anyway.

In 1445, artillerymen in Burgundy (then an independent principality, later part of France) were firing one of these monster bombards (early cannon) at invading Turks when a hoop burst. The crazy thing is, they fired it again. Two more hoops and a stave blew apart on the next shot.

In 1460, one of his own guns exploded and killed King James II of Scotland and many members of his royal party.

Battering down Constantinople's walls

Sometimes a big gun was just the thing. Remember how the Arabs (earlier in this chapter) failed to capture stout Constantinople? Deciding to meet the challenge with big guns, Ottoman Turkish Sultan Mehmet II hired a Hungarian gunmaker who built him a cannon that sent a ball flying a full mile.

In **1453,** the sultan fired that gun, nicknamed *Mahometta,* at the Byzantine capital's ramparts and kept firing. Like so many of these giants, this cannon cracked after the second day and became unusable after a week. But Mehmet had other big guns. After 54 days of pounding, the 1,000-year-old Byzantine Empire, a victim of technological advance, finally fell.

Refining the new weaponry

Although massive bombards worked, military leaders knew there must be less cumbersome ways to win battles using cannons. Weapons makers went to work devising guns that were more useful and more versatile — and that fit specific niches in the Renaissance arsenal.

Making guns lighter and more maneuverable

Eventually, artillery experts figured out that you could cast some guns in light-yet-strong bronze, rather than iron. Less-cumbersome guns that could be moved into place more quickly, fired more often (some of the big ones could deliver a shot only once in two hours), and that weren't so likely to explode, could do even more damage than the giants could.

Improving gunpowder with brandy

Guns got better, but gunpowder needed improvement because the sulfur, carbon, and saltpeter had three different weights. The saltpeter crystals settled to the bottom while the carbon came to the top.

Mixing the ingredients right before you loaded your weapon — the only way to ensure that the gunpowder worked — was difficult and time-consuming. Then somebody came up with a way to make the ingredients stick together by mixing the gunpowder with brandy and letting the resulting paste dry into *corns,* or grains, containing all three ingredients.

But what a waste of brandy. Soldiers tried substitutes, such as vinegar, which worked okay, but human urine worked even better — especially the urine from a soldier who had put that brandy to more pleasurable use. (It didn't improve the smell of gunpowder, however.)

Putting guns in soldiers' hands

Guns were first seen as replacements for the catapult and the battering ram — destructive, but not precise. As gunnery improved, however, it gained accuracy and usefulness.

Soon, gunmakers came up with models for use on the battlefield itself — both as light artillery (usually a horse-drawn cannon on wagon wheels), and also as weapons that soldiers could carry. Handcannon, as the smallest guns were called, scared the enemy's horses (and your own, for that matter) and perhaps intimidated a knight or two. But for quite a while handcannon did not seem a practical replacement for bows and swords. How did you hold a gun, aim it, and also effectively set fire to the gunpowder charge?

In the middle of the fifteenth century, the solution was a wick soaked in alcohol and coated with saltpeter, attached to a trigger. Pulling the trigger lowered this *slow match* into the gun's touchhole to light the powder charge.

The *matchlock,* shown in Figure 16-2, freed a marksman's hands to aim a weapon, including one called a *hackbut or arquebuse — variations on the German Hakenbuchse,* which meant hook-gun. Some had a hook that you could brace on the edge of a wall when firing over it. The hook caught some of the shock from the gun's powerful recoil.

The name *musket* comes from mosquito. It was supposed to irritate the enemy like its namesake. But muskets were anything but mosquito-like in size. Many a musket had to be propped on a forked rest, like a crutch, to be aimed and fired. So in addition to the heavy gun itself, a musketeer had to lug around this cumbersome prop.

Figure 16-2:
The matchlock added a fuse to ignite the gunpowder and free the soldier's hands.

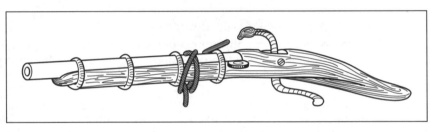

Striking sparks

Because a slow match (see above) could send off a spark that lit the charge too soon, the musket was dangerous for the musketeer. Gunsmiths came up with other ways to fire a powder charge, such as the wheel lock, a piece of flint held against a spring-loaded steel wheel. If you ever examined the moving parts of a cigarette lighter, you have a pretty good idea of how it struck sparks. Eventually the simpler flintlock, consisting of a spring-loaded hammer that struck a flint, became the dominant technology, lasting from about 1650 into the nineteenth century.

Floating a Fortress

After gunpowder redefined weaponry, naval battles became more and more about gunnery rather than ramming the opposing boat and then boarding it for a hand-to-hand battle on deck. The galley, once a formidable warship on the Mediterranean, became less useful because ships needed to bristle with gunports, not oars and oarsmen. Ships became floating fortresses.

Making Fortifications Star-Shaped

Ever since the earliest walled towns (see Chapter 15), a good defensive barrier was as tall as possible. Now cannonfire could topple such a wall. Architects came up with a new way to build a fort in the mid-fifteenth century. In Genoa, Leon Battista Alberti (see Chapter 12), drew designs for star-shaped fortresses with relatively low, but extremely thick walls. Figure 16-3 shows Castillo San Marcos, built by the Spaniards in St. Augustine, Florida, in the sixteenth century.

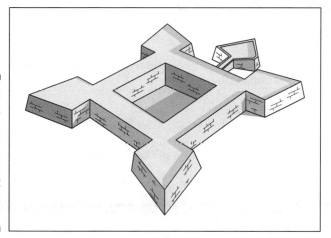

Figure 16-3: With thick walls and a star-shaped design, the Renaissance fort was built for cannon battles.

Jutting angles let a fort's defenders aim their cannons diagonally across the enemy lines so that a cannonball could skip down the line, wiping out more men, guns, horses, and equipment.

Adapting Old Strategies for New Weapons

Until the introduction of the breechloader — a gun loaded from the back (see Chapter 17) — a musketeer put everything, gunpowder and shot, down the barrel. You had to stand up to stuff all this material into the tube. Prince Maurice of Nassau, commander of the Netherlands troops in their religious war of independence against Spain (see Chapter 13) revived the *countermarch,* a Roman archery strategy. He put his musketeers in precise rows and had those in front fire all at once, then get to the rear to reload while the next rank fired.

Under Maurice and leaders like him — Sweden's King Gustav Adolph II (1594 to 1632) of Sweden and French Inspector General Jean Martinet (died in 1672) — armies emphasized rigid discipline more than ever. (Martinet's name became a synonym for an unbending authority figure.) Military commanders of the seventeenth and eighteenth centuries wanted soldiers to be more than fierce. They wanted the man willing and able to charge into concentrated gunfire. This trait — suicidal as it often proved — became a weird new definition of manly bravery.

Tracking the Centuries

Fourth century AD: Chinese cavalry begins using stirrups.

568 AD: Avar horsemen, using stirrups, win battles to take Danube Valley lands from the Byzantine Empire.

732 AD: At Poitiers, in Gaul, Charles Martel, king of the Franks, and his troops turn back invading Moorish horsemen from Spain.

Tenth century AD: European archers adopt the powerful crossbow.

1096: Pope Urban II condemns the crossbow as "hateful to God."

1241: About 80 men and boys die in tournament war games at Neuss, Germany.

1267: England's Roger Bacon has the recipe for gunpowder.

1396: Richard II of England marries the daughter of Charles VI of France, bringing a 28-year peace in the Hundred Years' War.

1460: A Scottish military cannon explodes, killing King James II and many members of his royal retinue.

Chapter 17

Reshaping Warfare in a Contemporary Mold

• •

In This Chapter

▶ Figuring out what's "modern" about *modern war*

▶ Applying nineteenth-century technology

▶ Enlarging the scale of armed conflict

▶ Hunkering down in trenches during World War I

▶ Returning to guerilla tactics in the nuclear age

• •

Modern war started with the U.S. Civil War in the 1860s. Or did modern war begin with the Crimean War in the 1850s? Perhaps modern war traces to several decades earlier, when a Prussian scholar-soldier began to teach the concept *total war*.

The Crimean War (see Chapter 8) has been touted as the first of the modern era's wars because it proved the wartime worth of new technologies, such as rifled muskets and telegraph lines to the front. The U.S. Civil War used such technologies and more, but it was a bigger and more devastating conflict. The U.S. Civil War seemed to personify the teachings of Karl von Clausewitz, who taught his young Prussian officers at the turn of the nineteenth century that they must conduct campaigns to do more than wipe out opposing forces — they must cripple entire regions. The Civil War's breadth and ferocity provided a glimpse of the future, previewing the global wars of the twentieth century.

Technology — from the rifle to the thermonuclear missile — fed every escalation in modern fighting styles, while backlash against the giant war-making capabilities of the post-World War II period revived age-old tactics, such as guerilla raids and terrorist sabotage.

Following Three Paths to Modern War

What's so modern about wars fought before armored tanks, airplanes, and the threat of nuclear explosions?

As I say in Chapter 2, historical terms are only good if they're useful. Maybe as the twenty-first century progresses, the term *modern war* will come to mean something new. Maybe a *modern* war will be defined as the kind of *surgical* air attack that the United States and its allies conducted in the late twentieth century, against Iraq, for example.

But for now, the term *modern* war reaches back to these three military milestones:

- ✔ Prussian generals, from the late eighteenth century through the nineteenth century, developed the concept of *total war* (a campaign of devastation) and *blitzkrieg* (lightning war, or a quick-strike campaign).

- ✔ The Crimean War began when England and France took on Russia in 1853, just when the armies of western Europe were rearming with faster-firing, easier-to-load weapons and employing such innovations as the steamship and telegraph to support the fighting.

- ✔ The U.S. Civil War followed South Carolina's 1860 decision that it didn't want to be part of the United States of America anymore. A massive death toll, and the devastation wrought upon an entire region, the South, and its economy, far surpassed the expectations of military commanders and civilians on either side.

Promoting devastation in Prussia

In the U.S. Civil war, which I talk about more fully later in this chapter, Northern troops resorted to burning crops and wiping out farmsteads so that ruined Southerners would be forced to surrender. These Northern soldiers' weary leaders, desperate to achieve peace, used extreme measures — *total war* — against a determined foe.

But there were other soldiers in the emerging German state of Prussia who saw *total war* not as a desperation strategy but as the model for how warfare *ought* to be conducted. The most influential was Karl von Clausewitz (1780 to 1831), director of the Prussian army school. He wrote a book called *On War,* a manual for fighting an all-out campaign — the "scorched earth" advance.

Helmuth Graf von Moltke, commander of Prussia's army, took Clausewitz's ideas and harnessed them to new technology — needle guns, new long-range artillery, and railroads. (More on nineteenth-century weapons advances with the Crimean War, just ahead.) Moltke reorganized and vastly enlarged his military. Then he used Prussia's forces to win wars against Denmark in 1864, Austria in 1866, and France in 1870.

Overwhelming in number and devastatingly efficient, the Prussians in the Franco-Prussian War advanced on Paris in a troop movement so quick it was called a *blitzkrieg,* or "lightning war." The Prussians surrounded the French Army, killed 17,000 in a rain of artillery, and took more than 100,000 prisoners, among them Emperor Napoléon III. (The *lightning war,* would emerge again, especially in World War II.)

Prussia's military preeminence allowed its prime minister, Otto von Bismarck, to unite Germany in 1871. Bismarck became the first chancellor of a new German Empire, a formidable military power through the age when total war would become *world war.*

Putting technology to deadly uses: The Crimean War

Why did France and Britain declare war on Russia to start the Crimean War? Well, for one thing, Russia was nibbling away at the crumbling Ottoman Empire. That was scary because other countries didn't want any neighbor too big or powerful.

The Ottoman Empire, dating back to the Ottoman Turks' conquest of Byzantine Constantinople in 1453 (see Chapter 16), was a wreck by the mid-nineteenth century.

As diplomatic friends of the Ottomans, France and Britain bristled when Russia marched troops across the Danube River into Turkish territory in Romania. Western European powers such as France and Britain didn't want Russia to control the Black Sea area and overland trade routes to India, much less establish a seaport on the Mediterranean.

Yet France and Britain didn't really want war, either. At an 1853 conference in Vienna, France and Britain tried to get the Ottomans to compromise with the Russians, but the Turks declared war instead. Ironically, the war proceeded even after Russia gave in to Austrian demands (and the threat of the Austrian army) and withdrew from the disputed parts of Romania — Wallachia and Moldavia. Austria mobilized its troops to threaten Russia into backing down, but Austria did not enter the Crimean War.

After Russia replied to the Turks' declaration of war by destroying the Ottoman fleet at Sinope, Britain and France saw no alternative but to weigh in and teach the czar a lesson. Britain and France, along with the Italian principality of the Piedmont (it means *foothills*), sent forces to confront the Russians on the Crimean Peninsula in southern Ukraine (between the Black Sea and the

Sea of Azov). What was at stake wasn't absolutely essential to any of the countries involved, so in some ways this was like many wars of a century earlier, the conflict-laden eighteenth (see Chapter 8). But technology made this a new kind of war.

Adding accuracy and speed with new rifles

By the time of the Crimean War, the flintlock musket (see Chapter 16) was old technology. A new device, the *percussion lock,* replaced the flintlock's old friction-spark system (see the sidebar "The clergyman's new gun"). In the percussion-lock weapon, the powder charge ignited within a reliable, easy-to-load cartridge.

What else was new about firearms? The rifled barrel was a big change. *Rifling* means to etch spiral grooves into the inside of a gun barrel, making the shot spin as it travels up the barrel and thus go straighter through the air. Think of the way a football thrown with a spin, or *spiral,* flies true, while one that doesn't spin develops a wobble.

For the rifled barrel to be most effective, you needed ammunition that fit the barrel tightly enough to engage the groove and take its spin. That kind of shot was difficult to load through the mouth, or muzzle, of the barrel. If the metal slug was tight enough to engage the grooves, the slug was also tight enough to catch on the way in, blocking the barrel and making the gun useless.

The *minié* bullet — named not for its size but for its inventor, Captain Claude-Étienne Minié of France — offered an early solution. Minié hollowed the bottom of a lead bullet, turning its back edge into a semi-flexible flange. When the explosive charge went off under it, the hollow expanded, pushing out the flange to fit more tightly against the sides of the barrel. The flange caught the rifling. The bullet spun and flew true.

The clergyman's new gun

The Reverend Alexander John Forsyth of Belhelvie, Scotland, wanted to shoot birds, not soldiers, when he came up with the idea for the percussion lock — a major advance in firearms technology.

Forsyth enjoyed hunting grouse and ducks. He did not enjoy missing a shot. You missed a lot in Forsyth's time (the early nineteenth century), even if you were handy with a musket, because the flash of a flintlock frightened the bird.

Frustrated, the reverend devised a self-contained gunpowder capsule that would ignite without flashing when the musket's hammer drove a firing pin into the capsule. This was the prototype for what would become a self-contained bullet, in which the powder charge and slug became one package.

Other advances followed after a few decades, resulting in the breechloading rifles used in the Crimean War.

Then came an even better solution for getting the bullet into the barrel. With the percussion lock and its self-contained powder charge, it became practical to load the weapon from the back, or *breech* end, instead of through its muzzle. A snug fit on the way in was no longer an issue. Even better, breechloading weapons eliminated the soldier's reliance on gravity to get the ammunition down the barrel. You no longer had to stand up when reloading. The rifleman could stay flat against the ground, presenting the minimum target.

The Prussian needle-gun (named for its long firing pin) came first among these breechloaders, followed by the French chassepot and the British Snyder-Enfield. With better weapons, range more than doubled — in some cases to more than 4,000 yards. Accuracy improved tremendously. Increased rate of fire allowed a skilled rifleman with a Snyder-Enfield to get off six shots in a minute.

How much difference did new firearms make? At the Battle of Inkerman in 1854, an early landmark in the Crimean War, the allies had breechloading rifles and the Russians did not. The score: 12,000 Russians dead to only 3,000 allies.

Transporting troops via steamship

Steam power (see Chapter 8) allowed shippers to deliver freight on time, keeping to a schedule instead of depending on the whim of the wind. The steamship did the same for military leaders.

When you deliver men, horses, and artillery by sea, they have a better chance of arriving fresh, rather than ground down from a long march. But a wind-powered ship sometimes stalled in becalmed waters for days or even weeks. If troops were aboard and supplies ran out, the soldiers arrived weak from hunger. With the steamship, ready troops could be shipped from England and France to Turkey and the Crimea faster and more reliably. Strategists could make plans with a reasonable certainty that the soldiers would arrive on or near the date promised.

Laying down railroad tracks to the front lines

There was no rail line handy for the British and French troops when they got to the port of Balaklava. So they built one to serve the inland battle head-quarters. This was the first railroad built to serve a war effort. The train did on land what the steamship did on water, providing a reliable way to get troops and supplies to a battle site.

Stringing telegraph wires to the battlefield

The most *modern* device employed in the Crimea, the electric telegraph, allowed commanders to communicate with their troops instantaneously. Support troops strung wires to wherever fighters were deployed.

MOVIE

Into the Valley of Death

The English of the mid-nineteenth century learned of the Light Brigade's mistaken charge through newspaper accounts. But they remembered it through verse. Lord Alfred Tennyson (1809 to 1892) landed the post of England's poet laureate in 1850 and was doing that job when he wrote a heroic verse that begins "Half a league, half a league, / Half a league onward, / All in the valley of Death / Rode the six hundred."

The poem caught the popular imagination as few poems ever have. There were the galloping horses and galloping cadences in the lines: "Cannon to the right of them, / Cannon to the left of them, / Cannon behind them / Volleyed and thundered." "The Charge of the Light Brigade" is one of the few poems ever to inspire a movie, and it inspired not just one, but two of the same title.

The first, made in 1936, stars Errol Flynn and Patric Knowles as brothers, both in love with Olivia de Haviland. The boys don't arrive in the Crimea until nearly the end. When they do, the audience is in for a strange interpretation of the Battle of Balaklava, which somehow involves an Indian Rajah on the Russian side. The recreated attack, however, is beautifully filmed.

The 1936 version remains better than British director Tony Richardson's ill-conceived 1968 effort of the same title. He wasted the talents of John Gielgud, Trevor Howard, Vanessa Redgrave, and David Hemmings, among many others.

Until this, armies communicated by messenger or sometimes by systems of signals, such as smoke puffs or semaphore code relayed by line-of-sight from station to station. With the electric telegraph, information and orders pulsed along at the speed of electric current.

Not only were commanders and field lieutenants in touch, but the governments in Paris and London also were connected with their armies by wire, for much of the distance, anyway. Getting a message back home no longer took weeks.

Civilians, notably the press, also could send messages quickly and easily — presenting a new public relations problem for British officers in the Crimea. W.H. Russell, an Irish reporter working for an English paper, became the first war correspondent to file a *wire report,* as many newspapers still call them. His stories in *The Times* of London told the English about the disastrous "Charge of the Light Brigade," a brave but muddleheaded British cavalry attack on Russian artillery positions during the Battle of Balaklava.

Russell witnessed and wrote of the way poorly equipped allied troops suffered through the long winter siege of Russia's fort at Sebastopol in 1854 and 1855, noting that some of their commanders spent that winter aboard private yachts offshore. Outraged readers demanded reforms.

Redefining armed conflict: The U.S. Civil War

If the Crimean War changed the tools of warfare, then the U.S. Civil War changed war itself by showing how big, deadly, and devastatingly costly a modern war could be. Four million men mobilized over its course and more than 600,000 of them died in widespread battles.

More Americans died in the Civil War than died in World War I, World War II, the Korean War, and the Vietnam War combined. That's right, *combined.* And if you think of how much smaller the U.S. population was then — fewer than 31.5 million by the 1860 census compared to about 273 million today — you can begin to imagine the devastation.

Waging total war on Sherman's march to the sea

For the South, the Civil War meant the wreck of an entire economy. This was the war in which a general, Ulysses S. Grant, commander of the Union Armies, first used the word *attrition* to describe his strategy. He announced his intention to pound the enemy until that enemy could do nothing but surrender. And so Grant did.

Although German theoreticians such as Clausewitz (earlier in this chapter) pioneered the concept of *total war,* the U.S. Civil war was the first large-scale demonstration of his idea. Before war's end, the Union wreaked brutal and absolute devastation — military, economic, and societal. Union General William Tecumseh Sherman (see Chapter 19) wiped out virtually everything in his army's path on an 1864 march from Chattanooga, Tennessee, through Atlanta to the coastal town of Savannah, Georgia. On this campaign, known to history as Sherman's March to the Sea, union troops destroyed farms, trashed machinery, spoiled any foodstuffs they could not steal, slaughtered cattle and chickens, loosed mules, scattered slaves, sacked and burned not just Atlanta but dozens of towns along their way, and in Sherman's words, "generally raised hell."

Sherman also gets credit for the phrase "War is hell." If he didn't actually say it, he acted it out.

Sorting through the Civil War's causes

Also called the War of the Rebellion and the War Between the States, the U.S. conflict started in 1860, although a violent prelude foreshadowed what was to come. The abolitionist John Brown (see Chapter 21), fresh from anti-slavery violence in the western territory of Kansas, came east with his men in 1859 to capture the U.S. armory at Harper's Ferry, in what was then northwestern Virginia (and would soon be the new state of West Virginia). U.S. troops commanded by Robert E. Lee captured Brown. Convicted of treason and hanged, he became a martyr for the abolitionist cause.

Abolitionists wanted to abolish slavery (see Chapter 7), the labor base of the American South. This issue, intertwined with that of state self-determination versus federal oversight, led to the South's rebellion at the end of 1860.

The rebellion erupted after Abraham Lincoln of Illinois, the Kentucky-born candidate of the new, anti-slavery Republican Party, won the presidency in 1860. In December, South Carolina resigned from the Union. Ten other states said "Us, too." The following April, troops of the newly formed Confederate States of America attacked Fort Sumter, a U.S. military post in Charleston, South Carolina. Neither side was prepared for what would follow. Who could be? Most Americans of the mid-nineteenth century had never seen war.

Exceeding each other's expectations with grim determination

In the summer of 1861, when Union troops marched south from Washington, D.C., intent on thrashing the Confederate forces camped in nearby Virginia, the capital's public treated the impending conflict as a lark. Sightseers toting picnic baskets tagged along behind the troops. Civilians and soldiers alike expected a neat victory, a quick peace.

What they got was a rout, and a shock. Before the day was over, many of the 18,000 Union soldiers who met the enemy at Bull Run near Manassas, Virginia, turned and ran for their lives. This war was not going to be easy, or predictable.

Spewing bullets from the machine gun

Ever since the cannon and musket became basic tools of warfare, inventors struggled to find ways to load and fire faster. Early attempts included weapons with multiple barrels or multiple charges to be fired in succession. The first practical design was the Gatling gun, named after American inventor Richard Gatling. An opportunist inspired by the U.S. Civil War, he used percussion lock technology and devised a hand-crank mechanism to feed charges into his gun's chambers, fire them, and then extract the spent cartridges. Gatling said it would fire 200 rounds a minute.

Although a Southerner, Gatling offered his invention to both sides in the war. Neither bought it. Only after the war did it become part of the U.S. arsenal. Britain, Japan, Russia, Turkey, and Spain all placed orders, too.

In the 1880s another American inventor, Hiram Maxim, came up with an improved machine gun that required no cranking. You could hold down the trigger and the gun would just keep firing, making this the first automatic weapon. It used the power of each charge's recoil to eject the cartridge and move the next one into the chamber. It could spit more than 600 bullets a minute. By World War I, the Maxim and imitators were a major part of just about any battle.

Believing fervently in their cause, Southerners thought that a decisive victory or two, like that early one at what would be called the first Battle of Bull Run (another battle followed there the next year) would convince the Union to turn them loose.

But the North had overwhelming economic advantages — factories, railroads, and a much larger population base — that the rebels lacked. And it had a deep-seated resolve of its own. The canny, articulate Lincoln convinced the public that the Union must be saved.

The Civil War evoked the kind of popular involvement that Europe saw in the French Revolution (see Chapter 7) and hooked it up to the new industrial technology. In some ways, the Civil War was a throwback to earlier ages, when sacking and burning were commonplace. But as the Civil War employed the same new technologies as in the Crimea — on a larger scale, over a longer time — it pointed toward a horrible future. Military leaders figured out, for example, that the improved range and accuracy of a rifled gun barrel added enormous risk to the infantry charge. Units learned to dig in. The spade, or *trenching tool,* came into tactical use. This was a preview of the grinding, static, morale-killing style of ground fighting that would characterize World War I.

Tying Tactics to Technology in the Twentieth Century

In Chapter 8, I tell you how twentieth-century wars spread European-based conflicts around the world, rearranging borders and bringing down economic and political empires. World War I reset the global stage for a new era in international relations, inspiring the world's first attempt at an organization to prevent war — the League of Nations — but it did that, at least in part, by demonstrating how war was changed by the killing trends of the nineteenth century.

World War II then speeded the process up, adding new weapon after new weapon to the technically sophisticated arsenal. Each perilous escalation in weaponry made industrialized nations better able to rain down death with an ease beyond any imagined by ancestors of even a century earlier. This *progress* brought civilization all the way to the perilous, fiery brink of the nuclear age.

Trapping valor in a trench: World War 1

With the Maxim machine gun (see the sidebar "Spewing bullets from the machine gun") and its *improved* descendents so widely used in World War I, the tactic of charging enemy positions, more dangerous with every advance in weaponry, now became suicidal.

Once this lesson sunk in, after the first Battle of the Marne, fought in France in September, 1914, the front lines of the war's Western Front turned into thousands of miles of parallel trenches across Europe — wet, rat-infested ditches in which cold, dirty, terrified men hid for days, weeks, months, and years. There they scratched at lice and warily watched the other side's trenches. On occasion, the horrible order would come. The men obediently climbed out and flung themselves into a barrage of bullets and exploding mortar shells. Trying to break the stalemate, both sides developed new weapons including hand grenades for lobbing into the enemy trench, mortar shells that could be fired up and over the opposite embankment, and exploding canisters of poison mustard gas, an oily chemical that left victims blistered and often permanently disabled.

One answer, thought up by a British officer in 1915, was to put an armored casing around the kind of tractor that ran on metal chain treads. The officer thought you could mount guns on this fortified crawler and drive it toward the enemy machine gun positions. The armored tank was born and by war's end, British units were using it to cross German trenches.

Revisiting World War II in outstanding films

The World War II way of war seems so familiar because it's still relatively recent, but also because you've probably seen all of the devices I mention in "Retooling and the WWII arsenal." They're all depicted in World War II flicks. There are loads of good movies about that war, from 1945's *The Story of G.I. Joe* through 1998's *Saving Private Ryan.*

The Story of G.I. Joe, starring Robert Mitchum, and *Saving Private Ryan*, starring Tom Hanks, both try to get at the war's brutal realities. The first, directed by William Wellman, examines the soul-deadening meaninglessness of a front-line infantryman's life, as seen through the eyes of war correspondent Ernie Pyle. (Pyle was a real news reporter, but actor Burgess Meredith portrayed him.) *Private Ryan*, directed by Steven Spielberg, uses 1990s special effects to capture the surreal horror of battle.

Also in 1945, John Wayne and Robert Montgomery starred in director John Ford's uncompromising *They Were Expendable*, about PT boat battles in the South Seas. Wayne, however, appeared more often in movies that simplified the war into nothing but heroic adventure, films such as the ridiculous *Fighting Seabees*, made in 1944. Part of Hollywood's role was to boost morale, and patriotic dramas about killing the "sub-human" Japanese while winning the girl (Susan Hayward) were just the thing for that.

Also in that war, a German engineer figured out how to time a machine gun to fire through a spinning propeller without hitting the blades. Fighter aircraft resulted. Airplanes began to drop bombs, too, although on nothing like the scale that was to come in World War II. The submarine, in the form of the German U-boat, showed its value in World War I as its crews enjoyed the advantage of underwater surprise.

Retooling the WWII arsenal

In World War II, technology in the service of mass destruction accelerated at a pace that would have astonished even General Moltke. Bazookas, aircraft carriers, anti-aircraft guns, anti-submarine depth charges, long-range fighter planes, missiles, radar, sonar, and atomic weapons all came out of that war.

What are all these things? Many of the names are self-explanatory — although *bazooka* is a weird name for anything. (It's a small, portable anti-tank rocket launcher that an individual infantryman can carry and fire.) Most of the inventions — even some of the most chilling among them — are now taken for granted as part of the modern world, and some serve peaceful purposes. Two examples:

- ✔ **Radar** (originally RADAR, an acronym for RAdio Detecting And Ranging) began as an idea based on the echo. Radar bounces radio waves off objects and then detects the pattern of the returning waves to *see* objects (especially airplanes) beyond the range of visual detection. Radar allowed Britain's outnumbered Royal Air Force to detect German bomber squads, spoiling Nazi plans to invade the British Isles. After the war, it was an invaluable tool for commercial aviation and, because radar can tell you how fast an object (such as an automobile) is moving, in traffic law enforcement.

- ✔ **Sonar** (SOund Navigation And Ranging) did much the same with sound waves underwater as Radar did with radio waves in the air. With sonar, a ship could detect enemy submarines. Numerous postwar uses range from salvaging sunken ships to fishing.

The United States dropped two atomic bombs on Japan in 1945 to end World War II (see Chapter 8). Historians, military strategists, and peace activists still argue about whether those attacks were justifiable. In any case, it's certain that those first "A-bombs," and the even deadlier nuclear weapons developed after the war, changed how war is perceived and fought.

Warring On Despite the Nuclear Threat

Some people thought that nuclear weapons would make any further warfare unthinkable. It didn't turn out that way.

A growing number of countries built and tested nuclear weapons (more about nuclear proliferation in Chapter 8), but in much of the world, the nuclear option remained irrelevant. This was especially so in South America, Southeast Asia, and Africa, where revolutions and civil wars raged on.

Despite the massive ability of the post Word War II superpowers (the Soviet Union, until its 1991 breakup, and the United States) to wreak large-scale mayhem, small-scale warriors — especially those that believed in their causes of revolution or retribution for perceived political wrongs — found ways to undermine the security of major nations. Often they reached back to pre-technological strategies such as the guerilla raid and the difficult-to-prevent terrorist strike.

Drawing strength from stealth: Guerilla tactics

Paradoxically, the nuclear age of the late twentieth century was also an era of a foot soldier treading softly in the night. Guerilla war is often fought by outnumbered, ill-financed bands of revolutionaries moving stealthily against better-armed powers. Guerilla units venture out under cover of darkness to conduct small-scale raids and set booby traps.

Guerilla, Spanish for "little war," first referred to the Spanish peasants who harassed Napoléon's conquering forces early in the nineteenth century. (See Chapter 8 for more on the Napoleonic Wars.) Then as now, guerilla tactics followed precedents as old as war itself — the same tactics that the sneaky Italian tribes who frustrated early Rome's Greek-style phalanx in Chapter 15 probably used. The improvisational soldiering of American revolutionaries sometimes caught Britain's infantry off guard in the 1770s. It too took guerilla turns. Americans fired from cover, for example, putting a marching formation of Brits at a disadvantage (see Chapter 7).

The British faced guerilla tactics again, more than a century later in South Africa. The Boer War began in 1899, when the Boers, descendents of Dutch colonial farmers, tried to take away land controlled by Great Britain in the Transvaal. Expecting to beat down this rebellion of farmers (*Boer* means "farmer") in a few months, the British failed to consider Boer determination and toughness. Frontier-raised, the Boers rode horses masterfully and knew the territory intimately.

Against Britain's superior weaponry, the determined Boers resorted to hiding, raiding, and bombing. Realizing that this foe would hold on indefinitely, the British were forced to do what Grant and Sherman did in the United States, to fight a war of attrition: burning farms and herding Dutch civilians into concentration camps where hunger and disease killed many.

Twentieth-century opposition forces ranging from the French Resistance in World War II to the Communist Viet Cong in 1960s Vietnam to the anti-Communist Contras in 1980s Nicaragua made effective use of backwoods evasiveness, quickness, mobility, and well-timed, small-scale raids against stronger foes.

Figure 17-1:
Guerilla fighters such as Vietnam's Vietcong stage raids against stronger foes.

© Bettman/CORBIS

Wielding the weapon of fear: Terrorism

While the targets of guerilla forces are generally military, or at least within an area at war, terrorist violence frequently seems indiscriminate and arbitrary — as in the bombing of a shopping mall, a city bus, or a commercial airliner full of tourists.

The perpetrators are usually minority groups who feel that violence is the only way they can advance their cause, often the overthrow of the established order. By definition, terrorists use terror — fear of the next unpredictable strike — as a weapon.

The Provisional Irish Republican Army (IRA), a nationalist group that wanted to reunite British-controlled Northern Ireland with the self-ruled Irish Republic, was frequently labeled terrorist in the period from the 1970s to the 1990s. Although IRA bombs were often directed at military targets, they also went off among passersby in English cities.

Terrorists, though often labeled criminals, usually consider themselves warriors — engaged in *honorable* acts of battle. Some are even sanctioned by governments. Iraq and Libya are two nations frequently accused of financing terrorist factions in the late twentieth century.

Terrorism is even more difficult to defend against than guerilla war. Toward the end of the twentieth century, it became theoretically possible to build a satellite-based missile defense system to automatically shoot down threatening nuclear missiles in flight. Yet no scientist had come up with a way to keep a terrorist from smuggling a bomb — conceivably even a nuclear bomb — across international borders in the hold of an airplane, or even the trunk of a car.

Tracking the Centuries

1833: Published two years after his death, Carl von Clauswitz's book *On War* is the manual for total war, an all-out style of fighting.

1854: French and British infantrymen armed with breechloading rifles kill 12,000 Russians while suffering only one-fourth that many casualties at the Battle of Inkerman in the Crimean War.

1899: British troops fight Boer rebels in the Transvaal, South Africa.

1914 to 1918: Parallel trenches define the Western Front of World War I, stretching from the North Sea to Switzerland.

1945: Atomic bombs devastate the cities of Hiroshima and Nagasaki, forcing Japan's government to surrender and ending World War II.

1973: The Vietnam War winds toward its conclusion as the United States begins to withdraw troops.

1980s: Right-wing Contra Rebel Army guerillas harass the leftist Sandinista government of Nicaragua.

Early twenty-first century: United States policymakers debate the value of a proposed orbiting antimissile defense system.

Part V
People

The 5th Wave   By Rich Tennant

MUSEUM EXIT

NEANDERTHAL MAN

"And believe it or not children, some of your ancestors could be related to this fellow right here."

In this part. . .

1 give you capsule glimpses into lives and legacies here. These snippets of biography tell you a little more about folks whose names pop up in other parts of the book and also add a few historical personalities that you don't find in other chapters.

Is this a complete list of everybody who ever made a difference in world history? Are these biographies complete? Are you kidding? The answers are "No," "No," and "You *must* be kidding."

Everybody in the following chapters deserves a whopping fat volume that delves deeply into motives and intrigues. Many of the historical figures in this part of the book have inspired a full-length biography, if not several full-length biographies. And there are more people — many, many more people — who could have and should have made this list if only I had some magic formula for jamming them all into these chapters. Watch for cross-references to help you connect lives and eras.

Chapter 18

Founding Something Lasting

● ●

In This Chapter

▶ Giving Rome a legendary start with a wolf-boy

▶ Uniting Anglo-Saxons under Alfred

▶ Marrying the kingdoms of Aragon and Castille

▶ Smothering Draco, the harsh Athenian lawmaker

● ●

*S*ocieties, nations, and cultures don't just happen. That is, maybe they do, but somebody always takes credit. Or . . . a few hundred years after the fact, somebody looks back and *assigns* credit for the founding of the city-state, the empire, the nation, or the culture. Sometimes it's an individual, sometimes a group.

In Chapter 2, I talk about the way historians label eras, movements, and trends, choosing what to include and what to leave out. Trying to make sense of the hodgepodge of human experience, historians have to make choices. In this chapter, I give you only a very few of history's founders — my choices, based on their impact in their own times and their political and cultural legacies. (Okay, a few made the cut just because I felt like putting them in.) When you notice glaring omissions, and you will, you're free to jot them in the margins — but *please* buy the book first.

Spinning Legends

Many historical figures, even in relatively recent times, take on mythic stature. Those from long ago can be so shrouded in layers of lore that the truth may never be known. Did a demigod really ever found a city-state? Did a wizard's spell ever grace an enchanted age? My educated guess is no, those things didn't happen. The following legends may all have been inspired by real leaders, or they could all be make-believe:

✔ **Agamemnon** (legendary, but probably based on a real king of the twelfth century BC): In the *Iliad,* a Greek epic poem, King Agamemnon commanded the alliance of fellow Greeks (or the pre-Greeks called *Achaeans*) who besieged Troy. Agamemnon, the wealthy ruler of Mycenae, was the brother of Menelaus, king of Sparta. The Greeks were mad at Troy because the Trojan Prince Paris stole Menelaus's wife, Helen. Because the *Iliad* is a poem laced with supernatural acts by the gods, nobody can say how much of it is literally true. Many centuries of Greeks found cultural identity in the tale. (For more about the *Iliad* and the Trojan War, see Chapter 1.)

✔ **Romulus** (probably mythical, although his legend could be based on a king of the eighth or seventh century BC): In a story about the founding of Rome, Romulus appears as one of the twin sons of Mars (the god, not the planet or the candy bar) conceived when Mars dallied with a Vestal Virgin. Romulus and his twin brother Remus, abandoned as infants, floated down the River Tiber until a she-wolf found them and suckled the babies. After they grew up, Remus cracked jokes as Romulus tried to get Rome built. (It took more than a day.) Romulus got mad and killed Remus. Later, a thunderstorm blew Romulus away. How much of this is true? Probably none of it, but Romulus still gets credit as the first Roman king. (Note: Romulus's brother is not the same as *Uncle* Remus, an American fictional character who told fables about talking rabbits, bears, and foxes.)

✔ **King Arthur** (perhaps sixth century AD): Maybe, just maybe, Arthur was a real person. Perhaps Roman-British war leader Arturus inspired the legend. Arturus supposedly united British (Celtic) tribes against invading Saxons. He may have promoted Christianity, too. Welsh chronicles say that he fought a series of battles in the early sixth century and died fighting in 537. Among the most famous Arthurian tales are those by Sir Thomas Malory.

Arturus may have inspired the Arthur legend, but don't blame him for the 1967 movie musical *Camelot.* Director Joshua Logan never figured out how to transfer the stagy romance of Alan Jay Lerner and Frederick Loewe's Broadway hit to the screen. Richard Harris, Vanessa Redgrave, and Franco Nero (as Arthur, Queen Guinevere, and Lancelot, respectively) look and sound painfully artificial. Among many other screen treatments of Arthur, Walt Disney's animated *The Sword in the Stone* holds up pretty well if you keep in mind that it's entertainment for children, never intended as a faithful rendition of its source. (Never expect a Disney movie, or *any* movie, to faithfully relate history or literature.)

Disney's source was not Malory, by the way, but the novel *The Sword in the Stone,* one of the four books in twentieth-century English author T.H. White's series *The Once and Future King.* White's books about Arthur — including *Queen of Air and Darkness, The Ill-Made Knight,* and *The Candle in the Wind* — also inspired lyricist Lerner and composer Loewe to write *Camelot.*

Vesta's girls

The Vestal Virgins waited on the Roman deity Vesta (goddess of home and hearth). Picked for the honor from a short list of suitable aristocratic girls, Vestal Virgins took a vow of chastity and served for 30 years each, cleaning Vesta's shrine and tending its fire. They got a place to live — the House of the Vestals — in the Forum, downtown Rome's public square. People trusted them and gave their wills to the Vestal Virgins for safekeeping. There was a down side: If a Vestal cheated on that vow of chastity, the authorities buried her alive.

Uniting for Strength

Many a founder is the one person strong enough for other leaders to rally behind. The leaders in this section made a difference through a combination of physical force and force of personality:

- **Saul** (eleventh century BC): Saul became the first king of the Israelites after Samuel, a holy man, poured oil on Saul's head. (As the pompadour was not yet in style, this was not a grooming aid.) By anointing Saul, Samuel signaled that Saul was God's choice to unite a tribal confederation of Jews. Saul defeated the Philistines and ruled the Israelites from his capital at Hebron. As king, Saul took over religious ceremonial duties, angering Samuel, the high priest. Samuel began to favor David, a brave young war hero. David was best pals with Saul's son and married Saul's daughter, making him a member of the family but also making Saul jealous of all the attention paid to David. Samuel secretly anointed David as the next king. After Saul and his son Jonathan died in another battle against the Philistines, David became leader of the tribe of Judah, later reuniting the Israelites as their second king.

- **Shi Huangdi** (259 to 210 BC): Shi Huangdi began as Zheng, Prince of Qin, an innovative warrior who adopted iron weapons before the rest of China and told his cavalry to ditch the chariots and sit right on top of those horses. This made them faster and more adaptable. Qin was just a little country whose rulers had to pay tribute to the Zhou family, which also ruled other Chinese vassal states. But then Zheng started branching out, taking neighboring provinces away from the Zheng until he could name himself Shi Huangdi (or First Emperor). As king, Shi Huangdi standardized writing and units of measure, including weights, across the lands he had conquered. This conformity helped successive dynasties rule China as a unified land. He opposed Confucian beliefs (see Chapter 9 to find out about Confucianism), burned Confucian books, and killed scholars while surrounding himself with officials and warriors. His tomb, full of terra cotta warriors to protect him in the afterlife, is an archeological and historical gold mine. Shi Huangdi's own Qin Dynasty survived him by only four years, until the long-lasting Han Dynasty came to power in 206 BC. Yet the name Qin (also spelled Chi'in) is the root of *China* (see Chapter 3 for more about early civilization in China).

- ✔ **Clovis** (about 465 to 511 AD): Roman officials, trying to hang onto Gaul (or France) after the western Roman Empire crumbled, had to give up when Clovis, the king of the Franks, took over. After he succeeded his father, Childeric, Clovis extended his rule over everything between the Somme and the Loire Rivers by 496 AD. That year, Clovis was the first Frankish king to convert to Christianity. Credit his wife, a princess from Burgundy. If Clovis ever said, "My wife is a saint," he was righter than he knew. The Catholic Church later canonized her as St. Clotilde. When Clovis converted, so did several thousand of his warriors. As Frankish leaders did in those days, Clovis had to battle Visgoths and Ostrigoths (both Germanic barbarian tribes) to stay in power.

- ✔ **Alfred the Great of England** (849 to 899 AD): The Danes were moving in on the Saxons when Alfred came to power as king of Wessex (the Western Saxons). Danes had their own kingdom in the north of England and they were expanding into such Anglo-Saxon parts of Briton (the main British isle) as Northumbria and East Anglia. Alfred put a stop to that at the Battle of Edington in 878 AD. Then he pushed back, regaining London in 886 AD and put together a standing army, navy, and network of forts that gave him the military advantage. Alfred got the Saxons together with other English peoples, descendents of fellow Germanic tribes such as the Angles and Jutes, so they could work together against the Danes. He emphasized Christianity (as opposed to Norse paganism), literacy, and codified laws. No other English king or queen is called "the Great."

- ✔ **Brian Boru** (about 926 to 1014 AD): Also called Brian Boroimhe ("Brian of the Tribute"), this Irish warrior was a chief of the Dal Cais (a clan) and fought his way to the crown of Leinster. The Irish were tired of absorbing Viking blows, which helped Brian rally support. He fought regional rivals until he united Ireland. That was the beginning of a nation (although many hard centuries lay ahead). Brian's forces beat the Vikings at Clontarf, but Brian died in the fighting.

Playing for Power

When the going gets tough, the toughest found dynasties. The guys in this list didn't need assertiveness training; they stepped forward to shove rivals out of the way as they made themselves, and their governments, the ultimate authority. Stand aside for military strongmen and emperors:

- ✔ **Augustus Caesar** (63 BC to 14 AD): Rome's first official emperor was Gaius Julius Caesar Octavianus, or Octavian, the son of a senator and a great nephew of *the* Julius Caesar. (See Chapter 19 for more about Julius Caesar, and Chapter 4 for more on the Roman Empire.) When conspirators killed Julius, who was dictator, Octavian was a student, but he closed his books, raised an army, dealt with the assassins, defeated his rival for power, Mark Antony, and forced the Senate to make him consul. Later that year, 43 BC, Octavian made a deal with Antony and another Roman big shot, Lepidus, to form a triumvirate (or ruling three). Octavian's part of the bargain was Africa, Sardinia, and Sicily. Later he got the entire western half of the Roman world and, after defeating Antony and the Egyptian queen Cleopatra at Actium in 31 BC, Octavian became sole ruler. The Senate gave him the name "Augustus," or "exalted." Under his rule, Rome saw peace, reform, and rebuilding. The Roman Senate declared him *Pater Patriae* (Father of his Country) in 2 BC. When he died, the Senate declared him a god.

✔ **Charlemagne** (742 AD to 814 AD): The Franks, like the Romans before them, had problems with intruders. Barbarians from up north kept horning in on Gaul (today's France) and there were rumblings from those Muslims down in Spain when Charlemagne (or Charles the Great) came to power — first as king of the Eastern Franks (his brother Carloman, got the western bunch), then as Great King of the Franks in 771 AD. The title *great king* meant that he ruled over lesser kings and princes, which was the feudal style of leadership. Charlemagne brought Europe together under one rule as nobody had since the Romans, fighting Saxons, Avars, and Lombards to do it. On Christmas Day, 800 AD, Pope Leo III crowned Charlemagne as *Emperor of the West* or *Holy Roman Emperor,* starting the Holy Roman Empire (which had nothing to do with the original Roman Empire). Charlemagne built palaces and churches and promoted Christianity, education, agriculture, and the arts. Commerce thrived under his administration, which came to be known as the Carolingian Renaissance — a *little* awakening hundreds of years before the big awakening. The empire fell apart after he died because Charlie's sons lacked his vision and authority. (For more about Charlemagne and his family, see Chapter 5.)

✔ **William the Conqueror** (about 1028 to 1087): When St. Edward the Confessor died, he really left a mess, because as king of England he apparently designated one noble — William, Duke of Normandy — and then another — Harold Godwinson — to succeed him. Harold took the crown as Harold II. But William thought that Harold promised to uphold *his* claim to the throne. William invaded, killed Harold at the Battle of Hastings, was crowned king on **Christmas Day 1066,** and forever after has been *the Conqueror*. He stayed in power by replacing all the leaders of the old Anglo-Saxon nobility with a new ruling class of French-speaking Normans, Bretons, and Flemings.

✔ **Genghis Khan** (born between 1162 and 1167, died 1227): Before he was Genghis Khan (also sometimes written as Chingis or Jingis Khan), he was Temujin, who at age 13, became chief of a desperately poor clan of nomadic Mongols. Temujin was hungry, so he went to work defeating other clans, including the Naimans and the Tangut (names that nobody much remembers anymore, but they were pretty tough in their time). In

1206, after the Turkish Uigurs bowed down to him, Temujin changed his name to Genghis Khan, which means "Very Great Ruler" or "Universal King." In several campaigns starting in 1211, he overran the empire of North China and other East Asian territories. By his death, the Mongol Empire stretched from the Black Sea to the Pacific. Genghis is shown in Figure 18-1.

Figure 18-1:
Genghis
Khan
assembled a
massive
empire
stretching
from
Eastern
Europe to
China.

✔ **Babur** (1483 to 1530): He was called Zahir-ud-din Muhammad before taking the name Babur, which means "tiger" in Arabic. The first Mogul (sometimes spelled Mughal) emperor of India, he was born in Ferghana, Kyrgyzstan. A genius at war, he invaded India and defeated leaders of its separate kingdoms to unite an empire and found a dynasty marked by its mixed Mongol and Turkish origins and by its attitude of conciliation toward the Hindu majority. Babur was interested in architecture, music, and literature. He passed these interests down through a line of successors whose empire remained strong until the early eighteenth century but eventually fell under the domination of the British East India Company in the nineteenth century. (See Chapter 7 for more on European influence in eighteenth- and nineteenth-century Asia.)

Building Bridges

The way to build something big — from a house to an empire — is to put together smaller components. As in carpentry, so in the hammering together of nations, regions, and cultures. The people in this section used means as diverse as battles and alliances to link geographic, religious, and ethnic components into new combinations. Some of them built so well that their constructions still stand:

✔ **Kublai Khan** (1214-1294): Genghis Khan's grandson established his capital where Beijing is now. As Mongol emperor of China and founder of the Yuan Dynasty, starting in 1279, he was vigorous and forceful in the way he used power, launching military campaigns against Java, Burma, Japan, and other Asian nations, although with only limited success (none at all against Japan). Kublai Khan, like many of history's most interesting people, was a study in contradictions. He was adaptable, making the Chinese style of civilization his own, yet he kept his Mongol ruling class separate from the Chinese natives and appointed many foreigners, especially Muslims, to high government offices while at the same time making Buddhism the state religion. Some accounts describe him as a cruel ruler, others as reasonable and merciful. His court is legendary for luxury and splendor.

✔ **Ferdinand** (1452 to 1516) and **Isabella** (1451 to 1504): When Ferdinand, king of Aragon (part of today's northern Spain) married Isabella, queen of Castille (also part of today's northern Spain) in 1469, their kingdoms, Aragon and Castille, got hitched too, coming together as the forerunner of modern Spain. Co-ruled by this happening couple, Spain finally ousted the last of its Moorish rulers in 1492 when Ferdinand and Isabella took over the Sultanate of Granada. That same year, Isabella sponsored Christopher Columbus, leading to Spain's supremacy in the New World.

In 1478, Ferdinand and Isabella began the Spanish Inquisition, a Catholic reform movement aimed at rooting out non-Christian (especially Islamic and Jewish) ideas that had dominated the Iberian Peninsula (Spain and Portugal) over centuries of rule by Moorish caliphates. (The Moors had been tolerant of Judaism.) The Inquisition also helped keep the Protestant Reformation out of Spain (see Chapter 13 for more about the Reformation). In 1512, after Isabella died, Phillip completed Spain's unification when he took the Kingdom of Navarre. (For more about Spain under Ferdinand and Isabella see Chapter 6.)

✔ **Nobunaga Oda** (1534 to 1582), **Hideyoshi Toyotomi** (1536 to 1598), and **Ieyasu Tokugawa** (1543 to 1616): The three great unifiers of Japan finally broke the cycle of warring feudal lords dominating the country. Nobunaga Oda, born into a noble family near Nagoya, subjugated Owari Province, threw out the sitting *shogun* (a feudal big boss), occupied the capital at Kyoto in 1568, and defeated the priests at Osaka, destroying the power of the Buddhists. Just to be sure Buddhism didn't bounce back, he briefly encouraged Christianity. When he died, he controlled half of Japan. That paved the way for his general, the lowborn Hideyoshi Toyotomi and Toyotomi's erstwhile ally, Ieyasu Tokugawa to finally unite the country. Toyotomi banned swords for anybody but the *samurai,* or warrior class. Tokugawa eventually turned on Toyotomi and his family and established the long-lived, but repressive and isolationist Tokugawa Shogunate, which lasted until the mid-nineteenth century.

✔ **James I of England/James VI of Scotland** (1566 to 1625): Scotland's King James didn't conquer neighboring England, he simply ascended its throne as the legitimate successor (through his English great-great-grandmother) to the childless Elizabeth I in 1603. This unified the crowns of the two realms — the first step toward the unification of the two kingdoms themselves (in 1707 when the Act of Union created the United Kingdom). When James I became their king, the English stopped trying to annex Scotland, as there was no longer any point. James was a scholarly type who wrote pamphlets and sponsored Shakespeare's acting troupe. He commissioned an enduring and beautiful English translation of the Christian scripture, known as the King James Bible. He imprisoned and executed Sir Walter Raleigh — not because he hated Raleigh's newfangled habit of smoking tobacco, which he did, but for other offenses against the crown. James also hated the extreme form of Calvinist-Protestant belief called Puritanism, which gained momentum in England at the beginning of the seventeenth century. (See more on the Puritans in Chapter 13.) James resisted Puritan pressure to purge Catholic practices from the English Church. Ironically, Catholic conspirators, not Puritans, tried to blow up the new king and Parliament in the Gunpowder Plot of 1605. (They almost succeeded; see Chapter 2.) James drew criticism for his habit of playing favorites.

✔ **Frederick the Great** (1712 to 1786): As a young prince, Frederick II of Prussia studied military skills, music (he even composed some), and French literature. As king, he fought the neighboring Austrians and other Germanic states, adding Silesia (along the Oder River in east-central Europe), part of western Germany, and part of Poland to his kingdom. (Poland had, until his father's time, ruled Prussia.) Prussia doubled in size under Fred's rule and became a leading power — both militarily and economically — the forerunner of modern Germany.

✔ **George Washington** (1732 to 1799): The first president of the United States of America set a remarkable precedent in 1796 when he declined to run for a third term of office. Many a new nation has stumbled over the issue of peaceful transfer of power, as the first administration balks at handing over authority to successors. Washington achieved this crucial transition gracefully. (He turned down Congress' earlier offer to make him king.) With natural authority rather than rhetoric, Washington brought disagreeing Americans together at two critical times. In the 1770s, the self-possessed Virginia planter and British military veteran was the clear choice to lead a revolution's army. In the 1780s, his willingness to revise the Articles of Confederation (the loose agreement by which the newborn country tried to operate) led to the drafting of the U.S. Constitution. (See James Madison in "Writing Laws.") It's hard to imagine the American Revolution succeeding without him. It's even more difficult to imagine the nation succeeding without his example. For more on George Washington, see *U.S. History For Dummies,* by Steve Wiegand (Hungry Minds, Inc.).

✔ **Nelson Mandela** (born 1918): Like George Washington, Nelson Rolihlahla Mandela could be listed along with other revolutionaries in Chapter 21, but his greatest legacy will be his commitment to reconciliation as the first post-apartheid president of South Africa. Raised to become a Thembu chief, Mandela was a college student when he started working to overturn apartheid, the legal separation of races. As a young Johannesburg lawyer in the 1950s, he organized a black underground. He was arrested and convicted of conspiracy to overthrow the government and sentenced to life in prison. During 27 years in jail, he became a worldwide symbol for justice. After his release in 1990, he helped negotiate the end of apartheid, shared the Nobel Peace Prize with F.W. de Klerk, and at age 75, succeeded de Klerk as president, becoming his country's first leader chosen in an all-race election. Never seeking revenge, Mandela consulted his former captors as he rebuilt South African society. When he left office in 1999, crime and poverty still plagued South Africa, but Mandela had seen the country through an extraordinary transition.

Writing Laws

Often a society's identity flows from the way it defines morality and administers justice. Consider that most modern jurisprudence is based on precedent. The way an issue was decided before becomes part of the current definition of what is legal or illegal, right or wrong. This precedence business doesn't date back just a few decades or even a few centuries. It's rooted in decisions about justice and punishment that go all the way to the foundations of human society. No wonder so many lawgivers — good and bad — are remembered in history. A small sampling follows:

✔ **Ur-Nammu** and **Shulgi** (twenty-second and twenty-first centuries BC): A ruler of the ancient Mesopotamian kingdom of Ur instituted the earliest code of laws that survives in written form. Which ruler? Researchers aren't sure, but it was Ur-Nammu or his son and successor Shulgi. Archeologists can read only five items from *Ur-Nammu's Code,* as it's known, but it supports other evidence that even 4,200 years ago, civilized people had a legal system requiring testimony under oath. They had special judges who could order a guilty party to pay damages to a victim. The code allowed for the dismissal of corrupt officials, protection for the poor, and punishment proportionate to the crime.

✔ **Moses** (fourteenth or thirteenth century BC): The Bible's book of Exodus says that God gave mankind the Ten Commandments through his servant Moses, a Hebrew reared as an Egyptian prince. Moses led the Israelites out of slavery in Egypt, on a meandering, 40-year route through the desert to Canaan. With his brother Aaron, he set up the religious community of Israel and founded its traditions, through practice and writings. Moses is considered the author of the first several books of the Bible, the only source of information about the above events. (For more about Judaism and Moses, see Chapter 9.)

Moses' story has inspired some bad films. The worst may be 1975's ill-conceived epic *Moses,* with Burt Lancaster in the title role and cheesy special effects undercutting his performance. Director Cecil B. DeMille did it better in 1956 when he made *The Ten Commandments.* In that one, Charlton Heston played Moses, heading an all-star cast speaking nonsensically shallow, pseudo-Biblical lines but photographing marvelously. A musical, 1998's animated cartoon *Prince of Egypt* may be the best version of the Moses story on film, even though the songs are forgettable.

✔ **Draco** (seventh century BC): Athens picked this official to write its laws, the first such written code in Greece, in about 620 BC. Draco's severe laws made the state exclusive prosecutor of those accused of crime, eliminating private justice, and many offenses merited death. The word *draconian* still refers to harsh punishment. Yet Athenians loved Draco. As Draco entered an auditorium to attend a reception in his honor,

Athenians gave him the customary celebratory greeting, showering him with their hats and cloaks. He fell down and was strangely still, so they pulled all the clothing off of him and found him dead — suffocated.

✔ **Solon** (about 630 BC to about 560 BC): Solon was an Athenian statesman and reformer, not to mention a wizard at reciting verse. This Greek's breakthrough as a public figure came when he spurred Athenians to military action against the Megarians with a rousing poem. His eloquence made Solon the choice to rewrite Draco's harsh code of laws. He had other talents, too. Solon reorganized public institutions, including the senate and the popular assembly, minted coins, reformed weights and measures, and strengthened Athenian trade. The result is that his name came to be a synonym for legislator, especially in twentieth-century newspapers where *congressman* wouldn't fit in a headline.

IN THEIR WORDS
"Four score and seven..."

✔ **Justinian** (482 AD to 565 AD): "The things which are common to all are the air, running water, the sea, and the seashores." That's a bit of Roman law, as interpreted and set down by the Byzantine Emperor Justinian in a series of books that have been an important source for legal codes every since. The word "justice" comes from Justinian's name.

✔ **Mohammed** (about 570 AD to about 632 AD): Son of a poor Arab merchant, Mohammed was orphaned at 6 and grew up tending sheep. As a young man, he led caravans owned by a rich widow. Later, he married her and became a merchant. But for a businessman, Mohammed (sometimes spelled Mohamet) was a bit of a loner who liked to go off and think. He was 40 when he said the Angel Gabriel commanded him in the name of God to preach the *true religion*. After a few years, Mohammed began attacking superstition and urging people to live a pious, moral life. He taught his followers to believe in an all-powerful, all-just God, or *Allah,* whose mercy could be gotten by prayer, fasting, and the giving of alms. Authorities in Mecca, alarmed by his growing popularity, threw him out in 622 AD, so he went to Medina, where he became high judge and ruler. Mohammed led a war against enemies of Islam, taking Mecca in 630. After his last pilgrimage in 632, he fell ill and died. His moral rules, set down in the Koran, remain a basis of law throughout the Islamic world. (You can find out more about Mohammed, Islam, and the Arabs in Chapters 5 and 9.)

✔ **James Madison** (1751 to 1836): His knowledge of history and keen ability to forge compromises served Madison well at a 1787 convention in Philadelphia. A graduate of Princeton (then called the College of New Jersey), Madison represented his native Virginia at the convention. The delegates were supposed to beef up the Articles of Confederation, governing relations between the newly independent American states. Instead, the convention threw out the articles and replaced them with the U.S. Constitution. Madison thought about governments including ancient Athens's democracy, the Roman Republic, and European federations such as the Holy Roman Empire. (You can find out about Athens in Chapter 3; the Roman Republic is in Chapter 4; and the Holy Roman Empire is in Chapters 5 and 13.) He knew that the United States needed a strong central government and he deftly managed agreements allowing the convention to hammer out a working document. Many of Madison's ideas became foundations of U.S. law, which is why he's called the Father of the Constitution. Madison's notes also contributed to the historical record, providing the most complete account of the Constitutional convention. Madison later became the fourth U.S. president. For more, pick up *U.S. History For Dummies* by Steve Wiegand (Hungry Minds, Inc.).

Tracking the Centuries

About 2200 BC: The king of Ur, a Mesopotamian kingdom (today's Iraq), institutes a legal system that requires testimony under oath and authorizes judges to order a guilty party to pay damages to a victim.

About 230 BC: Shi Huangdi, self-proclaimed First Emperor of China, standardizes writing and units of measure, including weights, across the lands he has conquered.

630 AD: Mohammed leads his army of Islam to capture Mecca.

1227: Genghis Kahn rules a Mongol Empire stretching from the Black Sea to the Pacific Ocean.

1469: Queen Isabella of Castille and King Ferdinand of Aragon, rulers of two kingdoms in the northern part of Europe's Iberian Peninsula, get married, forging their lands together into a forerunner of modern Spain.

1772: Frederick the Great of Prussia adds West Prussia to his kingdom in the first partition of Poland.

1787: At the Constitutional Convention in Philadelphia, James Madison's knowledge and bright ability to apply history's lessons earn him the title Father of the Constitution.

1990: Nelson Mandela walks out of jail after 27 years in the custody of the South African government.

Chapter 19

Battling Toward Lasting Fame

· ·

In This Chapter

▶ Sacking Jerusalem with Nebuchadnezzar II of Babylon

▶ Casting long shadows with Alex, Caesar, Napoléon, and Adolf

▶ Crossing the Alps by elephant with Carthage's Hannibal

▶ Fending off the English with Scotland's Robert the Bruce

▶ Commanding tanks across North Africa's desert with Germany's Rommel

· ·

"*W*ar is the father of all and the king of all," said Heraclitus, a Greek-Ephesian philosopher of the fifth century BC. "It proves some people gods, and some people men; it makes some people slaves, and some people free." War also makes people famous. Those in this chapter are among many more who owe their reputations to battles won or lost.

Neither complete nor absolute, these headings — like any historical labels — are arbitrary. That means I made them up. What's important is that you can find examples of some of history's feistiest fighters here. Many fierce types had other distinctions, too. (You may have already discovered Genghis Khan with other founders of empires in Chapter 18.)

Towering Over Their Times

Some historical figures are so huge that . . . that . . . well, they're just *big*, that's all. Alexander the Great, Julius Caesar, Napoléon, and Hitler each changed the world profoundly and each achieved monstrous fame — or notoriety – for ambitious, world-wrenching military conquests. I could have shoved them with other empire-building fighters later in this chapter, but I decided to give them a category to themselves.

✔ **Alexander the Great** (356 to 323 BC): By the time Alexander the Great died in Babylon, everybody knew about Macedon's brilliant young prince-soldier-general-king-emperor. (Macedon was north of Greece, now split between the Macedonian region of modern Greece and the Republic of Macedonia.) The son of Philip II, Alex thought he was descended from gods and loved the epic poems of Homer. Enjoying the best upbringing available, Alexander the Great studied under the philosopher Aristotle, his tutor. (See Chapter 10 for Aristotle.) As a teenager, Alexander commanded his dad's Macedonian-Greek forces, showing sharp military skills and remarkable maturity. After his dad's assassination, he took the throne as Alexander III and took the world by storm. Alexander (shown in Figure 19-1) was handsome, charismatic, and so popular that many of the peoples he conquered welcomed his rule, but he also had a temper and lashed at those closest to him. (To read about Alexander's casual murder of a close friend, see Chapter 2.) Alexander's brief empire stretched beyond the limits of what people of the time considered the known world (see Chapter 3).

Figure 19-1: Alexander's empire spread Greek ideas through the Mediterranean region.

© Araldo de Luca/CORBIS

✔ **Julius Caesar** (about 100 to 44 BC): Gaius Julius Caesar didn't become emperor himself (at least he didn't wear that title), but his ambition helped bring down the ailing Roman Republic and his death led to the new Roman Empire. A talented general, Caesar pushed Rome's frontier all the way to Europe's Atlantic coast in the Gallic Wars. In Egypt, he put Cleopatra VII back on the throne after her brother kicked her out. Why did Caesar help Cleopatra? The fact that she bore him a son (or said it was his) may provide a clue. In trouble-wracked Rome, he formed a three-man ruling body, or *triumvirate,* with Pompey and Crassus, but the arrangement dissolved into a power struggle. In 49 BC, Caesar led his troops across the Rubicon, a boundary of his province. That started civil war. (Rubicon has meant point of no return ever since.) He emerged with sole control, taking the title Dictator for Life. A group fed up with Caesar's airs assassinated him in **44 BC.**

✔ **Napoléon Bonaparte** (1769 to 1821): From the Italian island of Corsica, Napoléon's father sent him to military school in France, which led the lad into that country's service at age 16. The French Revolution of 1789 proved an opportune moment for a smart, ambitious young officer because just about every monarch in Europe declared war on the revolutionary government in Paris. Napoléon scored important victories, became a general, and in 1799 joined co-conspirators in a *coup d'état* ("stroke of state," or government takeover). Napoléon emerged as sole ruler of France and conqueror of neighboring countries until by 1807, he ruled Europe's largest empire since the Romans. His reforms improved education, banking and the legal system. (Many countries still base their laws on his Napoleonic *Code.*) Because wife Josephine had not borne him an heir, Napoléon dumped her for Marie Louise, an Austrian princess. When their son was born, Napoléon made the baby King of Rome.

Napoléon's biggest mistake was his 1812 invasion of Russia, in which thousands of his troops froze to death or starved. (For more on Napoléon's Russian disaster see Chapter 8.) The next year, Russia joined Austria, Prussia, and Sweden to crush Napoléon at Leipzig, Germany. His enemies exiled him to the Mediterranean island of Elba, where in 1814 he raised a small army and headed toward Paris. Napoléon ruled again for a famous *Hundred Days,* which ended at the Battle of Waterloo, Belgium, as English and Prussian forces delivered a defeat from which Napoléon could not rebound in **1815.** This time he was sent to St. Helena, an island in the south Atlantic, where he died six years later.

✔ **Adolf Hitler** (1889 to 1945) Hitler wanted to be an artist, but the Vienna Academy turned him down. Hitler, from Austria, attended a lesser art school in Munich, Germany, and served as an infantryman in a Bavarian regiment in World War I. After the war, he vented his rage at the terms of peace through right-wing politics. As leader of the extremist National Socialist German Workers' Party, he tried to overthrow the Bavarian government in 1923, and was jailed. Over the next several years he built support for his *Nazi* party, blaming *outsiders,* especially Jews, for weakening Germany. In 1932, Hitler won appointment as chancellor, then suspended the constitution. When President Paul von Hindenburg died in 1934, Hitler became president and supreme commander — *Der Führer* (the leader). He ordered Jews, Arabs, Gypsies, homosexuals, and "mental defectives" rounded up and sent to concentration camps, where hundreds at a time were gassed. Nazis killed at least six million Jews.

After forcefully uniting Germany with Austria, Hitler invaded Poland in **1939,** beginning World War II. (More about World War II in Chapter 8.) As Germany's war strategy deteriorated under Hitler's personal direction, a colonel on the German command staff tried to assassinate Hitler, shown in Figure 19-2, *Der Führer* purged the army of anybody he suspected of disloyalty. This weakened Germany further. As the Allies advanced on Berlin, Hitler hid in an air-raid shelter with his mistress, Eva Braun. He and Braun married, then killed themselves. After witnessing the ceremony, Nazi propaganda minister Paul Goebbels and his wife killed all six of their children, then themselves.

Figure 19-2:
Adolph Hitler started World War II in 1939 when he sent German troops into Poland.

© Hulton-Deutsch Collection/CORBIS

Building Empires

Many of history's most fearsome characters were out to gain territory (see "Towering Over Their Times," earlier in this chapter). The conqueror's motivation wasn't just to show how tough he was. Economic reasons included *booty* (goods stolen in warfare) tribute (money paid to a conqueror by the conquered), and trade advantages.

- ✔ **Nebuchadnezzar II** (about 630 to 562 BC): Before succeeding to the throne of Babylon, Nebuchadnezzar led his father's army to victory over Egypt. Crowned in 605 BC, Nebuchadnezzar launched campaigns against western neighbors. Babylonian forces captured Jerusalem and took thousands of Jews including the newly crowned King Jehoiachin back to Babylon as slaves. (Jehoiachin remained in captivity for 37 years.) Nebuchadnezzar appointed Zedekiah as his *vassal king* in Jerusalem. A vassal king's job was to govern as the deputy of an *overlord* or *great king*. After Zedekiah rebelled, Nebuchadnezzar came back and destroyed Jerusalem in 586 BC. Slave labor helped Nebuchadnezzar build the fabulous Hanging Gardens of Babylon, a wonder of the ancient world.

- ✔ **Wu Ti** (156 to 87 BC): Wu the Martial's original name was Lui Ch'e. An empire-building ruler of China's Han Dynasty, he annexed parts of Southern China, upper Vietnam, northern and central Korea, and the northern and western frontiers where the *Hsuiung-nu* nomads (a warlike people known elsewhere as Huns) roamed.

- ✔ **Attila the Hun** (about 406 to 453 AD): Attila, known as *The Scourge of God*, co-ruled the warlike, nomadic Huns with his big brother Bleda, controlling a region from the Rhine to the edge of China. In 445 AD, Attila murdered Bleda and assembled a vast horde of Huns based in Hungary. In 451, when Attila invaded Gaul (France), Roman commander Aëtius (you can find him in "Mounting a Defense") and Theodoric I, king of the Visigoths, resisted him. Attila pulled an end run into Italy, where Pope Leo I pleaded with Attila to spare Rome. The Hun Empire fell apart after Attila died.

- ✔ **Canute** (995 to 1035 AD): English monarchs haven't had names like *Canute* or *Ethelred* for a long time. Ethelred the Unready (it meant "ill advised" rather than "unprepared") lost control of the kingdom to Viking invader Sweyn Forkbeard in 1013. When Sweyn died, Ethelred tried to take back his crown, but the Viking's son, Canute, was on the case. Canute ruled England from 1016, becoming king of Denmark in 1019 and adding Norway in 1028. He achieved peace throughout this far-flung realm. It's sometimes said of Canute that he thought he was such big stuff that he tried to make the waves on the sea obey him. This is a bad rap. Canute was demonstrating that he was not some kind of god and he could *not* tell nature what to do.

✔ **Shaka** (about 1787 to 1828): The founder of the Zulu Empire conquered most of southern Africa with a military system that could deploy 40,000 well-trained, highly disciplined warriors — equipped, however, only with shields and short spears. A ruthless dictator, Shaka repressed his tribal rivals but died at the hands of his power-hungry half-brothers. Still, his tactics and empire survived for another half-century, until the British used modern weapons to break the back of Zulu power in 1879.

Two notable films, 1963's *Zulu* and 1979's *Zulu Dawn,* treat the clash between Britain and the Zulu Empire (after Shaka). Although the second admirably tries to tell the Africans' side of the war, *Zulu Dawn* is less effective than its 1963 predecessor — the story of a band of Welshmen standing against the spear-thrusting warriors. Michael Caine appears in his first starring role in *Zulu.*

Launching Attacks

No general can make do with one style of maneuver alone, but these men all made their names as audacious attackers, even though some of them lost crucial battles:

✔ **Xerxes I** (485 to 465 BC): Xerxes suppressed revolts all over the Persian Empire, including Babylon and Egypt. Because his dad, Darius the Great (548 to 486 BC), died trying to teach the Greeks a lesson, Xerxes thought he would finish the job. He burned Athens before going home to Persia, but the Greeks weren't down for long. They whipped the army that Xerxes left behind and burned the Persian fleet on the same day in 479 BC. His own captain of the guards, or *vizier* (Artabanus), murdered Xerxes.

✔ **Genseric** (birthdate unknown, died in 477 AD): During the last years of the western Roman Empire, Genseric was one of the barbarians who threatened it. King of the Vandals, he took over much of Spain and from there attacked North Africa. He captured Carthage from the Romans and made it his capital. He also sacked Rome, but stopped short of destroying the city in 455.

✔ **Harald III Sigurdsson** (1015 to 1066): Being compared to a saint is not what made this Norwegian prince ruthless. His half-brother became Saint Olaf (see "Instigating Inspiration"), but both brothers were Viking mercenaries and Olaf, who was king first, died in 1030 fighting Norwegian rebels allied with Denmark. Having to flee, Harald hired himself out as a warrior for the prince of Kiev Rus (an early edition of Russia, where Ukraine is now) before returning to Norway. There Herald became king in 1045, earning his nickname "The Ruthless" in wars against Denmark. He invaded England in 1066 to claim the throne after Saint Edward the Confessor died, but a fellow with a similar name,

Harold II of England, killed Harald. That would have been that, but William of Normandy (see Chapter 18), succeeded where Harald failed. Had it turned out differently, Harald III of Norway would be Harald the Conqueror and this book *might* be written in Norwegian.

✔ **Richard Lionheart** (1157 to 1199): Richard I was king of England for a decade, starting in 1189, but he spent only five months of that time in the country. No wonder his brother John tried to steal his throne. Called Richard *Coeur de Lion* (English rulers spoke French in those days, because they *were* French), he was the third son of Henry II and an outstanding soldier. Richard was on his way back from Jerusalem and the Third Crusade when he landed in a Vienna jail. (See Chapter 6 to find out about the Crusades.) His mom, Eleanor of Aquitaine, paid the ransom to get him released. Richard went on to fight, and die, for England's claim to lands in what is now France.

✔ **Erwin Rommel** (1891 to 1944): Rommel, a German field marshal in World War II, made his name leading a mechanized division that charged through France to the English Channel in 1940. Rommel led more attacks on allied forces in North Africa, where his inventive tank warfare strategies earned him the name "Desert Fox." Nazi officials suspected Rommel of conspiracy in a plot to kill Hitler. He was recalled from his post and forced to commit suicide by poison. (I talk more about World War II in Chapter 8. Hitler is in "Towering Over Their Times," earlier in this chapter.)

Mounting a Defense

Some fighters were at their best (or worst) when invaders came calling. Several of the people in the list that follows were just as aggressive, just as ambitious as any empire-builder known to history. It just so happened, however, that each of these fighters became known for an important defensive stand — whether it succeeded or not:

✔ **Flavius Aëtius** (about 350 to 454 AD): For 20 years this Roman general was in charge of keeping the barbarians at bay, often a losing battle. Coming from the *patrician* (or aristocratic) class, he became the empire's general-in-chief and was also a consul, the top government administrator. (To find out about Roman social classes, see Chapter 4.) Aëtius scored a big success at Châlons in 451 AD, when he commanded the allied forces that beat Attila the Hun (see "Building Empires"). Aëtius was flying high, the most popular guy in the empire, which ticked off Emperor Valentinian III. The jealous emperor stabbed Aëtius to death.

✔ **Charles Martel** (about 699 to 741 AD): The Carolingian kings of Charlemagne's family (see Chapter 18), started with Charles Martel, who ruled much of Gaul (France), but never got to call himself king. He was called *The Hammer,* however, for his military campaigns against Saxons and Frisons and other assorted rivals through the region. He fought the Muslims and kept them from penetrating Western Europe (beyond Spain, that is) at the Battle of Poitiers in **732 AD**. Charles Martel started out as Mayor of the Castle for the previous line of kings, the Merovingians.

- **Harold II** (about 1022 to 1066): The last Anglo-Saxon king of England had a short, violent, disputed reign. He fought off Harald Sigurdsson (more on Harald in "Launching Attacks") of Norway then turned around to take on the Duke of Normandy at the Battle of Hastings. (Find info on William the Conqueror in Chapter 18.) All it got poor Harold was an arrow through the eye.

- **Shagrat al-Durr** (birthdate unknown, died 1259): Also known as Shajarat, she was a onetime slave girl who married two of Egypt's sultans, ran the government from behind the scenes for years, and for two months wore the title sultan herself. In 1249, her first husband, Salih Ayyab, was out of town when Crusaders under Louis IX of France landed at the mouth of the Nile. Shagrat, acting for the absent sultan, organized Egypt's defense. Her hubby returned but soon died. Shagrat pretended Salih was still alive and kept acting in his name until her stepson Turan showed up and claimed his inheritance. Turan, with Shagrat's guidance, beat the Crusaders and took Louis prisoner. Egyptian army officers preferred Shagrat, a Turk like them, to Turan. They killed him and installed her as sultan. But the Caliph in Baghdad said "Nope," a woman wasn't allowed to be sultan. Shagrat resigned, then wooed and married her replacement, Aibak. She remained the power behind the throne until he decided to add a new wife to his harem, angering her. She killed Aibak in his bath. Riots broke out. Harem slaves beat Shagrat with their shoes and threw her into the palace moat. Egyptians later enshrined her bones in a mosque named for her.

- **Robert the Bruce** (1274 to 1329): In 1296, the Scottish Earl of Carrick, better known as Robert the Bruce, swore loyalty to the king of England, Edward I, who was trying to establish English sovereignty over Scotland. Then Bruce changed his mind and backed William Wallace, a Scottish patriot fighting the English. After Edward tortured and beheaded Wallace in 1306, Robert the Bruce advanced his own claim on Scotland's crown by killing political rival John Comyn with a dagger. Bruce was crowned Scotland's king and after a brief exile in Ireland (some people didn't consider this stabbing business to be fair) came back in 1307 and thrashed the English at Loudoun Hill. The Bruce and his lads trounced the English again at Bannockburn in 1314. Finally, the English signed the Treaty of Northampton (1328), agreeing that Bruce was the rightful king.

Heroic gloss and stirring cinematography bury historical perspective in Mel Gibson's 1995 film epic *Braveheart*. Gibson directed himself playing late-thirteenth-century rebel leader William Wallace in the sprawling war story and staged the wild battle scenes impressively.

Devising Tactics

A battle's outcome often hinges on strength, as in superior numbers or better weapons. But strategy and tactics just as often make the difference between winner and loser. When two forces are evenly matched, strategic advantage comes in second only to luck in determining the result. The following fighters all used wits and innovation — although not all of them achieved success:

- **Hannibal** (247 to 182 BC): In his mid-20s, Hannibal of Carthage subdued most of southern Spain. He blindsided the Romans in the Second Punic War (see the Punic Wars in Chapter 4) by invading Italy from the north, over the Alps mountain range, using battle-trained elephants. (The Romans assumed the African would come at them by sea.) Ultimately, the Alps invasion failed and Hannibal went home to work on political reform. He faced stiff opposition on that front too and eventually exiled himself. When it looked like the Romans would capture him at last (they held grudges), Hannibal did what good soldiers did in those days — he killed himself.

- **William Tecumseh Sherman** (1820 to 1891): "War is cruelty and you cannot refine it," said Sherman. Ohio born and West Point educated, Sherman resigned his U.S. Army commission in 1853 to become a California banker. The bank failed. He was superintendent of the Louisiana Military Academy when that state seceded from the Union. Sherman went north and rejoined the Union Army, commanding a brigade at the first Battle of Bull Run in 1861 (the North lost) then heading up defensive forces in the border state of Kentucky. After recovering from a nervous breakdown, he led units effectively at several decisive battles. His drive to capture Atlanta, destroying and burning towns and farmsteads along the way, stands as a definitive landmark of modern war. (To find out about the U.S. Civil War, see Chapter 17 of this book, or pick up a copy of *Civil War For Dummies* by Keith Dickson, Hungry Minds, Inc.)

Instigating Inspiration

A few of history's warriors inspired others with their bravery or dedication to a cause. Some soldiers inspired those who followed them into battle. Others left legends that inspired later generations of warriors.

- **Saint Olaf** (about 995 to 1030 AD): As a 15-year-old mercenary, Olaf joined Viking buddies in ripping down London Bridge in 1010. Three years later in Normandy, Olaf got religion. He went home to Norway, seized the throne (he was probably not yet 20), and worked to establish

Christianity in place of the old Norse gods, earning posthumous saint-hood. (To find out about the worship of multiple gods, see Chapter 9.) Danish-backed rebels killed King Olaf.

✔ **Peter the Hermit** (about 1050 to about 1115): Imagine joining an army led by a monk, Peter the Hermit, and an impoverished knight, Walter the Penniless. Thousands of Christians went for it in 1095, forming the People's Crusade, part of the First Crusade (see Chapter 6). Also called Peter of Amiens, he was an ex-soldier who fired up his followers about liberating the Holy Land from the Muslims. Most of Peter's followers — including co-leader Walter — died the first time they faced the Turks. Peter survived to join the better-armed branch of the First Crusade, which conquered Jerusalem in 1099. He later founded a Belgian monastery.

✔ **Robin Hood** (if he lived, it was sometime between the twelfth and four-teenth centuries): English ballads dating from about the fourteenth cen-tury credit the legendary Robin with protecting the poor and attacking corrupt officials. The stories may be rooted in discontent that led to the Peasants' Revolt of 1381 (see Chapter 6). Some accounts place Robin in the twelfth century, during the rule of the unpopular King John.

Robin Hood is the hero of many movies, as well as books, plays, and TV series. Maybe the lousiest Robin on the screen is Kevin Costner's. The actor seems out of place in 1991's *Robin Hood: Prince of Thieves.* (Perhaps it's the embarrassingly inept accent.) Sean Connery, more sat-isfying in 1976's *Robin and Marian,* plays an aging Robin who arrives home from the Crusades to learn that Maid Marian (Audrey Hepburn) is abbess of a priory.

✔ **Joan of Arc** (about 1412 to 1431): This 13-year-old girl (shown in Figure 19-3) heard the voices of saints telling her to rescue France from English domination during the Hundred Years' War. Tall order for a kid, but something about her seemed convincing. Charles VII, at that time the *dauphin,* or crown prince of France, let her lead the army against the English at Orleans. In white armor, she inspired her troops to victory and then escorted Charles to Reims for his coronation. She was cap-tured in her next campaign, handed over to the English, tried for sor-cery, and sentenced to burn. The Catholic Church canonized Joan as a saint in 1920.

Any collaboration between Hollywood's Otto Preminger and novelist Graham Greene, based on a play by George Bernard Shaw, is bound to be strange. And 1957's *Saint Joan* is just that. Jean Seberg plays Joan of Arc, with support from John Gielgud and Richard Widmark. Playwright Shaw, though from an Irish Protestant family, was an agnostic. Englishman Greene was Catholic. The overall tone of the movie is ironic.

A 1999 return to the Joan of Arc story, *The Messenger,* turned the heroine into a victim of post-traumatic stress disorder by having her witness the (fictional) rape-murder of her sister.

Figure 19-3: Joan of Arc led French troops to victory over the English in the Hundred Years' War.

63   JEANNE D'ARC.

A tale of two — or more — bridges

Olaf's teen vandalism probably did not inspire the children's song "London Bridge is Falling Down (My Fair Lady)." The wooden bridge that the Vikings demolished in 1010 was one of a series of early structures across the River Thames, linking London with Southwark (now part of London).

Perhaps the most memorable London Bridge (and the likely inspiration for the song) was a 19-arch stone bridge, built in the twelfth century. It included not just traffic lanes, but shops and houses along each side. Dangerously over-loaded, that bridge, like its wooden predecessors, began crumbling long before it was replaced in 1831 by another stone bridge.

The 1831 model was a handsome, no-nonsense, five-arch structure that stood until 1968. Then it was dismantled block by block and shipped to Lake Havasu City, Arizona. You can see it there. Its replacement over the Thames, today's London Bridge, is rather plain.

Because the name "London Bridge" is famous, people confuse it with Tower Bridge, modern London's best-recognized landmark. Tower Bridge, which opened in 1894, stands downriver from London Bridge, next to the Tower of London. Tower Bridge has tall, handsome towers. London Bridge has none (it's actually rather plain). Tower Bridge can be raised to let large ships pass beneath; London Bridge can't.

How widespread is the confusion over these two bridges? When I looked in an encyclopedia under "London Bridge," there was a picture of Tower Bridge.

Tracking the Centuries

586 BC: Babylonian troops led by Nebuchadnezzar destroy Jerusalem and take King Zedekiah prisoner.

479 BC: Troops from Greek city-states allied against Persia both defeat King Xerxes's army and burn his fleet in a single day.

49 BC: Julius Caesar leads his troops across the Rubicon, the stream that bounds his province, beginning a Roman civil war.

445 AD: Attila the Hun murders his big brother and co-ruler, Bleda, and begins forcibly assembling a vast horde of Hun warriors in Hungary.

1028: Canute, king of England and Denmark, adds Norway to his empire.

1431: Joan of Arc, convicted of sorcery, burns to death at the stake.

1828: His power-hungry half-brothers kill Shaka, emperor of the Zulu.

1853: William Tecumseh Sherman resigns his commission in the U.S. Army to become a banker in California.

1944: Germany's Nazi Gestapo, suspecting war hero Field Marshal Erwin Rommel of conspiracy in a plot to kill Hitler, recalls Rommel from his command post in Northern France and forces him to commit suicide by swallowing poison.

Chapter 20

Venturing Out: Voyagers

. . . .

In This Chapter

▶ Being the first to arrive doesn't guarantee an advantage

▶ Relaying information from around the globe

▶ Finding passages to different parts of the world

▶ Helping explorers find their way

. . . .

*M*any people made history by traveling to new places. Sometimes they went for the sake of going, more often for the sake of getting something they couldn't get at home — such as new territory or the glory of being first. You'll notice many people from the fifteenth to seventeenth centuries AD in this chapter — restless Europeans, in particular, were *discovering* the rest of the world during that time. (For more about the Portuguese and Spanish voyages that transformed the world, see Chapters 7 and 8.)

Arriving Before Their Time

Some discoverers arrived at new (to them) places before the world was quite ready for them to get there. Getting from point A to point B is always an accomplishment, but what if no cultural influence or trade links result? Some explorers didn't even know what they found.

> ✔ **Pythias** (fourth century BC): Ancient Greeks traveled and settled just about everywhere around the Mediterranean. Pythias, born in Massilia, Gaul, went farther — much farther. Around 330 BC, he sailed from Massilia (today's Marseilles, France) past Spain, out through the Strait of Gibraltar and up the Atlantic coast of Europe, passing the east coast of Britain as he continued north. Remarkably adventurous for his time, Pythias reached the island of *Thule,* which he said was six days' sail from Northern Britain. He probably was somewhere in Norway. (For more about Pythias and speculation about the people that he visited in the north, see Chapter 5.) Some people think he reached Iceland. Pythias's own account of the voyage is lost, but several later writers referred to it.

- ✔ **Leif Eriksson** (late tenth, early eleventh centuries AD): Icelandic sagas say that about the year 1000, this tall, strong, smart, and fair-dealing son of the murderous Erik the Red (see "Taking Advantage of Opportunity," later in this chapter) set out from Greenland with a crew of 35 to explore land sighted in the west. He found Baffin Island, just north of the Hudson Strait, then spied the coast of Labrador (calling it Markland) and camped on Newfoundland's northeastern tip. Eriksson called that place (now known as L'Anse aux Meadows) Vinland, probably for the wild berries that grew there. Captain and crew stayed all winter and would have come back again if Leif's dad, Erik, hadn't died, making Leif head of the family back in Greenland. More Viking boats traveled from Greenland to Canada, carrying other members of the clan, but a Norse settlement never took hold. Leif also brought Christianity to Greenland.

- ✔ **Zheng He** (birthdate unknown, died about 1433): A Muslim court eunuch (ouch!) in China's royal household, Zheng He was also an admiral, sea explorer, and ambassador. From 1405 to 1407, Zheng He commanded a 62-ship flotilla that went all the way to India. Then he led six more expeditions, into the Persian Gulf and eventually to East Africa. He brought back giraffes, ostriches, and zebras, but the Chinese never used the contacts that Zheng He established with the rulers of the countries that he visited to develop trade advantages or to wield political influence abroad. (You can read more about Zheng He, fifteenth century China, and why the Chinese were not very interested in the rest of the world, in Chapters 6 and 7.) Zheng He's name is also written Cheng Ho. Figure 20-1 shows many of many of Zheng He's voyages.

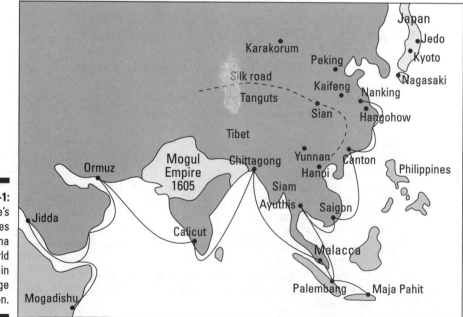

Figure 20-1: Zheng He's voyages made China a world leader in long-range navigation.

✔ **Christopher Columbus** (1451 to 1506): Some people celebrate Columbus while others vilify him for *discovering* America. But the tall, red-haired, eccentric sailor died never realizing what he accomplished. Born in Genoa, then an independent Italian city-state, Columbus was a crack navigator who sailed along the Atlantic coast of Africa and probably north to Iceland. He explored the Caribbean for Spain, becoming the first European navigator to land on the Bahamas, Cuba (he thought it was Japan), Haiti, Jamaica, and Trinidad before he stumbled on the South American mainland (Venezuela). Yet Columbus insisted that China, his real goal, was close by (see Chapter 6). Jealous rivals dogged his attempts to run colonial settlements. Spanish fortune hunters trumped up charges against him and hauled the Italian back to Spain in chains. Columbus's sponsors, co-rulers Ferdinand and Isabella (see Chapter 18), set him free and gave him another expedition. On his fourth trip, Columbus caught the illness that killed him. Columbus committed three major errors:

1. Thinking that Asia extended a lot farther east than it does.

2. Figuring that the Earth's radius is only three-fourths of what it really is.

3. Stubbornly refusing to re-evaluate what his discoveries meant.

Columbus has inspired really bad movies. Imagine Tom Selleck, the tall guy with the mustache from those *Magnum P.I.* reruns, gussied up like a Renaissance king. That's one of the highlights of 1992's *Christopher Columbus: The Discovery.* Selleck plays King Ferdinand of Aragon opposite Rachel Ward as Isabella of Castille. The cinematography features plenty of open sea as Columbus (George Corraface) searches for China and the screenwriters search for a plot. Just as bad, if not worse, was 1949's *Christopher Columbus.* Made in England, it brought this response from critic Richard Winnington: "[I]t contrives with something like genius neither to inform, excite, entertain, titillate, or engage the eye."

✔ **Neil Armstrong** (born 1930): Armstrong was supposed to say, "That's one small step for *a* man, one giant leap for mankind." It came out "one small step for man," which garbled the meaning a bit ("man" without the article "a" in those pre-feminist days often meant the whole human species), but his wording didn't diminish the fact that somebody finally walked on the moon. Ohio-born Armstrong was a U.S. fighter pilot and test pilot before training as an astronaut. After commanding the Gemini 8 orbiter in 1966, he was picked for Apollo 11, a moon-landing expedition.

On **July 20, 1969,** Armstrong climbed out of the landing module as all the earth watched on TV. Co-pilot Buzz Aldrin (also born in 1930) was the second guy to step on moondust. Just as Columbus's landing in the New World became a monumental landmark, so may the first moon landing prove to be a great turning point — after people eventually return to the moon or venture to other planets. So far, however, the 1969 moonwalk seems to be an achievement ahead of its time. Nobody, not even the inventive people at the National Air and Space Administration (NASA), was quite sure what to do on the moon or with the moon after they set astronauts on its surface. More U.S. Apollo missions followed, but then moon exploration dried up in favor of space shuttles and space stations.

Carrying Messages

Some people traveled to spread news. Most spread the word about where they were after they returned. Either way, travelers have always been important sources of information and even inspiration.

✔ **St. Paul** (about 10 AD to about 67 AD): First he was Saul, a Jew who came to Roman Judaea from his native Turkey. He became a rabbi of the strict Pharisee sect and believed in persecuting Christians, whom he saw as heretics (holders of religious beliefs that contradict official doctrine). Then, on a journey to Damascus to advise that Christians be rounded up, he said that Jesus came to him in a vision. Saul went blind for a while. Upon recovery, he was Paul, a traveling Christian apostle. He roamed widely as a missionary and participated in debates over whether *gentiles* (non-Jews) could be admitted to the Church (he was in favor), and if so, how. He wrote 13 New Testament letters. Other religious and civil leaders, both Jewish and Roman, still held Paul's earlier opinion that Christian ideas threatened the established order. Roman policy said those who spread Christianity should be jailed — or worse. Paul spent his final years as a prisoner, first in Roman-ruled Jerusalem, later in Rome.

✔ **Marco Polo** (1254 to 1324): Born to a Venetian-merchant family, Marco Polo tagged along with his dad and uncle on a trip to China in **1271.** By Polo's account, the Emperor Kublai Khan (see Chapter 18) appointed him as an envoy and then governor of Yangzhou before the Italian went home in 1292. A soldier for Venice against the Genoese, he was captured and thrown in jail, writing *The Travels of Marco Polo* while imprisoned. The book was widely read and broke through the provincial consciousness of many literate Europeans. Many of Polo's contemporaries thought the book contained lies. Many latter-day scholars also think Polo inflated his own Chinese resume, but the book's descriptions of the East stand as a cross-cultural milestone. (See Chapter 23 for more on Marco.)

✔ **Ibn Bttuta** (1304 to 1368): Some people call this writer the Arab Marco Polo, but that fails to do Ibn Bttuta justice, because he wrote about so many places. Born in Tangiers, Morocco, he spent almost three decades, from 1325 to 1354, covering more than 75,000 miles. Like Polo, he visited China and was well received. He also visited all the Muslim countries, writing about Mecca (in present-day Saudi Arabia), Persia (now called Iran), Mesopotamia (Iraq), Asia Minor, Bokhara (in present-day Uzbekistan), southern Spain, and the North African city of Timbuktu, as well as India and Sumatra. He then settled in Fez, Morocco, and dictated the story of his journeys. His book, *Rihlah,* is a memoir of cultural, social and political observations.

✔ **Amerigo Vespucci** (1454 to 1512): Florence-born Vespucci wrote about his 1499 voyage to Venezuela and points south. But Martin Waldseemüller (born perhaps in 1470, died 1518), a clergyman in northeastern France, is the one who tacked the navigator's name onto the New World. In a little publication called *Cosmographiae Introductio* (or *Cosmo*, for short), Waldseemüller spread the idea that there was a fourth part of the world beyond Europe, Asia, and Africa. He called this new mainland *America*, a Latinized tribute to Vespucci. The name stuck. Other mapmakers made it South America, using Vespucci's name for North America, too.

Vespucci later became a victim of historical libel, as the charge spread that he stole credit for discovering America from Columbus or that he was the mapmaker who egotistically applied his own name to the New World. These false accusations are perhaps rooted in the irrational dislike that an American philosopher, Ralph Waldo Emerson (1803 to 1882), held toward Vespucci. Emerson wrote about the Italian as a "pickle vendor" and "boatswain's mate in an expedition that never sailed." It's not clear where Emerson got the impression that Vespucci never traveled to the Western Hemisphere or that Vespucci was anything but a well-born and literate sailor with solid credentials in ocean navigation. Vespucci became pilot-major of Spain, the government's top navigator, in 1505.

Seeking New Ways to Get from Here to There

Many travelers left home in search of something specific — and many of these, especially in the sixteenth to the nineteenth centuries AD, were looking for sea routes between Europe and Asia:

✔ **Henry the Navigator** (1394 to 1460): Prince Henry had a singular vision of how important finding a sea route to India and China was. To that end, this member of Portugal's royal family founded a school of scientific navigation and sponsored expeditions along the west coast of Africa. In the same interest, he built Portugal's first observatory to advance the science that taught sailors how to steer by the stars. Although he died before his students sailed around Africa, the prince paved the way for his country's greatest nautical and commercial successes.

✔ **Juan Ponce de León** (1460 to 1521): Running a Spanish plantation on the island of Hispaniola (today's Dominican Republic and Haiti), this veteran officer (he may have been aboard during Columbus' second mission to the Caribbean) heard local Indians mention another tempting island. He sailed there, subdued the locals, and became Spanish governor of Puerto Rico. This inspired León to follow another Indian story that told of an island where a spring made anyone who drank from it feel young and healthy. Leon never found that island, or its "fountain of youth," but he did land on Florida early in 1513. He died of an arrow wound suffered on his second expedition to Florida.

✔ **William Clark** (1770 to 1838) and **Meriwether Lewis** (1774 to 1809): Better known as Lewis and Clark, these buddies crossed North America looking for the thing that so many seafarers failed to find — a northern water route between oceans. Lewis and Clark, backed by the United States government, wanted a route defined by rivers, with a manageable overland stretch at the continental divide. Nobody knew how high, steep, and wide-ranging the Rocky Mountains were: The American idea of a mountain range at the time was based on the Appalachians. The Lewis and Clark expedition was supposed to reach the headwaters of the Missouri River and then *portage* (carry their canoes and supplies) to the nearby headwaters of a westward-flowing river, which would carry them to the Pacific. Such a route, if practicable, would have been a commercial boon to U.S. traders, who wanted to establish a Pacific trading post on the West Coast (despite the fact that the United States had no territorial claims on the West Coast at the time).

U.S. President Thomas Jefferson chose Lewis, his private secretary, to lead the expedition in 1804. Lewis took Clark along as co-commander of a party that journeyed by canoe, horse, and foot up the Missouri River and into the Rockies, where they found the mountain crossing to the Columbia River too long and rugged for commercial use. They traveled down the Columbia to the Pacific, wintered in Oregon, and returned. Their observations of lands, people, plants, and wildlife were invaluable, although Lewis failed to publish their journals.

Lewis became governor of the Louisiana Territory in 1807. Strangely troubled, he killed himself while traveling through Tennessee. Clark went on to hold numerous government posts and negotiated several treaties with Indian tribes. For more information on Lewis and Clark's expedition, see *U.S. History For Dummies* by Steve Wiegand (Hungry Minds, Inc.).

✔ **Sir John Franklin** (1786 to 1847): British Naval officer Franklin fought in the Napoleonic Wars (see Chapter 8) and served as governor of Tasmania. He set out like so many sailors before him to find that illusive Northwest Passage — a northern sea route around North America. Franklin's expedition can't exactly be termed a success — he and his crew all died in their icebound ship. Yet they got so close — within a few miles — that Franklin gets credit for *discovering* the passage. Nobody successfully sailed the treacherous route until the Norwegian explorer Amundsen (see "Racing for First" later in this chapter) did it in the early twentieth century. An ice-breaking oil tanker was the first commercial vessel to use the passage, in 1969.

Arriving as Bad Company

Not all explorers had positive motives for seeking new worlds; some visitors just barged in and took over:

- ✔ **Vasco da Gama** (about 1469 to 1525): Check out Chapter 7 for the story of how Gama went from Portugal to Kozhikode (or Calicut) on India's Malabar (southwest) coast. Born in Sines, in the Alentejo region of Portugal, he was one in a series of Portuguese explorers trained and dispatched for the purpose of exploring the African coast, rounding the continent's southern tip, and establishing a trade route with the East. The first to succeed, Gama returned with a load of spices in 1499. Portugal followed Gama's success with a voyage by Pedro Alvarez Cabral (about 1467 to about 1520), who accidentally touched the coast of Brazil on his way south, thus establishing Portugal's claims in South America. Gama returned in 1502 as an enforcer, establishing a pattern for brutal European colonialism in Asia. When Portuguese authority in India slipped in the 1520s, the government called Gama out of retirement and sent him as a get-tough viceroy. He fell ill on that trip and died.

- ✔ **Francisco Pizarro** (about 1478 to 1541): Pizarro, a soldier from Trujillo, Spain, was crafty and brutal. He used both qualities to defeat the mighty Inca Empire of South America in the 1530s, capturing King Atahualpa by trickery and killing him. (For more about the Spanish conquest of the Inca, see Chapter 7.) Pizarro also fought with his fellow *conquistador,* Diego de Almagro (*Conquistador* is the Spanish name for the conquering commanders who beat up on American Indians and took their lands.) When Almagro (about 1475 to 1538), the conqueror of Chile, challenged Pizarro's authority in Peru, the ailing Pizarro sent his brothers to capture and kill Almagro.

- ✔ **Hernan Cortés** (1485 to 1547): Cortés helped his commander, Diego Velázquez de Cuéllar (1465 to 1524), conquer Cuba. After quarreling with Velázquez, Cortés, a proud nobleman from Medellin, Spain, accelerated his planned departure from Cuba to the mainland of Mexico, founding the port city of Vera Cruz before heading inland. Making allics of natives opposed to Aztec rule, he then marched on the Aztec capital. The Aztec King Montezuma welcomed Cortés as a god at first, but when the Aztecs became suspicious of the Spaniard's motives, Cortés took Montezuma captive. Velázquez sent an expedition to bring Cortés back to Cuba, but Cortés convinced the party's leader to join him and even burned their ships so that he couldn't be taken back to Cuba. After an Indian rebellion, Montezuma's death at the hands of rebels, and a brief Spanish retreat, Cortés conquered Mexico in 1521. He tried to conquer Honduras, but failed. (For more about Cortés' conquest of the Aztecs, turn to Chapter 7.)

Racing for First

As Jean-Luc Picard (not a historical figure but a science fiction character) once said, the explorer aims "to go where no one has gone before." (Yes, *Star Trek* fans; James T. Kirk said it first, but his gender-specific version — "where no *man* has gone" — sounds ironically dated now.) What's true in the make-believe future was certainly true in the real-world past, as explorers competed to be the first person ever to conquer a geographic barrier, or to slip the bonds of geography entirely. The following people fit that description and those that survived won the bragging rights that go with the title "first."

If you noticed that other explorers, in other sections of this chapter, were first to go where no one had gone before, congratulations. That means you're paying attention. A chapter about explorers is bound to be full of *firsts*. But, as I explain in Chapter 2, the study of history is divided up into arbitrary categories — valid only if you have to pass a history test or if they help you remember and understand the people and events you read about. The section titles in this chapter are just such arbitrary labels.

- ✔ **Ferdinand Magellan** (about 1480 to 1521): What Columbus dreamed — reaching the East by sailing west — Magellan accomplished. The Portuguese captain, sailing under Spain's colors, traveled from Seville, Spain, around South America, across the Pacific to the Philippines, where he died in a tribal dispute (see Chapter 7 for more about Magellan's achievement). His expedition, commanded by Juan Sebastian del Cano, continued, and a small, scurvy-weakened surviving crew completed the first trip all the way around the world. When Magellan first entered the *new* ocean west of South America, the weather stayed nice and the water calm for weeks on end, so he named the ocean the Pacific, or *peaceful*. The Pacific proved at least as violent as the Atlantic when a storm hit, but the name stuck.

- ✔ **Robert E. Peary** (1856 to 1920) and **Matthew A. Henson** (1866 to 1955): Peary and Henson, credited as first to get to the North Pole, in **1909,** may not have touched the exact geographic pole. It was tough to tell, since there's no actual pole to mark the North Pole, and no land either — just ice floating so swiftly that a campsite drifts miles overnight. Still, Peary's observations show that he and Henson (actually, Henson got there first) came within 20 miles of the pole and probably closer.

A U.S. Navy officer from Pennsylvania, Peary commanded several arctic expeditions, at least four aimed at reaching the pole. Henson, whom Perry hired as a valet (personal servant) in 1897, was his navigator, trailbreaker, and translator. They almost lost their claim of being first to the North Pole to former Peary-expedition–member Frederick A. Cook (1865 to 1940), who claimed to have reached the pole a year earlier. But Cook, who also said he climbed Alaska's Mt. McKinley, had a habit of exaggerating. (He later went to jail for mail fraud.) Peary's other projects included a surveying expedition in Nicaragua. Henson wrote the 1912 book, *A Black Explorer at the North Pole,* and is shown in Figure 20-2.

Figure 20-2:
Matthew
Henson
became
explorer
Robert
Peary's
indispensable
navigator and
collaborator.

✔ **Roald Amundsen** (1872 to 1928): Norway's Amundsen never finished the race for the North Pole, although he was first to locate the Magnetic North Pole (not the same as the geographic North Pole, a discrepancy that caused hassles for northern navigators who used compasses, which point to the magnetic pole, not the geographic pole). When he found out that Robert Peary (also in this section) beat him in the northern competition, Amundsen headed for the South Pole, reaching it in December 1911. Britain's Robert F. Scott (1868 to 1912) arrived a month later, only to find he was too late. Scott and all his party died on the way back. Amundsen's other accomplishments included sailing the Northwest Passage (see John Franklin in the "Seeking New Ways to Get from Here to There" section earlier in this chapter) and flying across the North Pole in a blimp.

✔ **Yuri Gagarin** (1934 to 1968): The first *cosmonaut* (Russian astronaut) died young, before the age of manned space exploration reached beyond its beginnings. Gagarin, of the Soviet air force, became the first human being to travel outside the Earth's atmosphere in 1961 when he made one trip around the planet in the Vostok spaceship. He was alive to see American John Glenn achieve sustained orbit by circling the earth three times in 1963, but Gagarin died in a plane accident the year before men first walked on the moon (see Neil Armstrong, under "Arriving Before Their Time," earlier in this chapter).

Playing "Name that Explorer"

To make learning and remembering history easier, keep in mind that explorers often got things — cities, rivers, and lakes for example — named after them. For example:

✔ **Sir Francis Drake** (about 1540 to 1596): Drake was an Englishman who fought the Spanish Armada and sailed around the world. His ports of call ranged from Virginia to the Caribbean to California, where a bay north of San Francisco bears his name.

✔ **Samuel de Champlain** (1567 to 1635): He was France's man in Canada — explorer, diplomat, and governor. He established French alliances with several Indian tribes and founded Quebec. The British captured Quebec in 1629 and Champlain was their prisoner until 1632. When Quebec was restored to French rule, he was its governor from 1633. Lake Champlain is named for him.

✔ **Henry Hudson** (birthdate unknown, presumed dead in 1611): Nobody knows anything about this navigator's early life, but he sailed for the Dutch and the English, making claims for both countries along the northeast coast of North America. Like France's Cartier before him, Hudson was looking for the Northwest Passage. He explored the river (in New York), the strait, and the bay (both in Canada) that now bear his name. Late in 1610, he found himself in Hudson Bay and decided to winter there. When the ship ran short of food, his crew rebelled. The mutineers set their captain, along with eight other men, adrift to die.

Guiding the Way

Some people just know how to get places. Out ahead of many a great explorer was a guide to show the way. Following are a couple of these:

✔ **Ibn Majid** (born early 1430s, died around 1500): When Portugal's Vasco da Gama (earlier in this chapter, also see Chapter 7) rounded the southern tip of Africa, sailing through the perilous waters between that continent's east coast and the island of Madagascar, he knew he would need help to travel all the way to India. He hoped to find an Arab ship pilot to guide him. Perhaps overqualified, the man Gama found in Malindi, Ibn Majid (also remembered as Ahmed Bin Majid) called himself the Lion-of-the-Sea-in-Fury. (Nobody has great nicknames like that anymore.) This greatest of Arab navigators wrote more than three dozen books about seafaring, oceanography, and geography. He specialized in the Arabian Sea, the Red Sea, and the Indian Ocean. His knowledge was precisely what Gama needed to open that part of the world to European sea trade. Many Arabs and other Muslims later regretted that Ibn Majid shared what he knew.

✔ **Sakagawea** (birthdate unknown, died in 1812): An Idaho-born member of the Shoshone tribe, she was treated as property, not an uncommon fate for women or American Indians in the late eighteenth and early nineteenth centuries. A rival tribe captured her from her village and sold her to Toussaint Charbonneau, a Canadian fur trapper, who married her by Indian rite and took her along when Lewis and Clark (see "Seeking New Ways to Get from Here to There," earlier in this chapter) hired Charbonneau as their expedition guide. Sakagawea proved a better guide than Charbonneau, and she also served as interpreter, trader, ambassador, and quick-thinking aide, once rescuing Lewis's priceless journal from floating down a river. Pregnant when they set out, she gave birth along the way and then carried the baby boy on her back. Her name, which means *Bird Woman,* has variant English spellings, including Sakajawea.

Taking Advantage of Opportunity

Traveling well often means grabbing your chance when it presents itself — turning a banishment into a chance to found a settlement, for example, or taking over the colony when you can. The following voyagers are among many in history that broke a few rules on the way to discovery:

✔ **Erik the Red** (tenth century): The Viking leader Erik Thorvaldson was banned from his native Norway for manslaughter. He sailed west to Iceland in 982, but after settling there and killing again, he was outlawed once more. Erik moved to a peninsula reaching west from Iceland. You guessed it. He killed somebody again and this time the sentence was a three-year banishment. Where could he go but farther west? He knew there was supposed to be land out there because a sailor named Gunnbjorn, blown off-course 50 years before, had reported it. So Erik sailed and found Greenland, rich with game and grassy enough (it was warmer then) to make good pasture. After his banishment was up, he and his crew returned to Iceland and rounded up 25 ships full of Icelanders eager for another new land. Erik would have commanded his son's expedition to North America (see "Arriving Before Their Time" earlier in this chapter), if he weren't thrown from a horse just before leaving and decided it was an omen against him. He told Leif to go without him.

✔ **Vasco Núñez de Balboa** (1475 to 1519): Balboa came to Darién (now part of Panama) as a stowaway on a Spanish ship. He seized power during an insurrection and extended Spanish influence into nearby areas. Extending Spanish influence took rough traveling through low jungle and wetland, but he found some high ground, too, and from atop a hill Balboa sighted what he called the Southern Ocean and claimed it for Spain. Later, the navigator Magellan (see "Racing for First," earlier in this chapter) would call this ocean the Pacific. Despite Balboa's industry, Spain appointed Pedro Arias Dávila (about 1440 to 1531) as governor of Darién. Balboa made the best of this, leading several expeditions for Dávila, but in 1519 Dávila and Balboa clashed, and the governor had Balboa beheaded.

Tracking the Centuries

Around 330 BC: Pythias of Massilia (today's Marseilles, France) sails out through the Strait of Gibraltar and up the Atlantic coast of Europe to what may have been Norway.

First century AD: St. Paul, a former Jewish rabbi of the Pharisee sect, travels widely through southern Europe and the Middle East, spreading the new Christian faith.

1354: Ibn Battuta, a scholar who has journeyed from Spain to Uzbekistan to China to Timbuktu over his nearly 30 years of wandering, settles in Fez, Morocco, to dictate his book *Rihlah,* a memoir of his travels.

1804: Sakagawea, whose name means *bird woman* in her native Shoshone language, helps American explorers Meriwether Lewis and William Clark find their way up the Missouri River toward the Great Divide.

1847: British Naval officer Sir John Franklin and all his crew die in their icebound ship just a few miles short of completing their navigation of the Northwest Passage, a sea route between the Atlantic and Pacific north of Canada.

1911: Roald Amundsen, a Norwegian explorer, arrives at the South Pole, the first person to reach this frigid goal.

1969: Neil Armstrong, an American, steps out of his lunar landing module to become the first human being to set foot on the moon.

Chapter 21

Overturning Societies

- -

In This Chapter

▶ Turning the tables as revolutionaries become rulers

▶ Inspiring the masses with martyrdom

▶ Putting ideology into action

▶ Making new rules

▶ Winning power only to lose it again

▶ Falling by the wayside

- -

Change happens. Usually, it gets a push. This chapter offers a tiny sampling of reformers, revolutionaries, and a few usurpers. These people — whether in power, wanting it, seizing it, or rejecting it — fought, plotted, labored, or all of the above, to usher in new eras.

Ruling Revolutionaries

The goal of any political revolution is to oust the people currently in power and replace them with new people. Usually, the leaders of the revolution become the leaders of the new political order. But forming a government and restoring order is a different job altogether from tearing down the old order.

The people in this section struggled to oust oppressors, then came up against a different set of challenges as leaders of a country. The way each was changed by the transition illustrates what a tricky business it is to wield power wisely and with grace.

> ✔ **Lucius Junius Brutus** (late sixth century BC): History knows this Roman hero by an unlikely nickname that became part of his formal name, proudly handed down to descendents (see "Falling Along the Way" later in this chapter). In the earliest days of Rome, then a city-state ruled by a king, "Brutus" meant *stupid*. Lucius Junius earned this title by pretending to be an idiot so that King Lucius Tarquinius Superbus wouldn't kill him. When Brutus's rich dad died, the king confiscated his property and killed Brutus's brother. He didn't bother to kill the "stupid" one.

After the king's son, Tarquinius Sextus, raped a nobleman's wife, she committed suicide. Public sentiment turned against the king. Brutus was among the Romans who declared a republic in **509 BC.** His fellow citizens elected "Stupid" to the top republican office of consul. But Brutus had two sons of his own who thought things were better back in the old days of the monarchy. They conspired with other monarchists to restore the Tarquin family (as Tarquinius Superbus's clan was called) to the throne. With the fledgling republic at stake, Brutus ordered his boys arrested and put to death. The Roman republic survived, but Brutus didn't — he died in one-on-one combat with Tarquinius Aruns, another son of Tarquinius Superbus.

✔ **Chu Yuan-chang** (1328 to 1398): When he was 17, after his entire farm-laborer family died in an epidemic, Chu entered a Buddhist monastery. Eight years later, he left the monastery to lead the province of Anhwei against China's Mongol rulers. After years of struggle, his forces occupied Beijing, the Mongol capital. At age 40, Chu Yuan-chang proclaimed himself the first emperor of the Ming Dynasty.

✔ **Oliver Cromwell** (1599 to 1658): Cromwell was a staunch Puritan (see Chapter 13), a disciplined military officer, and a persuasive member of England's Parliament during the reign of Charles I (1600 to 1649). Charles's religious and economic policies led to civil war. Cromwell originally defended the king, but then he put Charles on trial and signed his death warrant in 1649. After the execution, Cromwell stood looking at the king's lifeless body and muttered "Cruel necessity."

Touchy, touchy

Although Chu Yuan-chang had been a Buddhist monk and brought Buddhist monks into his court, he also promoted Confucian rituals and scholarship. (Turn to Chapter 9 for more on Confucius.) Among the Chinese of this time, few people felt that it was important to accept only one religious tradition while rejecting all others.

The emperor wasn't so tolerant about other things. He forbade any reference to his years in the monastery — not because of religion, but because he was sensitive about his humble origins. (You didn't dare mention that he'd grown up a peasant, either.) Once, two Confucian scholars sent Chu Yuan-chang a letter of congratulation in which they used the word *sheng,* which means "birth." The term was a little too close to the word *seng,* which means "monk." The emperor took it as a pun and had them killed.

Later, Chu got so touchy that he made it a capital crime to question his policies. When he thought the people of Nanjing didn't display a properly obedient attitude, he slaughtered 15,000 of them.

Cromwell replaced the monarchy with a *commonwealth,* ruled by Parliament. As Lord Protector of the commonwealth, Cromwell wielded enormous power and Parliament offered him a crown. Cromwell turned it down. He didn't hesitate to exercise his king-like power, however, quashing opponents, reorganizing the English church along more Protestant lines, and extending parliamentary representation to Scotland and Ireland (after his troops ruthlessly put down Irish resistance). After Cromwell's death, opponents restored the monarchy. (For more on the English Civil War, see Chapter 7.)

✔ **Vladimir Ilyitch Lenin** (1870 to 1924): Lenin put the economic philosophy Marxism (see Chapter 14) to work in Russia. As a law student in St. Petersburg, his underground leftist activities got him sent to Siberia. He came back as leader of the far-left faction of the Russian Social Democratic Labor Party. Lenin spent much of World War I in exile. After Russia's government collapsed in 1917, Germany, enemy of the Czarist government, helped Lenin return to his native land. Lenin rallied Russians with the slogans "Peace and bread" and "All power to the soviets." (A *soviet* is a council of workers or peasants.) In October 1917, he led the Bolshevik revolution and became head of the first Soviet government. (For more on the two Russian revolutions of the early twentieth century, see Chapter 8.)

Counterrevolutionary forces tried reversing what Lenin had done, which lead to the Russian Civil War of 1918 to 1921. Lenin's Communists — named for *communism,* the ideal Marxist economic state that they hoped to achieve — won the war, after nationalizing major industries and banks and seizing control of farms. The measures helped Lenin defeat the counterrevolutionaries, but they sent the fledgling Union of Soviet Socialist Republics (USSR) toward economic collapse and famine.

Lenin reacted by instituting a "New Economic Policy," permitting private production. This retreat from all-out socialism disappointed some of Lenin's harder-line Communist colleagues. The new policy was too late, because the farm economy recovered slowly and many thousands of Russians died in the famine of 1922 and 1923.

✔ **Ho Chi Minh** (1892 to 1968): As Nguyen Tat Thanh, he was a well-educated young man from French Indochina (as French-ruled Vietnam was called) who traveled widely and lived in England, the United States, France, and China. In Paris he became active in France's fledgling Communist Party. He went to the newly established Soviet Union (see Chapter 8), where the government recruited him as a foreign agent and sent him to Guanzhou, in southern China. There, Ho Chi Minh (the name means "He Who Enlightens") organized Vietnamese exiles, who had fled the colonial French regime into an Indochinese Communist Party.

After his party's first efforts against the French government of Indochina failed in 1940, Ho took refuge in China, only to be thrown in jail by the anticommunist Nationalist government there. Japanese forces occupied Indochina during World War II, and in 1943 Ho returned home to organize Vietminh guerilla forces to fight back. The Vietminh succeeded and Ho proclaimed the Democratic Republic of Vietnam in 1945, only to see French colonial forces return and overturn his new government. Ho once again fought the French. By 1954, the Vietminh ousted the French, but Ho's struggle was not won. Rival Vietnamese leaders seized control of the southern part of the country.

The Geneva Conference of 1954, officially ending the French-Indochinese War, partitioned Vietnam along the seventeenth parallel, with Ho in charge of North Vietnam. Ho remained committed to a reunited Vietnam. After a 1963 military coup left South Vietnam vulnerable to North Vietnamese takeover, the United States (as part of its anticommunist foreign policy) sent military assistance to South Vietnam. The resultant war — marked by U.S. escalation through the 1960s and into the 1970s — was raging when Ho died, but his side eventually won, as U.S. forces withdrew from South Vietnam in the 1970s. The former South Vietnamese capital, Saigon, was renamed Ho Chi Minh City as a memorial to the tenacious leader. Figure 21-1 is a picture of Ho and some young friends.

Figure 21-1:
North Vietnamese leader Ho Chi Minh found Communism as a young man in France.

(c) Hulton-Deutsch Collection/CORBIS

✔ **Fidel Castro** (born 1927): Castro, born into a prosperous Cuban family, was a law student in Havana and a gifted baseball pitcher — some say he might have made the pros — but he became convinced that the corrupt government of dictator Fulgencia Batista (1901 to 1973) had to be overturned. Castro joined a revolutionary uprising in 1953. It failed and he was imprisoned. Granted amnesty, he fled to the United States and then to Mexico, where he gathered support for another assault on Batista, which started in 1956. Castro and supporters finally forced Batista to leave the island in 1959. Castro ordered many remaining Batista supporters executed, raising concerns in Cuba and abroad. Failing to negotiate diplomatic relations or a trade agreement with the United States, Castro turned for support to the Soviet Union. In 1961, he declared a Marxist-Leninist government. His far-reaching reforms depended for decades on Soviet financing, especially because the anticommunist United States imposed an embargo on trade with Cuba. Yet Castro's regime survived the USSR's 1991 collapse.

✔ **Robert Mugabe** (born 1924): As a young teacher, Mugabe joined and helped form democratic political organizations in Rhodesia, a British colony in southern Africa with limited, white-controlled self-rule. With Ndabaningi Sithole (born 1920), Mugabe co-founded the Zimbabwe African National Union (ZANU), which sought black liberation. ZANU activities landed Mugabe in government custody more than once as pressure mounted for political change. Rhodesia's white government broke from Britain in 1965 but continued to subjugate blacks. Mugabe spent 1964 to 1974 under Rhodesian detention and then went to Mozambique, preparing to invade Rhodesia.

Although they were sometimes allies, Mugabe and Joshua Nkomo (1917 to 1999), founder of the Zimbabwe African People's Union (ZAPU), also shared a long history as rivals for power. In the late 1970s, their forces united as the Zimbabwe Patriotic Front and established the new nation of Zimbabwe in 1980. Mugabe won the post of prime minister, but his rivalry with Nkomo intensified almost to the point of civil war. After years of debate and frequent violence between their factions, the two men reconciled again with a formal ZANU-ZAPU Pact in 1987.

Mugabe became president of a reorganized government, moving away from his insistence on a one-party state in 1991 as the Soviet Union's government — and its foreign aid to communist-aligned countries — collapsed. Mugabe survived a crucial election in 2000, but opposition parties gained strength.

Raising the Icons of Rebellion

Rebellion carries a certain romantic cachet. "The Leader of the Pack" as the old pop song about a gang leader puts it, boasts a defiant magnetism — whether it's the appeal of a wild-eyed idealist or gritty guerilla toughness. Many movements have charismatic leaders who attract interest and galvanize support. The following may fit that label:

✔ **Toussaint L'Ouverture** (1746 to 1803): François-Dominique Toussaint (nicknamed L'Ouverture) was born to slave parents from Africa and rose up to free the blacks on the Caribbean island of Hispaniola. A fight for freedom is seldom simple, however. As a member and then leader of Haiti's French Republicans, Toussaint faced armed opposition from not only the Napoleonic French overlords, but from the British, whom he drove off the island; the Spanish who ran the other half of the island (today's Dominican Republic); and the *mulattos,* persons of mixed black-white heritage, who were opposed to losing their place in Haiti's racial hierarchy. Napoleon's agents captured Toussaint and shipped him to Paris, where he died in jail.

✔ **Simón Bolívar** (1783 to 1830): Caracas-born Bolívar is a national hero in at least five countries — Venezuela, Colombia, Ecuador, Peru, and Bolivia (a country named for him). Known as "The Liberator" and "The George Washington of South America," he was instrumental in wars of independence that ousted Spain from much of South America (see Chapter 8). He traveled the continent, leading campaigns of independence. Yet he clashed with other freedom fighters and, as the first president (actually dictator) of the Republic of Colombia (today's Colombia, Venezuela, and Ecuador), struggled with dissent and even civil war. Disheartened, Bolívar was headed into exile when he died.

✔ **Sun Yixian** (1866 to 1925): Chinese Communists on the mainland and Chinese Nationalists on the island nation of Taiwan may not agree on much, but they both honor Sun Yixian as the founder of modern China. Also known as Sun Yat-sen, he founded China's *Tongmenghui,* or United League, in Tokyo, Japan, in 1905, after studying medicine in Hawaii and Hong Kong. Sun lived away from China during the first decade of the twentieth century because he was exiled after his 1895 attempt to bring down the aging Qing Dynasty failed. The decaying imperial government saw Sun as such a threat that its agents kidnapped him while he was visiting London during his exile. (The English negotiated his release.) The Qing were right to fear Sun, because his Tongmenghui evolved into the *Kuomintang,* or Chinese Nationalist Party, which was instrumental in bringing down the Qing in 1911 and setting up a short-lived Nationalist government. Sun was briefly president in 1912 before stepping aside in favor of another revolutionary leader, who repaid Sun by banning Sun's Kuomintang. Sun set up a separate government in Canton in 1913 and oversaw an uneasy alliance with the newly formed Chinese Communist Party in the 1920s. He was trying to negotiate a unified government when he died. (For more about the Nationalists in China, see Mao Zedong under "Putting Theories into Action" and Jiang Jieshi in "Living by the Sword; Dying by the Sword," both later in this chapter.)

✔ **Che Guevara** (1928 to 1967): In the late 1960s, a popular poster on college dorm room walls showed the shadowy, bearded face of Ernesto Guevara de la Serna, a onetime medical student from Argentina. After helping overthrow Cuba's government in the revolution of 1956 to 1959,

Che — as he was popularly known — served in various posts in the Fidel Castro regime (see "Ruling Revolutionaries"). He left Cuba in 1965 to lead guerillas in Bolivia. His shaggy good looks, jaunty beret, and especially the timing of his 1967 arrest and execution made him a martyr of the 1960s left.

Putting Theories into Action

Ideas start revolutions, but thinkers don't always make the best revolutionaries. The men in this section were not just writers who synthesized the ideas that rallied supporters to their cause, but also doers who made momentous decisions involving others' lives and destinies. Transforming an idea into a practical result isn't easy, however, especially when there are politics involved. A sublime theory may bear sublime results, or it may bring tragedy. Examples of both follow:

✔ **Thomas Jefferson** (1743 to 1826): In 1774, Jefferson wrote *A Summary View of the Rights of British America.* This tract expressed the unhappiness that led him to become a delegate to the Continental Congress in Philadelphia. Jefferson wrote the Declaration of Independence, which was approved by that revolutionary congress in 1776. His public service also included serving as U.S. president (two terms), vice president (under John Adams), secretary of state (under George Washington), Virginia governor, and ambassador to France. As president, his nervy Louisiana Purchase more than doubled the size of the United States. He commissioned the Lewis and Clark expedition (Chapter 20 has more on the explorers), setting the precedent for U.S. expansion to the Pacific.

Jefferson was happiest in aesthetic pursuits, especially architecture. The University of Virginia and the Virginia statehouse are among his designs. His wife's death after ten years of marriage marred his private life. Four of their six children died young. DNA evidence reported in the late 1990s seemed to support the long-repeated rumor that Jefferson fathered children with a slave woman. Check out *U.S. History For Dummies,* by Steve Wiegand (published by Hungry Minds, Inc.) for more details on this relationship.

✔ **Mao Zedong** (1893 to 1976): Also spelled Mao Tse-tung, this longtime chairman of the People's Republic of China lead his party through a hard-fought struggle for power and led his country through a tumultuous stretch of the twentieth century. Mao, from rural Hunan Province, was just out of college when he landed a job in the library of Beijing University. Marxist professors there changed his thinking.

Mao became involved in the Chinese nationalist May Fourth Movement, which began with a **May 4, 1919,** student demonstration in Beijing, a protest against a trade concession that China's revolutionary government of the time granted to Japan. Within the May Fourth Movement, socialist ideas became popular and Mao attended the meetings that led to the formation of the Chinese Communist Party. As a newly converted communist, he moved to Shanghai in 1923 as a political organizer for the Kuomintang, or Nationalist People's Party, which was fighting to establish a new Chinese Nationalist government in place of the Revolutionary Alliance that had ruled since shortly after the Qing Dynasty's collapse in 1911. When the Kuomintang decided in 1927 that it didn't want communists among its fighters, the ousted Mao formed the Jiangxi Soviet, an outlaw guerilla force that watched the Nationalist take over, but finally emerged victorious from a post-World War II civil war against forces led by Nationalist President Jiang Jieshi. (See "Living by the Sword; Dying by the Sword" in this chapter.)

On **October 1, 1949,** Mao proclaimed formation of the People's Republic of China. As chairman of the new government, Mao left day-to-day administration to others, but he occasionally emerged with dramatic and disastrous reform proposals such as the Great Leap Forward, which lasted from 1958 to 1960. An ambitious drive for industrial and agricultural expansion, it resulted in crop failures and the starvation of as many as 13 million peasants. Mao, a stubbornly Marxist idealist, tried again in 1966 with the Cultural Revolution, a drive to reinvigorate the revolution and root out compromise and Western influences from every corner of Chinese society that resulted in widespread chaos and violence. A prolific poet and essayist, Mao was a much quoted source of leftist wisdom, especially in the turbulent 1960s. The plump chairman's jovial, Buddha-like portrait became especially popular.

Doing the Right Thing

Some people live by conscience; consequences be damned. The men in this section showed rare courage in standing up to the powerful and speaking out against injustice:

- **Martin Luther** (1483 to 1546): Turn to Chapter 13 for the story of how Luther, a German university professor and priest, started the Protestant Reformation. He was born in Eisleben and spent three years in a monastery before earning his degree. Initially, his big issue was the Church's practice of selling indulgences, which many people understood as a way to buy entry into heaven. Once he started taking on the papal system, Luther moved on to other issues, including priestly celibacy. He married Katharina von Bora, a former nun, in 1525.

- **Mohandas Karamchand Gandhi** (1869 to 1948): His fellow Indians called him the *Mahatma,* or "great soul." After studying law in England, Gandhi fought to end discrimination against Indian immigrants in South Africa. After two decades there, he returned to his native India in 1914. He led the

Indian National Congress, a group seeking independence from British rule. Inspired by the American writer Henry David Thoreau, Gandhi preached and practiced nonviolent noncooperation, or "civil disobedience." The colonial government jailed him, from 1922 to 1924, for conspiracy.

Gandhi helped shape independent India's first constitution. (Chapter 8 has more on India's independence.) Achieving his goal of self-rule for India in 1947, Gandhi's next challenge was to stop Hindu-Muslim violence. For that, a Hindu fanatic killed him. (Chapter 2 talks about how rarely virtuous people find a prominent place in written history.)

✔ **Martin Luther King, Jr.** (1929 to 1968): Named for the German who started the Protestant Reformation (see the previous entry for Martin Luther and Chapter 13), King guided the U.S. civil rights movement during the its most crucial years, from 1955 to 1968. As a young Baptist pastor in Montgomery, Alabama, he took over where Rosa Parks left off and led the 1955 boycott of that city's bus line to protest racial discrimination. Two years later, the newly formed Southern Christian Leadership Conference chose King as its leader. King looked to India's Gandhi (see the preceding entry) for inspiration as he preached and practiced nonviolent opposition to racism. Arrested, jailed, stoned by mobs, his family threatened, his home bombed, and his privacy ravaged by a hostile FBI, King continued to lead protests. He made his famous "I Have a Dream" speech at the Lincoln Memorial in Washington, D.C., in 1963 and in 1964 he was awarded the Nobel Peace Prize. An assassin killed King in Memphis, Tennessee, where he was supporting striking garbage collectors. (See *U.S. History For Dummies* by Steve Wiegand for more on King.)

Changing the Rules

Sometimes change, even radical change, comes from the top. The rulers in this section weren't content with the way things were and set about shaping their domain to fit their vision:

✔ **Akhenaton** (fourteenth century BC): As Amenhotep IV, he became Egypt's king in 1379 BC, but after six years, he changed everything — his own name, his capital city, and the state religion. Akhenaton was devoted to a cult that discarded Egypt's traditional array of gods (more on religions in Chapter 9) in favor of just one — the sun disc god, Aton. He put the new center of government at Amarna, which he called Akhetaton, 300 miles from the established capital at Thebes.

Art thrived under Akhenaton and his queen, the beautiful Nefertiti. (Many surviving sculptures depict her beauty.) But Akhenaton failed to take care of earthly business and Egypt's commercial and military fortunes declined.

✔ **Asoka** (third century BC): Also spelled Ashoka, this King of India was the last ruler of the Mauryan dynasty. Early in his reign, Asoka led armies but didn't like bloodshed. He swore off fighting, converted to Buddhism, and spread the religion throughout India and beyond. His policy of *dharma* (principles of right life) called for tolerance, honesty, and kindness. It was beautiful while it lasted, but after he died the empire went downhill.

✔ **Henry VIII** (1491 to 1547): Novelist Charles Dickens (1812 to 1870) looked back on big Henry as "a blot of blood and grease upon the history of England." You may remember this king as the fat guy who chopped off two of his six wives' heads, but he was also England's first Renaissance Prince — educated, handsome (before he put on the pounds), witty, popular (until he closed down the monasteries), and ruthless.

By *Renaissance Prince,* I mean that Henry was thought to meet the very high expectations that educated people had for a ruler during the Renaissance. (I talk about the ideas of the Renaissance, including the role of a king, in Chapter 12.)

As soon as his big brother Arthur died in 1502, a marriage was arranged between Henry, still a child, and Arthur's widow, Catherine of Aragon (1485 to 1536). Right after Henry became king in 1509, he and Catherine were married.

Chapters 9 and 13 give you the scoop on how Henry broke England away from Catholicism and founded the Church of England. It all started with the monarch wanting a divorce. While still married to Catherine of Aragon, Henry married Anne Boleyn. He had her executed and married Jane Seymour (not the actress from *Dr. Quinn, Medicine Woman*). When she died, he married the German princess Anne of Cleves. Henry told Parliament to annul that marriage (he could do that) so he could wed Catherine Howard. After two years, he decapitated her and married Catherine Parr, who outlived him. Three of his kids succeeded him, in turn, to the throne of England — Edward VI, Jane Seymour's son; then Mary, who was Catherine of Aragon's daughter; then Anne Boleyn's daughter, Elizabeth I.

✔ **Peter the Great** (1672 to 1725): As a kid, Peter I of Russia was a sort of co-czar with his mentally disabled half-brother. But this arrangement had their big sister Sophia calling the shots. In 1696, Peter sent Sophia to live in a convent, became sole ruler, and started changing things. He reformed the military, the economy, the bureaucracy, the schools, the Russian Orthodox Church, and even the way Russian people dressed and groomed themselves. He wanted Russia to mirror its Western European neighbors. How did he get Russians to do what he wanted? With brutality and repression. Peter's many wars, especially a big victory over Sweden, made Russia a major power and won it a Baltic seaport, where the czar built a new capital city, St. Petersburg. His wife succeeded him as Catherine I. (For more on Peter I and his reforms, see Chapter 8.)

Living by the Sword; Dying by the Sword

Often the person who gets power by force has it pried away by force.

✔ **Atahualpa** (birth unknown, died 1532): Atahualpa, last Incan ruler of Peru, was one of history's many sons who wanted a bigger piece of his dad's estate. Rather than being grateful for inheriting the northern half of the Inca Empire, Atahualpa overthrew the king of the southern half, who happened to be his brother. Just a few months later, Spain's Francisco Pizarro (see Chapter 20) captured Atahualpa and killed him. (For more about the Spanish conquest of the Inca, turn to Chapter 7.)

✔ **Maximilien-François Marie-Isidore de Robespierre** (1758 to 1794): He was called "The Incorruptible" and later "The Headless." Okay, I just made up that second name, but Robespierre, who energetically employed the guillotine upon anybody he thought threatened the French Revolution (see Chapter 7), also died under the falling blade. He was a lawyer and a member of the Estates-General, an official gathering of the three estates of the French realm (the Church, the nobility, and the commons). The Estates-General began centuries earlier as an occasional advisory body to the king, but had fallen into long disuse before King Louis XVI called it into session in May of 1789, with the unexpected (to the king) result of precipitating the French Revolution. Led by its radical fringes, the Estates-General transformed itself into the revolutionary National Assembly. Robespierre emerged as a leader of the revolution, becoming public accuser and, two years later, a member of the notorious Committee of Public Safety, directing a steady flow of executions over the three months known as the Reign of Terror. At this point, his ruthlessness scared even his former allies. The Revolutionary Tribunal, an institution he had helped create, sent him to get a fatally severe haircut.

✔ **Jean-Jacques Dessalines** (about 1758 to 1806): He was born in West Africa, taken as a slave and shipped to Haiti, where he proclaimed himself emperor. In Haiti's slave insurrection of 1791, Dessalines served as a lieutenant to rebel leader Toussaint-L'Ouverture (see "Raising the Icons of Rebellion"). With British help, Dessalines chased the French out of Haiti in 1803 and assumed the post of governor general. In 1804, he had himself crowned Jacques I. As monarch, he slaughtered whites and took their land. His former political allies, Henri Christophe (1767 to 1820) and Alexandre Pétion (1770 to 1818), couldn't tolerate his self-importance, cruelty, and immorality. They arranged for Dessalines's assassination.

✔ **Bernardo O'Higgins** (1778-1842): Though born in Ireland, Ambrosio O'Higgins (about 1720 to 1801) fought for the Spanish and became Spain's captain-general of Chile and viceroy of Peru. His son Bernardo, however, was on the side of those Chileans who wanted to break away from Spain. (For more about the revolutions in the former Spanish colonies of South America, turn to Chapter 8.) Bernardo O'Higgins planned and helped carry out the revolt that unfolded between 1810 and 1817. Then he became president of independent Chile. Yet another revolution threw O'Higgins out of office, and he was forced to flee to Peru.

✔ **Jiang Jieshi** (1887 to 1975): Also known as Chiang Kai-shek, he was the revolutionary leader who took over the Kuomintang, or Chinese Nationalist Party in 1926 after founder Sun Xixian died (see "Raising Icons of Rebellion," earlier in this chapter). The Kuomintang was largely responsible for the overthrow of China's decrepit imperial government in 1911. Struggling against rival revolutionary forces, Jiang ousted Chinese communists from the Kuomintang and in 1928 established his Nationalist government at Nanjing. (Westerners used to call it Nanking.) The Kuomintang had unified most of China by 1937, but World War II provided an opportunity for the Communists, who had regrouped under Mao Zedong (see "Putting Theories into Action," earlier in this chapter) to regain momentum. The Communists won the ensuing Chinese Civil war, forcing Jiang and his supporters into exile. In 1949, he set up a government in exile on the island of Taiwan and began to surprise the world with that nation's dramatic economic growth.

Falling Along the Way

Many rebels die for a cause. The failed revolutionary effort can make a lasting impact. The people in this section never rose to be presidents or prime ministers, but they left a legacy in the causes they championed and the sacrifices they made:

✔ **Spartacus** (birth unknown, died 71 BC): Born in Thrace, a northeastern region of Greece, Spartacus was a slave and gladiator who led the most serious slave uprising that Rome ever faced. Starting in 73 BC, Spartacus assembled a huge army of slaves and dispossessed people that more than challenged the mighty Roman army — his army actually scored numerous victories. Finally, a general called Crassus (about 115 to 53 BC) beat the rebels and killed Spartacus. Crassus had all the rebels crucified and left many hundreds of their bodies hanging along the Appian Way — the main Roman road.

Wouldn't Spartacus have been thrilled to know that Kirk Douglas would play him in the movie? "That's fantastic!" he would have said. "What's a movie?" Directed by Stanley Kubrick and with a smart and soulful screenplay by Dalton Trumbo, *Spartacus* explores issues of slavery and freedom and examines the awful realities of a kill-or-be-killed existence. Super thespians Lawrence Olivier, Charles Laughton, and Peter Ustinov show up among the cast, as does a lost-looking Tony Curtis. Too bad the sticky sentimentality of the ending mars the whole production.

✔ **Marcus Junius Brutus** (about 85 to 42 BC): This Roman politician's name means "stupid," but he wore it with honor. The name was handed down from a famous ancestor (see Lucius Junius Brutus in "Ruling Revolutionaries," earlier in this chapter). When Pompey and Caesar fought a civil war, Brutus sided with Pompey. He then bowed to the winner, Caesar, who appointed him governor in a region of Gaul (present-day France). Because the first famous Brutus had helped drive the last Roman king out of town, Marcus Brutus fancied the idea of being a king-breaker himself. That made it easier for a fellow politician, Cassius (who also died in 42 BC), to enlist Brutus in the conspiracy against Caesar in 44 BC. After they assassinated the dictator, the conspirators fought Caesar's avengers, Antony and Octavian. Antony and Octavian defeated Brutus at Philippi. Brutus killed himself and Octavian became Emperor Augustus (see Chapter 18). It was not the political outcome Brutus had in mind.

✔ **Wat Tyler** (birth unknown, died 1381): In 1381, English peasants rebelled against working conditions in Kent. They chose Tyler to lead them. He led a march to London to see King Richard II. The meeting ended in violence and William Walworth, Mayor of London, wounded Tyler. His supporters took him to St. Bartholomew's Hospital. Walworth had him dragged out of the hospital and behcaded. The uprising is called the Peasants' Revolt (which I tell you about in Chapter 6) and it proved to be ahead of its time.

✔ **Guy Fawkes** (1570 to 1606): Though born in York to Protestant parents, Fawkes converted to Catholicism and served in the Spanish army, fighting Dutch Protestants. Back in England, where Catholics were an oppressed minority, he conspired with fellow activists to blow up King James I and Parliament in 1606. Fawkes was caught red-handed in a basement full of gunpowder. He was convicted and hanged. Every November, on the anniversary of his death, the English burn him in effigy. (For how Fawkes's first name became the modern word "guy," meaning a regular fellow, turn to Chapter 2.)

✔ **Emelian Ivanovich Pugachev** (1726 to 1775): Political opponents killed Russia's weak Czar Peter III in 1762 and installed his widow, Catherine, in his place. Catherine rose to the challenge, but not without turmoil. *Cossacks,* semi-independent tribes of roving warriors in southern Russia, resented her authority. In the 1770s, a rebellion among rank-and-file Cossacks grew into a wider revolt, joined by peasants who flocked to support the Cossack soldier Emelian Ivanovich Pugachev when he proclaimed himself to be Peter III, the empress's murdered husband. With that claim, he led a fierce mass rebellion against Catherine, promising to strike down government repression. Catherine's officers captured Pugachev in 1774 and took him to Moscow where they tortured and killed him. His name long after stood for the spirit of Russian peasant revolution.

✔ **John Brown** (1800 to 1859): Brown's opposition to slavery dated back to his days as a youth in Ohio, but the tradesman and sometime farmer was in his fifties, the father of twenty children, when he decided emancipation must be won by force. With six of his sons and a son-in-law, he went to Kansas to fight slavery in that state. In retaliation for a raid on an anti-slavery town, Brown and his followers attacked the slavery stronghold of Pottawatomie Creek and killed five men. Then they headed east for the U.S. arsenal at Harpers Ferry, Virginia (later West Virginia). He took the arsenal in 1859, but Col. Robert E. Lee (future commander of Confederate forces) captured Brown. Hanged for treason, Brown became a martyr for the abolitionist cause. (See Chapter 17 and, *U.S. History For Dummies* for more on Brown.)

Tracking the Centuries

509 BC: Lucius Junius Brutus wins the top administrative post in Rome's new republican government.

71 BC: Roman General Crassus puts down a slave revolt led by the gladiator Spartacus. He executes Spartacus and hundreds of his followers by hanging them from crosses along the Apian Way.

44 BC: Marcus Junius Brutus, descendent of Lucius Junius Brutus, joins fellow conspirators in assassinating Roman dictator Julius Caesar.

1381 AD: William Walworth, Lord Mayor of London, orders the injured peasant leader Wat Tyler dragged out of a hospital and beheaded, ending England's Peasant Revolt.

1532: Atahualpa, ruler of the northern half of the Inca Empire, overthrows his brother, king of the southern half, to reunite Inca lands. Within months, Spanish conquerors will capture and kill Atahualpa.

1775: Officers of Russian Empress Catherine the Great torture and kill the leader of a widespread Cossack uprising, Emelian Ivanovich Pugachev.

1893: Mao Zedong, future founder and chairman of the People's Republic of China, is born in rural Hunan Province.

1922: The British colonial government of India imprisons nationalist leader Mohandas Karamchand Gandhi, known as the Mahatma, for conspiracy.

2000: President Robert Mugabe of Zimbabwe, who came to power as a revolutionary leader in 1980, survives a crucial election challenge.

Part VI
The Part of Tens

In this part...

Henry VIII had six wives. Anne Boleyn, his second wife, supposedly had twelve fingers. So, Henry had as many wives as Anne had fingers on each hand. What does this mean? Nothing that I can think of.

History, as I often remind you, is full of arbitrary judgments made by the people who gather it. Unlike Anne, I have only ten fingers, which is as good a reason as any for making the lists in this part of the book contain ten landmarks. History is full of big dates and important documents. Which are the *very* tippy-top biggest? In this part, I share my choices, but they aren't the *only* choices. Disagreements help make history fun.

By the way, if I cheat and try to sneak an eleventh or twelfth entry into one of these chapters, I'm sure you can make allowances. Just give me as much benefit of the doubt as Henry gave Anne. . . . Oh, wait. Forget I said that.

Chapter 22

Ten Unforgettable Dates

*I*f a teacher ever required you to memorize dates without bothering to get you interested in *why* whatever it was that happened that year (or that day and month and year, if the teacher was picky) means so much, then you know why I almost hate to mention them.

Still, dates give events context. They help you remember the order in which things occurred. Many dates serve as shorthand, standing for a broad change that hinged on a particular day or year. So, even if you hate memorizing dates (as I do), these are worth remembering.

If you don't think these dates are such biggies, feel free to choose your own.

460 BC — Athens Goes Democratic

The aristocrat Pericles turned Athens into a real democracy between **462** and **460 BC.** It wasn't the first-ever participatory government, but Athens became powerful during this time. (Chapter 10 talks more about the Greek city-states.) And Athens remains the early democracy that most inspired later ones. The founding fathers of the United States looked back to Athenian democracy as a model.

Athens's popular assembly, the principal lawmaking body, was open to any male citizen (but not to women or to slaves, who were ineligible for citizenship). In addition to the popular assembly, there was a senate made up of citizens over age 30. This senate operated as an executive council that drew up the government's agenda and administered law enforcement. These two bodies of citizen-rulers set a precedent for two-house legislatures in later democracies. Think of Britain's House of Commons and House of Lords and the U.S. House of Representatives and Senate.

Although Athens's democracy was rule by citizens, Athenian society hung onto some aspects of its former *oligarchy* (rule by a few) as aristocrats retained privileges won by birth or connection. The glaring example was the democratic aristocrat Pericles himself, almost an uncrowned king. (I talk more about Pericles's Athens in Chapter 10.)

Not all historians give Pericles credit for the shift to democracy. Pericles built on reforms that a predecessor, Ephialtes, brought about when he overturned an aristocratic council in 462 BC. Ephialtes may have been murdered for doing that, so it probably took courage for Pericles to take up the cause. Earlier yet, the statesman Cleisthenes pushed reforms that pointed toward democracy, after the fifth century BC rule of Pisistratus, a dictator. Some credit Cleisthenes with founding Athens's democracy.

323 BC — Alexander the Great Dies

Born in 356 BC, Alexander the Great succeeded his dad as king of Macedon (north of Greece) in 336 BC. Those were big dates. So were the years of his victories, as when he beat Persia's King Darius III in 334 BC. But the year of the conqueror's early death — **323 BC** — is most worth remembering. (Find more about Alexander's empire in Chapter 3 and more about Alexander himself in Chapter 19.)

Alex's conquests probably would not have ended while he lived. He was too ambitious for that. His victories stopped when a fever (probably malaria) killed him.

This death also *began* a remarkable period when Alex's generals became kings themselves and founded dynasties in places ranging from Macedon to Persia to Egypt. In Egypt, Alexander's general Ptolemy founded a dynasty that continued until Rome's Augustus captured Queen Cleopatra in 30 BC.

476 AD — The Roman Empire Falls

Rome wasn't built in a day and didn't collapse in one either. Civil Wars between competing military and political leaders rocked the Roman Republic from 88 to 28 BC, leading to the end of the republican form of rule and the beginning of government by one, strong emperor. (You can read about the first emperor, Augustus, and his fight to consolidate power in Chapter 18.)

Yet imperial rule eventually faltered, too, as third-century AD attacks on many fronts along the Roman Empire's far-flung borders, coupled with internal revolts, forced the Emperor Diocletian to take an extreme measure: Diocletian split the empire in two in 286 AD, installing himself as Emperor of the East (Egypt and Asia) with his colleague Maximian as Emperor of the West (Europe and northwest Africa). Although Diocletian still held authority over both halves, this system eventually led to the east becoming a separate empire, the Byzantine Empire, while the west went into a slow decline.

Huns, Vandals, Visigoths, and Ostragoths — all of them enemies of the Romans — kept pouring across the Rhine in the fifth century, eroding Rome's ability to defend its lands.

By **476 AD,** the empire had little authority left in Europe, so it wasn't all that big a deal when barbarians removed young Emperor Romulus Augustus from his throne that year. (Also known as Augustulus, or "little Augustus.") Yet 476 stands as the symbolic end, and the symbolic beginning of a feudal, fractured society from which the nations of Europe would eventually grow. (Find more on Europe's ascendancy in Chapters 6 and 7.)

1066 — Normans Conquer England

Wearing polyester half-sleeve shirts, plastic pocket protectors, and tape on their glasses, a band of guys named Norman rode into London and . . . oh, wait. These Normans were *French.* They wouldn't wear pocket protectors.

I don't know how Britain would have turned out if William, Duke of Normandy, had *not* won the Battle of Hastings on **October 14, 1066.** I *do* know that the Norman Conquest's effects were felt for a long time. William, crowned king of England on December 25, 1066, and his family ruled for almost a century, replacing English nobles with Normans (from Normandy, later northern France), Bretons (also France), and Flemings (from Belgium). From 1066 to 1144, England and Normandy had the same government and Normandy remained in English hands until France's Philip II wrested it away in the thirteenth century.

Royal family ties and conflicting claims kept the English and French linked — and often at war — for centuries. You can trace the Hundred Years' War of the fourteenth and fifteenth centuries back to the Norman invasion. (For more about the Hundred Years' War, see Chapter 16.)

1095 — The First Crusade

The Crusades, a prelude to worldwide European empires and colonialism, sent western Europeans surging into another part of the world — the Middle East — where they threw their weight around and acted self-righteous.

The Crusades started after Seljuk Turks took over a large part of the Middle East from Arabs and from the Byzantine Empire, which resisted. The Turks had become Muslim, like the Arabs. But unlike Arabs of the seventh to eleventh centuries, the Turks weren't tolerant toward Christians. The Byzantine emperor asked Pope Urban III, a fellow Christian, to help him resist this new Turkish threat. Urban also worried about reports of Christian pilgrims to Palestine, the Holy Land (now under Seljuk rule) being harassed.

On **November 26, 1095,** the pope called for Christian warriors to take on the Seljuk Turks. Two kinds of warriors answered. First, untrained, ill-armed peasants, and townspeople headed east, getting into trouble on the way, then getting themselves killed. The second type of soldier — well-armed nobles and their troops — defeated the Seljuk army defending Jerusalem in 1099 and massacred everybody in the city.

Later Crusades — which went on for centuries — were just as bloody and wandered even further from the goal of restoring holiness to the Holy Land. (To find out how the Crusades foreshadowed European imperialism of the sixteenth to the twentieth centuries, see Chapter 6.)

1492 — Columbus Sails the Ocean Blue

Even if you never memorized another date, you know this one. **1492** began Europe's involvement with lands and cultures that would forever after bear the mark of Spain (the country Columbus represented), Portugal (his home base for years), and other European seafaring nations.

Columbus's discovery rearranged the world — or at least the way everybody thought of the world — feeding a growing European hunger for conquest and helping bring about an age of imperialism that lasted into the twentieth century. Columbus's voyages (he kept going back to the New World, trying to establish that it really was part of Asia) also devastated the people who already lived in the New World, the people he called Indians. European diseases decimated their numbers and European immigration pushed them from their lands.

For all the changes it brought, however, Columbus's feat was disappointing at the time — especially compared to what Portugal's Vasco da Gama did by rounding Africa and reaching India, a coveted trade destination, in 1598. (For more about Columbus, Gama, and other European explorers of the fifteenth and sixteenth centuries, see Chapters 6 and 20.)

1776 — Americans Break Away

The spirit of **July 4, 1776,** when the Continental Congress adopted the revolutionary Declaration of Independence (see the next chapter for more on this revolutionary document) brought forth what would eventually be the most powerful nation in the world. But there's another reason this date is unforgettable.

The American Revolution, inspired by the Enlightenment thinking of the eighteenth century (you can read about the Enlightenment in Chapter 14), began an age of revolutions. It set the stage for the culturally shattering French Revolution of 1789 and for many successive revolts — in European colonies and in Europe.

Rebellion swept South America early in the nineteenth century, and the middle of the century — especially 1848 and 1849 — saw many more revolts in places such as Bohemia and Hungary. In the twentieth century, revolutionary fervor finally ended the colonial age. Revolutions also took on Marxist rhetoric and continued to overturn the old order in places as diverse as Russia and China.

1807 — Britain Bans the Slave Trade

In the eighteenth century, more and more free people in Britain and elsewhere realized how wrong slavery was. They focused on the worst abuses, especially the cruelty of the transatlantic slave trade. Denmark was first to outlaw the trade in 1803. But because of Britain's stature in trade and naval power, the British ban marked a huge international shift. Parliament took the crucial step with the Abolition Act in **1807.** In 1815, after the Napoléonic Wars, Britain leaned on France, the Netherlands, Spain, and Portugal to also stop trading in slaves.

The change grew out of Enlightenment ideas (I talk about Enlightenment thinkers in Chapter 14), notions about natural law and human rights that also fed the revolutions in America and France. Religious and political sentiment turned. England's Quakers formed a Christian abolition society in 1787. Britain's top judge, Lord Mansfield (William Murray before he became a baron) ruled as early as 1772 that fugitive slaves became free upon entering British soil. In the 1830s, Britain required its subjects to free remaining slaves.

Although idealism drove anti-slavery sentiment, the movement got a boost from economic pragmatism. By 1807, Britain's industrial revolution was taking off. The English saw more profit in Africa's natural resources and overseas markets than in slave labor.

1893 — Women Get the Vote

The democratic revolution is still happening. Women first won the right to vote in New Zealand in **1893,** but many other nations followed. Among them: Australia in 1894, Norway in 1907, and Russia in 1917. British women over 30 gained *suffrage* (they got the vote) in 1918. Voting age for women there was lowered to 21 in 1929.

U.S. women also won this right in 1918, although some U.S. states passed women's suffrage earlier. France was a relative latecomer to this party, granting women the vote in 1944. In Switzerland, women didn't gain suffrage until 1971.

The right to vote in itself is important. But this period — not much more than a century — also saw a rapid, generation-by-generation expansion of women's roles and status in many societies worldwide. In Western industrial nations, especially, women took on professions formerly reserved for men and excelled in science, medicine, law, and journalism, among many other pursuits. Women ran for and won elective offices. Major democracies — notably Britain, India, Pakistan, and Israel — all saw women prime ministers in the second half of the twentieth century. Women in other countries — especially some parts of the Muslim world — were just beginning to seek greater freedoms as the twenty-first century began.

1945 — The United States Drops the A-Bomb

Ninety thousand people died in the brilliant flash and impact that demolished 75 percent of the city of Hiroshima, Japan, on **August 6, 1945,** after a United States plane dropped the first atom bomb ever used in war. The explosion and the fire that followed wounded another 60 thousand people and many of those later died of radiation sickness and cancer. Three days later, Americans dropped a second atomic bomb on Japan, this one on the city of Nagasaki. Another 40,000 died instantly.

Two atomic bombs: Indescribable, indiscriminate death and destruction. World War II finally ended and the world entered the nuclear age.

These remain the only times nuclear weapons have been used against people. I hope they remain the only times. But the very existence of these atomic bombs, and the far-more-powerful thermonuclear weapons that succeeded them, make 1945 a huge turning point. Nobody knows how this one will turn out.

See Chapter 8 for more about World War II.

Chapter 23

Ten Essential Documents

Documents give humankind its history — that is, they preserve history. If no one ever invented writing, or started making formal records of battles, beliefs, laws, treaties, and so on, you'd have to sift history out of oral accounts.

Did you ever play the game where you whisper something into your neighbor's ear and she whispers what she heard to the next person, continuing around the room? If you have, you know how oral history changes from person to person, even in a span of a few minutes. Over centuries, people would be left with little idea of what really went down. As for contractual agreements, everybody knows that you need to get it in writing.

Documents are important, and some documents prove super important, not just in preserving the past but in shaping it. Documents set down basic tenets of understanding, societal identity, and principles of right and wrong.

The Rosetta Stone

As much artifact as document, the Rosetta Stone, a slab of black basalt, bears an inscribed text in ancient Greek and in two forms of old Egyptian writing: formal hieroglyphics (as seen on royal tomb walls) and the more common demotic script. In 1799, during Napoléon's occupation of Egypt, some of his soldiers found the rock on the Rosetta fork of the Nile River at Raschid, near Alexandria. The rock was carved about 2,000 years earlier, in 196 BC.

When the stone was recovered, nobody knew how to read hieroglyphics (more on hieroglyphics in Chapter 3). Ancient Egyptian history seemed lost forever.

Scholars Thomas Young and Jean François Champollion worked hard and long to decipher the stone, establishing that texts all said the same thing. Using his knowledge of ancient Greek, Champollion was able to announce in 1822 that he could read hieroglyphics. The Rosetta Stone provided an entryway into the remote Egyptian past.

You can see the Rosetta Stone in London's British Museum.

Confucian Analects

In the Western world, people attribute the Golden Rule to Jesus. But 500 years before Jesus, a humble Chinese teacher, Kung Ch'iu, told his students "Do to others what you would have them do to you."

Kung lived from about 551 to about 479 BC. He became a government official as a teenager, in charge of grain stores and pastures at 15, and worked his way up to high office. His ideas for reform made him popular with the public but also angered some privileged people.

After enemies forced him to leave his native province, Kung traveled and taught his ideas about respect for others, reverence for ancestors, obedience, shared values, loyalty, and self-improvement. He stressed the concepts of *li* (proper behavior) and *jen* (sympathetic attitude). His students gave Kung the respectful title *Futzu* ("venerated master"). You can find more about Kung Futzu's teachings in Chapter 9.

Late in Kung Futzu's life and after he died, followers gathered his sayings into the *Analects,* a tremendously influential source of Chinese thought. Confucianism (from the Latin version of Kung Futzu: *Confucius*) shaped Chinese character — blending with other philosophical and religious schools such as Taoism, Buddhism, and Legalism. (Chapters 9 and 10 look at religion and philosophy.) Until the twentieth century, every student training to be an official in the Chinese government had to study the *Analects*. Confucianism also influenced other Asian cultures, including Japan's.

The Bible

This is a package deal — a treasure chest of documents all wrapped up into one volume. Which Bible you're talking about depends on which tradition you follow. But regardless of how you know the Bible, this is an indispensable document for understanding the course of many world events.

The Bible — in its Christian form, anyway — includes writings that are at the heart of two major religions — Judaism and Christianity. (Chapter 9 talks about world religions.) The Bible contains the *Pentateuch,* or Jewish Priestly Law (the written *Torah*) and both the Ten Commandments (Old Testament) and the Christian Golden Rule (see the "Confucian Analects").

Bible stories stand as an important historical source, even as some historians challenge them. The Bible's teachings have shaped the courses of great nations, including the Roman and Byzantine empires, as I discuss in Chapters 4 and 5.

The Bible also figures in a huge technological change, courtesy of Johannes Gutenberg, who chose it as the first book to come off of his revolutionary printing press.

The Bible played a role in important linguistic changes too. Both the German and English languages were shaped by early major translations of the Bible into those languages. For German, it was Martin Luther's 1530 translation. For English, it was the King James edition of 1611. (It may sound funny to you, but the way you talk right now owes a lot to a 400-year-old book full of "thee" and "thou.")

The Koran

A holy book like the Bible, the Koran is the foundation of not just religious practice, but daily life, formal law, and government policy in most of the Islamic world — a huge, wealthy, and powerful part of humanity more than a millennium ago and today, too.

The book defines Islam's place in history. The Koran's verses spurred the Arab conquests of the seventh and eighth centuries and the verses continue to shape the worldview of Muslims today.

Muslims believe that the Koran (or Qu'ran) is God's direct, infallible word, and that the angel Gabriel revealed it, as written in heaven, to the Prophet Mohammed, founder of Islam, in the seventh century AD (see Chapter 9). Muslims consider the text sacred. To touch sacred text without being ritually pure is forbidden. If you imitate its style — in which God (Allah) speaks in verse — you have committed a sacrilege.

In addition to its vast impact on world events, the Koran is also the book from which Muslims traditionally learn to read Arabic. That makes the Koran perhaps the most widely read of all books, ever.

The Magna Carta

The divine right of kings idea (covered in Chapter 11) was based on the understanding that the monarch, as God's deputy, had to care for creation's lesser children. Obedience was repaid with protection.

It didn't always work like that. John, the most unpopular of England's kings, upset his barons. They rebelled and in **1215,** the barons got the upper hand, forcing King John to sign a contract, the Great Charter, or in Latin (official language of thirteenth-century Europe) the *Magna Carta.*

By signing, King John agreed to specific rules on respecting his subjects. The *Magna Carta* contained 63 clauses, most relating to John's misuse of his financial and judicial powers. Clauses 39 and 40, the two most famous, say:

> 39) No freeman shall be taken or imprisoned except by the lawful judgment of his equals or by the law of the land. [A *freeman* was an adult male subject of the crown who wasn't a serf or slave.]
>
> 40) To no one will we sell, to no one will we deny or delay right or justice.

This first formal try at separating kingship from tyranny didn't solve all the problems between King John and the barons, but the charter set a precedent for laws regarding rights, justice, and the exercise of authority in England, the British Empire, and beyond. The Great Charter pointed toward constitutional freedoms guaranteed by the founders of republics such as the United States of America.

The Travels of Marco Polo

When thirteenth- and fourteenth-century Venetians called Marco Polo *Il Milione,* they were repeating one title of his well-read book about his travels and his life in China. (Polo's book appeared under other titles in various translations and editions.) *Il Milione* referred to the vast wealth (millions) possessed by China's emperor, Kublai Khan.

But some of his fellow Europeans also used the term *Il Milione* to mean that Marco Polo told a million lies. Many could not believe his tales of Kublai Khan's magnificent empire. Cathay, as people called China, seemed as remote as another planet. Well, not quite. A few other Western travelers of the thirteenth century saw Beijing, including Polo's father and uncle, who took the lad along on their second journey east in 1271. They got back to Venice 20 years later.

Marco's knowledge of the East and its riches gained believers because he put his experiences in writing. More and more people became fascinated by his reports. His book, known in English as *The Travels of Marco Polo* became a fourteenth-century must-read. It fed a hunger for silk, ceramics, and other exotic goods. His book drove the quest to find a sea route to transport those goods. As historian Daniel J. Boorstin put it in his 1983 book *The Discoverers*, "Without Marco Polo . . . would there have been a Christopher Columbus?" You could go so far as to trace the age of European conquest and colonialism to Polo's account.

The Declaration of Independence

When in the Course of human events, it becomes necessary for one people to dissolve the political bands which have connected them with another . . . they should declare the causes which impel them to the separation.

Say what? It's my pared-down version of the opening sentence from a great document, written largely by Thomas Jefferson (Chapter 21 has more on Jefferson) and signed by the Continental Congress on **July 4, 1776** (see previous chapter).

The Revolutionary War was already on, so this declaration wasn't about war as much as it was an *explanation* of why America's colonial leaders felt they had to do what they were doing. It's full of specific grievances against George III. But Jefferson — with assists from Benjamin Franklin and John Adams — also did a brilliant job of summing up some of the most compelling political and social philosophy that came out of the eighteenth century philosophical movement, the Enlightenment.

Thomas Jefferson wrote:

We hold these truths to be self-evident, that all men are created equal, that they are endowed by their Creator with certain unalienable Rights, that among these are Life, Liberty and the pursuit of Happiness.

The Declaration doesn't mention women and didn't apply to all men — it excluded slaves. Still, Jefferson's were powerful words. The Declaration said that people had not just a right but a *responsibility* to stand up to government when the exercise of authority is unjust. Those words echoed through the rest of the eighteenth century and the two centuries that followed it.

Chapter 14 of this book has more about revolutionary philosophies. To explore the American Revolution, see *U.S. History For Dummies,* by Steve Wiegand, published by Hungry Minds, Inc.

The Bill of Rights

Drawn up in **1789** and added to the U.S. Constitution on **December 15, 1791,** the first ten Constitutional amendments were powerful afterthought, intended to limit the power of government and to guarantee certain rights — civil liberties — to everybody.

Freedom of speech, *freedom of the press*, and *freedom of religion* come from the First Amendment, which specifically guarantees those freedoms. The Second Amendment, the one that begins "A well-regulated Militia, being necessary to the security of a free State . . ." is the one that gun control advocates and gun-rights advocates argue about more than 200 years after it was passed.

People argue all the time about the Bill of Rights. Everyday citizens, members of Congress, talk show hosts, and judges interpret and reinterpret this essential American document. Supreme Court justices spend much of their time deciding what the framers of the Constitution meant when they wrote these amendments.

Debatable, but indelible, the Bill of Rights provides a permanent curb on what government can get away with. Like the Declaration of Independence, these amendments have been copied and elaborated upon by many other democracies around the world.

Also in **1898,** the revolutionary French National Assembly proclaimed a similar set of liberties, called the Declaration of the Rights of Man and Citizen. (See Chapter 7 for more about the French Revolution.)

The Communist Manifesto

The **1848** *Communist Manifesto* and its **1869** sequel, *Das Kapital*, seem discredited now. The biggest governments founded upon *Das Kapital*'s arguments collapsed (the Soviet Union in 1991) or made concessions to private property and individual incentive (the People's Republic of China).

Still, the worldwide impact of this economic-political treatise by Karl Marx and Friederich Engels (Chapter 8 has more on them) has been incredible — inciting numerous revolutions and reshaping societies drastically.

The *Communist Manifesto* attacked government, religion, and traditional culture as tools of a repressive *capitalist class,* defined as people who owned factories and mines and used other people to get profit from these properties.

Marx and Engels presented communism — with collective ownership of industry and farms and equal distribution of resources among everybody — as the only economic system fair to everybody. Communism struck a powerful chord among working people worldwide. Despite the Soviet collapse, socialist ideas linked to Marx's theories are still powerful influences on workers' rights and government responsibility.

The Origin of Species

Charles Darwin's theory of evolution by natural selection, set forth in his **1859** book *The Origin of Species,* underlies the way scientists, ever since Darwin, approach the study of living things. Modern biology, anthropology, and paleontology are all based on the idea of evolution.

In the nineteenth century, most naturalists thought that plant and animal varieties were unchanged since God created the world. Others saw change, but thought a trait acquired in life could be passed on to offspring — as in a mare with a bad hoof giving birth to a limping colt. In his 20s, Darwin (1809 to 1892) traveled around the world as a naturalist aboard a British naval survey ship. His observations made him doubt both theories.

The idea of species evolving by natural selection is called *Darwinism*, even though Darwin himself recognized at least 20 other scientists who had proposed similar ideas. What Darwin did that the others didn't was support his theory with boatloads of hard data from all over the world.

Darwin also wrote in plain enough language that anybody could read *The Origin of Species.* This brought him fame, but also attracted opposition. Many religious people decried any theory of life that did not rely on direct divine intervention. Some religious conservatives were especially shocked at the notion — suggested within Darwinism — that humankind evolved like other animals.

Index

(continued)

YOUR ONLINE RESOURCE

WWW.DUMMIES.COM

Discover Dummies Online!

The Dummies Web Site is your fun and friendly online resource for the latest information about *For Dummies* books and your favorite topics. The Web site is the place to communicate with us, exchange ideas with other *For Dummies* readers, chat with authors, and have fun!

Ten Fun and Useful Things You Can Do at www.dummies.com

1. Win free *For Dummies* books and more!
2. Register your book and be entered in a prize drawing.
3. Meet your favorite authors through the IDG Books Worldwide Author Chat Series.
4. Exchange helpful information with other *For Dummies* readers.
5. Discover other great *For Dummies* books you must have!
6. Purchase Dummieswear® exclusively from our Web site.
7. Buy *For Dummies* books online.
8. Talk to us. Make comments, ask questions, get answers!
9. Download free software.
10. Find additional useful resources from authors.

Link directly to these ten fun and useful things at
http://www.dummies.com/10useful

For other technology titles from IDG Books Worldwide, go to
www.idgbooks.com

Not on the Web yet? It's easy to get started with *Dummies 101®: The Internet For Windows® 98* or *The Internet For Dummies®* at local retailers everywhere.

Find other *For Dummies* books on these topics:
Business • Career • Databases • Food & Beverage • Games • Gardening • Graphics • Hardware
Health & Fitness • Internet and the World Wide Web • Networking • Office Suites
Operating Systems • Personal Finance • Pets • Programming • Recreation • Sports
Spreadsheets • Teacher Resources • Test Prep • Word Processing

IDG BOOKS WORLDWIDE BOOK REGISTRATION

We want to hear from you!

Register This Book and Win!

Visit **http://my2cents.dummies.com** to register this book and tell us how you liked it!

- Get entered in our monthly prize giveaway.

- Give us feedback about this book — tell us what you like best, what you like least, or maybe what you'd like to ask the author and us to change!

- Let us know any other *For Dummies®* topics that interest you.

Your feedback helps us determine what books to publish, tells us what coverage to add as we revise our books, and lets us know whether we're meeting your needs as a *For Dummies* reader. You're our most valuable resource, and what you have to say is important to us!

Not on the Web yet? It's easy to get started with *Dummies 101®: The Internet For Windows® 98* or *The Internet For Dummies®* at local retailers everywhere.

Or let us know what you think by sending us a letter at the following address:

For Dummies Book Registration
Dummies Press
10475 Crosspoint Blvd.
Indianapolis, IN 46256

™ FOR DUMMIES

BESTSELLING BOOK SERIES